FIDEL &CHE

A REVOLUTIONARY FRIENDSHIP
SIMON REID-HENRY

SCEPTRE

First published in Great Britain in 2008 by Sceptre
An imprint of Hodder & Stoughton
An Hachette Livre UK Company

I

A CIP catalogue record for this title is available from the British Library

Hardback ISBN 978 0 340 92343 6
Trade paperback ISBN 978 0 340 92344 3

Typeset in Sabon MT by Palimpsest Book Production Limited,
Grangemouth, Stirlingshire

Printed and bound by Clays Ltd, St Ives plc

Hodder & Stoughton policy is to use papers that are natural, renewable and
recyclable products and made from wood grown in sustainable forests. The
logging and manufacturing processes are expected to conform to the
environmental regulations of the country of origin.

Hodder & Stoughton Ltd
338 Euston Road
London NW1 3BH

www.hodder.co.uk

For Papous Apostolis

CONTENTS

PART 4

I had a brother.
We never saw each other,
but it didn't matter.
I had a brother
who passed through the hills
while I slept.

I loved him in my fashion
I took his voice
free like water,
I sometimes walked
close to his shadow.

We never saw each other
but it didn't matter,
my brother awake
whilst I slept.

My brother showing me
from beyond the night
his chosen star.
Julio Cortázar, 'I Had a Brother'

Abu Is'af is more than a brother to me, as you know.
Being comrades-in-arms is something that time can't
erase; after you haven't seen him for twenty years, your
comrade-in-arms turns up and you discover he still has
his place in your heart.

Elias Khoury, *Gate of the Sun*

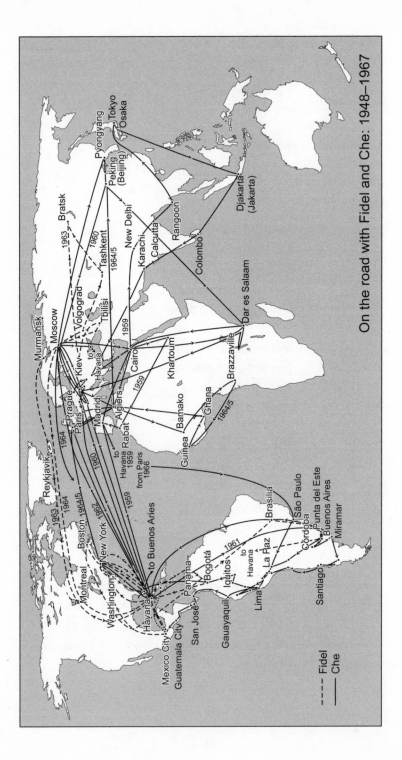

On the road with Fidel and Che: 1948–1967

Pyongyang
Tokyo
Osaka
Peking (Beijing)
Bratsk
1963
Tashkent
1960
Volgograd
1964/5
New Delhi
Tbilisi
Karachi
Calcutta
Rangoon
Murmansk
Moscow
Djakarta (Jakarta)
Colombo
Reykjavik
1959
Dar es Salaam
Kiev
to
1959
Havana
Prague
Cairo
Paris
Khartoum
Brazzaville
Madrid
1959
Algiers
Bamako
Ghana
1964
1960
Rabat
Guinea
1964/5
Montreal
1963
1964
Boston 1964/5
to
New York 1962
Havana
1959
Washington
1959
from Paris
1966
Mexico City
to Buenos Aires
Brasília
Guatemala City
São Paulo
San José
Panamá
Córdoba
Punta del Este
Bogotá
1961
Buenos Aires
Gauayaquil
Iquitos
to
Miramar
Lima
Havana
La Paz
Santiago

- - - - Fidel
——— Che

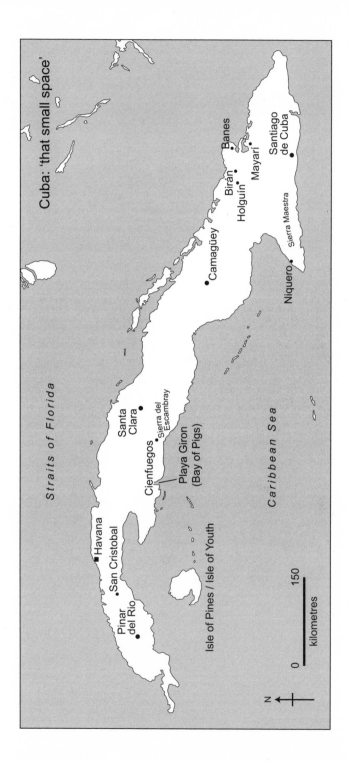

Cuba: 'that small space'

INTRODUCTION

FIDEL CASTRO IS 'addicted to the word', as his good friend Gabriel García Márquez puts it. This makes it all the more surprising that during his half-century in power – by far the longest effective rule of any recent head of state – he has said so little about his twelve-year friendship with Ernesto 'Che' Guevara. Yet theirs was a friendship that spanned the beginnings of the Cuban revolution and the high point of the Cold War, a friendship that for a time was the most important relationship in both men's lives, and a friendship whose secrets hold the key to understanding some of the most significant events of the twentieth century.

In October 2007, on the occasion of the fortieth anniversary of Che Guevara's death in Bolivia, Castro looked back at the 'sad and luminous days' he and Guevara once shared. The phrase was not his, but in a certain way it belonged to him. Two years before he died, Che had scribbled it down on a sheet of lined paper as, forever in a rush, he penned a last-minute farewell to Fidel, his comrade of the previous ten years. This unusual goodbye was not the ending of their relationship, and the circumstances in which it was written were themselves to play a part in the denouement of their story. But Castro never publicly replied. Even forty years later, and himself then lain up in bed, suffering from the intestinal problem that would see him officially retire from office, the great orator maintained an effective silence.

Such reticence to open the past is unusual for someone with Fidel Castro's avid interest in history. Castro has regularly staked his revolution on the popular appeal of the island's history of rebellion, and he will always be associated with the famous line: 'Condemn me, it does not matter, history will absolve me!' But he has also always – and with not inconsiderable success – discouraged serious historical research into his own past. He has been especially protective about his relationship with Che Guevara, limiting his comments to the occasional 'exclusive' (if not always revealing) interview or the republication of some of his earlier speeches.

Guevara too tended to smudge the detail of his own life. His now much-publicised diaries are fascinating insights into the revolutionary process and the radicalisation of an ordinary boy from a middle-class background as he journeyed further into the more impoverished parts of the South American continent and ultimately well beyond. But they are all the versions that he rewrote after the events, and accordingly they fit with the vision he wanted to portray. They retain much of value and insight, but are not as objective as perhaps he would have liked to think.

It is not all that surprising, therefore, that for many years serious accounts of these two highly colourful and important characters of the twentieth century were a scarce commodity indeed. Vitriolic and impassioned accounts of both men arose to fill the gap, often authored by those with some personal involvement in their story. But it was not until the 1980s that more serious biographies of Castro began to emerge, and in the mid-1990s a spate of works on Guevara followed suit as doors opened and a light was finally cracked on to at least some of the archives. But the depth and subtlety of their relationship escapes even these earlier, pioneering works. There has been no major new account of either life for some time.

Like the 'grey blur' that Stalin became for historians, the relationship between Fidel and Che has thus, for decades, failed to register as more than a ghostly flicker. As this book shows however, that relationship was of paramount importance to both men during those critical years; as important in its way as the intellectual camaraderie of Engels and Marx, or indeed the great clash of egos that was the partnership of Trotsky and Lenin. Fidel and Che had at least something in common with these other historical pairings, and more besides, for they were not just comrades but *compañeros* who found common cause at a remarkable historical moment when the Cold War intersected with the nationalist struggles of their own and other countries. Their relationship differs from many other political double-acts however, in that it was a full-blooded friendship first and foremost, and it was lived out during just a few short, intense years. It was, as one biographer put it, quite simply 'unmatched'.

This book is about that unmatched relationship and the coming to prominence together of Fidel Castro and Ernesto 'Che' Guevara 'in that small space, where two of the great epics of our time coincide'. It is based upon archival research in Havana, Washington, Moscow, Miami, Princeton, Boston, London and Berlin. Drawing also on interviews with some of the major players in this history, it brings together a novel range of sources to tell for the first time at full length the story of one of the most remarkable political friendships of the twentieth century.

PROLOGUE
A FATEFUL CROSSING

IN THE EARLY hours of the morning of 25 November 1956 there was unusual activity at the small port town of Tuxpán, one of the few settlements situated between Veracruz and Ciudad Madero on the long, sweeping arc of Mexico's eastern coast. Soaked by a wind-blown drizzle that foretold an approaching storm, a small group of men were busily carting biscuits, water and medical supplies up a precarious gangplank to where a small pleasure craft was moored along the river that flowed down into the port. Two attractive young girls gave a hand as Hershey bars, oranges and a couple of hams were stowed among the rifles, ammunition and anti-tank guns already on board.

Overseeing these last-minute preparations, was the six-foot-two figure of the Cuban lawyer Fidel Castro, one of the country's most promising basketball players in a life that could have been; a largely unsuccessful practitioner of law turned politician and now amnestied revolutionary in the life that increasingly was. Tonight was the most important moment in Fidel's young life to date. Everything he had worked for since walking out of Jesuit school in Havana – his gangster days, his enrolment in armed operations, his months of solitude in prison and, more recently, the long nights of clandestine preparations in exile – all were staked on the success of the next few hours.

Standing nearby in the darkness was the much leaner figure of the Argentine doctor Ernesto Guevara, until then a reluctant medic and researcher who was at heart a traveller and a poet: a free spirit shackled to a burning desire to do something. But what, until he had met Fidel, he did not quite know. He too stood that night on the brink of a new period in his life, one from which there would be no return but which he had sought, perhaps without quite knowing it, all his life. The two men did not speak as the silent mobilisation got underway.

More than a hundred other men had been summoned to Tuxpán. Many had arrived in ones and twos from the various safe houses and sparsely furnished back-street hotels in which they had been lodged since the group's release from prison a few months earlier. Guevara himself arrived in an old Ford Pontiac. Its tyres crunched over the loose dirt of the road as someone wheeled it off to be hidden. Some of the men around him embraced each other silently in the dark, but nobody spoke. Like men on a prison break, their task for the moment was simply to lie low, keeping out of sight in the small warehouse next to where the boat was being loaded.

Castro, the mastermind of the whole operation, was among the few men standing outside in the rain. He wore a black cape, and a Thomson machine gun rested across his thighs. He looked concerned and kept glancing at his watch. Not all of his men had yet arrived and, despite having continually shuttled them from one safe house to another, he was fearful the Mexican police might have been alerted to his plans. It was not just them he had reason to fear. In the last few months his group had been tracked by Cuba's feared SIM agents – the dictatorship's notorious Military Intelligence Service – as well as Mexico's own Federal Security forces and the United States' Federal Bureau of Investigation.

The governments of all three countries had watched the activities of Castro's group closely since he had publicly declared his intention to overthrow the incumbent Cuban regime. Their fears had only been heightened when the group were temporarily detained in a sting operation, and the secret ranch where these men had been training was uncovered. Fidel had managed to secure their release, but the communist credentials of one Dr Ernesto Guevara had been splashed all across the Mexican newspapers by editors who caught, amongst the growing Cold War tensions of the country, the unmistakeable scent of a good scandal.

Fidel had chosen their point of departure with these recent events in mind. Tuxpán was a desolate place, a small port town hopefully poised at the opening of a river. Here neither customs house nor immigration controls existed, allowing the would-be revolutionaries a degree or two of freedom in their preparations. For now at least, they were also aided by the weather. The previous day had been one of the stormiest of the year and tonight everything in the half-lit town receded even further into the moonless night.

It was here that Fidel had found the boat that would take them to Cuba and every now and then, as the men loaded equipment on to it via the single plank, it was illuminated in the reflection of the lights on the water: the *Granma*, a shabby, sixty-three-foot wooden craft with two sickly diesel engines for propulsion. Far from Castro's first choice – in fact, the only craft available in the rapid escalation of events that had engulfed his small band of rebels over the previous weeks – she had already sunk once during a hurricane in 1953. The boat had been prepared with two days to spare by one of Castro's men, tortured during the group's arrest five months earlier, and a Mexican gun smuggler named El Cuate (buddy) who had sourced half of their weapons as well. But with only the patchiest of repairs carried out by the two men, working at night by a bare bulb so as not to rouse suspicion, she looked as though she might well sink again.

'You'll not get more than a dozen men on that,' Melba Hernandez, a loyal member of the Cuban resistance and one of the young women helping with the preparations, told Fidel when she saw it. In many ways she was right, but Fidel refused to believe it. 'She'll take ninety,' he declared obstinately. In any case it was too late now to find another craft to carry them to Cuba. When the order to board was given, eighty-two men shuttled out of the warehouse and managed to squeeze themselves below deck. Some, armed with the few machine guns that El Cuate had obtained, took up their positions on the deck. Fearing arrest if he waited any longer for the last few men, Fidel gambled on luck staying with him and set about making the final preparations.

* * *

Guevara's official capacity on the expedition was medical officer and head of personnel. Despite being personally and ideologically committed to the domineering figure of Fidel Castro ever since they had met the previous summer, and though, as he put it, for such a noble cause it seemed 'worth dying on some foreign beach somewhere', he had his reservations about the course they were taking. These were not fears of failure – though any common-sense appraisal would suggest that success was unlikely. Like all the other men crouching in the shadows that night, Guevara had an optimism bordering on blind faith that they would achieve their aims. His suspicions rested instead on the fact that, once successful, the revolution would go the same way as most other attempts to overthrow corrupt governments across Latin America. Given time, Guevara thought, this Cuban revolution would succumb to Western dollars and bourgeois greed just like the rest. But he put these thoughts to one side for now, and focused on the task at hand.

The young Guevara had already made his rushed farewells to the wife he had met during the second of his two epic journeys around the continent. 'Is something going to happen?' Hilda had asked her husband when one of the movement's members came nervously to the house and asked for him. Another comrade had just been arrested again, and his papers and some weapons taken. 'No, just precautions . . . ,' he replied, gathering his things but not looking at her. When he was finished, he went over to the crib where their baby daughter was asleep and caressed her. 'Then he turned, held me, and kissed me,' Hilda recalled. 'Without knowing why, I trembled and drew closer to him. Afterward I would remember how he tried to remain natural at that time, and I knew how much he must have forced himself. He left that weekend and did not come back.'

It was really only Fidel who had any idea at this point what was going to happen, or at least what he hoped would happen. Deep in thought about the arrangements he had made in Cuba to receive them, he made his own less emotional farewells. For once he avoided the theatrics and the speeches, never straying from the task at hand. He put his arm around his good friends and fellow underground conspirators de Cárdenas, his wife and Orquidea Pino, before issuing his final order to them: 'Hide, all of you, hide yourselves, and don't go out until you hear we either got there or were arrested.'

The only message Fidel was concerned to send after that was a coded one to alert his supporters on the island. Once the men were safely on their way, with their supporters following them along the coast in blacked out cars, that message – 'Book ordered out of print' – would be duly cabled to Santiago de Cuba, along with a couple of others to Havana and Santa Clara. After a final hug with Melba, Fidel took up the gun he had handed briefly to a comrade and ordered the last of those who were coming to follow him on board when they had loosened the ropes. With that he bounded up the gangplank to the ship's cabin and ordered the boat to cast off. It was nearly two in the morning, and already it was time they were gone.

* * *

The event that would soon come to play such an important role in the Cold War and that would reshape the political landscape of Latin America was underway. Although various intelligence agencies were tracking the movements of Fidel's group of rebels, the governments in Washington and Moscow were themselves largely unaware of what was afoot. Rumours of rebellion were constant traffic in this part of the world and Washington gave the activities of Fidel Castro no particular attention: its primary concern was whether any uprisings were communist in nature, and though Castro had by then made something of a name for himself he had never publicly said anything about communism. Despite their having an embassy in Havana and a consulate in Santiago de Cuba, one of them just a few miles away from where Castro planned to land, the US government had no idea of the extent of Fidel's underground movement on the island.

The Soviet leadership too was occupied with other matters. As the *Granma* prepared to sail tanks were still grinding their way around the streets of Budapest where Nikita Khrushchev, Stalin's successor, had deployed them to crush an uprising just weeks before. Hungary was not Khrushchev's only concern. Communist China under Chairman Mao was growing increasingly powerful and restless at the presumed primacy of the Soviet Union within the socialist bloc countries and the Soviet Premier had just been roundly criticised by the West for voicing his infamous 'we will bury you' speech to a group of Western diplomats in Moscow.

Only a year before things had looked so much better for Khrushchev and his prime minister, Nikolai Bulganin, as they made a state visit to India. So positive had their reception been in Calcutta, where the two Soviet leaders had been completely engulfed by a vast gathering of more than two million, that their security guards had violently elbowed and jack-booted their way through the crowds to 'rescue' them, lifting the two statesmen up above their heads and carrying them back to the safety of their official limousines like precious dolls. Khrushchev had been impressed by the whole experience that had left him with a tantalising sense of the possibilities the USSR might yet exploit in some of the recently independent nations around the globe as it sought to retain its international standing relative to the Americans and the Chinese.

Though Khrushchev did not know it, a young affiliate of

the Soviet embassy in Mexico, Nikolai Leonov had in fact already made friends with Che and with Fidel's brother, Raúl. Khrushchev would not learn of Leonov's 'contact' with the Cuban rebels under Fidel for some time yet. Nor indeed was Fidel to realise the full extent of his brother's and Che's involvement with the communists until several years later. For the moment, Fidel Castro, Ernesto Guevara, and the other men aboard the *Granma* sailed into a new and as yet undefined era largely unwatched by either of the superpowers and unencumbered by the finer details of their political programme.

* * *

Today in Tuxpán – a town with little else to sell itself by – there exists a small museum recording the 'great historic expedition' of the *Granma* and its crew. On the night of 24 November 1956, however, no one in the town had any idea of the importance of the events that were beginning to unfold as the boat slipped down the river to where it opened up to the sea. Squall warnings had been posted along the Mexican coast and the streets of the town were empty. Through the portholes of the overloaded vessel, sitting low on the water, the men could see the occasional light slip by as the boat crossed the harbour and turned out into the rougher waters of the Gulf of Mexico.

As the rebels hit the full force of the storm, the boat yawed precariously against the waves and soon all inessential items had to be thrown overboard. To make matters worse, the engines were playing up and they were shipping water. Fidel's plan was to head towards the western tip of Cuba before making a wide turn south of the island, passing along the coasts of Jamaica and Grand Cayman. This way, he had reasoned, they could avoid being in Cuban waters for almost the entire journey before making a quick dash at the last minute for the southernmost tip of the island, which juts out like the skull of a hammer-head shark, and from where they could scramble up into the sanctuary of the mountains that limn the southern shores of the island.

But no sooner had they left the Mexican coast than the rebels all but ran into a Mexican navy frigate. Fortunately the frigate failed to spot the *Granma* low in the water as the rain poured down. When the coast had receded a little further Fidel deemed it safe to put on the boat's lights. A few hours later, in spite of the waves that continued crashing against the small craft 'like mountains', the tension of the initial departure eased somewhat and the men on board began to sing. Guevara joined in with the Cuban national anthem as if it were his own as cries of '*Viva la Revolución*!' and '*Abajo la Dictadura*!' were hurled out into the night.

Then, all of a sudden, their voices fell silent. Aware that they were alone in the vast blackness of the open sea, the men stood looking at each other through the rain and the spray for a short but undoubtedly memorable moment. Perhaps now that they were a band again, after months of isolation in cramped safe houses, they were reminding themselves of who they were and who, for now, they were with as they headed out on that dark stretch of water towards the unknown: a journey, a war, their freedom or their death.

Meanwhile, the small boat continued to be thrown about. Rain and spray poured from the roof, and it seemed as if the *Granma* might list into the dark waters at any moment. Someone ordered the bilge pumps to be turned on, only to find that they didn't work properly; the men took to baling the craft out with buckets instead. Amid the renewed confusion Faustino Pérez, one of Fidel's inner circle, sought out his leader, busy shifting water, to suggest that they sail closer to the coast. 'This is lost!' he shouted to Fidel over the storm. But Fidel seemed not to hear him.

* * *

In the town of Santiago de Cuba, near to where the *Granma* was due to land, the members of underground revolutionary movement on the island swung into action. Celia Sánchez, daughter of the doctor at a vast sugar mill whose first-hand experiences of conditions there had given him the sharp sense of injustice that he had imparted to his children, and Frank País, the son of a Baptist minister and a radical young student leader, were busy implementing the final elements of the carefully prepared plan. They had received from Fidel the coded telegram 'Book ordered out of print', and the two of them now set about organising an armed uprising and strike to coincide with the *Granma*'s landing.

The President of Cuba, Fulgencio Batista y Salvidar, was informed too. Castro and Batista had met on a number of occasions when Fidel had been an aspiring politician, but since Fidel's more radical turn Batista had kept a close eye on the man whom everyone acknowledged to be as brilliant as he was unpredictable. Batista had long been abreast of Castro's plans, but he was confident that any attempt to land a small group of men on the island would be picked up long before they reached the coast. There would be no invasion by 'gangsters', he had assured his people in *El Mundo* newspaper just three days before. The army was 'alert, competent and fully capable of handling any insurrection that might take place'.

The telegram Castro had sent as they departed had told País, Sánchez and their men to expect Castro before dawn on 30 November. So that morning, as people were getting up, País's small force, armed with 'rifles, machine guns, grenades, and Molotov cocktails', attacked key points in Santiago. With the element of surprise in their favour around three hundred men in uniforms and the red and black armbands that indicated their adherence to Fidel's movement took control of the radio station. For much of the day the town was closed down, the inhabitants either shut up their shops or stayed at home. And while the army and the police remained in their barracks, unsure of the situation, País had created a perfectly executed diversion for Castro's landing.

All that day País's men waited, holding their positions, but the

Granma was nowhere to be seen. As afternoon turned to dusk the government forces went on the counter-attack. By nightfall, País knew he had to withdraw. On the coast near Niquero, where they were expecting Castro to arrive, Celia Sánchez had also got together around a hundred men. But again, having successfully mustered a sizeable rebel force and waited for the promised landing they too had to withdraw, as army reinforcements flown in from Havana began scouring the countryside in pursuit. With the disbanding of Sánchez's men went Fidel's last hope for a diversion.

* * *

Some time later, Che himself described the *Granma*'s travails across the Gulf of Mexico: 'The entire boat had a ridiculously tragic aspect: men with anguish reflected in their faces, grabbing their stomachs; some with their heads inside buckets, and others fallen in the strangest positions, motionless, their clothes filthy from vomit.' He was suffering more than most on account of the asthma that had plagued him since childhood and because, in the hurry to depart, the expedition's doctor had left his own medicines behind.

Half way to Cuba the situation worsened. Fidel learned that, while the carefully planned strikes and mobilisations had indeed brought the country to a standstill, the *Granma* was still three days short of her destination. As their rations ran low and the salt air edged their hunger, the men could only listen impotently to the ship's radio telling them of the gradual crushing of the uprisings. Already in Santiago, which was Fidel's home town, dozens of men now lay dead. 'I wish I could fly!' he shouted in anguish to Faustino as the *Granma* chugged on at its infuriating slow pace and the occasional plane overhead kept the men in a state of constant tension.

Shortly before 5.00 a.m. on 2 December the craggy green coastline of Fidel's beloved island finally came into view. It was the first time Guevara had set eyes upon it. But the final landing, at the appropriately named Purgatory Point, was more of a ship-wreck than anything else. The boat beached on a sandbank nearly a mile out and the men were forced to climb down into the chest-high water. Checking their rifles, many found that the seawater had jammed the parts. But these were the only weapons they had, and they could ill afford to discard them. With guns held aloft, they began an exhausting trudge towards the shore.

As they scrambled out of the water the men encountered swampy wasteland that was hardly any easier to traverse. 'Some comrades had to be carried by the stronger men in the group,' one of them later wrote. 'As soon as we reached solid ground we threw ourselves on the abundant grass, exhausted, hungry, and totally covered with mud.' By then the coastguard boat had successfully alerted Batista's men. 'They shot at us persistently from the air and the coast', Guevara recalled, 'and after a while only half of us were alive, or only half-alive if we take into consideration our condition.'

Those who were able to headed for the cover of the nearby mangrove trees. But without maps, or the guides who had been supposed to meet them and provide reinforcement, they were utterly lost. As their clothes baked dry in the sun they could do nothing but stumble on, breaking up into ever-smaller groups of men, some of them wandering in a half-delirious state after seven days with little to eat or drink. The haggard rebels were easily tracked down by the spotter planes that circled overhead and the patrols that were hot on their tail.

'We were an army of shadows, of ghosts, who walked as if following the impulse of some dark psychic mechanism,' Guevara recalled. That dark mechanism would prove enough to keep himself, Fidel and just eleven others alive. The rest would be caught and summarily executed, or else subjected to the brutal interrogations that Batista's army had come to specialise in. But even for the lucky ones the seven days of hunger at sea were about to be followed by three more days – 'terrible ones' – lost and adrift on land. The Cuban revolutionary war had begun.

* * *

A few days later, when some of the rebels had managed to regroup, Fidel was ecstatic, however improbable it might have seemed. 'Now we have already won the war,' he declared jubilantly. But for the family and friends whom the would-be revolutionaries had left behind in Mexico, Argentina and elsewhere in Cuba, the news when it finally came the following week was everything that they had feared. 'INVASION OF CUBA BY BOAT – Fidel Castro, Ernesto Guevara, Raúl Castro, and all other members of expedition dead' ran the headlines in Mexico's *Novedades* paper the day of the landing.

The reports would later prove to have been exaggerated, of course. And in just over two years' time Fidel Castro and Ernesto 'Che' Guevara would not only have won the war alongside the rest of the *barbudos* – the bearded ones – who came to power with them, they would already have become two of the twentieth century's most iconic figures. But for all that the war had by then shaped them and their friendship, they remained two utterly different individuals who, for most of their lives before they met, had seemed to be travelling in almost the opposite direction. This book begins with their lives before their meeting in Mexico City. These early years set the scene for everything that followed.

PART 1

1. FAITHFUL AND
THE PIG

IT WAS NOT inevitable that they should meet: Fidel Castro and Ernesto Guevara were born to very different families, a little less than two years apart, and at opposite ends of a vastly unequal continent. Their meeting was not the product of fate. They were drawn together by the geographical circumstances of the times and by the way they had each been touched by one of the very few things that their lives by then had in common.

In the first half of the twentieth century, Latin America was a continent that had been undergoing profound change. The former colonial powers, primarily Spain, had long been ejected by the independence movements led by figures such as Simón Bolívar. But in place of outright colonialism had then come the neo-colonialism of economic dependency, leaving those same nations now reliant upon foreign capital, much of it coming from North America, to sustain them.

Governments that looked to all the world despotic and corrupt but which made the resources of their countries available to foreign interests were, by the mechanisms that tied financial power to a position of influence, kept in place. Resentment was on the rise. Mexico had witnessed a full-fledged revolution during the first decades of the century, and by the time Fidel Castro and Ernesto Guevara were born, in 1926 and 1928 respectively, other revolutions were brewing.

Growing up in Oriente, the eastern and most impoverished

region of Cuba, the young Fidel Castro was intimately familiar with just such a picture. His father, Angel, was a former cavalry quartermaster who had fought for the Spanish in Cuba's war of independence. At the close of the war in 1898 Angel returned briefly to Spain but caught a steamship back to Santiago de Cuba in December 1903. He began selling lemonade on the wharves there before working on the country's vast sugar plantations. He married, worked his way through the sugar cropping hierarchy and settled on a comfortable ranch in eastern Cuba, near the town of Mayarí.

Lina Ruz González, Fidel's mother, was from the west of the island. She arrived in Oriente along with her father, a travelling salesman, carried in the small cart in which he used to store his wares. Lina was offered work by Angel and his wife, but she and Angel were soon having an affair. Like Angel, Lina was of working-class roots, with, in later life, a matronly appearance topped by a beaked face and heavy-rimmed glasses. In the blossom of youth, however, she was Charleston-thin and persuadable. In the only photo of her to have been released, an older Lina looks unimpressed, made up but with heavy eyes. The photographer seems not to have her attention.

One who always did was their second son, Fidel Castro Ruz, born on a clear August night in 1926 to the sound of contented cattle underneath the stilt-framed house, and of hens scrabbling around for space in the nearby pens. For all the peace of the setting, however, the child was born into turbulent times. The first quarter of the century since the war of 1898 that had first brought Angel to Cuba, was marked by a series of rebellions and uprisings.

In 1925, less than two years before Fidel's birth, Gerardo Machado y Morales, a former meat man turned business magnate, had risen to power on the back of a surging world market for the island's principal export of sugar. But the Great Depression was already gathering on the horizon, and as the economy faltered, Machado – who with his wing-collared suits and thick round spectacles looked every inch the university intellectual – donned the heavy boots of the dictator.

Under the terms of the 1901 Platt Amendment by which, following their involvement in the Spanish–American war of 1898, the United States had secured effective control over the island in exchange for turning power over to a Cuban government, Cuba's leaders came and went in accord with Washington's interests rather than those of the Cuban people. American policy favoured order and control over social progress so as to safeguard its own substantial investments on the island. Machado – that 'tropical Mussolini' – like those who had come before him was thus given a relatively free rein.

The community at Birán, where Fidel would spend his first few years, was a mixture of all the classes: a community of around a thousand workers from the surrounding Caribbean islands, Europe and America. During the sugar harvest, the centre of this small and relatively isolated community was the cock-fighting pit. Every Sunday the immigrants who worked on the farm would gather to watch the fights, betting as much as their meagre wages would allow. Those who won would cele-brate into the early hours with rum and dancing until they could stand no more.

These were the parents of the children whom Castro and his brothers and sisters would play with – though never quite as equals. With them, Fidel – their 'little Lord Fauntleroy', as one biographer described him – would go riding around the estate, down to the river or across to the foothills of the sierra, searching for birds to shoot with their home-made catapults. Fidel especially liked to ride his horse up on the plateau at Pinares de Mayarí, 'savouring the sweet air and the perfect climate', and looking out across the American-owned land all around. Despite his subse-quent years of fine schooling, Fidel would always carry with him the echo of these rural surroundings of his youth.

The school where Fidel took his first lessons, in a seat at the front of the class, was just a few yards from where the cocks would peck and scratch their owners to financial ruin on Sundays. Here the young Castro clan had their own sort of war with the teacher. In fact they got through about four or five teachers, the war being the only consistent element of their otherwise potholed education. As Fidel himself later put it, somewhat euphemistically, 'We responded according to how we were treated.' The son of a relatively rich man brought up among the children of the poor, the young Fidel was ever the ringleader of these playtime plots.

Accordingly, he was despaired of as much as he was doted upon. When his sisters caught him red-handed one day, after he had dragged a shotgun into the yard and despatched a sizeable number of the family chickens, Fidel tried (unsuccessfully) to avoid their telling his father by offering to show them how to fire the weapon themselves. It was around this time that Angel decided to send Fidel, along with his sister Angelita and brothers Ramón and Raúl, to a religious boarding school in Santiago.

* * *

If Fidel was born to a rich family among the poor his future comrade in arms, Ernesto Guevara de la Serna, was born to a family fallen from the rich. Argentina was nothing like Cuba. Though part of the South American mainland, it had less in common with the rest of the continent than Cuba did. Argentines tended to see themselves as better off and more independent than their brethren elsewhere in Latin America.

When Ernesto was born, the Radical Party of Hipólito Yrigoyen that had been ushered in to replace Argentina's corrupt governing oligarchy was still in power. It was a short-lived period of political advance in which all men were granted the right to vote, irrespective of their social status or class (women would have to wait until 1947) and one that greatly bolstered the aspirations of a new middle class. The military and traditional ruling classes were already plotting their return, but Ernesto's family circumstances would ensure he would live out much of his younger life isolated from – and indeed uninterested in – the seismic political shifts going on around him.

Ernesto's father, Ernesto Guevara Lynch, was the grandson of one of South America's richest men, while his mother, Celia de la Serna Guevara, was descended from a Spanish viceroy. His paternal grandfather had been a geographical surveyor, diligently marking out the borders between countries that the grandson would make a career out of disrespecting. Both the Guevaras and the de la Sernas were somewhat fallen in wealth and standing by the time Ernesto was born to the noble lineage, however, and his parents were in any case uncompromising heretics when it came to the conventions of their class: he would inherit neither the wealth nor the social values of his forebears. The values they handed down were those of the aspiring middle classes whose ranks they now joined, accompanied by a certain inbuilt sense of entitlement that would match Fidel's.

Ernesto's parents had met in Buenos Aires in 1926. Celia, 'a dramatic looking girl of twenty with an aquiline nose, wavy hair, and brown eyes', had recently graduated from high school. She was 'well read but unworldly, devout but questioning. Ripe, in other words, for a romantic adventure.' Ernesto Guevara Lynch may have been drawn to a 'snowy neck kept bare with beads' as one family friend put it, but what he got was a very modern, iconoclastic woman – 'She was the first woman', one of her nieces recalled later, '. . . who had her [hair bobbed] like a boy's, who smoked and crossed her legs in public.'

Celia had asked for her inheritance to be released early in order to fund her husband's plan to develop a tea plantation in the remote and somewhat mysterious region of Misiones. The family had refused and so the day after their marriage Ernesto and Celia de la Serna Guevara absconded to Misiones where the already three months pregnant Celia would give birth to Ernesto in May 1928.

There were strong differences between the parents, however, that came to a head when Ernesto developed asthma at the age of two. Guevara Lynch privately harboured the belief that it was his wife's insistence on taking the child swimming in cold water that had caused it. 'She had a particular character', he later wrote, trying to be understanding. 'It wasn't so much that she was irresponsible as that danger attracted her.'

These early years, in a region of thick impenetrable forests cut through with fast rivers and traversed by pumas, yaguaretes and lianas, and as far from Buenos Aires as Fidel was from Havana, were thus 'difficult but happy', as Ernesto's father recalled. And though the effect of the damp climate on Ernesto's asthma soon forced them to return to the city, those days would remain forever like a favourite family holiday, spoken about in the house for years after the event, its imperfections glossed, its freshness repeatedly aired, the details of life there carefully logged. The only echo of it that young Ernesto would retain, however, was a lifelong love of the yerba maté tea that they tried, with little success and less profit, to grow there.

Where the Castros' world was based on the solid routine of the farm at Birán, the Guevaras lived more of a peripatetic life as they moved from country to city and back again, propelled one way by the father's business adventures and the other by the son's asthma. Ernesto's parents tried everything to cure his asthma, subjecting the child to a barrage of bizarre treatments – anything that looked, smelt or felt as though it might do the trick. Medication and herbal teas came first. When they failed, witchdoctors with their cats and sandbags to be placed in his bed, were ushered in upon the convalescent scene.

Already demonstrating that he had inherited his mother's wilfulness, the child refused to succumb to his asthma. When out with friends he would fight his tightening chest to the point where he had to be carried back home by his playmates, who would do their best to haul his prostrate little body along by taking an arm or a leg each. 'When he was really delicate we would go to his house and look at him for a bit through the window,' Enrique Martín, a school friend, recalled. 'If he couldn't come out, or we saw he was really ill, we would leave straight away because his father didn't like us bothering him. Poor kid, sometimes he looked half-dead. All the same, two or three days later he would be back out running and jumping around.' This was the essence of Ernesto.

In the autumn of 1931 the family (now with a daughter, Celia, and the recently born second son, Roberto, in tow), moved to the central highlands of Córdoba, settling in the small spa town of Alta Gracia. In a fitting scene of what was to come, the congregation of this predominantly Catholic town were returning from mass as the Guevaras roared into town in the family's Chrysler Voiturette. The new arrivals had brought their 'little creature' – as Guevara Lynch was accustomed to calling his first-born son – to recuperate for a spell in the fabled dry climate of this quiet, steepled town, with its bullfights and friezes and the unmistakable atmosphere of old Spain.

While political turmoil was being stirred up elsewhere in the country, as the workers railed against the government and the government in turn railed against the British businesses that exerted considerable control over the Argentine economy, things were all rather mute in Alta Gracia, where five o'clock tea and *déjeneur concert* at the Sierras Hotel were the order of the day. But the Guevaras' lifestyle of 'impoverished aristocrats' made them a strange sight in such a conservative town. Celia in particular raised eyebrows almost anywhere she went, with her cropped hair and her trousers and her tendency to 'often speak openly with her husband'. Always the quixotic outsiders, they were known to the locals as the 'live how you likes', after the Spanish title of the popular film You Can't Take It With You: *Vive Como Quieras*.

Unlike Fidel, who was boarding from the age of six, Ernesto did not go to school regularly until he was almost nine years old. Instead, he was tutored at home by Celia, his 'old girl' as he liked to call her. She was always his confidante, his father recalled, and the young lad in turn was the one she would turn to for consolation. If his frequent asthma attacks kept Ernesto away from school they did not, however, keep him from developing into one of the brightest children among his peers. Like Fidel, he simply learned to study on his own. And given the lack of peace and quiet in the family home, he would often scuttle outside and hide in the chicken run with a pile of books; the result was crumby pages but, unlike Fidel, he left the chickens well alone. Such isolation endowed him with a scholarly mien that for now said little of a more deep-rooted boisterousness. It may also have exacerbated a natural impatience that would chase his decision-making throughout life.

But the voluble side was always there for those who cared to see it. When Ernesto finally began full-time at the local Escuela San Martín in March 1937 he was nine, two years older than the others. He was well ahead of them academically, too. On being assessed on his first day, he was passed straight into second grade, skipping the two preparatory years. Spared these years of rote and register, he also soon became that pupil who always thought he knew better than the teacher. Much to the teachers' chagrin, and undoubtedly to his doting mother's delight, at least some of the time he did. When he was asked primly, having been speaking over the teacher, whether he would like to show the other children how to do a complex new equation she was trying to teach them or keep quiet, Ernesto opted for the former and promptly gave the correct demonstration. An exasperated but quietly approving teacher could only respond: 'Do like Guevara, children. Don't learn, know!'

A constant feature of the Guevaras' countless homes, even when they moved from Alta Gracia to Córdoba where Ernesto would spend his early adolescence, was an impromptu and always chaotic library. Wherever they lived, every nook and cranny was filled with books, and Ernesto's father would spend much of his free time pottering about the house, pulling one of the books from the shelves or piles to peruse it in some comfortable if sparsely furnished corner. His son picked up the habit, both of reading and of paying scant attention to his surroundings. Salgari, Stevenson and Dumas were among the writers he had read by the age of twelve. He loved books about discovery and adventure in particular, and soon began to keep a list. His somewhat pre-cocious 'Catalogue of Books Read in Alphabetical Order' reveals a particular affinity for Jules Verne, with twenty-three titles recorded under this heading.

Another habit he picked up was his father's fascination with graphology, the analysis of handwriting. Given the importance that writing would play in Ernesto's life – his diligent keeping of diaries and reading lists, his philosophical notebooks, his jour-nalism and his historical tracts – it is more than a little ironic that his own 'belle lettre' should be quite such a bilious beast. Allusions to his hopeless handwriting pepper his later and very voluminous correspondence. At times it is almost as if he takes a wilful pride in obscuring his prose.

Despite the best efforts of those who have sifted patiently through them, Che's letters, when they have appeared in print, are often marked by the same problems: 'Illegible word, could be *pelotudos* [stupid] . . .', or, as elsewhere, 'In the [illegible word] already narrated, I encountered . . .'. Sometimes just a space appears, in place of the 'illegible word', signalling something that might have been. It became something of a running joke in the family. In a letter which the twenty-five-year-old Ernesto wrote home from Guatemala, he commented with his usual dryness on a rather short missive he had just received from his father: 'Your letters, very Guevara, big script, generous characters, page immediately full.'

Many years after his son had perished, Guevara Lynch – pottering about the house as ever – came across some of his old graphology texts in which he found the annotations of the young Ernesto who, it seemed, had set himself to analyse his own impen-etrable scrawl. The sentence he would write out year after year to spot the changes was: 'I believe I have sufficient strength – and I feel it in these moments – to rise to the scaffold with my head raised up. I am not a victim, I am a drop of blood that fertilises the land of France.' Clearly these words made an impression on Ernesto, but as with everything from this time they ought not to be read too closely. They were just another set of clothes he was trying on, all the time figuring out how he wanted to dress his life.

* * *

Fidel had rather less choice about the path he was expected to follow when he arrived as a schoolboy in Santiago de Cuba. The city, whose buildings were still painted in the bright pinks, ochres and blues of the colonial era, had a strongly Caribbean feel to it. People spoke more quickly here than in Havana, they dropped their Rs, and Bahamian English could be heard mixing with the Yoruba and Hausa carried over from the days of the slave trade. Here was where Fidel would spend all but the summers of the next ten years or so, shuttling between the mean and impoverished house of his guardians, where he would often be locked into his tiny attic room to study, and periods at boarding school, first at a place called La Salle, then at the larger, Jesuit-run Dolores.

They were dangerous years in the city. Santiago was at the sharp end of an incoming era of social change. Sometimes bombs went off in the area where Fidel lodged, keeping him up at night. One day, sitting in the doorway of the house he stayed in opposite the high school, he watched as a number of students were chased down the road for having insulted a small group of soldiers. Before long the boys were being dragged back down the street and hauled into jail.

Fidel now began his own run-ins with authority. 'I knew all the scholastic tortures,' he later recalled. 'Every day he fought,' his brother Raúl remembered, even with the priests. One time, a quarrel with the teachers' pet at La Salle came back to haunt him when the boys were assembled for benediction in the chapel. Halfway through, the sacristy door opened and a priest called Fidel outside to ask him what had happened. Just as Fidel began to tell him, the priest struck him with such force that it was remembered, nearly eighty years later, as a 'vengeful' and 'cruel' thing to have done, a 'great and shameful pain'.

Dolores, a Jesuit school just up the hill from La Salle, was no less strict. A photo from the time shows the students dressed in their white military uniforms with leather sashes and carefully pitched caps. During his time here Fidel wrote a letter to President Franklin D. Roosevelt which turned up many years later during a sweep of the White House files. 'Send me a ten dollar bill, American?' Fidel precociously asked. Roosevelt never replied, but the acknowledgement from his office was pinned up outside the classroom for weeks. 'I didn't know you had written to Roosevelt,' one of his fellow pupils said to him on seeing it. 'Yeah, well,' a now altogether more angular Fidel – he was at this age all elbows and knees – replied. 'He won the election. But the Americans are assholes. I asked for ten dollars and they didn't send me a cent.'

Dolores was an important period in Fidel's younger life. It was only a small preparatory academy and boarding school – there were just 238 boys when he was there – but it was a place accustomed to producing the country's next generation of leaders. As one account suggests, 'To be a Dolores boy was to walk through the Plaza Dolores as if you owned it, and to step right past students in the uniforms of other *Colegios* without comment.' Like Ernesto, Fidel too learned a sense of entitlement at a young age. Enclosed behind high walls, with its students locked in at night by an iron key, Dolores, like all Jesuit schools, was based on a military structure. At 7.45 a.m. a handbell would be rung by one of the borders (a *regulador*), calling them to order. It gave them and the day pupils who had by then arrived precisely 270 seconds to get to their places for mass first, then classes.

The tenets of the Jesuit curriculum, the *Ratio Studiorium*, perfected in the fifteenth century and adhered to ever since, were well summed up by the famous nineteenth-century Jesuit scholar Father Luís Martín. 'The mere acquisition of knowledge is not enough,' he said. 'Our special obligation is to develop the natural talents.' Boiled down, that meant, as one of Fidel's fellow pupils said, '[T]hey got in your head and prepared you for a triumphant life.' Jesuits wanted not only learned men, but men of character (and civic virtue thereby). Castro's later life was to be an object lesson in how to reverse this logic: he took the learning and used it to develop his own vision of civic virtue. He was an arch-pragmatist from the start.

After the boys were called to attention in the morning, they would give a military salute before snaking out of their lines and into the chapel. The Jesuits they saluted wore high-collared black robes except on the hottest of days and spoke with posh Castilian lisps that highlighted the divide between the school and the rest of the city. Punishments for those who transgressed the school's strict code of conduct – and that included Fidel, of course – were inventive, reaching well beyond ear-pulling and ruler-whipping. 'Two boys who antagonised each other, routinely and endlessly, were ordered to climb up to the *solar*, or sun room, that made a kind of fourth floor, and fight it out.'

Fidel would later speak admiringly of his education, and, though it seems finally to have tamed his wilder side one of his fellow pupils recalls his increasingly dominant personality from this time. The 'little rooster', as he called him, 'acted as if he ran the school, rather than attended it'. Certainly Fidel was one of the brightest, another recalls. In particular he set himself to succeed at sport, becoming not only the school's top athlete but later one of the country's top pitchers and basketball players. Through sport, Fidel found a means to channel his competitive spirit. 'When it came to sports everyone thought he was great.'

Off the sports pitch, however – and perhaps this was the reason he first took to it – Fidel suffered from bullying about his bastardism, rumours of which had spread north to Banes from the Las Manacas ranch in Birán, and then south to Santiago, along the lines of money and influence of his father's circle. Here, Fidel's very name did not help matters. An unusual name, it was drawn not from his forebears but from his father's attempt to gain the good favour of a wealthy local businessman – also named

Fidel – by asking him to be the godfather of his son. It seems the businessman did not much care to be associated with the lad born to the housemaid, however, and Fidel would remain unbaptised for some years, until a suitable replacement (the Haitian consul in Santiago) could be found. Fidel – which in Spanish means faithful – was thus a peculiarly inappropriate name.

Rumours of this story arrived at Dolores, along with the visiting parents and family members of other children from near Mayarí. The young Fidel simply responded by trying to prove himself quicker and more daring than the other pupils. For a bet one day he rode a bicycle head first into a wall, putting himself in the infirmary for several days. Other accounts have him flinging himself off the top storey of the school building with only a sheet to break his fall. Perhaps more believable than at first it seems, he had actually worked through the problem beforehand like a diligent stuntman, finding just the right place where the hill rose up round the back of the school to make his fall a lot shorter than it appeared.

Fidel's fellow pupils also all concur that, from even a young age, he had a 'fabulous' memory. 'We would say, "Fidel, what does the sociology book say on page forty-three?" and even if the page ended on half a word, he would say it,' one recalled. 'He had a photographic memory,' affirmed another. It was an ability which, added to his great intelligence, would become Fidel's saving grace time and again. And if he was by no means a model student, nor even – for all his evident intelligence – much of a student at all, he was, as he would later in all earnestness warn young students not to be, an exceptionally good crammer.

Life at school was thus a maelstrom of contradictions for Fidel, and as turbulent as the times themselves: born to the 'right' class, but out of wedlock; the privileged kid from the country brought up in the wrong part of town; ebullient because of his intelligence, but seen as an outsider by many. He was a bully to some, and he was bullied by others. But whatever it was he was always to be found in the thick of things, and as he learned to control his temper he was better able to channel his energy into what had by his teenage years begun to emerge as his favourite project: always, and at any time, to be the best at everything.

* * *

Ernesto's aims were rather less ambitious. The family's new house in Córdoba, another strongly Catholic town in a predominantly Catholic society, was notable for the cracks that appeared in its walls – as they now also did in Don Ernesto and Celia's marriage. The darkening family atmosphere aside, young Ernesto's teenage years were relatively typical for a boy of his class. He had grown into a handsome young man, but his classmates still nicknamed him *pelado* (baldy) or *huevara* (egghead) for his characteristically short and fuzzy haircuts. Ernesto's continual failure to care about his appearance meant he would never quite shed the nickname that he carried with him from Alta Gracia and that he would take with him into adulthood: *chancho* (pig). Of all his names, this was the one to which he himself was most drawn. He would play up to it, donning his favourite shirt for days on end so that it too earned its own nickname of *la semanera* (the weekly).

In 1943 the years of tension that had been held in check in Argentina erupted into the first of a series of military coups. It darkened the atmosphere in Córdoba considerably. At Ernesto's school, some teachers suspected of being reformist were plucked from their jobs. One who was under no such suspicions set about proudly explaining to the class one day how the new military government was going to educate the people. Ernesto immediately began to laugh uncontrollably. The others shuffled a little, and nervous chatter broke out. When the teacher called Ernesto to account he responded, 'So, teacher, how do you think the military are going to educate the people? If they succeeded, the people would throw them out.' Furious, and totally outclassed, the teacher threw Ernesto himself into the corridor. Ernesto did not jump to rebellion as quickly or as instinctively as Fidel did, but the potential was always there. It seems that all he ever needed was a push.

In Cuba, Fidel had begun to take control of his own future. When his period of schooling at Dolores was up he asked his father if, rather than return to the ranch, he might go on to study at Belén College in Havana, arguably the best school in the country. With its fountained courtyards and finely detailed wooden ceilings, Belén was the place to be for an aspiring young Cuban. All of which did not come cheap for Angel, who now had to raise Fidel's allowance – which he would in effect go on paying until his son was fighting in the mountains as a thirty-year-old – to $50 a month.

It was at Belén, under the influence of one of its younger professors, Alberto de Castro – a man with goggle-eyes, but a fantastic orator – that Fidel took to the study of politics and public speaking with a hitherto unrealised passion. A friend of Fidel's at Belén, José Ignacio Rasco, recalls that now, 'The two of us were very interested in politics, and especially Latin American problems.' The public speaking was harder, though. For the great orator and voluble elder statesman he would become, Fidel was, in his later teenage years, a 'tremendously shy' man. '[I]t wasn't easy to get on with him,' concurs another classmate, Juan Rovira. But Fidel was determined to succeed, and would practise speeches by Desmosthenes and Cicero in front of a mirror. He came to see oratory 'as a sort of verbal warfare'.

Havana was a fractious city at this time, and towards the end of his time at Belén Fidel discovered a rather different sort of politics; one that was rather more immediate than the classical kind emphasised at Dolores, or the rumours and commentary he had picked up about the recent Spanish Civil War that the Spanish immigrant workers in Birán had followed so closely. As Ernesto set off on his first series of travels, Fidel was soon to have a run-in with the gangs that ran wild about the city from their base in the university, an almost law-free zone. It was to be a very particular sort of education.

As the first half of the twentieth century drew to a close, the elements that would shape the two young men's lives were, like a puzzle, being gradually worked out at the margins. They had grown up in, and come to know, very different parts of the continent. But it was only really as young men that they would develop, in complementary register, a sense of belonging to those places. As they both adhered staunchly to their own, highly individualised creed, they would for the next few years follow paths that seemed to be leading them in almost the opposite direction. In following these different paths, though, they would each also absorb the experiences with which they would forge a revolutionary project together.

2. ZARPAZO!

THE BURLY YOUNG man, dressed incongruously in a dark blue wool suit and tie despite the late summer heat, burst into the café. The year was 1947. It was still almost a decade before Fidel and Che would meet for the first time, and the still somewhat awkward-looking Fidel Castro was in his third year at Havana University. 'I was sitting inside having lunch with a journalist,' Alfredo Guevara recalled. Alfredo, no relation of Ernesto, was perhaps Fidel's closest friend from university. The café, on the corner of L and 27 Streets, was a regular hangout for its students being just to one side of the famous stone steps – the *escalinata* – that lead up to the university perched atop a hill like a Caribbean acropolis. From the top of the steps a statue of the Alma Mater sits with robes billowing about an august chair, her back to the campus and her arms outstretched as she gazes across the city.

'I have to speak to you,' the youth in the suit said to Alfredo. Even from a distance the young man's distinctive gait – loping and sloven but with a briskness – would have made it clear who he was. Fidel Castro was already known as an agitator around the university campus and his demeanour verged on the theatrical. His suit, which would reappear many decades later as he declared his country open for business, was in this first incarnation a kind of uniform, his personal trademark. He was rarely seen without it, and he always had it carefully arranged.

Fidel wanted to look different, a cut above the rest, if not too obviously so. Accordingly he wore the jacket open, with his patterned tie at half-mast, and he exhibited not a trace of the military staunchness that in later life would complement his trademark olive-green tunics. His next few years, however, would see him find a voice in national politics, marry and set up a home in which he would never really manage to settle down. He would taste exile for the first time, and come close to losing his life more than once.

The moment he bounded into the café to see Alfredo was the culmination of a period of intense activity for Fidel that had begun the moment he left Belén. Havana was the epicentre of Cuban politics and the university was at the heart of the systematic corruption that supported it. This grand city of half a million people, the largest in the Caribbean, lay cupped around a great harbour where in past centuries Spanish ships laden with gold and other riches of the earth used to congregate before setting sail as a fleet for Europe. The most regular comings and goings in the 1940s, however, were of the omnibuses as they ferried people in and out of the *reparteros*, the surrounding suburbs, to the old colonial heart of the city with its cramped streets and alleys that opened on to the plazas, the parks and the sea.

Within a half-hour's stroll from the university, along the great harbour road, the Malecón, Fidel could take in at a glance from those he passed the different classes and not a few of the nations of the Americas. By the late 1940s Havana had become a tropical playground for the rich but discontent simmered deep within the city as the corruption of Cuba's then government of Ramón Grau San Martin spread to all parts of life. There was a growing restlessness about the city during the years that Fidel spent at the university. It was as a student there, he later claimed, that he became a revolutionary. Fidel, it seems, was never set to experience more peaceful times.

For the last few weeks chants of 'Down with Grau!' echoed around the porticos and streets of the city. It was just a tremor of rebellion, but for Fidel, who was looking for a way to make his name on the campus, not a single opportunity was to be missed. Like Ernesto, Fidel was finding that he needed always to keep on the move. But he achieved this without setting out on some great journey. Nervously energetic by nature, he simply kept himself constantly tapped into whichever event was making headlines. He was the one who could never resist trying his hand and he was always seeking new depths to his understanding. If he could add complexity, he would do so. Breadth and novelty had not the interest for him that they held for the far more introspective Ernesto.

Perhaps a little warily that day at the café, though of all people it was he who had the most faith in the endlessly ambitious schemes of his conspiratorial young friend, Alfredo agreed to talk with Fidel. Alfredo Guevara was himself head of the Young Communists at the university. As he recalls, during these years it was 'quite usual' for Fidel to drop in on a social gathering and call one of the students outside to discuss some idea of his. 'We went outside to where another youngster was waiting', Alfredo said. The journalist remained alone inside. 'What is it?' Alfredo asked. 'I need your help,' Fidel replied. 'We're going to go to Manzanillo,' he declared, 'to bring back the bell of Demajagua.'

It was an outrageous suggestion even for Fidel, who since arriving at the university had gained a reputation for his often outlandish schemes. The bell that he was referring to, from the Demajagua sugar plantation near Manzanillo in eastern Cuba, was famous for having been rung in 1868 by Carlos Manuel de Cespedes, the island's great revolutionary hero, as he gathered together a rebel force, freed his slaves and invited them to join him in the struggle for independence from Spain. The ringing of this bell had marked the beginning of ten years of bloody conflict. It was a profound historical event, firmly anchored in popular memory. Fidel told Alfredo that he intended to bring the bell right to where they now stood and hoist it to the top of the university steps. 'He presumed that this would attract a large crowd that we would then arm and use to take the palace. He was going to Manzanillo to see about the bell,' Alfredo recalled, 'and he asked me to obtain the arms and to be ready.'

Three days after leaving Havana for Manzanillo Fidel returned, posing for pictures in his trademark suit and tie, which he had for once knotted neatly for the benefit of the photographers shoving through the crowd of several thousand students thronging to see them. It was a remarkable coup, and he gleamed with pride as the bell was paraded around the streets of Havana in a convertible that came to meet them at the station. It was, as a fellow student, Max Lesnick, would recall, 'A transcendental achievement of national notoriety'. But more importantly, it put Fidel's name on the political map. Within the small and often violent world of student politics in Havana he was now a force to be reckoned with, 'one of the most colourful and charismatic students of his generation'. For the twenty-one-year-old Fidel Castro, student agitator and political avatar, the first stage in a meticulously planned operation had been successfully completed. He could go home for the day and rest well. He would need to. The bell was about to be stolen.

* * *

Nothing could have been further from Ernesto Guevara's mind at university than student politics. He failed even to pay much attention to Perón's assertive rise to power. But, like Fidel, he managed to spend his six years of official enrolment in the Faculty of Medicine at the University of Buenos Aires preoccupied with other things.

His decision to study medicine, having always professed an interest in engineering, was the result of a constellation of unhappy events. Before they left Córdoba to live in Buenos Aires his mother had been diagnosed with breast cancer, and in the summer after he graduated from college, while working in Vialidad Province in northern Argentina he received a letter informing him that his favourite grandmother, Ana Isabel, was dying. Ernesto was the last of the family to arrive at her side. He scarcely left her during the two weeks in which she quietly slipped away, and was in an emotional state throughout. 'It must have been one of the great sadnesses of his life,' his sister Celia later observed.

From almost the moment of his arrival at university, Fidel had sought out the limelight, but Ernesto kept to the shadows during his studies. It was a distinction that would mark their entire youths before they met and ultimately press upon the nature of their political partnership. Though studying medicine was an obligation that Ernesto had imposed upon himself in order to 'do' something about a confluence of events – his mother's, his grandmother's, and his own illnesses – it was also one that his instincts would always rebel against. He had no intention of being 'trapped in the ridiculous medical profession', he wrote to a girlfriend in 1952. It seems strange, then, that the librarian in the medical faculty recalls that in his first year at university Ernesto was one of the most diligent students, regularly spending entire days in the library.

Perhaps what the librarian failed to notice – but certainly it explains the lower grades that Ernesto was now attaining – was that his reading consisted not only of medical books. Alongside the anatomy notes and the basics of chemistry that he spread out over his desk in the library lay what was for him far more exciting reading: the political and philosophical writings of the Argentine Marxist Aníbal Ponce, as well as works by Jean-Paul Sartre and William Faulkner. All of this extra-curricular reading he carefully – one is tempted to say lovingly – commented on in the philosophical notebooks he continued to keep. He did so with such method that one presumes he must also have spent time poring over them in whatever spare time was left to him: as he rode on one of the old *colectivo* buses – those heaped curves of colourful tin with their wooden-framed windows – while heading to class, or sitting at a café waiting for an engagement with one of his young *porteño* friends – the progeny of the city's cultural elite who filled most of the places at the university.

This new world of radical thought he explored with a plain, mop-haired but not unattractive-looking girl from his class. The first that this young girl, Berta 'Tita' Infante, knew of Ernesto was when she heard a 'warm and deep voice' in the anatomy room of the Faculty of Medicine. As she recalled, it was a voice which 'for its accent was provincial', but which, she soon realised, came from a handsome but graceful figure; one, like her, who had recently arrived in Buenos Aires. The two hit it off immediately. They were both somewhat sensitive individuals and each was going through difficult times at home. 'Ernesto had great affection for her,' his sister Celia recalled. But she 'was very in love with him'.

It did not seem to matter. Their whole relationship was based on their differences. They had not friends, nor interests nor political views in common. But they spent hours talking in the city's noisy cafés, slumped over books in their rooms at home, or in the contemplative stillness of the Museum of Natural Sciences where they would meet on Wednesdays to study the nervous system. If, during their studies, something surprised them – as it frequently did given their range of interests – they would repeat to each other as a lesson a line from the poem 'La Victoria' by the nineteenth-century Argentine poet and doctor Ricardo Gutiérrez: 'Don't sing victory hymns on the sunless day of the battle.'

This little billet-doux refrain was a highly incongruous one for such a studious young pairing. Ernesto in fact continued to show little interest in politics. He would sit on the fence when it came to political discussions – 'He was neither for, nor against, anything,' Tita herself mused. 'Marxists,' as he had said to her, were 'inflexible sectarians'. But if Ernesto remained uninterested in politics *per se*, he was becoming increasingly absorbed in his own private study of politics in the philosophical sense. He wanted to know the reasons behind the things he saw around him, and he began searching for the answers ever more systematically in his reading.

※　※　※

On entering university, before he had even conjured up his plan to parade the bell of Demajagua about the city, Fidel had sought almost immediately to gain a seat on some student body. He was first elected class representative in the anthropology of law (softening up the class's professor with two crates of 'magnificent oranges' from the family estate) before being elected as the year representative for the entire Faculty of Law. As Fidel knew well such elected positions were a passport to political power more generally: presidency of the students' union, the Federation of University Students (FEU), brought with it a guaranteed national political post afterwards, for example. But they carried little weight without the support of one or other of the main rival campus gangs: the Insurrectional Revolutionary Union (UIR) of Emilio Tró and the Socialist Revolutionary Movement (MSR) led by Rolando Masferrer.

The university was effectively run by these two gangs and they in turn answered to President Grau: he called them his 'fire eaters'. Though an officially elected government, Grau's Autentico (authentic) party was mired in corruption and violence. 'I bathe myself, but I also splash,' Grau once said. And much of his dirty money found its way into the campus politics of the university: the Education Ministry itself saw its 15,000 peso 'discretionary' budget – out of which the sinecures to various gang leaders were paid – increase to two million pesos by the time Grau left office in 1948. As the Dean of Social Sciences put it, the university was now awash with 'pseudo-revolutionary gangsterism'.

In furtherance of his political ambitions, Fidel had no great ideological scruples about obtaining the patronage of the university gangs. As friends of this time recall, he had 'no real ideological attachment' at all. He was emerging, rather, as 'a revolutionary in the traditional American sense of the term' – he was after influence, the means by which he obtained it mattering somewhat less. For some time, therefore, as he sought to make headway through this political minefield, the young Fidel tried keeping both the UIR and MSR on side. Just in case, he began also to carry a gun. This landed him in a pistol duel one day, when he replied to the campus police who asked him to remove it, 'If you want it, try and grab it by the barrel.' The police were themselves thickly involved in the university's web of gangland vendettas and sinecures, and the policeman whom Fidel turned up to face at the university sports ground had carefully rigged the stage beforehand. Fidel realised just in time, fleeing down the street to safety. As he later recalled, 'It was a miracle I got out of that alive.'

At the end of his second year at university, in the summer of 1947, Fidel took another step on the ever more radical path he was embarking upon when he signed up to a planned expedition, organised by a group of Dominican exiles led by future president Juan Bosch in cahoots with some of Grau's top officials and the MSR, to overthrow neighbouring Dominican dictator Rafael Trujillo. Trujillo ruled the Dominican Republic with a mad-eyed conviction in his own greatness. He strutted around in brush-capped helmets while signs in the country's churches announced: 'God is great, but Trujillo is on earth.' The planned expedition, an open secret from the start, had a good deal of popular support in Cuba but it soon became embroiled in controversy. For six weeks, while plans for the expedition were finalised, Fidel and the other recruits were kept fed and watered on a secluded cay, Cayo Confites, infested with mosquitoes and searing hot in the daytime. Many of those who had signed up were members of one or other of the university gangs, however, and loyalties soon tipped over into feuds and internal fights.

When word of their son's involvement in this improbable scheme filtered through to Fidel's parents, they could take it no longer. Throughout the year they had read reports in the national press of their son's flirtation with the Cuban underworld. Now it appeared he was rushing headlong into a suicidal farce that could not be anything but a diversion from the proper work of a student at the country's premier site of learning. Calling him to Havana to meet with them, they insisted Fidel stay away from Cayo Confites and come to see them. 'If Trujillo doesn't get you, Salabarria will,' Lina emplored her headstrong progeny referring to one of the gang leaders behind the operation, Mario Salabarria, who had recently been promoted to head up the Investigations Department of the National Police and whose path Fidel had already crossed. But Fidel would have nothing of it. He just stood there scuffing his feet at the doorway, intent on seeing the project through.

Though the expedition was eventually called off, Fidel arrived back at the university from his parents' home, where he had gone to rest afterwards, too late to enrol for that year. He seemed unconcerned and opted to sit his courses out of attendance. This would free up more time for politics, and Fidel took immediate advantage. In October, he made one of his by now rather more impassioned and flowing speeches at the funeral of a high-school student who had been shot dead by the bodyguard of a government official during an overheated demonstration. And by November he had pulled off his coup with the bell of Demajagua. In just his third year at university, the Jesuit-schooled boy with the razor-sharp mind and the volatile temper was becoming one of the principal voices of his generation.

✻ ✻ ✻

Ernesto, meanwhile, was ever the provocative oddball, the one who arrived late at parties, his clothes unkempt, in deliberate contrast to the primped and manicured attire of most of the other boys of his age and class (well-fed young dolts who fussed over the latest slacks from America or the newest style of pullover from Britain). He could not dance, and ignored the fact that his appearance made people turn their heads and talk about him.

He persisted, too, with a surprisingly stern refusal to get involved in political issues. When both his close friend Alberto Granado, and another Córdoban acquaintance, Fernando Barral, were caught up in the crackdown on dissent under Perón, Ernesto refused outright to support Granado. He never once paid Barral a visit during the seven months he was held in police custody before, as a foreign national, he was booted out of the country. Ernesto was never one to get involved if he didn't want to. He was still working things out. The problem was his huge range of interests, which made it seem as if he might never figure out exactly what he wanted to do.

By the end of his time at university his philosophical note-books were filling up. Having worked his way through his father's twenty-five-volume *Contemporary History of the Modern World*, he now moved on to more challenging works of social philosophy, covering a wide range from Sigmund Freud to Bertrand Russell. He was also increasingly interested in books by political figures – being highly enthusiastic about Nehru's *The Discovery of India* – and beginning, now, to delve into work by socialist writers: Emile Zola and Jack London, and, closer to home, the 'flamboyant' Argentine socialist Alfredo Palacios.

In combination with his striking good looks, it was his grasp of literature that drew Ernesto's first love to him. In October 1950 he met a very pretty young girl called Chichina Ferreyra at the wedding of his cousin Carmen Aguilar. 'I saw him in that house,' Chichina later recalled, 'he was coming down the stairs and I was thunderstruck. He had an impact on me, a tremend-ous impact, this man was coming down the stairs and then we started talking.' They would in fact spend the whole night talking, and what they talked about above anything else was books.

But Ernesto was no shy scrivener. He began his first letter to her just a few days later on a promissory note: 'For those green eyes, whose paradoxical light announces to me the danger of losing myself in them . . .' This was to be the most important romance of his youth. On receiving such ardent prose from the dashing Guevara, he of the pale skin and dark, haunting eyes, the sixteen-year-old Chichina was hooked.

At the age of twenty-two, Ernesto too was ready for love. But he was also desperate to explore horizons beyond his native land. Just two months after the young lovers met, Ernesto enrolled in the merchant marine. Serving as nurse on the *Anna G*, he travelled down to the tip of South America and north as far as Brazil and the Caribbean. Marx, it seems, was a constant travelling companion. In February of the following year, a few weeks into his journey, he wrote from Porto Alegre on the Brazilian coast to his Aunt Beatriz. As ever, he taunted her for her bourgeois life in 'boring' old Buenos Aires, signing off with his best wishes 'from these lands of beautiful and ardent women'. He asked after her 'poor bourgeois soul' again from Trinidad, where he wrote of the 'café coloured sirens' now tempting his heart.

* * *

It was not yearning but necessity that finally drove Fidel from Cuba. After the bell of Demajagua had been stolen from the Hall of Martyrs, where Fidel had left it overnight before his planned procession to the palace the following day, a note was found in its place. It read: 'The bequeathed relics are not for politics. They are venerated.' It seemed that the Manzanillo authorities were not the only ones unhappy with Fidel. He had also incurred the wrath of the UIR. In a comment directed specifically his way, the UIR now called on its supporters to fight 'the intrigues of Creolo Stalinism' and Fidel found himself at the centre of a rather bloody situation that caused even the normally sanguine FEU to denounce 'the climate of violence that prevails'.

Fidel realised he needed to go underground or get away from Havana for a while to let things cool off. The opportunity arose early in 1948 courtesy of the changing political climate on the mainland. Perón's rise to power in Argentina might have stoked liberal resentment among families like Ernesto's, but the cries that travelled furthest across the continent were his own anti-imperial ones. Perón was masterminding a Latin American student leaders' conference that would run alongside (and, he hoped, upstage) the upcoming, and critical, first meeting in the Colombian capital, Bogotá, of the Organisation of American States (OAS). The OAS was to be the lynchpin of United States policy toward the region and Fidel was only too happy to take one of the places for Cuban students that Perón was offering.

He arrived in Bogotá, along with his friend Alfredo Guevara, a student leader named Rafael del Pino and Enrique Ovares in March 1948. A police tail had been assigned to Fidel from the moment of his arrival. According to the report of the Chief of the Department of Security in Bogotá, written about a year later:

> Around these same days arrived in Bogotá the known Cuban communists Fidel Alejandro Castro and Rafael del Pino; they provoked meetings of known leftist students in the University City, from which they frankly rejected all elements marked as rightist. They were taken with their papers to the immigration office and were interrogated. They came on holiday and propagandising against colonialism in America; their papers confirmed this version and they were freed.

The labelling of these two young men in this post-hoc report as 'known' communists – and there is no evidence at this point to paint Fidel as anything more than an occasional visitor to the Marxist library on Carlos III Street in Havana – probably only came about because of what Fidel and del Pino did after sneaking into a performance put on for the diplomatic delegations to the conference. During this event hosted by the Colombian President, Mariano Ospina Pérez, Fidel and del Pino threw down from the mezzanine level leaflets bearing the words: 'From Cuba, of notable communist character'. It was this 'little immature' activity – though, from the way Fidel himself later described it, evidently a rather satisfying one – that got them arrested.

It was but a warm-up for what was to follow. On the morning of 9 April – and with uncanny timing – Fidel was set to have a meeting with Jorge Eliécer Gaitán, the hugely popular leader of the progressive wing of Colombia's Liberal Party. Only days before, Gaitán had led over a hundred thousand people in what was known as the March of Silence, to protest against the last two years of Conservative government and the growing violence across the countryside. As Fidel strolled towards the meeting, Gaitán was shot while leaving his office. The assassin was caught fleeing the scene and beaten to death by an angry mob, his body dragged through the streets and placed outside the presidential palace.

The first Fidel heard of it was that all of a sudden 'there appeared people, running frantically in all directions . . . people who appeared crazy, people shouting, "They killed Gaitán!" "They killed Gaitán!" . . . . Angry people, indignant people, people reflecting a dramatic situation . . . telling what had happened, word that began to spread like gunpowder.' Gaitán's murder, in that fractious city, was sufficient spark to set off a spontaneous popular revolt that many credit with having tipped Colombia towards its long-term slide into civil war.

It also set something off in Fidel. As the crowds rioted in an orgy of pent-up frustration that would later become known as the Bogotazo, a 'restless, impassioned' Fidel Castro was in his element. Fidel later described himself then as 'quixotic, romantic, a dreamer, with very little political know-how but with a tremendous thirst for knowledge and a great impatience for action'. But this was more than just the 'day Castro ran wild' – and at various points, full of 'revolutionary fever', he certainly seemed wild, jumping on to a bench to harangue a nearby troop of soldiers into joining the revolution, waving his rifle around frantically and commandeering a bus with a teargas shotgun. This was Fidel's first taste of rebellion – a formative moment in his young life. He was still not twenty-two, and he would learn much from it – above all, that 'What April 9 lacked was organisation'. Interestingly, in this comment made many years later, he did not say it lacked an ideology or purpose, which assuredly it also did.

Later that same year, after he had organised a strike against bus fare price hikes and was implicated in the murder of a policeman, Fidel decided to marry. His wife to be was Mirta Diaz-Balart, a pretty, dark-haired philosophy student he had been seeing for some time and who had joined him for part of the time in New York. She was from a very well-to-do family in Banes, the town just north of the Castros' holdings in Oriente. They were very much in love – and for a man of his political aspirations her family's social standing was a clear advantage – but it was to be an awkward and ultimately impossible marriage for both of them in many ways.

The Diaz-Balarts were powerful: Mirta's father was a lawyer to the political elite and his clients included Fulgencio Batista, the former president who would later take power in a military coup and become Fidel's arch-enemy. In fact, Batista was among the well-wishers who donated money ($1000) for their honeymoon, which was to be in New York. There was so much about American culture and the buzz of the city that appealed to Fidel. And in any case, with the escalation of violence between the UIR and MSR that summer it was not safe for him in Havana, caught up, as he was, in the crossfire between them.

The wedding took place on 12 October 1948 in Our Lady of Charity Catholic church in Banes. It was a small affair, overshadowed in some respects by the heightened security. According to some accounts, Fidel's father did not even attend. Mirta's parents did, though, and to be on the safe side her father had a word on their behalf with the local chief of the Rural Guard. That even the wedding presents were searched for possible bombs gives an indication of why the Diaz-Balarts were less than enamoured with their daughter's new husband. The newly-weds travelled first to Miami before moving on to New York. Little more is known about this period, though it is said that Fidel took to studying the language and that one day he was seen walking out of a New York bookshop carrying an armful of works by Marx and Engels.

By the time the couple returned to Havana Fidel's constant attendance at rallies, his writing of speeches and denunciations and his attendance at almost any debate that mattered, as well as his two lengthy sojourns in the United States, had left him, even more than Ernesto, terribly behind at university. To begin their new life together, he and Mirta moved into a hotel room at 1218 San Lazaro Street in the shadow of the university. But it was really just more of the same: Fidel crammed and Mirta put up with the lack of comfort and attention.

Before long Mirta was expecting their first child Fidelito, born in September 1949, but Fidel was scarcely ever around, spending whatever time was not taken up by his studies in furthering his political connections, forming alliances and, of course, standing up and making sure he was counted every time a political misdemeanour or act of injustice took place.

That summer of 1949, President Grau's successor Carlos Prío signed what would become known as the 'Gangs' Pact'. In return for an end to their internecine and by now highly unpopular fighting the leaders of the main gangs had been promised top political positions and sinecures. It was a case of fighting fire with fire.

A group of students organised a committee to denounce the increasingly institutionalised favouritism towards the gangs. Though Fidel was not included among the original membership – he was, after all, part of the gang system himself – he perhaps sensed an opportunity not to be missed, and put himself forward for the frankly unenviable task of being the one to deliver the committee's coup de grâce: an unmasking and denunciation of all those involved in the Gangs' Pact. At a meeting in the aptly named Martyrs' Gallery on campus at the end of November Fidel took the floor and according to one fellow student who was there, delivered 'a demolishing denunciation of the whole gangster process'. He then proceeded to name all of those who had been involved in gang activity – which, with his contacts, was a pretty comprehensive list. It was an act that was as foolhardy as it was brave.

The effect of Castro's denunciation was 'absolutely stunning'. Before he had even finished cars were arriving with people who wanted to kill him, and his friend and political aspirant Max Lesnick, who had himself just arrived in a red convertible, was forced to speed him away to safety. Fidel was now one of the most wanted men in Havana and hid out at Lesnick's apartment for two weeks. When it was safe enough he came briefly out of hiding and fled into exile in the United States, where he would spend the first few months of 1950.

Far from feeling isolated, Fidel would spend those months feeling as if he were truly walking in the footsteps of his political idol José Martí (1853–95), the independence hero who is to Latin Americans, and Cubans in particular, a revered figure – a kind of secular saint. Fidel would later seek deliberately and unabashedly to model his life and political career on that of Martí. It would have pleased him greatly that his hero had spent a period of exile in New York. Fidel returned to Havana later that year. He even managed to graduate as a doctor of law in September 1950. He hadn't bothered to go to classes in the end – there wasn't time – but his great ability to cram had seen him through.

* * *

During his trips on the *Anna G*, Ernesto experienced not just the freedom that travel can bring but also its solitude. Notwithstanding his provocative and light-hearted letters home, behind the scenes the now twenty-three-year-old Ernesto was feeling depressed. He wrote a short piece of prose entitled *Angustia* (Anguish) – a series of writings on themes that begin with a quote from Ibsen. In them he conveyed his frustration and despair, arising from an inner turmoil that seemed to knot his insides but which he could still not quite bring out into the light in order to understand.

Though he speaks in *Angustia* of overcoming this depression, on his return to Buenos Aires Ernesto still appeared to be in a despondent state. 'Many times I saw him looking concerned, low or deep in thought, but never really sad or bitter,' Tita recalled. Like Fidel, but for wholly different reasons, Ernesto needed a period of time in which to straighten his thoughts. The form that it took was the now famous half-year road trip he embarked upon with his old friend from Córdoba, Alberto Granado.

Before Ernesto and Alberto – whom Ernesto nicknamed Mial (My Al) left on the clapped out motorbike they ironically christened *La Poderosa* (Powerful One), Ernesto wrote to his much-trusted (and in love, still tested) friend Tita. In that letter he makes mention of the effect that his travels up to that point had had on him. In an elusive and much-debated passage, its meaning muffled by his atrocious writing and the ambiguity of the Argentine expressions he uses, he speaks of his growing sense of inserting himself into a 'mother' of a problem. But it seems at least possible, and perhaps probable – given that he speaks of piety, of the *patria*, and his 'future political family' – that Ernesto was aware that his journeys had their destination rooted not in some place, but rather in a particular state of mind. He signed off with the phrase, 'Salen baby, as your friends like to say', mimicking the local pronunciation of 'So long, baby'. This attempt at a departing flourish was not quite as emphatic as he might have liked. He would return from this trip – he had at the very least promised his mother he would – but not, as he himself soon realised, quite as the same person.

The two young travellers, Ernesto and Alberto, left Buenos

Aires on 4 January 1952. They passed a few days in Miramar, where Chichina's family were spending the summer, so Ernesto could say farewell. From here they cut round the bottom of Argentina before heading across to Valparaíso in Chile. The inappropriately named bike gave up on them before they had gone too far, and they carried on as hitch-hikers. Their route maps out a gliding circle of intent, first around the more familiar Argentine provinces, then taking a more adventurous swoop from Chile up almost along the spine of the Andes to Colombia and Venezuela before Ernesto struck out alone on the final leg to Miami.

What Ernesto, admirer of Jules Verne and Jack London that he was, sought along the way was adventure. But not simply adventure. He had a volatile and eager mind, and neither his medical studies, nor even his readings with Tita had thus far been able to satisfy him. The one feature that, above all others, distinguished Ernesto Guevara from his contemporaries was his facility for ruthless self-criticism. If he was renowned for being harsh on others, he was yet harsher on himself. But he had one weakness which he seems never to have recognised, and almost certainly because it was also the cause of his great strength: he was as a youth, and would remain as a man, utterly incapable of exercising patience. It is for this reason that he took with such gusto to travel – not because he wanted to escape, but because he needed the flow of constant movement to keep him steady. While most people find travelling either tires or releases them, empties their mind or fills it, for Ernesto travelling simply allowed him to sustain the constant barrage of novelty that his sharp but impatient mind required in order to think things through. One need only compare his travel diaries with the prose written in his more sedentary moments to appreciate the effect of movement upon his thought. He saw things far more clearly on the go.

Toward the end of their trip, the two by now seasoned travellers arrived in Bogotá. Four years earlier, in 1948, when Fidel passed through, he had been caught up in the tumultuous events of the Bogotazo and in many ways the country was still reeling from its effects. Ernesto had a fine knack for pen-sketches of the places he saw, and his diary makes it clear that he found Colombia unappealing. 'This country is that in which individual rights are most suppressed of all the countries we have seen, the police patrol the streets with rifles on their shoulder and demand of everyone their passport. It is a tense atmosphere which makes you think there will be a revolt some time soon.' Unlike Fidel, if there was going to be a revolt, he wasn't waiting around long enough to see it, this different response marking clearly the differences between them. After the police picked up Ernesto and Alberto for not having their papers in order the two Argentines were given forty-eight hours to leave the country. They only needed half the time.

Ernesto was scarcely more enamoured of Miami, where he arrived on his own after having left Alberto to a medical post he had taken in Caracas. Ernesto had accepted the rather long detour in exchange for a free flight back to Argentina on a plane carrying race horses for one of his wealthy uncles. He spent most of his time in Miami in student digs, wandering about, visiting the public library, living off a daily milky coffee until he began picking up some free food at a local diner, and longing all the while to head back south once more. He was disappointed when informed he would have to spend a month there awaiting some crucial repairs to the plane. As with Bogotá the two future revolutionaries had responded to their first experience of the United States somewhat differently: Fidel had rather enjoyed his time in New York, but Miami stretched Ernesto's patience to the limit – though he gave the place little chance to impress him.

When Ernesto arrived back in Buenos Aires, he was pleased and relieved to be home, but he sought to take advantage of the opportunity it provided to cast himself anew among his family and friends. No longer could he relax in the moral isolation that the physical and mental distance from such acute poverty afforded his more sedentary peers; he had squeezed poverty and riches into the same few months, and had carefully noted how they were connected.

He had also fallen far behind in his studies. In order to make up the necessary grades to qualify in his final year everything else was for a while pushed into the background. The relationship with Chichina, already over, rested quietly in that place between love lost and friendship found. They met a few times and exchanged, as she recalls, a few lingering glances. But overall he had little time for his friends. 'He would spend fourteen hours studying in the library, alone. One would see him only at moments . . . he would disappear for long periods and then reappear,' one recalled.

But there was one thing he did find time for apart from preparing for his exams. Establishing a pattern that he was to keep for life, he now began to edit his diary and to reflect upon his travels. 'Wandering around our "America with a capital A" has changed me more than I thought,' he wrote. Travel and writing went hand in hand for Ernesto. It is as if the two are connected, and, like some great dynamo, he needs the charge of movement to wind out his thoughts. He concluded, 'The person who wrote these notes died the day he stepped back on Argentine soil. The person who is reorganising and polishing them, me, is no longer me, at least I'm not the me I was.'

*　*　*

Graduation finally brought about a period of relative calm for the ceaselessly active young Fidel. Shortly after finishing his studies Fidel set up a relatively low-key operation with two former fellow law students, Jorge Azpiazu and Rafael Resende. Their firm was dedicated to helping the poor against more powerful opponents. And if it seemed strangely quotidian to some of his friends, it was not quite the change in direction it might have looked. Fidel wanted a platform for his future political career now, and he desired a record of good works to go with it. The law firm would provide the perfect vehicle to indulge his genuine social views in a way that would also support his future political aspirations.

The trio set themselves up in the commercial district of Habana Vieja, near to the harbour and given the pitiful state of their finances struggled even to rent the most basic office for their firm. But with the little money they had left over from the rent, they sent a carefully staged picture to the newspapers to advertise their new business. The sign above the door read: 'Office of Aspiazu–Castro–Resende: Asuntos Civiles, Criminales y Sociales'. The 'office', portrayed in the advert with a solid dark wooden desk decked out with a card file and inkpot and with two swivel chairs behind it, was rarely used by Fidel. Its small, chest-height bookshelf was merely functional, and half empty. But it was crested with a pineapple-sized bust of Martí, which gave a truer impression of where Fidel's real interests still lay.

Over the three-year life of this enterprise, before Fidel became completely sidetracked by his revolutionary career, the three lawyers made a little over 4000 pesos from just two successful cases. Their third major victory – a law suit against the American-owned Cuban Telephone Company – did not come through until Fidel was already in prison for having begun his armed struggle. At the point Aspiazu–Castro–Resende began, however, Fidel was still some way from taking up arms as a means of furthering his political ambitions. Those ambitions were for the time being channelled into the Ortodoxo party that had set itself up in opposition to the governing Autentico party founded by former President Grau and the incumbent President Prío.

Fidel developed a particular attachment to the Ortodoxo senator and national political icon Eduardo Chibás. The two had a lot in common. Chibás had also been described as 'too volatile, too unreliable, for the entrenched leaders of the official party'. He had been known to call for a duel when his honour was slighted. But above all, Chibás was a magnificent speaker –

something Fidel always admired – and he used his popular Sunday radio shows, during which his 'impassioned, emotional and sincere temperament' came to the fore, to denounce the ever-persistent corruption in Cuban politics.

In August 1951 Chibás took to the airwaves to defend his name from a smear campaign that, this time, had been launched against him. People tuned in by the thousand, eager to hear how Chibás would draw blood in response to this latest political wheeze. But that day was to provide an even greater surprise. Towards the end of his show, as Chibás declared live on air, 'This is my last wake-up call [to you]!' he pulled a revolver from his jacket and shot himself twice in the stomach.

Whether Chibás had meant to kill himself was hotly debated in the press, but the outcome was clear. For many Chibás *was* the opposition, and his death marked the end of an era. It also left a vacuum in the national leadership, and when Fidel stood in the front row of the guard of honour lain on for Chibás the twenty-five-year-old was making a statement of political intent. Indeed, not long after Chibás' death Fidel tried to gain election to the House of Representatives. But he was not successful because he lacked the support of the rest of the Ortodoxo leadership who saw him as too much of a wild card.

Adapting his mentor's own approach, Fidel then sought a more direct political mandate for himself and began using his law practice to undertake a series of scandalising investigations into the increasingly corrupt Prío regime. On one occasion he even posed as a gardener to take the photos that would show how Prío was 'prostituting the spirit of the Presidential office' with his 'voracious appetite for land' and his 'palaces and pools'. It was the beginning of a long campaign. Next, Fidel set about trying to document the full extent of this 'corruption and misery'. He made a careful inventory of four of Prío's ranches and noted just how they had come into his hands. Then Fidel threw down the gauntlet to Prío, inviting him to respond to the accusations before the nation. 'I said that I would avenge the disgrace that this vile regime brought upon Chibás,' Fidel wrote triumphantly, '. . . and we are doing so week by week.'

But Fidel's brief period holding Chibás' mantle aloft was soon brought crashing down. Batista, former president and now family friend of Fidel's in-laws, the Diaz-Balarts, had been standing in the elections that were scheduled for that summer. When he saw that his chances were dwindling, and amid rumours that Prío was going to do something unconstitutional, Batista decided to take action himself.

Though he always claimed surprise, Fidel might just have known beforehand about the coup that took place on 10 March 1952 and set him firmly on the road to revolution. He had well-placed sources in the army, and he knew Batista's mind after having paid him a visit in the summer of the previous year. The meeting got little further than a few carefully worded pleasantries, but as Fidel perused Batista's well-stocked bookshelves he was unable to resist conveying his surprise that the Machiavellian former army sergeant did not have Malaparte's *Technique of the Coup d'Etat*. Batista replied wanly that it was something he would have to speak to his librarian about.

It seems he didn't need to. On the morning of the 10th, Batista took control first of the army and then, with resistance from the beleaguered administration proving minimal, the entire country. Whether apprised of his plans or not, Fidel was furious. Aware that his own safety might be at risk as a known opposition member, he immediately went into hiding, first at the apartment of his sister Lidia and then at the apartment of a friend, Eva Jiménez, who ran a safe house in the middle-class Almendares district of Havana. Then, inspired perhaps by his recent writing activities, over two days he set himself to defining a response.

Fidel chose the title of this reply to Batista's coup – *Revolución no, Zarpazo!* – very carefully. A *zarpazo* is a punch, and not just a lightweight's jab but a proper bone-busting heavyweight smack. Fidel responded with all the indignation that Chibás might have mustered, condemning Batista to one hundred years of prison for having infringed – and he cited them – Articles 147, 149, 235, 236 and 240 of the Civil Defence Code.

Fidel was not alone. Other voices of the underground now surfaced too. After years of internecine warfare the students' union, the FEU, brought back its newspaper, *Alma Mater*, to denounce Batista, and on 2 May an edition of the clandestine *Son los Mismos* (They Are the Same) was put out, edited by Abel Santamaría and Jesús Montané Oropesa – two men who would soon be swept along with Fidel's now rapidly evolving ideas. As Raúl Chibás, brother of Eduardo, said: '[T]he 10 March determined everything that came after.'

3. BULLETS AND BACKPACKS

FROM THE MOMENT Batista seized power in March 1952 Fidel Castro gave up on the slow and, he now deemed, futile work of constitutional opposition. As he would later put it, he simply 'stepped out' from party politics. He was not the only one to reach this conclusion. A rising tide of similarly disaffected young people – left-wingers and radicals drawn from the popular and workers' parties, especially the Ortodoxos, in the main – did likewise. As he met many of these, often in Havana's vast Colón cemetery which was a focal point for speeches and secret political meetings, Fidel quickly drew a group of like-minded people about him: Abel Santamaría (who would become Fidel's second-in-command), Abel's sister Haydée, Jesus Montané (an employee of General Motors whom Castro met when trying to exchange his car for a more serviceable one) and Melba Hernández. As was perhaps inevitable, *they* would immediately be cast as *his* supporters.

Slowly, this impromptu and rather ad hoc movement began to grow. It was a largely shapeless grouping for now, and for some time it would lack even a name. What shape it did have was given form primarily by Fidel's magnetic personality. 'When this young man began to talk,' Melba – who was seven years older than Castro – later recalled, 'all I could do was listen to him . . . Fidel spoke in a very low voice, he paced back and forth, then came close to you as if to tell you a secret, and then you suddenly felt you shared the secret.' Ties of personal loyalty and trust were thus a feature of Fidel's political organising from the start.

During these months of clandestine activity Fidel worked at what was to become his trademark frenetic pace: composing and disseminating pamphlets, organising the group's structure and week by week developing its mandate. He was constantly busy whether seeking out radio transmitting equipment or writing rhetorical broadsides to be wound out by hand on their small mimeograph machine and later distributed along with the movement's underground publication, *El Acusador* (The Accusor). The line taken was always the same – down with Batista. And at the same time as he tried to figure out just how they might achieve that, Fidel was trying to maintain the semblance of a family life with Mirta and their young son Fidelito.

'We are going to take up arms against the regime,' he began to tell new recruits from the end of that summer. Meanwhile, the clandestine presses thrummed with indignation as they catalogued the growing atrocities of the new regime. By the beginning of 1953 Fidel had at his fingertips a movement of some several hundred members, carefully organised into cells and partially trained in the use of arms. Finally, by the summer of that year he was ready to launch his attack against the regime.

The date set was 26 July, the Sunday of carnival weekend in Santiago where the main thrust of Fidel's plan was to capture the infamous Moncada barracks. There was also to be a secondary objective, the barracks at Bayamo. The heat in Cuba is at its worst at that time of year, and even just before dawn on the Sunday it was almost unbearably hot and sticky. But the Saturday night's festivities were still in full flow. Carnival-goers with painted faces and in brightly coloured costumes crowded the streets, dancing charangas and cha cha chas.

Just after 5.00 on the Sunday morning, as the last of the revellers stumbled down the crooked lanes, their feet sore and their ears buzzing from the racket of trumpets and drums, Fidel gave the group of men who had gathered for the attack the order to begin. A cavalcade of sixteen cars filed out of a ranch in a place named El Siboney, on the outskirts of the city, and began making its way down the dirt roads toward the town. 'It was so dusty you could only see a couple of yards,' one of the drivers recalled.

Packed into the train of Buicks, Cadillacs and Pontiacs were ninety men, their mouths dry with fear and their fingers nervously clutching the mixture of light hunting rifles and small-calibre sports guns that had been handed to them from a secret stash at the ranch. Dressed in poorly fitting military fatigues, some with their two-tone shoes lucent beneath them, they were no less a spectacle than the worst of the drunks at the carnival. One of the men, José Luis Tasende, was still wearing his civilian belt with its glittering 'J'-shaped buckle – an unfortunate error that he would very soon come to regret.

No sooner had the rebels' cars driven out of the ranch towards the Central Highway that would take them to Santiago than things began to go wrong. The plan had been to place the vehicles in a predetermined order once on the motorway, but when some of them got lost, or simply drove off the wrong way, this proved impossible. In the second vehicle, manoeuvring down the steep and winding lanes into the city, Castro cursed and fumed at the disorganisation that was unfolding around him.

As they approached the barracks, the front group of cars filed off towards its side entrance. Behind them, the sniper contingent broke off to take up their places on the roof of the Palace of Justice, while the third group headed towards the nearby Civil Hospital which would also provide a good position from which to supply covering fire. Fidel's planning at this stage had been meticulous. The men knew when the patrols passed by, and with the carnival still winding down – the leader of the garrison himself was the worse for wear – it was the perfect time to attack. But Fidel had planned with only a thin margin for error.

At 5.17, precisely two minutes behind schedule, the first attack car, a Mercury driven by a young man named Marerro, throttled up to gate no. 3, a side entrance to the barracks. Following the plan Fidel had outlined at El Siboney, Renato Guitart, the leader of this contingent, whose car had been disguised as an official vehicle with the military's Fourth of September flags draped around it and a photograph of General Batista taped to the front windshield, bellowed authoritatively, 'Clear the way, the General is coming!' As the confused guards drew to attention the car stopped and three other rebels, Jesus Montané, Ramiro Valdés and José Suárez, jumped out to disarm them.

The first of the rebels then rushed into the building while the second car, driven by Fidel, confronted an unexpected two-man patrol walking the perimeter of the barracks. Fidel slowed down and fired his Luger at the two men, Private Silva Domínguez and Luis Triay (a man known to his fellow soldiers as Goat Face). The soldiers returned fire with their Thompson machine guns, shots which 'rudely awakened' Sergeant Eulalio González, at home with his wife and infant child, as they 'stitched a row of holes across the upper wooden wall of their living room, killing their parrot on its perch'. The volley of bullets also caused Fidel to swerve violently. The car struck the kerb at such an angle and with such force that the left front axle was completely smashed.

By now the alarm, 'a loud and continuous electric bell at all four entrances', had been raised. The entire garrison, and half of the city, would be aware that an attack of some sort was taking place at the Moncada. The element of surprise was lost. Blocked by Fidel's car, the rest of the rebels could only side their cars to the barracks, or take cover behind their vehicles' huge winged doors, to return what fire they could with their peashooter rifles.

At the nearby Palace of Justice, overlooking the barracks, Raúl Castro and his squad of fighters – presided over by Léster Rodríguez – were headed for the roof to provide covering fire. 'What is happening?' they were asked by a corporal from the barracks as they approached the Palace of Justice. 'Batista has fallen!' responded Raúl. They rang the doorbell and entered, taking the concierge who opened the door hostage as they did

so. 'That's when we started hearing the shots from our companions and the soldiers,' Léster recalled. Rounding up the rest
of the security staff inside, they bundled them all into the elevator
and hauled the prisoners along with them to the roof. But they
had a nasty shock when they realised that the height of the
building's retaining wall prevented them from firing downwards.

The group led by Fidel's second-in-command, Abel Santamaría, had meanwhile successfully taken over the Civil Hospital.
The two women – Melba and Haydée, Abel's sister – along with
Mario Muñoz, an older man and a doctor by profession,
eventually turned up in their black Lincoln after first heading the
wrong way on the Central Highway. They arrived at the hospital
under what another of the rebels, Severino Rosell, described as
a 'hail of bullets'. Once inside, they smashed open the drug
cabinets to treat the injured and put on medical uniforms as
planned to disguise themselves. But they too were unable to offer
any useful covering fire once the garrison's machine gun set to
work, and they found themselves also fighting off resistance from
armed security guards inside.

Fidel's carefully thought out strategy was rapidly coming
undone. Central to his plan had been that all the cars would file
into the main courtyard of the barracks, under covering fire from
the surrounding captured buildings. The rebels would then rush
up the stairways that led into the main barracks, capturing soldiers
and weapons and temporarily taking over the fort and its radio
transmitter before fanning out through the city to arm the presumably willing population. It was a strategy based upon careful
observation of the fort and a good dose of faith in the historical
belligerence of Santiagueros.

As the rebel cars crumpled under the pounding of the machine
gun Fidel stood in the street behind his Buick, waving his pistol
and shouting, 'Forward, boys! Forward!' He stayed there for 'five
or six minutes' desperately trying to regroup his men. But with
the loss of speed and surprise he knew that the battle had already
been lost.

The few rebels to have penetrated the barracks were soon holed up in its barber's shop. They tried waving a handkerchief out of the window to indicate surrender, but that action was only answered with more bullets from the machine gun and then a squad of soldiers was sent in. The soldiers tossed a grenade into the barber's shop, killing one of the rebels on the spot. Two managed to escape, but the remaining three were soon captured and taken outside where they were clubbed to death with rifle butts.

One of the two to make it back outside was Ramiro Valdés, who sprinted towards their car – now with its tyres blown out after half an hour of incessant crossfire – and managed to start it up. Seeing this, Fidel too realised there was now nothing for it but to retreat. Valdés wheeled off in reverse on the rims, slamming into Fidel's car, before turning and rattling along a few blocks to the home of a physician who was known to the conspirators. Two of those fighting alongside Fidel, Severino Rosell and Gerardo Granados, did the same and ran for another car. As they started it up, Fidel dived through the still open door. Before they hurtled off, eleven others managed to squeeze in alongside them. The attack had not lasted more than an hour and some of Fidel's men had not even found their way to the barracks, but already his dream of bringing down Batista was over.

* * *

A long way from the stifling heat of Fidel's failed attack in Santiago, it was snowing in Buenos Aires. A small group of people stood waiting on the platform of the city's vaulted Belgrano railway station, gifts of an oven cooked chicken and two litres of wine clutched in their cold hands. It was two weeks before Fidel's attack would make headlines around the world and ten months since Ernesto had returned from the now famous journey he had made with 'Mial', whom he had promised to rejoin in Venezuela. In April Ernesto had walked proudly out of the university buildings brandishing his doctor's certificate, and since then he had been eagerly planning his next trip with another childhood friend, Calica Ferrer.

'My helper's name has changed,' he wrote on the first page of a still crisp new diary. 'Alberto is now called Calica. But the trip is the same: two separate wills moving out through the American continent, not knowing the exact aim of their quest nor in which direction lies their objective.' As they clambered into the train carriages Ernesto sensed, quite accurately, that here were 'a couple of odd-looking snobs loaded down with baggage' whose 'fine clothes, leather coats etc.' were drawing 'strange looks' from the peasants who made up the vast majority of second class.

But 'strange looks' were precisely what he was after. He wanted once more the thrill of the new, the excitement of discovering things previously unimagined. And if he wasn't yet sure exactly what he was searching for, he was none the less certain of what he did not want to be: precisely one of those 'semi-scientist, semi-bohemian, semi-revolutionary' products of his class that had come to see him off. Of all the smartly dressed friends and family waving handkerchiefs at them and pressing gifts to them from the platform edge, his mother was the most expressive. 'Minucha, I am losing him forever, I will never see my son Ernesto again,' she had confided to her daughter-in-law Matilde Lezica the day before, and when the moment came she was distraught. 'When the train pulled out, Celia ran, ran, ran along the platform next to the train,' Matilde recalled.

Though he was never given to overt expressions of his own feelings, and like any young man leaving home behind he would have shied from such an emotional outburst from his mother, Ernesto fully reciprocated his mother's adoration for him. And he was sad to say goodbye to faithful old Tita, who had also come to see him off. The differences were more clearly marked, however, between Ernesto and his father. Guevara Lynch looked on with what comes across in his writings as a certain disdain at the antics of his wife. He seems in fact to have erased entirely from his memory the picture of his wife crying over her special son, focusing instead on the more portentous image of a young soldier with a kitbag slung over his shoulder. As Ernesto's father recalled, 'instead of boarding the train he ran alongside it for a few metres, and then raising the arm in which he carried his green bag, cried: "Here goes a soldier of the Americas!"'

They did not understand this gesture, Guevara Lynch later recalled, until after his son had joined forces with Fidel. But what was clear was that the little 'creature' that he had tried to raise was gone, and of the son that remained there was little that he would ever really understand. For Ernesto, the chance to be back on the road again, to leave behind this comfortable but constraining life, was a relief. As the train reached La Quiaca on the Argentine–Bolivian border, he noted, 'Two flags face each other across a tiny little railway bridge, the Bolivian new and brightly coloured, the other old, dirty and faded, as if it has begun to understand the poverty of its symbolism.'

'[N]ight falls and everything is lost in the gradually spreading grip of the cold,' Ernesto scribbled with numb fingers into his diary as their train trundled towards their first destination of La Paz. The cold hardened the water in the travellers' drinking bottles and iced over their boots. It also broke Calica's initial resolve to stick it out in second class. On his insistence, they upgraded themselves to first. Not that it was any warmer. Unwashed and slowly freezing, they trudged to the dining carriage where they passed most of that day looking out over the sparse scrub as the train passed through the countryside and eventually up and over the rim of craterous hills around La Paz. From there they descended into a 'small but very beautiful city' that 'lies scattered about the rugged background terrain, with the perpetually snow-covered figure of Mount Illimani as its sentinel'.

Bolivia was a country in the throes of revolutionary upheaval. When Ernesto arrived, the nationalist revolution there was noisily celebrating the Agrarian Reform Law and he spent many of his afternoons observing with interest the marches and parades led by the Bolivian miners. But on the train to La Paz the two youths had also met the son of a well-known Bolivian aristocrat, Isaías Nogues, former governor of the Argentine region of Tucumán and now a sworn enemy of Perón. Nogues was at the centre of the Argentine community in La Paz and afforded the two an easy entrée into almost any place they desired: 'The best people of La Paz invite us to lunch . . . they drive us around the city and have invited us to a party . . . We went to a boite, the Gallo de Oro, owned by an Argentine. They haven't let us pay for any of this . . . All the time it's tea, meals in the Sucre and the Hotel La Paz, the two best ones . . . This afternoon we're having tea with a couple of rich girls, and tonight we're going to a dance.'

Bolivia was thus to prove a contradictory experience for Ernesto. He spent his days exploring the complex social dynamics at work: 'The Indian continues to be an animal for the white mind, whichever holy order they belong to,' he noted after a trip out of the capital and down a treacherous mountain pass to Las Yungas. But nights involved all the delights that high society in La Paz could offer them, and after just a couple of days of Nogues' hospitality Ernesto felt obliged to refresh his description of the city. This was 'the Shanghai of the Americas', he corrected himself in his diary.

It was at Nogues' house that Ernesto and Calica met another Argentine, Ricardo Rojo, a 'tall, beefy man with a balding pate and a moustache'. Córdobans being incapable of letting a possible nickname slip, he was immediately, and for the rest of his and Ernesto's long and usually reluctant acquaintance, referred to as 'Fatso Rojo'. Rojo had recently escaped from prison, where he was being held on suspicion of having been involved in a planned series of dynamite explosions intended to interrupt a speech that Perón was to make to a crowd of workers in the Plaza de Mayo in Buenos Aires. *Life* magazine ran a story on it and thereafter, along with his exile's special pass, he always carried a clipping around with him like a badge.

It was at one of these rather broadly educational evenings –

there were reports of some of the guests disappearing to the toilets to snort cocaine – that Ernesto heard of the events that had recently taken place at Moncada. Whether he realised it or not, though instinctively he seemed to be groping his way towards it, Ernesto was gradually being drawn into this world. At this moment, however, he still looked upon foreign intervention in the affairs of Latin American nations with not much less scepticism than he viewed some of the responses that were made to them. But the balance was beginning to shift.

* * *

With his attack at the Moncada, Fidel instantly achieved the wider recognition he had long sought. But right then, his life was in very grave danger. After fleeing the barracks Fidel had regrouped with the small number of others who had managed to escape. What his exact intentions were at this point have never been clear. Together they trudged towards the mountains, stopping at the *bohios* of sympathetic peasants, picking fruit when they could find it. On the second day planes began circling overhead looking for them, as they tuned in to the radio at the farm of a peasant named Feliciano Heredia and heard the names of the dead – far more than they recalled – they realised that their comrades were being murdered.

The scene that those who were able to escape left behind at Moncada – as at the secondary objective at Bayamo where the attackers met with a similar fate – had quickly become a far bloodier affair than it was at the close of battle. Venting their fury on the prisoners, 'the soldiers went looking for vengeance'. Dozens of the captured rebels were led in small groups to the target practice range inside the barracks and machine-gunned at point-blank range. Among those murdered was José Luis Tasende, he of the shimmering 'J' buckle, who having so deftly escaped from the barracks by jumping out of a window had been captured on account of his unconvincing uniform. He made no sound as he was carried by four soldiers to the target range, dropped on the ground and then quickly shot through the head.

Fidel was right to be fearful, therefore, when he was finally detained at a farm in the hills outside Santiago. Indeed, the private who captured him had lost a brother in the attack, and when he realised that it was Fidel he had before him the soldier levelled his gun to shoot him in cold blood. Fidel was fortunate that the commanding officer, Sarría, had no such vendetta and had read his Sarmiento. 'You cannot kill ideas,' Sarría said to Fidel, quoting the Argentine educationalist as he disarmed the furious private and ordered him to back off. As they were transported back to the base Fidel turned to the officer and whispered, 'Why didn't you kill me?' '*Muchacho*,' Sarría replied quietly, 'I am not that kind of man.' Once again, Fidel's luck had held. He was *that* kind of man.

Fidel was held at the nearby Boniato prison until the much-publicised trial of the Moncada rebels was due to begin. On Monday, 21 September 1953 he was taken to the first session of their trial, to be heard in the very Palace of Justice that the rebels had taken over during the attack. An army cordon was drawn around the building, but the usually empty chamber where the trial was to take place was packed with hundreds of friends, relatives and onlookers. Fidel was driven to the courtroom in a Jeep, his handcuffs clamped down to the bone, with three buses bringing the rest of his men behind. He had planned for both a clinical strike and a powerful symbolic action in his attack at Moncada. Though it had proven not to be the former, Fidel was determined that it might still be made into the latter.

'This is the most difficult case the Cuban justice tribunals have encountered,' Juan Mejías, one of the three presiding judges, had told the waiting reporters before the trial. 'It is also the most important of all that have been known in political matters.' He was quite right. Fidel, for his part, knew that the trial would enable him to espouse the revolutionary platform that their failure to take Moncada had denied him. He would also be ensured of the full attention of the nation, which had been enthralled by the events in Santiago. By making it such a public trial, Batista had unwittingly given Fidel the perfect opportunity to turn a courtroom drama into a political act – and Fidel was never one to miss an opportunity.

Fidel was the last to enter as the court drew to attention. 'Look at him, so tough when he attacked the garrison, and now he is shitting his pants in fear,' one of the soldiers said. Fidel turned round, fixed his gaze on the soldier and then, without responding, turned back to face the court again. The soldiers were not his quarry today. Just as he had planned meticulously for Moncada, so Fidel had prepared well for the trial. Though kept in isolation, the men had secretly supplied him with crucial evidence that had emerged in the eight weeks since the attack. Using these reports of the subsequent atrocities, Fidel's strategy was to turn their own trial into a judgement of Batista himself.

Fidel was asked, first of all, to explain his movement, which of course he was only too happy to do even though it still lacked a name. He was sanguine in the answers he gave as to why they had attacked Moncada and how they had ultimately failed. It was, he said, 'the only solution to the present national problem'. Once he had been questioned by most of the twenty-four defence attorneys, Fidel then asked to assume his own defence. He donned a robe, and took up his position in front of the bar before the court adjourned for the day. For the next two days Fidel questioned his co-defendants in detail, logging in public the atrocities committed against his men – some of whom, as he declared, had been dragged behind cars with nooses around their necks, while others, like Tasende, had been murdered in cold blood.

When he learned that Fidel was turning the court into a political arena in this way, Colonel del Río Chaviano, the Commanding officer at the barracks, was furious. And when he heard that Fidel had called upon him to testify, he became extremely nervous too and privately forbade Fidel to be allowed back into the court. There was an eerie silence at the roll call the following morning when the register reached Fidel's name. The court clerk looked up at the chief judge, who signalled for him to proceed. The defence attorneys raised an objection, but an army lieutenant then produced a letter informing the court that Fidel was sick. This was the opening he had been hoping for.

'Dr Fidel Castro is not sick,' cried Melba as she approached the bench, drawing a folded note from her bosom. It was a letter from Fidel who had smuggled it out of his cell. He certainly was not ill, he informed the court; he was being prevented from attending by the army. Fidel demanded that a physician should come and see him to verify his health, and that copies of his letter should be forwarded to the appropriate authorities. As before, he was deliberately seeking to win the three presiding judges over to his cause so as to keep the army at bay. 'The performance of the court until now and the prestige of its magistrates,' he went on ingratiatingly, 'accredit it as one of the most honourable in the Republic, which is why I expound these considerations in blind faith in its vigorous action.'

The judges, duly convinced of their own greatness, called for a recess. But they were at a loss. Yet again Fidel's foresight, combined with his sheer nerve, had pulled the rug out from under the military. Aware that he had effectively derailed the process, the judges ordered Fidel be safeguarded, that all his conditions in the letter be met, but that henceforth he should be tried separately. With Fidel out of the way, the remainder of the trial proceeded quickly. The leaders had agreed to confess to everything, so as to allow some of the others to be let off for lack of evidence. The leaders were then sentenced to thirteen years' imprisonment. The judge rang his desk bell and the court rose.

* * *

With his 'passe partout' Rojo had glided effortlessly north to arrive in Ecuador some time before Ernesto and Calica, whom he had agreed to meet there. They had taken a rather more long-winded route, as Ernesto insisted on dragging his suitcase full of books everywhere they went. 'It felt like a ton of bricks,' he wrote in his diary, a problem which, after 'a hell of a row' at the Peruvian border, was eased somewhat as the weight of *Man in the Soviet Union* and another publication that made the customs guard loudly accuse him of being 'red, red, red!' were taken off him. Ernesto's experience of the South American continent was now being filtered through a more deliberate engagement in Marxist literature. Indeed, both his reading of Marxism and his experiences on the road seemed to make more sense to him when absorbed alongside one another.

In Guayaquil, Rojo was waiting to greet them. He had joined up now with a further group of Argentines, Andres Herrero, Eduardo (Gualo) García and Óscar Valdovinos, all of them lawyers. Guayaquil was a fruit-ferrying port, 'an excuse for a city without a life of its own', as Ernesto described it, and he and Calica soon realised that they had little option but to join in with Rojo's living arrangements – this time, however, in one of the poorest parts of town.

The group settled into a shared room in a hostel by the port with views of the tugboats and fruit container ships. It was a dreary scene that spoke to Ernesto of the sad plight of this and other small republics prostrate before the demands of the world market. Prevented from doing very much by their current lack of finances and a complete lack of things to do, there was plenty of time to mull things over. At the prompting of some of the others, Ernesto decided to continue north towards Panama and Central America with this new group, rather than, as he had promised, head with Calica to visit Alberto in Venezuela. The things he saw in these countries angered him to be sure, but they fascinated him in equal measure and he wanted to see more.

Waiting to leave with Gualo García in the port of Golfito – a town dominated by the American-owned United Fruit Company – Ernesto noted the fractious social landscape: 'As ever, the class spirit of the gringos makes itself felt,' he noted bitterly. It was all the more poignant for being set against the physical beauty of the place, where 'hills a hundred metres high rise almost from the sea shore, their slopes covered with tropical vegetation', surrounding a town 'divided into clearly defined zones with guards who can prevent anyone from moving across, and of course the best zone is that of the gringos'. 'It looks a little like Miami,' he said – in Ernesto-speak, a sure-fire insult.

After a journey up the coast that he spent 'caught between the dodges and smirks of [a] black woman' whom he had found in port before they left, an ever more footloose Ernesto arrived in Costa Rica where he began, really for the first time in his life, to set about deliberately exploring the local political scene. Walking into the Soda Palace Hotel one day, with his rucksack on his shoulder, Ernesto met some of the Cubans who had taken part in the Moncada attack with Fidel. They included Severino Rosell, who had escaped from the barracks in the same car as Fidel. The hotel was known as 'the international', given that on almost every table could be found a group of young exiles, just like themselves, conversing conspiratorially in different languages. And theirs were all stories for Ernesto's increasingly willing ear.

At the hotel Ernesto also met the Dominican exile Juan Bosch – on whose expedition to unseat Trujillo, Fidel had enrolled – and the Costa Rican communist leader Manuel Mora Valverde. He had now begun actively to seek out leaders whenever he arrived somewhere new, and seemed to be looking for some combination of testimony and explanation from them. Valverde he found a 'quiet man, indeed slow and deliberate . . . [but] He gave us a thorough account of recent Costa Rican politics.' More interesting perhaps than the account – which, though populated with intellectuals ruined by whisky, plans for invasions of Nicaragua and double-dealings, none the less runs to little more than a pat analysis of indigenous higher classes turning against their own – were the copious and detailed notes that Ernesto took of it. He was using these conversations to translate the ideas that he was reading about into an increasingly concrete understanding.

What he was beginning to put together was a means of explaining the range of experiences he was encountering in Central America, and it made intuitive sense to him.

The same kind of situation occurred when, after a day of 'boredom, reading, insipid jokes' and a touch of medicine on the side (a pensioner from Panama came complaining of tapeworm), Ernesto finally got to meet the former Venezuelan President Rómulo Betancourt. He caught the measure of Betancourt immediately: 'He strikes me as a politician with some firm social ideas in his head, but otherwise capable of swaying and bending for what promises the greatest advantage.' This was not a comment he would have made even a few months earlier. Ernesto's understanding of politics, gradually learned while on the road, had come on in leaps and bounds.

He now stood on the brink of an important period in his life, and he seems to have sensed it. From San Juan on 10 December 1953 he sent a typically playful letter to Aunt Beatriz. 'In Guatemala I will improve myself and obtain what it is I lack for being an authentic revolutionary.' He signed off 'With hugs and kisses, your loving nephew, he of the iron health and empty stomach and the shining faith in the socialist future, Ciao, Chancho.' As he and Gualo trekked that way, through a thoroughly unappreciated drizzle, they were for once quite pleased when a car that approached from the other direction skidded to a halt and none other than Fatso Rojo jumped out, as ever with a few more hang-alongs in tow, and offered them a lift to the border.

* * *

On 16 October, Fidel was finally tried with two further co-defendants who had missed the joint trial due to their injuries. Ostensibly for this reason – though in all likelihood so as to keep Fidel away from the public – this second trial took place in the Civil Hospital and not the Palace of Justice. Military police stood guard at the doors of the cramped room, bayonets fixed, while the defence attorneys sat behind a mahogany desk that had been rather grandly squeezed in for the legal proceedings. A handful of reporters, among them Marta Rojas – who had rushed to the Moncada barracks from the carnival when she first heard shots that clearly could not just be firecrackers and had followed the trial ever since – crowded in to sit on folding wooden chairs.

Despite the scant audience, Fidel had donned a robe – albeit one that was too small for him and creaked at the arms every time he moved – to conduct his defence. He had been up all night practising, just as he used to at Belén, and with his small pile of notes, his book of beloved Martí quotations and a copy of the Cuban penal code he went immediately on the attack. 'Castro spoke at length without being interrupted,' one of the judges recalled. A lot of what he said was rhetoric, but Fidel knew he was damned if he did and damned if he didn't, so he had planned to speak his mind – as indeed he warned the judges. When he began to speak, 'even the soldiers who had been dozing in the heat now began to pay attention,' Rojas recalls. 'Thank you,' Fidel said ironically when he saw them stirring. 'Hopefully the country will pay as much interest as you.'

'I must admit that I am somewhat disappointed,' Fidel began. 'I had expected that the Honourable Prosecutor would come forward with a grave accusation ... But no. He has limited himself to reading Article 148 of the Social Defence Code ... Two minutes seems a very short time in which to demand and justify that a man be put behind bars for more than a quarter of a century.' The prosecutor, Mendieta Hechavarría, visibly shrank on hearing this. 'Do they hope that I, too, will speak for only two minutes?' Fidel asked rhetorically, satisfied that his audience knew the answer already. 'I warn you, I am just beginning,' he added to make his position quite clear. Having got into his stride, he then turned to his defence proper.

Fidel began by refuting the legal basis on which he was being tried. 'The article in question reads textually,' he said, picking up the penal code to quote from the same passage he had used

to condemn Batista just a year before, '"A penalty of imprisonment of from three to ten years shall be imposed upon the
perpetrator of any act aimed at bringing about an armed uprising
against the Constitutional Powers of the State. The penalty shall
be imprisonment for from five to twenty years, in the event that
insurrection actually be carried into effect."'

'In what country,' he asked indignantly, putting down the book,
'is the Honourable Prosecutor living? Who has told him that we
have sought to bring about an uprising against the Constitutional
Powers of the State?' Far from it: neither was Batista's regime –
and he took some pleasure in pointing this out – constitutional,
nor had their attack been directed at the various powers of the
state. They had merely been after its one cancerous head.

For the next two hours he set out an impassioned and indignant history of his movement. No, they weren't military strategists,
he declared with pride when rebuffing the prosecution's accusations of professional assistance. But we still gave them a 'good
beating', he quipped. He embellished the truth more than a little
when he complimented his men on having been the better
marksmen, but historical truth was not what Fidel was after. This
was political theatre – 'epic narratives', as he called it – and he
dressed up the scenes of chivalry and murder accordingly.

In setting out the tenets of the kind of government he would lead,
Fidel said, 'The problem of the land, the problem of industrialisation, the problem of housing, the problem of unemployment,
the problem of education and the problem of the people's health:
these are the six problems we would take immediate steps to
solve, along with restoration of civil liberties and political democracy.' This social programme he drew largely from Chibás – it
was much tamer than the actual Manifesto to the Nation he
would have read out over the radio had they been successful –
while the rhetoric and the anti-imperialism to support it were
from Martí. 'More than half of our most productive land is in
the hands of foreigners,' he went on.

It was not, in truth, a particularly original platform – though

Fidel made sure to show off a little, taking in Montesquieu to thumb his nose at despotism, and citing just about everyone from Thomas Aquinas and John Knox to Jean-Jacques Rousseau and the American Declaration of Independence to justify the overthrow of those who ruled as despots. But for the most part it was what the people would have wanted to hear. He had captured fully their frustrations and hopes, and he was certain they were going to thank him for it.

As he drew his speech to an end, he forgave the judge for having to reach such an 'unjust decision' against his person and the judge's own better sense of justice before concluding, 'I am not asking for my liberty . . . . The silence of today does not matter. History, definitively, will say it all.' Later, from his prison cell, he would work this ending up into the curdling cry of resistance that would become one of the most eloquent passages of political rhetoric of the twentieth century: 'I know that imprisonment will be harder for me than it has ever been for anyone, filled with cowardly threats and hideous cruelty. But I do not fear prison, as I do not fear the fury of the miserable tyrant who took the lives of seventy of my comrades. Condemn me. It does not matter. History will absolve me.'

In a little over two hours the twenty-six-year-old Fidel Castro had set out his life's course and his revolutionary platform, and he had somehow turned the disastrous events of 26 July somewhat to his advantage. In return he was handed down a fifteen-year prison sentence (the maximum for a coup was thirty, but the judges seem to have bought Fidel's argument that Batista's government was itself non-elected). Before he left, Fidel shook hands with the judges, as if to thank them for their forbearance, and asked them bluntly what they thought was the safest way for him to be taken to prison. 'In an aeroplane,' was the reply, '. . . on a train, anything can happen.' Fidel had no choice, of course, but he had assured his safety simply by raising the matter with the judge. And with that, he was handcuffed and led away.

The Cuban magazine *Bohemia* later named Fidel Castro as

one of the twelve most outstanding figures of 1953, alongside the newly crowned Queen Elizabeth of England, the Shah of Iran and Lavrenti Beria, the Soviet KGB chief shot by Stalin. Fidel was delighted at his inclusion. He might be going to prison, but he was going as a well-known man; he had made his mark at last.

4. THE MONKEY
AND THE BEAR

ERNESTO ARRIVED IN Guatemala just before Christmas 1953. The leftist President Jacobo Arbenz had come to power two years before and the large American corporation, the United Fruit Company, which had long considered itself the de facto head of this minuscule Central American state, had been watching closely. Arbenz, a former army sub-lieutenant who had already refused to sign up to the Rio Defence Pact – the United States' strategic holding pattern for South America – had, since June 1952, been making a thorough nuisance of himself in American eyes by expropriating United Fruit land. There was talk of communist infiltration and plans were afoot to topple Arbenz.

Guatemala was therefore also attracting the interest not only of the American security services, but of a good number of the continent's radical political exiles as well. The atmosphere, as Rojo put it when he arrived, was 'electric'. Ernesto's stay here would be a watershed in his political awakening. If he was going to 'make up for what it was he lacked', as he had written to his Aunt Beatriz just before arriving, he would do so with the icy grip of the Cold War upon him.

In Guatemala Ernesto had reached the very heart of the political faultline that ran through the American continent: the land of 'McCarthyism Internationalised', as one Cuban historian has put it and the land of the 'red threat' as it was perceived at the time by the US State Department. Initially, however – and it revealed his continued introspection – the atmosphere in Guatemala did little to encourage Ernesto. 'I am still following the donkey's path,' he wrote again to Aunt Beatriz shortly after his arrival; before summing up his first days in the Guatemalan capital with the line: 'I haven't met a single interesting person with whom to have a conversation.'

That wasn't strictly true. By Christmas he had in fact met the woman who would become his first wife. Hilda Gadea was Peruvian and a leader of the youth wing of Peru's American Popular Revolutionary Alliance (APRA) party founded by Victor Haya de la Torre. Unlike Ernesto she was a seasoned political exile and, somewhat older than he was, calm and constructive in adversity. She was, at this point in his life, therefore more or less everything he wasn't. Since she was someone to know, Rojo of course had her on his books, and it was he, as ever, who had introduced them. Before long the three were dining out regularly together. Now that Ernesto was becoming a little more confident in his political views, as often as not he and Rojo would argue bitterly about what was to be done to cure the continent's ills.

Ernesto's failure to mention Hilda to his aunt conveyed one inescapable truth, however. Their relationship was not, for either of them, a case of love at first sight. 'Guevara made a negative impression on me,' Hilda wrote later. 'He seemed too superficial to be an intelligent man, egotistical and conceited.' He in turn would first describe her to his parents as 'a young aprista who, with my characteristic suaveness, I tried to convince was affiliated to a useless as shit party'. She began to change her mind, though, as during the evenings of endless political and cultural debate they shared it became clear that he was more than capable of subjecting her every idea to a merciless critique. By the time she had reconciled the intellect with 'those dark eyes', she was hooked. From those first days, 'I . . . knew that I was going to help him,' she recalled in her memoirs. And she would prove to be an important influence on Ernesto: certainly greater than he ever really acknowledged.

Quite how long Ernesto planned to stay in Guatemala was not clear, even to himself. His most usual answer was that it would be long enough to pay off his mounting debts. He tried constantly to find employment as a doctor, but the endless bureaucracy required to register his certification in the first place prevented him from doing so. On the other hand, these days of 'neither troubles nor glory', as he put it, left him with plenty of time to see what was going on around him. And as the weeks turned into months, his immediate circle of friends gradually expanded: to Gualo and Hilda were added Hilda's friend Myrna Torres and her father, the Nicaraguan exile Edelberto Torres, and Rojo remained too, bringing a constant supply of new contacts.

As of the New Year, 1954, a small number of Cubans who had been at Moncada but escaped also joined the group. Hilda was impressed. 'The Cuban exiles from the Moncada were quite different from all the others,' she recalled. 'They were lively, had none of the theoretical airs that the rest of the bunch Guevara had fallen into had. [M]ost of all,' she went on, 'they stood out because they had actually done something.'

The one who most stood out, even among his spirited compatriots, was Ñico López – partly on account of his willowy six-foot six-inch frame and his circus ring moustache, but due also to his deep convictions and wicked sense of humour. Ñico, a former labourer at Havana's Central Market, was a devoted follower of Fidel and would tell anyone who joined them in the evening soirées at their various pensions or out at some fiesta just why that was so. Ñico's faith was so great, Hilda recalls, 'that whoever listened to him was forced to believe him'.

'So, you're the Argentines,' he said to Ernesto and Gualo at a party at Myrna Torres' house in the New Year. 'Hilda told me about you.' To which Ernesto replied, laughing – and doubtless with a conspiratorial wink to Hilda, 'And you're the Cubans, of

course. We knew about you from Hilda too.' Ernesto was immediately taken with his tall new friend with the wrenching
Caribbean accent. Ñico was likewise 'delirious' about the
Argentine – and he found Ernesto's accent no less strange. He
took to calling him by a new nickname that would soon become
his only name, and indeed, much more than a name: the word
that Ernesto, like many of his fellow Argentines, had the habit
of pronouncing over and again throughout his sentences – Ernesto
'Che' Guevara.

* * *

On 17 October 1953 Fidel arrived at the Men's Model Peniten-
tiary on the Isle of Pines with another rebel, Fidel Labrador, who
had stayed on in Santiago during Castro's trial in order to have
a new glass eye fitted – he had lost the original during the assault
on Moncada. There they joined the twenty-six other combatants
who had arrived four days earlier at the prison, which lay some
56 miles off the Cuban coast. As would certainly have occurred
to him, Fidel appeared once more to be following in the footsteps of José Martí, who had been imprisoned here in 1870. While
Ernesto's mental horizons were finally, and by sheer weight of
experience, beginning to open up, Fidel's were now drastically
narrowed down. The change would be ultimately useful to them
both. The extrovert would develop a more contemplative style,
and the introvert would find his voice.

Fidel did not keep entirely to himself, of course: it was not in
his nature. He sent a good many letters from prison, writing
them on the wooden plank which he used for much of his studying
and correspondence. As he confessed to his brother in one of
them, it was not such a bad place: they were not being robbed
or exploited, he said, and 'there seems to be good will on the
part of the authorities'. But that did not preclude his regularly
falling into a state of near despair. As he reflected near the end
of his sentence, to be a prisoner was, ultimately, 'to be condemned

to silence'. For Fidel, that was a torture in itself, and there were times when he fumed at their being held in this 'tropical Siberia'.

In the 1920s the Isle of Pines had been a notorious hellhole – a place of a 'thousand screams' – capped by four large round tower blocks crammed full with cells. Things had improved by the 1950s, but not much. Where the Moncadistas were, in the medical wing, life was hard but not as brutal as it was for the other inmates. The routine soon took its toll, though, as Fidel grouched in a letter to an unknown correspondent. 'At 5.00 a.m. sharp, when you think you've just shut your eyes, a voice yells, "Line up!" accompanied by handclaps, and we remember – if we forgot it for a moment while we slept – that we're in prison. The lights, left on all night, glare more harshly than ever; our heads feel heavier than lead; and we have to get up!' At 7.30 another prisoner would throw on to the floor of each shared cell a sack of bread and a can of milk for breakfast; lunch and dinner were served in the same way at 11.00 and at 5.00 p.m. respectively, with silence ordered at 10.00 p.m. It was medieval, monastic almost, and, as would later prove fatal for Batista, precisely what Fidel needed at this moment to muster both his thoughts and his men. Before going to prison the rebels had worked largely in isolation from each other; now they began to cohere into a group.

'Special assemblies shall begin at 7.45 p.m., after the conclusion of the reading group,' decreed one of the prisoners' own articles of behaviour, to which they conformed more readily than to the prison's code of conduct. The reading group was another Castro innovation. In memory of their fallen comrade, the prisoners had founded the Abel Santamaría Ideological Academy. It was a modest institution, composed of just a blackboard and the wooden benches at which they ate in the yard, but in its name debates and lectures on famous events, political economy and works of literature were held on a daily basis.

By December, the group of rebels who had entered jail inexperienced in everything but the one action that had brought them here had begun to learn a little more of the world and a lot about each other. 'More than friends, we are brothers,' wrote one of them, Armando Mestre, to his uncle. That sort of camaraderie was invaluable, and Fidel now had full liberty to cultivate it. Prison was to be his movement's training ground. 'Those who learned how to handle weapons are now learning how to handle books,' he wrote approvingly on 22 December. 'What a fantastic school this is.'

By now Fidel, who under Cuba's peculiar legal system had already been able to launch a series of law suits against the government (they would rumble on indecisively until he was released) was once more focusing his attention outside the prison walls. Smarting still from the loss of so many comrades after the Moncada attack, he wrote constantly to anyone in a public position who he thought might be sympathetic enough to denounce what had taken place. He wrote also to the families of those killed in his name at Moncada and Bayamo. In December, he replied to a letter from the father of Renato Guitart, who had been shot during the initial attack.

> It is hard for me to begin to address you, to find the word that expresses at the same time my gratitude, my emotion, my deep appreciation for your letter, so heartfelt, so kind, and so full of paternal and loving affection. You address me as 'dearest Fidel.' What might I call you? Few times in my life have I felt as honoured, or felt so encouraged to be good, to be decent, to be loyal until the last instant of my existence as when I received your lines.

In a letter to Luis Conte Agüero, a radio commentator and journalist who would for the next eighteen months be Fidel's principal voice on the mainland, he gave further vent to the anger bottled up inside him. 'I write with the blood of my dead brothers,' he declared, raging at the lack of publicity his attack was receiving and accusing the opposition of encouraging the government with its 'shameful cowardice'. He signed off indignantly, 'Luis, we still have the strength to die and fists to fight.'

* * *

For his part, having fallen in with the Cubans, Ernesto decided 'to stay a little while' in Guatemala. During one of many group picnics in the country, as they all took a walk before settling round a fire for the evening Ernesto caught up with Hilda. 'Are you completely healthy?' he enquired as he approached, somewhat to her surprise. 'Is your family in good health?' he clarified. She looked at him, still puzzled, unable to understand the question, much less find an answer. Then she burst out laughing. 'Are you writing my clinical history?' she said, before adding more seriously, 'Yes, I am very healthy, and so is my entire family. Why are you asking me such things? Is your interest entirely professional or are you perhaps going to propose?' Ernesto smiled. 'Maybe it's not such a bad idea . . . what do you think?' 'It's too soon to tell,' she replied before they rejoined the others. She realised later that he did not wish his children to be as afflicted with hereditary health problems as he had been.

Picnics were not the only order of the day, however. Over the next couple of months, the group began to attend more and more of the marches and protests that marked the hardening of the stand-off between President Arbenz and the United States. Ernesto's failure to secure a medical post because of visa problems increasingly ceased to worry him. Indeed, he now began to see such a job as undesirably bourgeois and reactionary. Of far more interest was what was going on around him. The progress of Arbenz's social reforms was almost always one of the main topics of discussion among the men at the group's dinner parties and soirées, despite the best efforts of some of the women – never Hilda, of course – to distract them. As for Rojo, with him the discussions now ended in near fist fights, particularly when Ernesto proclaimed the achievements of the Soviet Union and

Rojo vehemently argued that the electoral process offered the right solution.

Returning from a commemoration of the assassination of the Nicaraguan guerrilla Augusto César Sandino at the end of February, Ernesto wrote in his diary, 'I felt very small when I heard the Cubans making grand assertions with total calmness. I can make a speech ten times more objective and without banalities; I can do it better and I can convince the public that I am saying something true. But I don't convince myself, whereas the Cubans do. Ñico left his heart and soul in the microphone and for that reason fired even a sceptic like myself with enthusiasm.' In what was perhaps the most liberating insight he would ever have, the young Che Guevara seemed to have realised he needed to aim a little less high – to start somewhere, no matter how small; no matter, in fact, if it be with something not of his own choosing.

Fidel too had grown increasingly frustrated, in his case with the lack of attention to his attack at Moncada. But in February 1954, an unexpected opportunity arose for him to take some of his frustration out on Batista rather directly. The men were informed by one of their guards – known as Pistolita, or Little Gunman, on account of his 'buffoonish, provocative poses' – that they would have to stay confined within their cells that day. They wondered what was up. Standing on the shoulders of a cellmate to see what all the fuss was about, Juan Almeida peered out of the barred windows set high into the wall and reported that there was a visitor and it was none other than Batista himself. Ever impressed by the pomp and ceremony of government, Batista was on an official visit simply to open a new electricity plant.

Fidel could not resist taking a pot-shot at his adversary and wasted no time in thinking up what could be done. Just as Batista was preparing to leave, twenty-six lusty male voices bawled out a vigorous rendition of the Freedom March that had been composed for the moment they took over the radio transmitter at Moncada. On hearing the singing emanating from the cell windows Batista stopped short, thinking at first it was a tribute to him. But as he caught the words his smile faded.

> Marching inward toward an ideal,
> We're certain to carry the day;
> In furtherance of peace and prosperity
> We'll struggle so freedom will win.

> Forward, all Cubans
> May Cuba ever prize our heroism;
> We're soldiers united, fighting so our country may be free,
> Our weapons destroying the evil that has plagued our troubled
>   land
> Of errant, unwanted rulers and of cruel insatiable tyrants
> Who have dragged us down in the mire . . .

Before they could get much further, the Cuban President exploded into a rage and stormed off. He was still fuming that evening as he boarded his yacht to return to the mainland. Meanwhile, inside the building Pistolita ran around cursing, 'I'll kill them; I'll kill them.' To the men's great surprise nothing happened all that day, or on the next, a Saturday. Perhaps they had got away with it? On the Sunday, however, the names of the known leaders within the group were read out: 'Ramiro Valdés, Oscar Alcalde, Ernesto Tizol, Israel Tápenes.' They were all moved into the isolation wing. Fidel followed them there in the afternoon, and the following day Agustín Díaz Cartaya, the composer of the song, joined them. It had taken him just a week to compose it, but he would suffer somewhat longer than that for the first public performance of his art.

The isolation wing was effectively run by a long-term inmate who was deranged – 'short, chubby, and big bellied, completely bald and [with] small round eyes that were almost lost in his pudgy face', as Tápanes recalled twenty years later. This individual was known to all in the prison as Cebolla, or Onion – perhaps because he stank, or because he made people cry. 'So you're the author of that piece of shit,' Cebolla said to Díaz Cartaya when he had been brought into the cell. 'Well now you're going to sing it for us.' That night Cebolla returned with three of the guards. 'They opened the door to my cell and jumped me. They stripped me, beat me with ox-dick whips, kicked me, and pummelled me all over,' Díaz Cartaya recalled. He remained unconscious in his cell until morning.

With just a small bookcase and a cooking stove for comfort, Fidel began his time in isolation. He slept on a cot that one of his few visitors, the Havana judge Waldo Medina, described as 'an island, surrounded by books'. The happier times would now be when he lost himself in his reading: 'I forget all that exists in the world and I refocus on the effort of learning something new and useful even if it is just to better understand humankind.' The worst times were when it rained, as often it did, and the water, leaking through the ceiling and walls, threatened to ruin his precious pile of books. After seventeen days of isolation he wrote, 'I still have no light . . . But last night it was not just the darkness and solitude but also the rain . . . . I did what I could to protect my books by putting them inside the suitcase and covering it with a blanket. Meanwhile, the bed got soaked, the floor was flooded, and the cold, wet air penetrated everywhere.'

But the rains also produced ideal growing conditions on the island for citrus fruits, the inspiration for Fidel's most audacious plan to date. The prisoners all appreciated fruit, but the prison authorities never quite seem to have noticed Fidel's particularly voracious appetite for the stuff, lemons in particular. Perhaps that is why they also failed to notice the constant stream of communication he kept up with his supporters on the outside – above all with Melba and Haydée after their release from the women's prison in February – all of it written in lemon juice between the lines of his letters. The words remained invisible until a hot iron was passed over them beyond the prison walls.

By such means, as well as with the assistance of a few well-disposed (or easily bribed) prison guards, the prisoners were soon back in constant communication with the outside. Other signals were devised for use within the prison walls. Raúl Castro and Pedro Miret learned to communicate by hand signals, dangling their arms between the bars. The men all became proficient at rolling and unrolling cigars containing small messages. They would walk to their monthly visits with messages tucked safely at the mouth end of a lit cigar, putting it out just before the minute sheaves were cindered.

In between these visits, Fidel kept up his correspondence, licit and illicit, directly and indirectly, with various interlocutors: Conte Agüero, the Ortodoxo writer Jorge Mañach and the editor of *Bohemia*, Miguel Ángel Quevedo. His most revealing correspondence, however, was with his mistress Naty Revuelta. They had met at the end of November 1952, while Fidel was in the thick of his clandestine planning for the Moncada attack. She was the young wife of a prominent and wealthy cardiologist, a socialite and a regular at the exclusive Biltmore Country Club. Both she and her husband were also fervent and passionate supporters of the Ortodoxos, and after Batista's coup they had decided to help the clandestine opposition. Naty was a beautiful woman, with deep green eyes, even deeper pockets, and a weakness for the impassioned theatrics in which Fidel specialised. She lived just a few blocks away from Fidel's wife and child but she came from an entirely different world, one much closer to Fidel's own heart.

Naty refused to visit Fidel in jail, but they kept up an intense exchange of letters. True love, he wrote her, was indestructible, like a diamond, 'the hardest and purest of all the minerals'. As early as November Fidel had proposed that they read books together. 'I'm going to choose carefully and calmly the best works of Spanish, French, and Russian literature. You do the same with English. Literature should be your forte . . . I who lack your fine taste, and will never falter, shall deal with the dry and impenetrable fields of political economy and social science . . . Music will be your responsibility . . . It should be easy to improve ourselves, thinking of a better world. Do you like the idea? With fifteen years in prison, we should have plenty of time!'

Fidel's reading had already got off to a flying start and it is not clear if Naty ever kept up. 'After having knocked heads a good while with Kant, I find Marx easier than the "Pater Nostrum",' he wrote. 'Both he and Lenin had a powerful polemical spirit and I'm having a fine time with them, laughing and enjoying my reading. Fidel was in fact working his way through a vast number of other thinkers too. Political and social science began with Weber and ended with Mannheim; literature began with Thomas More's *Utopia* and was topped by Tolstoy, Oscar Wilde, Shakespeare and his favourite – Dostoyevsky. This still left time for Thackeray, Turgenev and Balzac. He worked his way through Freud, Ramiro Guerra's ten-volume *History of the Cuban Nation* and biographies of his favourite historical figures: Bolívar and Bonaparte both figured large (he compared Marx's and Victor Hugo's analysis of Bonaparte, favouring that of Marx), as did Trotsky's *Stalin*, which led him into an amusing exchange with the prison censors. Fidel took considerable cultured pride in informing them that if they were holding this book back because they thought it was in any way Stalinist they really had no need to worry!

All this reading occasionally lifted his spirits. On 4 April, reading Lenin's *State and Revolution* (of all books) put him in the mood, so he wrote Naty, for a bit of a spring clean. 'I fixed up my cell Friday. I scrubbed the granite floor first with soap and water and then with scouring powder, then washed it down with detergent. Finally I rinsed it with a disinfectant, aromatic solution. I put everything in perfect order. The rooms at the Hotel Nacional are not as clean. . . .' He went on: 'When I go out in the morning in my shorts and breathe the sea air, I feel like I'm at the beach, and that there's a little restaurant here. They're going to make me think I'm on vacation. What would Karl Marx say about such revolutionaries?'

In the same letter he went on in the more serious register that really animated his thoughts: 'How I would love to revolutionise this country from head to toe.' Confirming his rejection of the democratic process, he now condemned those interminable and 'fanatical' political rallies – the late-night harangues he himself had once felt so much at home delivering – in no uncertain terms: 'I have come to the conclusion that our people are infinitely patient and kind. Thinking of it here in this lonely cell, I cannot understand how they applauded instead of hurling their chairs at the charlatans.'

By April, Fidel was ready to begin rebuilding his movement, even if that had to be done from inside his prison cell. He wrote to Melba, asking her to be his eyes in the community of opposition groups in exile. Fidel was aware that these groups – the very ones Ernesto was now getting to know better in Guatemala – who were constantly conspiring against one another and presented as much of an obstacle as the government he hoped one day to overthrow. 'Maintain a soft touch and smile with everyone,' he advised Melba. 'There will be time enough later to squash all the cockroaches together.'

* * *

'Already March of 1954,' Ernesto headed a letter to Tita on his return to Guatemala City after a brief trip to renew his visa. 'Almost a year since I left and I haven't advanced much in anything.' He had not been completely idle, however. 'I'm preparing an extremely pretentious book,' he declared with his usual self-deprecating tone. It would take him, he thought, two years of work. 'Its title is: The Function of the Doctor in Latin America'. 'I only have the general plan and two chapters written,' as he confessed to Aunt Beatriz in a letter, 'but I believe with some patience and a bit of method I could say something good. An iron hug from your proletarian nephew.'

Hilda thought the book a wonderful idea and set to helping Ernesto with it. At the same time, the two now settled into a comradely domestic routine based around just the sort of reading programme Fidel had embarked upon with Naty. When they weren't at work on his *magnum opus* they would discuss poetry: Hilda lent him a copy of César Vallejo's poems and he shared with her his great love for Pablo Neruda, Jose Hernández and Sara de Ibáñez. They also read political works together: Engels, Marx and Sartre in particular. 'We shared a sense of the "agony of life",' Hilda recalled.

By mid-March it had become quite obvious that not just Hilda but Ernesto too was in love, and he proposed. This time it was for real – sort of. He had found her at the house of Señora de Toriello, where Hilda was attending a small birthday party; she was dancing and he tried to call her over. 'I didn't realise you were so frivolous!' he said, a little sullenly. It wasn't frivolity, she explained. She just liked to dance. At which point the cause of his sullenness became clear. He handed her a poem in what was for once quite a readable scrawl: it was a formal proposal of marriage. As she later described it the poem was, like the proposal itself, 'short but beautiful and forceful'. When Ernesto decided to confess to Hilda that because they had not been an official couple he had been having an affair with a nurse at the general hospital, she told him to go with the nurse if that was more his thing. Theirs would be an on-off relationship for some time.

Though they kept attending the parties held by members of the exile community, Ernesto would frequently take himself off on his own, sometimes straight after a party, with his flask of maté, his sleeping bag and a pile of books on history and culture such as Franz Blom's *Life of the Mayans*, and spend a weekend alone in the countryside. One imagines him on these trips settling down under a tree, immersing himself in the lonely beauty of his surroundings. Ernesto was always, and would remain, just such a man – a thinker first and foremost, who wanted little more than to disappear for a while to mull things over. But he was coming now to be something else as well. Ernesto was beginning to give serious thought to the political situation in Guatemala, where the stand-off between Arbenz and the United Fruit Company had become tense.

Enduring his forced isolation in prison in Cuba, Fidel too was keeping his eye on events across the continent. That summer, an article in Cuba's monthly magazine *Bohemia* was accompanied by seven pictures of Fidel in jail. In one of them he was reading about Guatemala. He had the men debate the theme one evening, and their conclusion was that Arbenz's programme of national-isation must be supported at all costs: 'If she [Guatemala] triumphs in her titanic struggle, she will become a beacon guiding us to true freedom, equality among peoples, and social justice.'

A titanic struggle on a rather more personal level was now beginning to unfold for Fidel himself. During their conjugal visits and in his letters, he had in various ways asked Mirta to denounce publicly the conditions in which he was being held. In mid-July she did so at a public event to pay tribute to the radio presenter Luis Conte Agüero. Obediently, Mirta read out a statement from her husband which – in his inimitable style – branded Batista a despot and a tyrant. But Mirta's brother, Rafael Diaz-Balart, the deputy Minister of the Interior, had provided her with a sinecure since Fidel had been imprisoned, and the Ministry was extremely vexed to learn that these words should be conveyed to the public by someone on their payroll.

The Ministry's response was as nothing, however, compared to Fidel's when he discovered while huddled over his radio set that evening that Mirta had been on the Ministry's payroll in the first place. Initially he refused to believe his ears, writing to suggest she 'initiate a criminal suit for defamation' against the Ministry. At the same time he wrote to Conte Agüero for help assuring him that 'Mirta is too level-headed to have ever allowed herself to be seduced by her family.' He believed it all to be a plot against his person concocted by the Minister of the Interior, Hermida, and his deputy. 'I am ready to challenge my own brother-in-law to a duel,' Fidel assured Agüero. 'It is the reputation of my wife and my honour as a revolutionary that is at stake. Do not hesitate:

strike back and have no mercy. I would rather be killed a thousand times over than helplessly suffer such an insult.'

Four days later, however, his sister Lidia wrote to him to confirm the truth of the story. She added that Mirta was now asking for a divorce. In truth she had long been furious with her husband, ever since the prison censor had forwarded in her direction one of the rather warmer letters he was sending to Naty. There is nothing to suggest that she would have left him, however, until he lashed out at her indiscretion. But Mirta knew well that Fidel never forgave if he felt he had been betrayed.

'Don't worry about me, you know I have a heart of steel,' Fidel replied to Lidia a few days after receiving her letter. But as a result of what for him was the 'vilest' of all possible betrayals, he was at his lowest point when he was paid a visit by, of all people, the Minister of the Interior, Hermida on 26 July, the anniversary of Moncada. Fidel could not understand the reason behind it and wrote afterwards to Conte Agüero to try to get a handle on the meeting. It is surprisingly domestic and frank for a Latin strongman, prudish, and emblematic of the way in which Fidel assumed that his own concerns were automatically those of others.

Luis:

Enclosed is the text of the most essential part of the interview with Hermida.

I was in my cell at approximately 1:15 p.m., lying down in my underwear reading, when a guard called for my attention ...

'Castro, the Minister of Governance is here and wants to greet you, but ... he doesn't know how you will receive him.' I replied, 'Comandant, I'm not some spoiled boy capable of an act of rudeness. Now, because I was offended by some of the Minister's comments, if I speak with him it would be only to ask him for an apology.' The warden said to me, 'I think it would be best if you do not bring up that issue.' 'Then, Commandant, it would be best that I not see the Minister,' I replied.

But, having come all this way, Hermida was not going to return empty-handed. As he entered Fidel's cell he told him he had come to assure him that his incarceration was nothing personal – he was just enforcing the rules. Fidel too, somewhat meekly, agreed that he had never considered it a personal struggle (overlooking perhaps the moment when he had declared what a hard time the Devil would one day have deciding to which of Dante's circles of hell – that for criminals, thieves or traitors – to consign Batista). But Hermida too had once been imprisoned on the Isle of Pines for his part in the uprisings of the 1930s: 'Don't be impatient,' he told Fidel before he left. 'Everything will pass.' In this he had touched on one source of Fidel's apparent great luck: connecting his struggles in the present to those of the past allowed him to traverse seemingly unbridgeable divides with erstwhile opponents and somehow always to have a friend in the right place.

On that score, Fidel had spent his year in jail profitably. He had diligently reconstructed from memory and then scratched out in lemon juice his entire courtroom defence speech from the previous July. This he was writing at exactly the same time as Ernesto was working on his own book about social medicine. But where Ernesto lacked the patience for such an undertaking and was inexorably diverted as he constantly sought out new and better references, Fidel had learned in his time alone to keep focused on the immediate task and to make use of whatever was to hand. He had spruced his speech up where he felt it was lacking, and peppered the prose with some of his more recent reading. Then, line by bitter line, it had rematerialised outside the prison in the heat of the iron that Melba and Haydée passed over his letters. Until their falling out, Mirta too had been in on it. In fact a vast, secret mobilisation had been under way since he had begun the writing in April of 1954, as funds were raised, clandestine printers found, and a storage and distribution network put into place. By October, copies of Fidel's speech were hitting the streets of Cuba in their tens of thousands. It was the first decisive strike back from the man who would not be silenced – 'the bear' as some referred to him – and it had all been organised from the confines of his solitary cell.

* * *

On 14 June 1954, just as events in Guatemala were coming to a head, Ernesto celebrated his twenty-sixth birthday. Two days later mercenary planes financed by the CIA began bombing the capital and Ernesto's life began to veer inexorably towards a more radical path. The political situation in Guatemala had hardened substantially over the past few months, and there was a good reason for the many farewell parties he and Rojo had been attending. Slowly but surely, their group of exiles in Guatemala was beginning to trickle away to safer places as it became clear that the CIA was positioning the opposition to launch a coup against Arbenz. In February, Gualo returned to Argentina. Valdovino and his wife Luzmilla also moved on, and soon Myrna Torres did too. Even Rojo himself made plans to go and study in the United States.

On the 18th the invasion itself began, as a force of four hundred men directed by a former general, Castillo Armas, from his base at Copán in Honduras, followed in Ernesto's own tracks to Guatemala City, thundering across fields and quiet settlements towards the capital. As the invasion punched into the interior, the port cities of Puerto Barrios, where Ernesto had shifted crates of bananas on one of his solo excursions, and San José were fire-bombed. On the 20th, as the capital came under fire, resistance groups began to be organised.

The Guatemalan government itself denounced the attack before the UN Security Council, but otherwise did surprisingly little. Ernesto, who had lauded Arbenz's bravery many times, was bitterly disappointed. He immediately enrolled himself both as a medic in the Red Cross health committees that were providing medical services and in the communist youth brigades that

patrolled the streets at night to ensure the curfew was maintained.

From the roofs of the houses where he was stationed during
his night guard, Ernesto was well positioned to see events
unfolding around him. Of this he later wrote, 'The planes came
to bomb the city. We were completely undefended, with no planes,
no anti-aircraft artillery and no escape. There were a few deaths,
not many. Panic, however, flooded the population, especially the
"valiant and loyal army" of Guatemala.'

Ernesto and Hilda did not remain untouched by these events.
Hilda's pension overlooked the back of the Presidential Palace,
and one of her windows was broken by machine gun fire from
the planes strafing the building. Ernesto railed at them. 'Sons of
bitches,' he cursed as the owner of the pension moved them to
an interior room for safety.

The seriousness of the situation became more apparent when
word got out that any of Arbenz's supporters who were caught
by the advancing troops would be executed, along with their
families. Hilda was advised by many to flee, but she and Ernesto
remained and kept in regular contact with the now increasingly
underground opposition. Ernesto attended the secret meetings of
the Alianza Juventud Democrática, the Democratic Youth
Alliance, one of the relatively few opposition groups which were
considering taking any action. But he was frustrated at their
dithering. During one meeting, 'Ernesto was really pissed off to
see that nothing was being done and . . . said: "Gentlemen, the
only way of defending this government is if we take these rifles
that are here. . . . I think there are three or four, we'll go to the
police station and take the arms that they have too. It's the only
way of defending this process. The rest is a farce and we won't
embarrass ourselves with it!"' It was the closest he had yet come
to taking action, but most of those present were entirely opposed
to 'such a crazy idea'.

In hiding at Hilda's, as he fumed and they waited to see what
would happen, he composed a short article entitled 'I Saw the

Fall of Arbenz'. He dictated it to Hilda over a period of three afternoons. All copies of this document appear to have been lost, though the essence of it was reconstructed in Hilda's memoirs. The article, so she says, begins with an uncontroversial analysis of the world situation which Ernesto saw as a product of the struggle between the two camps, East and West, corrupting the local bourgeoisie in places like Latin America and turning them into puppets. But he saw the third position, or moderately radical middle way – that of the Peruvian APRA party founder, Victor Haya de la Torre, or Venezuela's Rómulo Betancourt – as a betrayal too, for though reformist and social democratic both were also anti-communist. The only alternative was to struggle against the entire capitalist system that enslaved so many in this part of the world and to do so with arms. If Arbenz had armed the people, his government would not have fallen. Ernesto was certain of it.

This was the new and authentic voice of the young Che Guevara. It was also highly compromising stuff. Returning to her apartment one day, Hilda found the police waiting outside in the street and all her belongings scattered around, with her friends standing about looking worried. Seeing all this as she approached the house, she tried to walk on by nonchalantly – but they were already on to her. Word of the couple's political leanings must have got out. As they led her away, the first question the police asked was whether she knew where Ernesto Guevara whose essay they had evidently read, might be found. Ernesto now had no choice but to take refuge, like so many others, in the Argentine embassy. 'The embassies are full to the brim and ours, along with that of Mexico's, is the worst,' he wrote home. He too was now finally full to the brim. The final sentence of the article that had raised police eyebrows read, 'The struggle begins now.'

In the Argentine embassy Ernesto was one of the 'group of twelve' – the communists who were kept apart from the other exiles and forbidden to speak to others. This new status of notoriety seemed to energise him. On 4 July he wrote a characteristically blunt letter home about the recent events. He had lost his hard-earned medical post, he explained to his mother, but also his debts, deciding somewhat entrepreneurially to write them all off for reasons of *force majeure*. His excited tone, however, stems not from his account of this financial legerdemain but from the war. 'I'm a little embarrassed to say but I had as much fun as a monkey,' he wrote. 'That magical sensation of invulnerability while the people fled like mad just as the planes arrived, or at night when, during the blackouts, the city was filled with gunshots. I'll tell you that the light bombers are pretty imposing. I saw one released over a target quite near to where I was and you could see it getting bigger while, from the wings, tongues of fire shot out. . . .'

On the 22nd he wrote much the same to dear old Aunt Beatriz: 'Here it has been very entertaining with shots, bombings, speeches and other hues that have brought to an end the monotony in which I was living. The revolution arrived just in time, for I was about to have to work – something which at these heights of life I might have found most inconvenient.' The rest of his letter was more serious, consistent with his habitual self-reflection: 'I don't know where I'm going now but wherever it is I will be ready to take up arms.'

In such a frame of mind Ernesto had decided not to return home to Argentina on the plane sent to pick up his compatriots. He sent instead a letter of introduction to his parents for many of those who would be returning without lodgings or a job and insisted that they, in turn, should now finally stop fussing about him. The truth was that he relished the idea of staying on with the remaining – more intransigent – exiles.

Meanwhile he made occasional sorties out of the embassy, especially after Hilda was released from custody in late July. Having finally got his papers in order in September, he arranged for his books to be sent home and for his own onward passage to Mexico. Now that Arbenz had fallen, this was the next most obvious place for the sort of radical that Ernesto now believed himself to be. His father knew an important figure in the film industry in Mexico City, he told Hilda as he left. 'I'm going to realise my artistic aspirations after all: I'll start as an extra and then, little by little. . . .' It was a joke, to be sure, but doubtless with a kernel of truth within it: he had indeed just been an extra, and while he would show no interest in either his father's contact or an acting career, in Mexico he would finally stumble upon a whole cast of like-minded players.

Before leaving he sent home with the last of his things another couple of articles he had just written in which he analysed what was happening around him. Though never published, these articles saw him trying on the prose of a radical and finding that it fitted rather well. The first was called 'The Guatemalan Dilemma', the second 'The Working Class of the United States: Friend or Foe?' The former offers relatively little of note, but the latter a roughly hewn analysis of the different strands of capitalist imperialism around the world, offers an intriguing glimpse into his thinking at this time. It stands as testimony to his vast reading and his preference for the bigger picture over the details. In it, he argued rather lucidly that, as the head of the 'so-called' free world, the United States was not able to intervene in other countries without a very good reason, and that therefore it was increasingly developing such a reason: international communism. The demonisation of communism was thus inherent to capitalism, he argued. Conflict, Ernesto concluded, could not be avoided. The only option available, he reaffirmed, was to fight.

* * *

Fidel was learning a rather different lesson. In August his brother Raúl was moved in with him and they were both given access to a small patio – some space at last. But Fidel was voluble even at his most downbeat, and Raúl now had to share a cell with a man buoyed up by the sense of having overcome his greatest personal challenge to date. Never being one for small talk, Fidel must have tried his brother's patience a thousand times over. 'I have heard enough of Fidel for a lifetime,' he would later recall. As he paced up and down their cell during those months, Fidel berated the predictable descent of the November elections in Cuba into a farce as the former president, Grau, who had put himself forward as a candidate, withdrew the day before leaving Batista to be crowned again, this time as an 'elected' president.

But by the beginning of the New Year, 1955, an amnesty campaign led by some of the mothers of the imprisoned rebels was gaining national attention and more and more calls for the release of the 'Moncada Boys' could be heard at rallies, in broadcasts and on news-sheets around the country. Aware that their time in jail might soon be over, Fidel began to turn his thoughts to the outside. In March he wrote to his sister about the unfolding legal battle for his son. To win custody, he said, 'I . . . am prepared to re-enact the famous Hundred Years War. And win it!' He finished the letter by adding that she should bring Fidelito to see him.

In March Fidel also wrote to Luis Conte Agüero again, to explain why he would not accept the 'amnesty' that was being demanded for himself and his men. 'For there to be amnesty a priori, a compromise of acquiescence to the regime is required,' he argued. And compromise was something Fidel could not countenance. Citing Cuba's independence hero, Antonio Maceo, he declared: 'From our enemies the only thing we gladly accept is the bloody executioner's block.'

But it was by then clear that very soon, with or without Fidel's requesting it, an amnesty was going to be granted. And by May he was busy preparing for the moment. His sisters wrote to say they had found a flat for the four of them, Lidia, Emma, Raúl and Fidel. Fidel viewed the idea with deep reluctance – he was terrified, as he tried without success to put diplomatically, of the women fussing unduly around him. 'I have a bohemian temperament, which is unorganised by nature. Apart from that there is nothing more agreeable than having a place where one can flick on the floor as many cigarette butts as one deems convenient without the subconscious fear of a housewife, vigilant as a sentinel, setting the ashtray where the ashes are about to fall.'

Ungrateful it may have been, but it was a strong hint that on leaving jail he intended immediately to take up the fight once more. None the less he was, as he was at pains to tell them, a changed man: 'Why should I wear linen *guayaberas* as if I were a rich man, an official or a professional thief?' His ragged old grey suit would do just fine, thank you very much. Fidel went on to scold his sister for being a touch too meddlesome.

> You do not seem to be able to be satisfied unless in some way you show your concern and care for us, but we are strong as oaks ... we are less in need of your sacrifices than you are of our sincere reproaches. What need do we have that your love – which needs no more evidence – be made evident at every instant? Not by words alone. These are realities we must perceive. I am very moved by the effort to offer to us the greatest number of small joys. But that may be obtained as well without material benefits! Do you want an example? The wish that my books be arranged and in order when I arrive comforts me, gladdens me and brings me more joy than other things.

Just a few days later, on the morning of 22 May, Fidel left prison wearing the grey suit his sisters so despaired of. He was sweating profusely in the heat as a result, but they were absolutely delighted to see him. Relatives who had been shuffling anxiously at the gates all morning thronged around him. Emma and Lidia patted his head, sinking their own heads into his chest. Melba and Haydée ran over to embrace him too, tears streaming down their cheeks. Wherever he went, between then and the press conference he immediately called in the nearby Nueva Gerona Hotel, he was surrounded. 'I am not leaving Cuba. I will fight for the unity of the forces of good,' he said in words reproduced on many of the following day's front pages. 'I have no ambitions, I don't aspire to anything. All that interests me is a better and happier Cuba.'

PART 2

5. A COLD MEXICAN NIGHT

IN THE 1950s Mexico City was on the brink of great change, its once quiet colonial plazas and winding lanes yielding to the skyscrapers and eight-stream highways of today. It was then just a fraction of its present size, but the influx of people that had begun with the revolution of 1910 was already producing rapid growth and a fractious, shifting population. Since the establishment of the left-of-centre National Revolutionary Party in 1929, Mexico City had attracted thousands more exiles fleeing the rising tide of fascism in Europe. All this made it a cosmopolitan if sometimes dangerous hub of artists, writers and political radicals. Cuban communist leader Julio Antonio Mella had come seeking refuge in the 1920s, before being gunned down in 1929. Trotsky too had lived out his final years here before Stalinist agents murdered him with a pickaxe in 1940. By the mid 1950s, Mexico was beginning to attract the interests of the Soviet Union and the United States, both of whom had substantial embassies and growing Cold War interests in the country.

It was here that Fidel Castro and Ernesto Guevara both fled when they were forced into exile within a year of one another, and it was here that they would finally meet one summer evening in 1955. By then they had both taken different paths and had accumulated almost entirely different experiences. But in their own ways they had both determined to fight against a common adversary: the long arm of foreign intervention, which they rejected not because it was foreign but because it was interfering and because it often propped up corrupt, wasteful and sometimes violent political regimes.

It was the United States that figured largest on their horizons in this way, though for now they had rather different views about that country. Fidel, though he was drawn to many aspects of American culture, was also convinced that to loosen the grip of the ruling elite in Cuba he would have to undermine the American patronage that those elites enjoyed. But Ernesto, who had developed a more general sense of the social consequences of North America's involvement in the South, wanted a more wholesale, root-and-branch overhaul of the system. As of yet, neither had found the means to make much of their ideas: Moncada, for all that it had been a sensational event, would never have succeeded. But, despite their individual setbacks when they met they were both of a mind to keep trying.

As befits such a conjunction of position as opposed to personality, their lives had begun to slot together before they themselves realised it. By the time Fidel Castro arrived in Mexico City Ernesto Guevara had already become a personal and political *confrère* of his fledgling rebel movement, albeit signed up in the rather general and non-committal terms that had drawn him to the radical trades union movement in Guatemala and roused his interest in the miners' strikes in Bolivia. Why settle on this one? Why make his stand alongside the Cubans and not the Guatemalans, or the Bolivians, or his own countrymen? The answer turns upon his meeting with Fidel and its immediate effect on him. Guatemala had been the first turning point for Guevara, but it was not in itself sufficient: the meeting with Fidel would complete the process. For Fidel, on the other hand, the meeting with Guevara provided him with some early encouragement in exile and perhaps also a framework for his revolution. For him, the real benefits of the union would come later.

* * *

The train that carried Ernesto over the border from Guatemala pulled into the fog and rain that shrouded Mexico City's main Plaza de Buenavista railway station one October morning in 1954. The Argentine carried sparse luggage but his head was full of the experiences of his eventful year in Guatemala, as well as his preceding great trek through the continent from his own country to Central America. On the way he had seen so much that had affected him, and in a cross-sectional way condensed the continent's ills into a single, comprehensible narrative. For Guevara the lessons of that narrative were clear. What had happened in Guatemala was related to the poverty he had seen in Panama; the difficulties confronting the miners in their revolution in Bolivia were the same issues as those confronting the workers with whom he had stacked crates in Puerto Barrios. All this he laced together with the thread of American imperialism and concluded that the whole continent was fettered with the same curse.

'The atmosphere one inhales here,' as Ernesto himself tried to capture it upon his arrival, 'is completely different to Guatemala. Here too you can say what you want, but on condition of being able to pay for it on some side; which is to say one inhales the democracy of the dollar.' Even before he left Mexico City a little over two years later, and as a direct consequence of having by then encountered Fidel Castro, Guevara would have refined this perception somewhat. 'The air of freedom is, in reality, a clandestine air,' he wrote in 1955, 'but this does not matter: in any case it gives the most interesting shade of a mystery film.'

Ernesto's life would soon take on more than a little of the feel of a mystery film. For now, though, as the immediacy of his experiences in Guatemala faded, he slipped back into his usual lassitude: 'My aspirations haven't changed and my immediate north remains Europe, or the middle east,' he wrote to Tita, before adding after pause for thought, 'how is another story.' As he remarked to Aunt Beatriz, 'the city, or better said, the country of the *mordidas* [bribes] has received me with all the indifference of a big animal, neither caressing me nor showing its teeth.'

In his ever-constant struggle to obtain money, Guevara rotated a series of part-time jobs: an occasional stint at the General Hospital, where he would often sleep over on the night cots, some research work in a downtown laboratory and, with the Zeiss camera he had bought himself on arriving, taking portraits of the Sunday picnickers and strolling couples in the plazas and parks for a few pesos apiece.

His letters make it only too clear though: these were yet more 'zero days'. Despite enjoying the attentions of his new hosts' attractive young daughter, Marta Petit de Murat – a 'nice' girl, albeit with 'a typical clericaloid bourgeois education' against her – he clearly felt rather alone. Even though Hilda was temporarily imprisoned in Guatemala (not that he took the trouble to find out much about her situation) he made little attempt to contact her. Having finally secured her release and safe exit from Guatemala, Hilda however made sure she caught up with Ernesto. They soon slipped back into the old routine, each with their own – as ever, incompatible – understanding of the affair. In the last week of November, the couple went to see a Soviet production of *Romeo and Juliet* at the ballet. Hilda maintained in her memoirs that the discussion it prompted that evening as to the universality of Shakespeare resulted in them 'making up'. If so, it captures the peculiar nature of the bond between them: he insisting that they marry, while forgetting things like Christmas presents; she holding him to his promises and forgetting that he never kept them.

Eventually, she suggested that they marry the following March, exactly one year after they had become 'proper' friends, as she put it. 'You and your dates. Why does it have to be exactly a year after?' he replied. 'It could be now, it could be at the end of the month. Why does it have to be March?' But then Hilda found a small photo of the Petit de Murat girl when it fell out from, of all things for him to have kept it in, a work of Einstein's that the two of them had been translating together. She slipped the photo into an envelope and wrote Ernesto a tart letter announcing that she was breaking off their engagement, and indeed all contact between them, once and for all.

But there were new distractions in Ernesto's life now. He had once again begun bumping into some of the members of Fidel's revolutionary movement, who had been steadily congregating in Mexico City since the start of the previous year when Fidel had smuggled out of prison an order that they should do so. Ernesto was reacquainted first with Ñico López, with whom he had got along so well in Guatemala, then José Angel Sánchez Pérez, who had been one of those to attack the Palace of Justice opposite the Moncada barracks with Raúl. Pérez was installed in the room next to Ernesto in his pension in Calle Tigris, and the two of them would often head out together across town to Calle Guttenberg where some of the other 'Moncadistas' were staying. Ernesto wouldn't say much at these meetings, which were based on endless games of dominoes and what were probably rather embellished accounts of their exploits. He preferred on the whole just to listen: 'he wasn't much of a talker', as Sánchez Pérez later recalled.

Ernesto also accompanied these young men to the house of María Antonia González, an expatriate Cuban who lived not far away on the rather nondescript Calle Emparán with her husband, the Mexican boxer Dick Medrano. The couple's apartment had become a focus of refuge for Cubans over the previous months, and the unofficial heart of Cuban exile operations. Here, recently arrived members of Fidel Castro's 26 July Movement – it had finally been given a name, after the date of the Moncada attack – crashed out on makeshift mattresses on the floor where they would wake to the smells of María Antonia's cooking. Ernesto looked just like all the other young *muchachos*: half-starved, restless and on the make. '[H]e was very young, very thin, always with the same clothes. He would come here when he had gotten tired of taking photos.' María, much loved though she was by the Cubans, had a filthy tongue, which doubtless would have appealed to Ernesto's sense of humour. But it was her husband for whom he reserved a special fondness. 'Old girl,' Medrano would call out to María when Guevara arrived, rake thin 'make something for Che to eat – the poor thing, he's dying from hunger.'

By April, around the time Fidel was released from prison in Cuba, Ernesto was earning a pittance of 150 pesos a month at the hospital. This he supplemented during the Pan-American games when he worked as a photographer for the Peronist news agency Agencia Latina. With Severino Rosell, one of Fidel's side-kicks whom he had also got to know in Guatemala, Che set up a small photographic business. But he remained poor and would even sleep rough in garages at times.

In the meantime, Hilda had resolved to give their relationship yet one more try. When she called in at the Cubans' apartment one day during the games she found Ernesto there and in good spirits. After she had left, his new friends ribbed Ernesto merci-lessly. 'Hilda came, now you're happy Che,' they teased him. It was true: he was. As ever, their accounts of the subsequent reunion diverge. As she recalls it, a few days later he gave her an ulti-matum. They were to be married or nothing. As he had it, the proposal of marriage was her idea. 'I said no, that we should stay as little lovers until I beat it to hell and I don't know when that will be.' Whoever initiated things, it was perhaps a fitting solution: the proposal that neither really made but both were happy to accept.

While Ernesto was scouting around one morning for likely subjects to part with a few pesos for a photo, he chanced to see Ñico López walking past the Hotel Prado on the grand Avenida Juárez. Ñico was with Raúl Castro, who had arrived just a few days before via asylum in the Mexican embassy in Havana. The younger Castro had already taken warmly to the local passion for bullfighting. In addition to spending many hours at the *corridas* over the coming months he would also develop the pecu-liar habit of pretending to fight cars as they crossed roads, holding out his jacket with a flourish and a cry of '*Olé!*' Such oddities aside, once he and Ernesto got chatting they soon realised they had much in common – notably a strong interest in Marx that the older Castro did not yet share – and a 'strong friendship' immediately ensued.

With Raúl and Medrano Ernesto would often go along to the local Library Zaplana, not to read books but to watch the Soviet films that were shown around the back. Raúl and Guevara also went to the Mexican–Russian Cultural Exchange, in Calle Edison, where Raúl re-established contact with a young Soviet language student, Nikolai Leonov. Raúl and Leonov had become friends during a long journey back by boat from Italy after Raúl had attended a communist youth conference in Vienna. Leonov had been heading to Mexico to study and to work at the Soviet embassy. It was a typical friendship of the time between like-minded young men in that part of the world: sincere, often educational – coming from such different cultures as they did – and quite often later proving to have been uncannily prescient. Leonov's friendship with Raúl fitted this mould perfectly. Ernesto too hit it off with Leonov, who lent him a number of Soviet books he asked for. Innocently, he tucked his business card in among them for when Ernesto wished to return them.

These were all new and pervasive influences on Ernesto, but it was during these months, the angst and tension of Guatemala behind him but not quite out of his system, that he wrote the following poem. It captures something he had grasped at but was not yet in a position to act upon.

> The sea beckons with a friendly hand
> My meadow – a continent –
> Unrolls itself softly and indelibly
> Like a bell tolling at eventide.

How deceptive this rather tranquil poem was. It hid entirely the urgency with which he was yet again wanting to escape the routine he had fallen into. When he finally received some money that the Agencia Latina owed him for having covered the Pan-American games for them, he wrote a desperate missive to his faithful old friend Tita saying that he wanted 'to invest it quickly in a trip to Europe' and asking her to help him make the necessary arrangements. 'I would like to be in that continent before the first of August,' he announced. He never made it, however, because the vortex that was Fidel Castro was about to enter his life with his conviction, his insistence and his sheer inability not to envelop all those around him in his plans. The days of talking and reading were numbered for Ernesto, whether he was quite ready for the change or not.

* * *

Fidel arrived in Mexico just four weeks after his release from prison. Under threat of assassination, with bombs going off in Havana and the press being shut down wherever they gave Fidel a voice, he had reached the conclusion that he needed to leave. His final message, declaring the necessity for revolution, was penned off the cuff in the offices of the last publication still prepared to run his articles, *Bohemia*. Calling upon the island's popular history of rebellions, Fidel declared: 'I no longer believe in general elections . . . there is no option but that of [18]68 and that of [18]95.' After tearful farewells to family and friends in Havana, he had boarded an aircraft that brought him from the muggy Cuban heat via Venezuela to Veracruz on the east coast of Mexico. From there, after a night spent surrounded by plaster casts and busts of José Martí in a modest sculptor's studio that doubled as a safe house for Cuban exiles and fugitives from Batista's regime, he caught a bus up to Mexico City where the air was much cooler. He was met there on the afternoon of Friday, 8 July with hugs and introductions to some of his old compañeros and some new ones who had joined the movement in exile.

Fidel was pleased to see them all, but he had arrived in a terrible mood. 'My body aches all over,' he complained in a letter to Melba Hernández, and that was before he picked up a cold.

Worst of all, he could find no Cuban cigars. He felt alone and far removed from the rush of events in Cuba: 'I feel more isolated than when they had me in solitary confinement,' he moaned.

What ailed him was rather more than just the climate. It was an intense and deeply felt frustration. Before leaving Cuba, Fidel had made a speech that was to mark a turning point in his life:

I am leaving Cuba because all the doors of peaceful struggle have been closed to me.

Six weeks after being released from prison I am convinced more than ever of the dictatorship's intention, masked in many ways, to remain in power for twenty years, ruling as now by the use of terror and crime and ignoring the patience of the Cuban people, which has its limits.

As a follower of Martí, I believe the hour has come to take our rights and not beg for them, to fight instead of pleading for them.

I will reside somewhere in the Caribbean.

From trips such as this one does not return, or else one returns with tyranny beheaded at one's feet.

During those first days in Mexico City Fidel struggled simply to keep his own head, however. He was further than ever from power, adrift not only from Cuba but from his own revolutionary movement which he now had to hope would function without him. Even Fidel's indomitable spirit was down. He desperately needed to make contact with the wider network of exiles in Mexico to garner support for his movement.

Fidel began to write a stream of letters that were intended more to keep his own spirits up than to make any concrete suggestions about what to do. In one such letter to Faustino Pérez ('Médico'), sent like the others via an intermediary and addressed to his collaborators' underground names back in Cuba, Fidel wrote, 'Right now I am getting to grips with the revolutionary process under [former Mexican President] Cárdenas. Later on I think I will set down the complete revolutionary programme that we will present to the country, in the form of a *folleto* [pamphlet], that it will be possible to print here and introduce clandestinely to the country.' But he received no reply to this communication, nor to any other: a channel for letters into Mexico had not yet been established. The following week, still unanswered, he wrote again, this time to Melba, using her pseudonym: 'Dear Doctora, I am going mad with impatience to know how work is going. . . . Here I really need collaborators, on all fronts.' He was frustrated, anxious for his movement and desperate to meet people.

Two days later, a little more settled, and quietly engrossed in his own thoughts as he set about cooking a seafood pasta dish, Fidel Castro was being watched closely from across the room by a scrawny, fuzzy-haired youth in an oversized brown suit who was leaning against the wall. It was 26 July, two years since the Moncada attack, and a date Fidel would normally have used to vocalise his plans and deliver up some verbal tirade at the incumbent government in Cuba. Now that he was effectively underground, though, it had for once been a quiet affair: flowers left at the tomb of the Heroes of Chapultepec – a memorial to the young military cadets who defended the city against invading US forces in 1847 – and attendance at an event organised by the Continental Indoamerican Movement, before a small gathering back at the house of Eva and Graciela Jiménez.

Ernesto Guevara, the youth closely observing the newly arrived Fidel Castro that night, picked up very little of this. Ever the shy individual in a crowd, Guevara appears to have remained in the shadows that first evening. The two did not as a result properly get to meet, though they may well have exchanged greetings or caught one another's eye. But both kept within their own world, Guevara most likely observing with his quiet smiles and dark eyes as Castro, by force of habit, quietly took charge of the evening and of those around him whom he knew well.

A few days later, however, Ñico and Raúl agreed to bring Che over to María Antonia's apartment. It was 'one of those cold, Mexican nights' and Fidel had been suffering from flu, but her apartment was now the hub of his new world and it was already crackling with activity. Fidel himself was busy socialising with his expanding network, gleaning further contacts, trying out ideas, testing loyalties. Despite the flu, his mood had picked up considerably since his early depression and he was now throwing himself at his work with more typical gusto. In that small apartment he moved gracefully among the suits and their belles and, amidst the rising tide of chatter and debate, a tap on the shoulder from Ñico perhaps and a casual regrouping of conversations and the two men were properly introduced.

Then still close-shaven and looking every bit the lawyer he had trained to be, with his brilliantined hair and thin moustache, Fidel was in sparkling form for the shabbily dressed traveller from the South. He made an impression that Ernesto would never quite forget. Full of indignation and passion, Fidel grabbed the newcomer gently by the shoulder, pulled him over and immediately began telling him of their plans. He found a ready listener in the Argentine, but he also subjected him to relentless questioning. Perhaps understandably, Fidel was wary about admitting a foreigner to the group. Why indeed, he asked Ernesto after they had been introduced – most likely now jabbing him conversationally with his finger in that distractive Cuban style – was a medical doctor working as an itinerant photographer?

Fidel was most interested to hear of Ernesto's experiences in Guatemala and about other aspects of the South American political scene. Ernesto was, of course, only too happy to tell him what he thought about all that and soon the two men were eagerly trading ideas on Latin American and international politics, their respective experiences of various uprisings and their passion for the great revolutionary thinkers of the continent – José Martí and Simón Bolivar – and, of course, for Karl Marx as well. Here at least one suspects that Ernesto might have got a word in, his reading on Marxism having been far more dedicated than Fidel's at this point.

'There was nothing extraordinary about that first meeting,' María Antonia recalled, 'they simply got to know each other. "Look, Fidel, this is Ernesto Guevara, Che, the Argentine doctor". And then, nothing, they dealt with each other normally, as any two people would after meeting. Here in the house there were other *muchachos*. They spoke in general. But really, I don't know what they spoke about. The conversation lasted a long time.'

Raúl, Fidel and Ernesto decamped later that night to a restaurant just around the block, and stayed there talking until the early hours. Ernesto headed home thoroughly impressed with Fidel's optimism and resolve. Unlike some of the other exiles who were content to bicker and bemoan the fate of their countries, Fidel had no sooner arrived in exile than he was planning a way back, or so it seemed to the Argentine. Fidel's 'plan' at this moment in fact amounted to little more than 'an unshakeable faith that once he left he would arrive in Cuba, that once he arrived he would fight, and that once he began fighting he would win.' But maybe that was enough. Fidel's recollection of the meeting was the more pragmatic of the two and gives a strong indication as to his priorities at the time: 'it was Che Guevara's combative temperament as a man of action that impelled him to join me in my fight . . .'

They had arrived at a similar conclusion via different routes. For Guevara, the sum of his experiences in Bolivia and Guatemala (the two countries he knew best outside of Argentina) was that South-American armies were corruptible and unreliable at bringing about political change and there was no alternative in the current climate but to start from scratch by arming the people. This was what Fidel – who had far greater experience, of course – had tried at Moncada. The question was how to put this idea into practice.

If their meeting was not quite the thump and flare of instantaneous ignition that Cuban historians would have us believe, it contained none the less some outward affirmation of the inner faith, or perhaps fatalism, which both men posessed and to which they had, in their own ways, become attuned. But above all it seems that Fidel, by then the more mature, the more developed of the two of them, evaluated Che's ability and possible worth to him more or less immediately. As to whether he could trust this Argentine, he took the chance that he could. But perhaps just as importantly he made no demands of Ernesto, asked him to swear no bonds of allegiance, but simply determined to set him among the rank and file and see what would become of it.

For Ernesto, that immediately made Fidel stand out from the other would-be revolutionaries he had met. 'Ñico was right in Guatemala, when he told us that if Cuba had produced anything good since Martí it was Fidel Castro. He will make the revolution,' Ernesto told Hilda shortly after their meeting. 'We are in complete accord,' he went on. 'It's only someone like him I could go all out for.' When he asked Hilda soon afterwards what she thought of Fidel's 'crazy idea', she agreed it was crazy but thought it was also important to support it. 'I think the same,' Guevara said, having long since made his mind up, 'but I wanted to know what you would say.' He then told her he had decided to stand and fight alongside Fidel.

*　*　*

Shortly after that first meeting, Ernesto and Hilda invited Fidel over for dinner. They also invited the Puerto Ricans Juan Juarbe and Laura Albizu Campos, the wife of Puerto Rican nationalist Pedro Albizu who was imprisoned. There were so many exiles in Mexico City at this time that it is remarkable that Fidel found the time to meet them all. But meet them he did, by day and by night, until finally he began to find his feet again. 'Dear sisters,' he wrote to Melba and Haydée on one of these nights. 'It is already four or five in the morning and I am still writing. I have no idea how many pages I have written in all! I have to get them to the messenger at 8.00 a.m. I don't have an alarm clock and if I fall asleep I will miss the mail. So I shan't go to bed.'

It was perhaps inevitable, therefore, that Fidel turned up late for dinner that night at Hilda's flat. He was so late, however, that Hilda's flatmate, the Venezuelan poet Lucila Velasquéz, who was hoping to attract Fidel's attentions, had already gone to bed in despair. Hilda's first impressions – never excessively elaborate, given some of the people of whom she had the opportunity to form first impressions – were of a man who resembled a 'handsome bourgeois tourist'. After dessert she asked Fidel why he was in Mexico, since his struggle – so he said – was in Cuba. 'That is a good question,' Fidel replied. 'Very good,' he added. 'I'll explain.' His answer took four hours of pacing and pontificating, as he surveyed the recent political scene in Cuba and outlined his plans for an armed invasion.

One imagines the effect of this oratorical grandeur upon Che. But Fidel's performance in Hilda and Lucila's apartment was not entirely spontaneous. It was a synthesis of the thoughts he had been preparing for his first political statement in exile, *Manifesto Number One*. 'To those who accuse the revolution of upsetting the economy we reply: for those peasants who have no land, the economy does not exist; for the million Cubans who are out of work, the economy does not exist; for the railworkers, the dockers, textile workers, bus drivers and workers from other sectors for whom Batista has reduced their salaries, the economy unmercifully does not exist.' The Manifesto looked just the sort of document it needed to be: a political 'wanted' poster, its text and title printed in heavy type, whose denunciations of Batista's so-called constitutional government made one thing abundantly clear: the only viable opposition was the 26 July Movement, and the 26 July was Fidel Castro.

The second document he produced at this time, a *Message to the Ortodoxos*, was an altogether more accurate window on these early days and weeks in exile, the manuscript written on thin paper in Fidel's slanting hand. It called on the Ortodoxos to accept that participation in the political process played into the hands of the regime. Both documents were printed on the clunky old machine of a friend of María Antonia and Medrano, Arsenio 'Kid' Vanegas, a stocky wrestler who would prove as loyal and as solid as he looked. Though only a few copies were smuggled over to Havana, Fidel was optimistic. He wrote to Melba, still working clandestinely and devotedly for him in Havana, that his group would keep sending them 'every fortnight at the least'.

When read out by Fidel's trusted assistant Faustino Pérez, to the five hundred assembled delegates at that summer's conference of Militant Ortodoxos in Havana with its challenge to Batista that if he did not resign 'we shall sweep you and your clique of infamous murderers from the face of the earth', the message caused a sensation. At the end of the document Fidel posed a rhetorical question: 'The opposition has called for general elections AS THE ONLY FORMULA FOR A PEACEFUL SOLUTION. What will it do if, as is probable, Batista refuses to concede this SINGLE FORMULA FOR A SOLUTION?' But there was another road, Fidel declared, one cleansed of any concessions to the incumbent regime. It was a classic Fidelista ploy: in rephrasing the concept between the first capitalised phrase and the second (presumably the words to which Faustino gave special emphasis) he omitted the part he found inconvenient. And just as it was the word 'peace' that disappeared between the two lines, so, in what he was proposing, it now dropped off the agenda. At the conference the delegates jumped up as the word that signalled the other path was voiced, repeating it aloud as they broke into chants of 'Revolution! . . . Revolution! . . . Revolution!' Exile had confirmed for Fidel the necessity of a violent path forward.

* * *

At around this time, Hilda broke the news to Ernesto that she was expecting a child. Despite their on-off relationship the news was not unwelcome, and the couple decided to get married as a matter of some urgency. The following day Ernesto bought her a silver

121

bracelet studded with black stones, saying, 'This is for the baby,' as he kissed her. Despite the gesture, it does not seem to have been an especially romantic moment for him. He describes it in his journal as an 'uncomfortable episode'. 'I am going to have a child and I will marry Hilda in a few days. The thing had dramatic moments for her and heavy ones for me. In the end she gets her way – the way I see it, for a short while, although she hopes it will be life-long.' Never one to want to feel tied down, Ernesto now had some rather more personal hopes invested in Fidel's planned expedition.

Despite his doubts, Ernesto and Hilda were married on 18 August 1955. Fidel and some of the other Cubans were invited. It was a Thursday, but they did not have jobs to go to and Ernesto and Hilda travelled to the historical city of Tepotzotlán accompanied by Raúl, Jesús Montané – Fidel's 'short, flap-eared' treasurer – Lucila Velásquez and a few of Ernesto's friends from his other life at the General Hospital. The marriage itself was conducted with no great fuss at a registry office. In a clear indication of who he felt his most significant friends to be, Ernesto had asked that either Fidel or Raúl should be the witness. But for reasons of security Fidel had stayed away from the ceremony itself (memories of the atmosphere at his own wedding perhaps also guided his decision), and at the last moment Raúl decided not to sign the register. Fidel came later to the lodgings where the wedding group had retired for the evening and where Ernesto was preparing an Argentine *asado* of roasted meats cooked over an open fire.

As for his new in-laws, however, Ernesto would never meet them. The newly-weds wrote to tell their parents only once they had moved into their new lodgings in a five-storey Art Deco building on Calle Nápoles in Colonia Juárez, still a rather humble affair, but larger at least for the coming child. They received a rebuke from the Gadeas for not having told them before the wedding so that they might have attended, and, rather more welcome, a bank draft for $500. But, as Hilda herself was beginning to recognise, 'All [our] plans and prospects had changed, of course, forever, with that conversation with Fidel.'

As summer turned into autumn Ernesto and Fidel met with increasing frequency at the social gatherings of the Cubans. Fidel was always keen to explain, to teach: he regularly took his comrades down to the Antonio Mella memorial where he gave accounts of the Cuban communist's life and struggles, 'nothing mystical . . . just the historical facts', one of them recalled. Ernesto, of course, was always keen to learn. They must have shared their passion for books because Ernesto was still editing his philosophical note-books and Fidel was busy acquiring a library of his own.

'Hey Che, you're very quiet. Is it because your controller's here now?!' Fidel shouted out one night at dinner, in reference to Hilda. Hilda knew that her husband and the Cuban had been spending a lot of time together. Ernesto was shy in a large group, but once someone had entered into his confidence he put up no further personal barriers. Fidel, of course, was adept at settling himself within the personal space of others. On this occasion Ernesto uttered private words of reassurance to Hilda: 'I'm your boy and don't you forget it.'

Fidel would now often find a reason to call in at Ernesto and Hilda's house on Calle Nápoles. Though Guevara was still not yet actively a member of the M26, as the 26 July Movement was often referred to, their apartment was one of the few places where Fidel could share time with like-minded trustworthy folk and let off a little steam. In September, as Ernesto and Hilda contemplated whether to buy a car or take a trip with the money her family had sent them, Fidel advised them to take a trip. Failing that, a record player, he told them; but in any case 'not an automobile' – as they had been considering – 'too many prob-lems here in Mexico . . . better to buy something for the house'.

* * *

'We're mourning the developments,' the Peruvians Raygada and Gonzalo Rose and the Puerto Rican poet Juan Juarbe – all of them fellow exiles – said in greeting, as if doffing their hats, as

they arrived at Ernesto and Hilda's flat one day. They were referring to the news that Perón – who after nearly ten years in power
in Argentina, much of that with his wife, Evita, at his right hand
– had just been overthrown. Later, Fidel and Ernesto mulled over
the situation together. Many people – the middle and upper
classes especially – viewed Peronismo with distaste. But for these
two exiles, what stood out above the swill of corruption and
heavy-handedness was Perón's populist welfare state at home and
his anti-imperialism abroad. Perón's formula was one that would
ultimately prove unsustainable, even with the support of the military. But for now the two men both seem to have instinctively
taken note of the same thing: that one could both be radical *and*
attain power. The greater problem would be keeping it.

Fidel's thinking on how to attain such power was becoming
more developed by the day. He gave an impassioned and eloquent
speech on that theme on 9 October in Chapultepec Park. His
audience consisted of just a smattering of the hopeful few, though
Fidel later confessed that he had been more nervous about this
speech – in which he set out, for all those who cared to listen,
his new revolutionary platform – than any other in his life. 'The
present American generation', he told his audience, 'is obliged
to take the offensive; is obliged to light up once more the spirit
of democracy; is obliged to drop words and to raise deeds. . . .
America is growing tired of the *politiqueros* and traitors and
oppressors it is suffering from. The ideas of Martí and the sword
of Bolívar will once more sparkle across America. I have faith in
America!'

It was precisely this sort of rhetoric – conveyed that day through
the hatched tones of the microphone, but into Ernesto's ears
more often via Fidel's soft voice over dinner, that began gradually, yet with a growing insistence, to draw him into action. The
notion of revolution was predominantly still a romantic one for
Ernesto, but as he himself suggested later to the Argentine journalist Jorge Masetti, what Fidel made him realise at this point
was that 'you had to stop whining and fight.' Ernesto had in fact

always been aware of this dilemma. It lurks in almost all his writings from his youth. What was really beginning to happen, rather, was that Ernesto was seeing in Fidel *how* to stop whining and fight.

A rather more serious interest in revolution was thus emerging in Ernesto as Fidel left that month on a fund-raising trip to the eastern United States. The night he was due to leave, and accompanied by Melba and Jesús Montané, Fidel went to Ernesto and Hilda's for a farewell dinner. By October, most of the Movement's high command – save for those still running operations back in Cuba – had now also left for Mexico. Melba and Ernesto had got off to a frosty start, when they were introduced by Montané at the hospital. Dr Guevara looked up and down at her fine clothes and jewellery, and retorted bluntly that this could not be a revolutionary given the way she dressed herself. A revolutionary, he lectured her, adorns herself on the inside, not the outside. She, who had seen her brother's eyes in the hands of his torturers, and who had already served a prison sentence for her conviction to fight alongside the men, was understandably furious at the cheek of this Argentine upstart, and Montané had had to pull her away as she cursed and fumed at Ernesto. Guevara's often insensitive bluntness alienated a good many of the Cubans at first as they came to understand why he had once been nicknamed 'sniper'.

The dinner that last night was a calmer affair as they enjoyed typical Peruvian and Venezuelan dishes prepared by Hilda and Lucila. Fidel noted approvingly that the Guevaras had bought a record player, as he suggested. It was a night when, for once, politics was not the centre of attention. Lucila was catching Fidel's eye, and Melba and Jesús used the occasion to announce their engagement. 'Tell me, Hilda, how did you snare Ernesto.' Lucila asked provocatively. Hilda could tell from his expression that Ernesto was going to make some sort of mocking response – which of course he did, taking them back to Guatemala and saying, 'She went to jail in my place so out of gratitude I married her.' The couples stayed talking and listening to music until the early hours, when Fidel, joined now by Juan Manuel Márquez – the forty-year-old former Ortodoxo president of the Marianao municipality of Havana, who had been beaten by the police there for his association with the Fidelistas and was now one of Castro's chief advisers – left on the coach for Texas.

* * *

Fidel's third visit to the United States was to be a turning point in his revolutionary career. This time he was received by large crowds as he established essential support networks for the coming struggle. But on a more personal level, it seems to have marked the moment when Fidel began to believe he might finally have caught up with the spectre of José Martí that he had lived with on his previous visits. Now he felt he was actually carrying on something of Martí's legacy.

After whirlwind stops in Philadelphia, Union City, and Bridge-port Connecticut, Fidel arrived in New York. There, in Central Park, the Cuban photographer Osvaldo Salas took photos of him for *Bohemia* magazine as he walked around some of Martí's favourite spots. In a packed theatre at the Palm Garden Hotel, Fidel was at pains to demonstrate that he and his followers were serious: 'We are digging trenches of ideas, but also trenches of rock . . . . I can tell you that in 1956 we will be free or we will be martyrs.' But his most consistent point throughout this speaking tour followed on from the theme of a letter he had written to the Ortodoxo party executive committee in New York before he left, in which he had argued for the need for 'a radical and profound change in national life'. It was a message that struck a chord with the large Cuban exile communities of the cities he was working his way through.

By November Fidel had travelled down the East coast to Florida, where he made an impassioned speech in Miami's Flagger Theatre – putting across his usual two-fold pitch of Martí and Chibás –

for which he received a standing ovation. He and Márquez had brought recordings of Chibás with them to set the scene for Fidel's own speeches at the various venues; donations were placed in upturned cowboy hats on the top table (beneath, whenever they could arrange it, a portrait of Martí). Throughout this tour Fidel limited his rhetoric to the task at hand and kept, for once, out of sight of the authorities (he was stopped just the once, for a routine traffic check). But his reception was sufficiently warm to prompt Batista to let it be known that he too had friends in America. The two remaining dates on Fidel's tour, in Tampa and Cayo Hueso, would be sabotaged to a greater or lesser degree by Batista's agents. It was too little too late, however. Fidel's American trip had further consolidated his reputation in Cuba. As one editorial back in Cuba stated, if Fidel were ever to come to power, he would be 'God and Caesar in one man.' The article did not go unanswered, of course.

Leaving the Movement's organisation in the United States to the Mexicans Alfonso Gutiérrez and Orquídea Pino, Fidel prepared to return to Mexico City. He also had to leave behind his six-year-old son, who had been brought over by Fidel's sister Lidia on the first of a series of flying visits he would make to his father. It resulted in one notable moment when, playing with the dollar bills stashed into the cowboy hats as he sat next to his father during one of the events, he was reprimanded with the words: 'Don't touch that, Fidelito, because this money belongs to the Motherland.'

It had been an intense few weeks, and after the final event in Florida Fidel spent a few days resting and writing at a boarding house on Truman Avenue in Key West before flying home. It would be his last period of rest for a long time to come. As their plane made a stop at Nassau in the Bahamas, he finalised the Second Manifesto of the 26 July Movement. Partly a reflection on why he had named the movement after the date of the Moncada attack, it was also a succinct outline of his revolutionary philosophy that the ends justify the means. In this he most certainly followed Martí in deeds, even as he sought to deny such an approach in words: 'In the revolution, Martí said, "The methods are secret and the ends are public." But how are we to demand resources of people if we don't tell them why we want them? If the revolution asks for the help of interest groups, it will be compromised before obtaining power. [But] to pronounce the revolution out loud will give, without doubt, better fruits than to speak of peace in public and to conspire in secret.'

Fidelito was not the only person who came to find Fidel in Miami. Naty Revuelta, his long-term lover who had supported him through his preparations for Moncada and during his imprisonment on the Isle of Pines, turned up too. She had come ostensibly to carry out a mission for the underground movement, but probably also to tell Fidel that she was pregnant. When she arrived at the house of the collaborator Álvaro Pérez however, she was told that Fidel had already left. Five days later and without having been able to find the man she loved, Naty returned to Havana.

By the time Fidel himself returned to Mexico he had set up the beginnings of an M26 movement in exile and, through the establishment of donation committees there, a means of securing income and popular support for the coming struggle. The money accrued so far was needed right away to pay off debts already incurred on the lodgings and living expenses of the men; the support would be needed to keep the money coming in later.

* * *

Ernesto had confronted a major decision in Fidel's absence. He had been inspired by the Cuban, of that there was no doubt. Ideas of revolution and, above all, the possibility of his taking part in it, filled his head. But as yet he had still done precious little to act upon them. He continued to sit on the sidelines, unable to will himself to take the final step.

In November, he and Hilda took their long-delayed honeymoon in Palenque. True to Guevara's natural instincts they had left with no firm itinerary in mind: they just planned to head south and fit in as many architectural sites as they could. Palenque, Chichén Itzá, Uxmal: Ernesto could never get enough of these ancient ruins with their stone friezes, sculptures of gods and steles. He clambered enthusiastically all over them, dragging a four months' pregnant Hilda by the hand as she became more and more tired and more and more grumpy.

The visit inspired him to set down a poem but, indicative of the conflict welling up inside, he was too frustrated to settle on the piece. The situation wasn't helped by a recurrence of his asthma, which the higher altitude of Mexico City had been keeping in check these last months. The result was a somewhat velvet set of verses slashed apart, Fontana-like, with personal and political swipes. They were directed at a telling range of targets: Hilda, capitalism and Yanqui tourists, the last of which he compared in his diary to 'a slap in the face'.

In her memoirs Hilda remembers the trip as one of 'happy days', but despite her perpetually optimistic prose the strains in their relationship were still apparent. Ernesto shouted at her violently one day as she tried to give him his medication. 'I'm sorry,' he apologised, after he had administered the injection himself, 'it's this disease that gets me out of sorts.' He was up and down the whole trip, but perked up considerably when they arrived at Veracruz to find an Argentine boat in dock from whose captain Ernesto was able to acquire a few kilos of his favourite maté tea. Having decided to make their way back down the coast by boat, they were hit by a violent storm. Well accustomed to the sea since his time as a ship's hand, Ernesto whooped around on the deck like a boy of half his years while, furious at his adolescent behaviour and inattentiveness to her condition, Hilda went below deck. A remorseful Ernesto followed her there soon afterwards.

On their return Ernesto learned he had finally been offered a permanent research post in medicine. But it seems not to have pleased him and he turned it down. Indeed, he now began to set aside many of his former interests. Even of his much-loved scientific work he declared, that 'most of what I've done is second rate and unoriginal – copied from Pisani'. Confirmation of this opinion was received when someone at the French embassy noted that, as he was the fifth author of a four-page article, he had probably written just the bibliography – and it was particularly bad. Ernesto was indignant, but too honest not to see the truth in it. His scientific work, like his poetry, was something he worked hard at, but lacked the patience to excel in. He needed something more immediate.

Some time later a letter arrived for Ernesto from the Leper Hospital of San Pablo. It was from his old friend *Mial* and brought with it fond memories of their travels together. Alberto congratulated Ernesto, who was deeply touched to receive news from his former, and now increasingly distant, life. But he did not reply this time; nor did he write to his usual correspondents about what was really happening in his life. Something had begun to change, and indicative of the transition was yet another poem he wrote about this time – one that has tended to be cited as proof of his deeply felt rage at the poverty and injustice of the South American continent, and thereby taken as evidence of his growing revolutionary conscience. In fact, it tells us rather more about the psychological battle he continued to wage with himself.

'Old Maria, you are going to die' is a keening lament for a patient Ernesto had been treating these last few months at the hospital: an old laundress, racked with asthma, who died as her no less afflicted doctor sat by her bedside holding her hand one winter's night. It was the second time Ernesto had made vows to himself at the bedside of a dying woman. The first time, when he had watched his grandmother die, he had turned to medicine as vocation. This time, it was as if he had decided finally to turn away from it.

'Don't ask for clemency from death / your life was horribly dressed with hunger / and ends dressed in asthma', Ernesto writes before lines in which one imagines him leaning forward to whisper in her ear what appears to him still to be a secret: 'But I want to announce to you / in a low voice virile with hopes / the most red and virile of vengeances / I want to swear it / on the exact dimension of my ideals . . . Take this hand of a man which seems like a boy's / between yours polished by yellow soap / Scrub the hard calluses and the pure knots / in the smooth vengeance of my doctor's hands'. He finishes the poem with the assurance: 'Your grandchildren will all live to see the dawn', adding, as a sort of afterthought, and, revealingly perhaps, in capitals just as Fidel had used to emphasise his points: 'I SWEAR'.

It was in this state of mind that Fidel Castro found his new *confrère* Ernesto Guevara when he arrived back in Mexico City shortly before the end of 1955 to return the favour of the farewell dinner. Fidel himself, energised by his US trip, was holding forth on his plans for Cuba after the revolution triumphed. 'He spoke with such certainty and naturalness that one had the feeling we were already in Cuba carrying out the process of construction,' Hilda recalled. Then, as if the realisation had suddenly dawned on them, they all fell silent. 'Yes, but first of all we must get to Cuba,' she said, voicing what they were probably all thinking at that moment. 'It is true,' Fidel replied gravely, and the room sank back into thought.

6. FELLOW TRAVELLERS

THE NEWSPAPERS IN Cuba began the New Year of 1956 with a series of statements by Antonio Blanco Rico, chief of Batista's secret police, accusing 'doctor Fidel Castro of hatching a subversive plan against the country from abroad'. This was entirely true, of course – though, frustratingly, the Cuban authorities did not yet have the evidence to prove it. More frustrating for them still, their precipitate claims merely opened the door for Fidel to publish a trademark stinging rebuke in *Bohemia*. But what the Cuban secret service did not know was that as a result of his American trip, and with the clandestine development of the 26 July Movement in Cuba itself, Fidel was now beginning to receive the means with which to launch just such a subversive plan.

Long gone were the days when Fidel could complain, 'each of us lives on less money than the army spends on any of its horses'. Pedro Miret, his old friend from school and now the Movement's principal arms expert, had arrived with $1000 in December. Faustino Pérez had brought $8000 with him in February, and then a further $10,000 arrived to bless the Movement's coffers by way of a revolutionary-minded man of the cloth. And in January the first new recruits – forty men in all – had arrived too. Along with Fidel, Raúl, Ñico, Ernesto and the others, there were now more than sixty of them. Having pronounced publicly in America that they would return before the end of the year, Fidel urgently needed to develop the military side of his operation, to turn his men – mostly 'humble, ordinary people – store clerks, labourers, students at business schools or at the secondary school' – into a fighting force. In this he was to find a special use for Ernesto Guevara, the one that almost all the Cubans now called Che.

For now Che kept up his work at the hospital, but when he came off duty he would travel across town to where the men were already training hard in the gymnasium of Arsenio Vanegas, Fidel's printer of manifestos. He also threw himself into the study of anything that 'might be useful', be it learning to type or how to-cut hair. And he embarked with renewed enthusiasm on a reading programme that covered Smith, Keynes, Hansen – in fact anyone who had written on political economy. In the evenings he would saunter to the Russo-Mexican exchange to find litera- ture appropriate to his developing tastes. This he shoehorned into his philosophical notebooks, editing them into a manageable, transportable form. As he told Hilda, he had to be ready to move if need be. She knew by now that her husband was always ready to move; it was staying put he found most difficult.

Fidel's time was mostly taken up with writing the unending stream of epistolary directives required to keep the different sinews and strands of the 26 July Movement advancing as one body. One of the first things he had done in Mexico before embarking on his US promotional tour was to make contact with a Cuban-born expert in guerrilla warfare, General Alberto Bayo, who had agreed to train his men. Bayo was a veteran of the Spanish Civil War and of insurrections in North Africa. Securing his not inconsiderable expertise was no mean feat given that, as the general recalled, at the point of asking him Fidel appeared to have 'neither a man nor a dollar' to his name.

A respected, feared or reviled figure, depending on whom you asked, Bayo was in all cases an extraordinary man. A one-eyed stunt pilot adept with both 'the gun and the lyre of the trouba- dour', as the introduction to a book of his poetry reads. He was elderly and white-haired when Fidel met him and made his pitch, but he had lost none of the indignant fury of his youth. Bayo responded first with incredulity but ultimately with a conviction that surprised even himself: 'Come now, I thought, this young man wants to move mountains with one hand. But what did it cost me to please him? "Yes", I said. "Yes, Fidel. I promise to instruct these boys the moment it is necessary."'

With the arrival of Fidel's new recruits in January, Bayo's services were now required. The training began with drill exercises and military classes in the evenings, Bayo scuttling between the safe houses into which the men had now been moved on the pretence of being a language tutor. Then they moved out on to the streets and into the gymnasiums, where the old warrior would growl at them to 'stop acting like señoritas' as he began pounding them into shape.

To improve their fitness, he also marched them up and down Mexico's long Insurgentes Avenue at dawn and hired rowing boats on Chapultepec Lake, where, in an ironic turn of events, the Rio Pact – a 'reciprocal assistance' treaty designed to keep the Soviets out of South America – had been signed in 1947. For several weeks visitors to the park were greeted by the sight of some fifty men ceaselessly thrashing up and down on the water amid the peaceful views of willow trees, balloon sellers and sweet vendors.

In February, Fidel booked the local Los Gamitos shooting range and filled it with live turkeys so that the men could improve their shooting skills. He also drafted in two experts – Miguel Sánchez, known as El Coreano because he had fought with the US forces in the Korean War, and José Smith, another Cuban-born US army veteran. The would-be rebels now learned the finer details of shooting: lines of fire, deviation rates, equipment maintenance.

Away from the intensity of their new regime – in which, as Bayo kept pressing on them, they would need to learn properly what military culture was all about if they wanted to survive what Fidel had planned for them – daily life continued for the young rebels. In the dual existence to which they were all becoming accustomed, daytime training went hand in hand with evening dinner parties. Fidel, Raúl, Ñico, Universo Sánchez, Juan Almeida and Calixto García, Doña Laura and her daughter, Juan Juarbe, the Torres family, Alfonse Bauer Paíz and the Jiménez sisters formed the main group.

The political situation in Cuba was heating up, however, and that spring Fidel had word that he was being targeted for assassination by Batista's regime. Utterly engrossed in his plans, Fidel took these threats to his life in the same stride as the more well-meaning attempts of his friends to get him out on a date – 'Fidel, we are not going to talk about politics; we are going to pay attention to the girls,' Raúl coaxed him one evening before the brothers went out together. On Valentine's Day, they finally got Fidel sitting down to tamales courtesy of a date who had convinced Fidel, who was notoriously fussy about accepting any money not destined for the Movement itself, to think of it as no more than a loan.

In contrast it was a quiet start to the year for Che and Hilda, she awaiting the birth of their child while he kept up his medical research at the General Hospital. On the same evening that Fidel was enjoying his tamales, and after a whole day of moving apartment, Hilda went into labour. Ernesto took her to the clinic and the following day, 15 February, their daughter Hildita Guevara was born. Her middle name was Beatriz, in honour of his long-suffering aunt. 'My communist soul expands plethorically,' he wrote in his usual sardonic tone to his father in early April. 'She has come out exactly like Mao Tse-Tung.' With his Córdoban fondness for nicknames, she was soon known to her father as his 'Little Mao'. Aunt Beatriz would not have appreciated the association.

After Che had brought his two girls home, Fidel was the first to come and visit. By all accounts, he was almost as enraptured with Hildita as Che was himself, though as ever he drew a political point from the occasion. 'This girl is going to be educated in Cuba,' he said as he held her up. Che's thoughts were more of the moment. 'This is what was needed in the house,' he declared proudly of the new situation. It was but a fleeting moment of marital bliss, however, as he confessed to Tita just a fortnight later: 'For a moment it seemed to me that a combination of the enchantment of the girl and consideration for her mother (who in many respects is a great woman and loves me in an almost infectious way) could turn me into a boring old father figure with [but] a small history of a once free life that grates at every moment with the daily reality; now I know that it won't be this way and that I will follow my bohemian life until who knows when . . .'

Che's certainty stemmed partly from his growing confidence in Fidel. What he had found alongside Fidel and his devoted men was the sense of comradeship and loyalty that he had sought, without quite realising it, in all his relationships. It was, as he freely confessed, the one thing that continually kept his relationship with Hilda together; and it had been something that he had learned at the earliest age with his mother. But it was principally, and overwhelmingly, something that was developing now between himself and Fidel. Indeed, it seems very likely that Che was going along with the secrecy and the training primarily in order to be alongside Fidel and to have the opportunity to take up arms, and not because he was yet completely sold on the 26 July platform.

Fidel was a shrewd judge of character and doubtless recognised this. But he had enough faith in Che to name him head of personnel, and to have him work alongside Bayo supervising the men's training. It was Che whom Fidel had sent – disguised as a Salvadoran colonel and with Bayo as his 'assistant' – to secure the purchase of a ranch at Santa Rosa, in the Chalco region south-east of Mexico City. By all accounts the disguise was fairly lamentable, but it did the trick and the men were moved out there to begin the more serious phase of their training for guerrilla war.

Life there was a spartan affair, involving exhausting night marches among the 'cactus, woods, and poisonous snakes' of the local terrain. It was an environment in which Che, with his long-developed self-control, thrived, and his real worth now began to become apparent to Fidel. In Bayo's report on him, Che was described as 'an excellent shooter, with approximately 650 bullets [used]. Excellent discipline, excellent leadership abilities, physical endurance excellent. Some disciplinary press-ups for small errors at interpreting orders and faint smiles.' Clearly he was having fun with his new comrades.

When Fidel came to the ranch one day to check how things were progressing, he offered Che as an example for the rest of the men. 'We were terribly tired, having practised all day,' Melba, who also took part in the marches, recalled. 'Having had only a half orange each for food, most of us just relaxed . . . . The only one to go on working with Fidel was Che. When they finished, Fidel gathered us, telling us with infinite sadness that the struggle ahead was very long, that if we became exhausted so easily we wouldn't be able to keep up, and that he was very upset that Che, an Argentine, a foreigner, hadn't got tired.'

As head of personnel Che made his own reports on the men, and in the evenings kept Bayo on his toes with repeated questionings and discussions about their training. When one of the men, Calixto Morales, refused to go on during a march, Che put him in detention and called for Fidel to be brought from the city. At a court martial held at three o'clock the following morning those in judgement called for the death penalty, commuted at the last minute to his being placed instead under permanent guard. Morales had in fact stopped because he was suffering from a bone condition, not because of lack of discipline, but nobody knew this at the time. Discipline was something on which neither Fidel nor Che would ever make concessions. Fidel began to take note of this other, 'harder' side to his new friend that Alberto had got to know and remarked upon during his travels with Ernesto and that was now beginning to show through more frequently.

While training progressed, Fidel was still mostly busy organising affairs in the city, but on the few occasions he visited the ranch he would sit with Che and review the men's reports. It was a glimpse of what was to come later, the two men putting their heads together in concentrated thought. The information in some of these reports was distilled from questionnaires which asked the men to identify those whom they thought suspicious and those who might join the group's leadership. A good number of them mentioned the Argentine doctor, 'el Che', as a future leader of the group.

Many formed the opposite view, however. Not everyone was as enamoured of the quirky and often arrogant Argentine as were Fidel, Raúl and the Movement's high command. New recruits soon realised that the days of 'talc' and 'toothpaste', as Universo Sánchez put it, were over. Che's tendency to impose strict discipline and order seemingly endless marches also caused a near mutiny before the end of February. Fidel was called out once again to preside, this time in defence of Che. In a tense atmosphere, some of the men let it be known that they felt life at the ranch resembled a 'concentration camp'. Che would have none of it; the first recruits had had no such problems, he insisted. Fidel then spoke out in his defence. When one of the guards on sentry duty approached to warn Fidel that he could be heard outside the ranch's perimeter, he turned and gestured to him to be quiet. Already, as Faustino Pérez, a close associate of Fidel, noted, there was a 'confidence like that of an old friendship, between him and Fidel'. The tit for tat by which the two men would knock each other into shape had begun.

* * *

By March Fidel's organisation comprised a growing clandestine network spanning Cuba, Mexico and the United States. It was now sufficiently independent that he no longer needed the protective umbrella of the Ortodoxo party for shelter. On the 19th he broke with it publicly, denigrating its members for their 'cowardice' and submission to the regime. It was a shrewd move that afforded him greater room for manueovre in the context of an increasingly belligerent opposition to Batista on the island. In April the Cuban secret police uncovered plans for an uprising of liberal army officers, known as the 'Conspiracy of the Pure'.

Around the same time a group from the Students' Revolutionary Directorate attacked a television station in Havana, resulting in the death of one of the students, while a group of militants pertaining to former president and now exiled opposition leader, Carlos Prío, launched an assault on the Goicuría army barracks in Matanzas, at which fourteen were cut down by machine gun fire in a bloody scene reminiscent of Moncada.

Fidel now needed to accelerate his plans for the departure to Cuba – something he had already set his operatives on the island to work on. According to the Cuban authorities observing him closely, his lodgings saw a constant stream of visitors from actual or intended collaborators. He was also now receiving yet more money from his supporters in Cuba and the United States, which he used to secure the services of a Mexican arms dealer known as El Cuate (Buddy). El Cuate would equip them with the more serious accoutrements of war that would be needed.

Things appeared to be going well until Fidel was unexpectedly arrested on the night of 20 June in a joint action by Mexican Federal Security agents and representatives of the Cuban embassy. Fidel had known for some time that the Cuban government had been plotting to assassinate him, but he had not realised the extent to which they might be able to act via the Mexican secret police. On the night of his arrest he and some companions had been to visit one of his men when, looking out of the window, the Cubans noticed two figures checking over their car, a crumpled 1942 Packard which had arms stashed in the boot. Fearing the worst, Fidel decided to make a run for it and crept out of the house with Universo Sánchez and Ramiro Valdés, his bodyguards for the day. But to no avail – the police were on to them. Fidel, who was armed, tried to draw his pistol but Universo and Ramiro had already been taken and were used as shields. All three were bundled into a police cruiser before being driven around the city and questioned. Eventually, they were dropped off at Federal Security Headquarters.

Elsewhere in the city other safe houses were being raided. That night twelve rebels were rounded up, two of whom were detained and tortured by being made to stand under freezing water with their hands tied behind them. When the Federal Security Agents arrived at María Antonia's door they knocked three times – the Cubans' usual code. Without thinking she opened it and the agents burst in, arresting all those present. Since most of the rebels were caught, the police rapidly discovered the extent of the operation Fidel had been masterminding over the last few months. They learned of the ranch, of the many safe houses and the names of most of those involved. Batista had failed to dispose of Fidel in person, but it looked now as if he might not need to: the whole movement in exile appeared to have been smashed.

Having detained Fidel and his key operatives, the next person on their list was 'Sr Guevara, of communist affiliation'. Officers were sent to the Guevaras' new flat, where Hilda was alone with Little Mao before going off to work. She was taken to the police station, along with the baby, for questioning. Hilda, not at all fazed – though she had no idea where Che might be – had managed to put out word to alert people before her arrest, but Fidel had already decided it would be better if they all turned themselves in. He would try to talk their way out of this one.

The whole group was to be held at the Interior Ministry's detention centre on Miguel Schultz street. One of the first visitors to see them there was the novelist and actress Teresa Casuso, widow of the famous Cuban poet Pablo de la Torriente Brau, himself one of the generation of Cuban revolutionaries of the 1930s who, like Fidel, had been imprisoned on the Isle of Pines. Casuso had heard of the events in the papers and came with her young and, by all accounts, enchanting new lodger, Lilia, to see the fate of her countrymen.

The two arrived just after visiting hours began at twelve. They weren't the only ones. Over the few weeks of their detention Fidel held court with numerous visitors, lawyers and journalists who passed through each day. 'There were over 50 reporters,' recalled Sánchez, 'everyone came to see about us.' The men probably took particular notice of the two women, though, and Teresa Casuso suggests why. 'Lilia, who I had only been able to arouse from her profound childlike slumber by threatening to go alone, looked like an elegant model, with the rims of her enormous innocent, greenish-brown eyes darkly accented in what she called the Italian fashion . . .'

Casuso picked out Fidel 'by his look and bearing' – he struck her as 'like a big Newfoundland dog': eminently serene, inspiring confidence and a sense of security. His greeting was warm 'but not overdone' – he knew who she was, Cuba being a small country. His manner, there in the prison yard, she found calm; his expression, however, was grave. 'He had a habit of shaking his head,' she recalled.

Fidel was distracted when Casuso introduced him to Lilia, and afterwards kept glancing over to where the young woman was chatting with a photographer she knew. Eventually Fidel took Teresa over to the other side of the yard to meet Che, dressed in turtleneck sweater and looking more the young academic than the revolutionary conspirator for which he had been taken into custody. He had settled himself in a quiet, sunlit corner, for once engrossed in a medical book. Then Hilda arrived with Little Mao. Che picked her up, held her up to the air, and the three of them swung away for a while.

Before she left, Casuso gave Fidel her card; 'if ever you should need it,' she said, perhaps not yet aware of his habit of holding people to their word. Then she retrieved Lilia from the men thronging about her, and the two women left to the sounds of the men's enthusiastic rendition of the Cuban national anthem which they sang, huddled together, at the end of every visiting session.

The men stood accused of training a group of 'commandos' to assassinate Batista. Fidel's response was uncompromising: 'The simple elimination of a man does not solve the problem. That is a desperate measure that revolutionaries who count on the support of a whole country do not require,' he said. He was fortunate, however, that former Mexican President Lázaro Cárdenas – a staunch nationalist who had welcomed Trotsky in exile from Stalin's Russia – interceded and managed to secure the release of most of the men. By 9 July all but Fidel, as leader, Che, for his ever-incorrect paperwork, and Calixto García, one of the Cubans, who also lacked the right visa, had been released.

For the next two weeks it was just the three of them, until Fidel was released on the 24th. During that time Fidel busied himself with picking up the threads of his movement and limiting the damage done to weapons stores and finances. Che for his part wrote a series of letters home in which he finally and unequivocally signed off on his former bohemian self and committed himself to fighting alongside Fidel first, and to something further, grander, less clearly defined, after that. In between they passed the time with games of chess and endless conversation. Meanwhile, members of 26 July stood guard outside the entrance to the prison, in case the Mexican or, more likely, Cuban authorities tried to use the opportunity to assassinate Fidel.

* * *

These few weeks in jail underlined two things about the relationship between Fidel and Che: on the one hand it brought out the differences between them, on the other it revealed the mutual respect that was developing despite those differences. Outwardly, Che was for much of the time rather uncharacteristically boisterous, as he debated with and challenged his captors at every opportunity. Because of his communist affiliations he had already been singled out for special treatment, and he was perhaps responding in kind. The police threatened him that his wife and child would be tortured if he did not answer their questions. 'Up to now I have answered your questions, from now on, I won't,' he replied. 'Since you're so savage as to jail a woman with an infant, nobody can expect justice from you.' This did not endear him to his captors, though it gained him a measure of respect among the men. Compared to that of some of the others his interrogation was relatively painless, but he was confidently defiant when pressed about his communist affiliations. Imperialism contained the seeds of its own destruction, he told them. He was, he confessed proudly, in complete accord with the Marxist doctrine.

From prison, Ernesto wrote to his mother saying much the same thing as he told his jailers. He proudly described the group's 'communist morals', asserting that 'In these days of prison and in the previous ones in training I have come to identify totally with the *compañeros* of the cause . . . . It was (and is) beautiful to be able to sense this feeling of removal that we have.' Celia immediately wrote back both with concern and reproach at what she saw as her son's increasingly dangerous hot-headedness.

Inwardly, however, Ernesto was more contemplative. Strangely for someone in jail, these were for him 'days of sun and happiness'. He was content with the transition that had begun to take place within him, and was keen to show off the link between his inner, Marxist convictions and his new-found outward confidence: he spoke of his shining faith to anyone who would listen. He went around, said Carlos Franqui, one of the members of the underground movement in Cuba who caught something of his state of mind, 'without a shirt on . . . switching between Stalin and Baudelaire, poetry with Marxism'. This did not go down at all well with Fidel, who was at that very moment busy trying to deny that the group had any connections to the communists (on the whole, a truthful statement) in order to limit the political fall-out from the whole affair: 'Enough lies already!' was the title of the piece he wrote denying such accusations.

On 26 June, when both Che and Fidel were whisked off to the Procuradia General yet again for interrogation, Che's answers were direct and stayed away from political denunciations. Fidel, who stood there handcuffed alongside him, had clearly had a word. But it was too late. The following day the Mexican daily *Excélsior* accused the Argentine of links with the communists, ignoring his latest statements. But it was Raúl's and Che's young Soviet friend, Nikolai Leonov, who would suffer most of all for this. It was his business card the police had found among Che's possessions and that led to the claims. He was called in to explain to his superiors, and within a matter of weeks found himself on the British passenger ship *QEII* returning to Russia.

Despite their different approach to the problem – Fidel nimbly strategising, Che wilfully puffing out his chest – what became clear at this moment was that Fidel had decided to bring his hot-headed friend along at any cost. The sensible thing for him to have done, given that Che's communist credentials stood to jeopardise months of careful planning, would have been to leave Che out of the future plans of the Movement. Fidel had already prevented men of other nationalities from joining up, and was even now trying to prevent any more Cubans from getting involved. But Fidel would not abandon his new Argentine friend. As Che wrote later, 'these personal attitudes of Fidel with the people he is fond of are the keys of the fanaticism he inspires around him'. Indeed, when Che and Calixto were finally released on 31 July, all the available evidence points to Fidel having paid a hefty fine to secure their release.

A few moments from these crucial weeks are recorded in the first images known to exist of Fidel and Che alone together. The photos come as a pair, like stills from a film. The first shows just the two of them in the large cell, with facing rows of beds, that they had been sharing with the other men. It conveys their two characters at that point in time almost perfectly. Fidel stands to the left, wearing a tie and fastening his jacket, eyes focused on the ground as he prepared to go and speak to the press; Che, his shirt off, belt loose and arms clasped behind his back, leans over as if trying to leave the frame on the right. Seemingly unsure, he looks expectantly at Fidel. The second photo, taken just a few moments later, shows Fidel having advanced towards the photographer. Now he is the one looking at Che. All around them are strewn the detritus of shared accommodation: clothes thrown down on beds, papers falling off the table at which they worked. But what stands out from all of this is the unmistakeable message of Fidel's pose. He is waiting; he is not leaving without Che.

* * *

'Having expressed his decision to leave the country', as the official statement of Fidel's release somewhat credulously put it, Fidel might have been expected to show up at Teresa Casuso's door soon or not at all. As it was, he came knocking within two days of his release, expounding at length on his plans and slowly letting her know in the process that he needed her support. With the young men and women of his generation Fidel had an almost innate appeal, but Casuso had heard these sort of theatrics before; she was less moved than most, merely gazing back 'implacably', as she recalled, while Fidel encouraged and cajoled and told her of his plans. As ever Fidel was in luck. Since the arrival of her young lodger, Lilia, Casuso had been looking for something to believe in again, and had taken an interest in Fidel's group despite herself.

It soon became clear that Lilia had stirred something in Fidel, too. In addition to enquiring after the woman with the immaculate eyes that had caught his own across the prison yard, Fidel asked Casuso if she could store some things for him. She agreed and showed him a cupboard in a room that had been prepared for another friend who was about to visit her. It was fine, Fidel said, 'but you must get rid of that [friend]'. Slowly but surely Casuso's house was given over to Fidel's work: weapons (a full seven carloads of munitions that first night) and then men were stored, or put up there as the police closed in once more during the final months before their departure for Cuba.

It was now a race against time. Batista was intensifying his clandestine operation against Fidel, continuing to work through the ever-buyable Mexican police and using his own SIM agents to infiltrate Castro's network. There was also a traitor within

Castro's inner circle, Rafael del Pino – Fidel's old accomplice from the days of the Bogotazo – who had recently been caught smuggling arms in the USA and was now working for the FBI. When Che was finally released from the Miguel Schultz centre on 14 August Fidel had already confirmed, in an exclusive inter-view to the manager of United Press in Cuba, Francis L. McCarthy, his claim that before the end of the year he and his men would either be martyrs or they would be free.

Che was now determined to leave Mexico with Fidel. When Hilda came home one day soon after his release to find him 'a shadow behind the door', as she put it, her words were pecu-liarly apt. He looked perfectly adapted to family life, playing with his daughter as she lay in her cot, but the next three days, as he set about organising his papers and writing home, would be the last time they really spent alone together. On the fourth day he packed his bags and said goodbye, promising to keep in touch.

Che's decision to fight alongside Fidel was a decision inevitably linked to another – his determination now finally to leave Hilda. With his characteristic brevity, he confirmed both sides of the problem in one stroke. 'From now on,' he wrote to his parents, in reference to having an 'heir' to his name, 'I would hardly consider my death more than a frustration, like Hikmet,' refer-ring to the twentieth-century Turkish poet whose life mirrored so many aspects of the one Che was about to embark upon, and whose famous lines Che then quoted: 'I will take to my grave / only the sorrow of an unfinished song'. Only someone with the most austere convictions would see the presence of a young child as a reason to leave, rather than to stay, but austerity was a new strand to his character that his brief spell in prison seemed to have fostered. Already he was not the youth who had arrived in Mexico just the year before.

In his own forward-looking interview with Francis McCarthy, Fidel confessed to having had to change tactics somewhat. With insufficient time to rise above all the island's opposition groups, Fidel was now seeking to unite the various strands of militant opposition in Cuba, and glossed over his own group's recent imprisonment. Such things were 'occupational hazards' and he blamed not the Mexican police, for whom, despite the torture of some of his men, he had a generally high opinion, but the Cuban embassy which was buying off sections of the police force for its own ends. Fidel was ever a master at dividing his opponents, and in any case he had by now developed a useful working relationship with Gutiérrez-Barrios, chief of the Mexican Federal Security services.

Discreetly cultivating such inside help was but one part of what Fidel had been doing since his release. Something he sought to achieve rather more publicly was unifying the opposition back in Cuba through a series of meetings and negotiated agreements with leaders of the Students' Federation and with the Revolutionary Directorate, whose head, José Antonio Echeverría, came to visit Fidel at the end of August. He even held secret, if non-committal, meetings with the Cuban communists. Fidel also held a series of meetings with his own Movement leadership on the island, above all with the young schoolteacher and leader of the 26 July underground in Cuba, Frank País. País's clean-cut, patient and studious demeanour could not have contrasted more with Fidel's grimed appearance, reflecting his nocturnal existence, when the two met in a safe house late one night. But they shared a bottomless energy and immediately set to work, hunched over maps and charts, on the details of the invasion.

Fidel made one other, very secret accommodation at this time. With the decimation of his movement's resources after their arrest, he had known he would need to find cash from somewhere and in desperation he had turned to the only readily available source, the ex-President and until now one of his principal adversaries, Carlos Prío, whose palaces and pools Fidel had excoriated in print when Prío was in power. Fidel had sent word to Prío from prison to the effect that he was prepared to accept a loan from him – but 'no cheques', he added, in a tone that suggested he was wise to those sorts of tricks: 'the loan needs to be in proper cash'.

Prío, whose vast funds had lubricated many a revolutionary project over the years, was, despite the two men's unhappy past relationship, willing in the present circumstances to meet Fidel. It was Prío whom Batista had replaced with his coup, and Prío had vowed revenge. The only problem was that Prío was not allowed to leave the United States, and Fidel was no longer officially in Mexico. There would be no chance of either man securing exit papers to go and visit the other.

For these reasons, on 1 September, somewhere near the city of Reynosa, Fidel stripped naked and waded into the cold waters of the Rio Bravo that marked the border between Mexico and the United States. He was met on the other side by a small group of conspirators who gave him dry clothes and drove him under cover of darkness five miles north to McAllen, the small capital of Hidalgo County. Years later, Castro described the encounter with Prío in McAllen's Palm Hotel as 'a bitter experience'.

Fidel walked into the hotel dressed as an oilman, in Stetson and jeans, and was met by Faustino Pérez and the traitor Rafael del Pino, who took him up to the room where Prío was waiting with Juan Manuel Márquez. Once the two former adversaries had agreed terms on the exchange of $50,000, Fidel asked Prío if perhaps he would like to come along. He had no desire of Prío's company, of course, but it served to make his point that Prío was a spineless fool whose money but not his mandate he would accept. Prío politely declined: he thought Fidel no less foolish. Fidel was then whisked back to Mexico while the dependable Márquez stayed on to supervise the handover of the money.

The trip was a success, and so too by then was Fidel's courtship of the effusive Lilia; thoughts of his mistress Naty seemed by now to have been put from his mind. Double-dates with Casuso and Candido González had segued into a full-blown romance, and Fidel had obtained Lilia's parents' permission to marry her. He was ever the traditionalist in matters of love, and Casuso recalled that 'as part of her trousseau, he had equipped [Lilia]

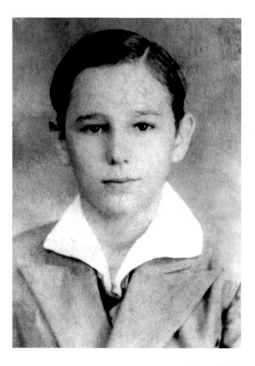

The young Fidel Castro during his time at La Salle, the first of two boarding schools he attended in Santiago de Cuba, before moving on to Belén – the island's most prestigious school – in Havana.

Ernesto Guevara, 'Ernestito', several years before he first went to school at age eight. The family kept numerous homes during his boyhood years.

Soldiers walking among the bodies of rebels killed during the July 1953 assault on the Moncada barracks. Post-university and frustrated with constitutional politics, Fidel had planned for the attack since army sergeant Fulgencio Batista took power in a coup d'état on March 10, 1952.

Castro walks out of prison on the Isle of Pines in May 1955, just two years into his fifteen-year prison sentence for orchestrating the Moncada and Bayamo attacks. Responding to popular pressure, Batista had signed an amnesty for the prisoners' release. Fidel soon fled to Mexico.

A beardless Fidel Castro in the Mexican countryside in late 1955, where his group of rebels in exile – recently joined by Ernesto Guevara – had begun basic military training. After his second stint travelling around Latin America, Guevara too had fled to Mexico from Guatemala, where he had witnessed first-hand the CIA-sponsored overthrow of Jacobo Árbenz in 1954.

The first known photo of Fidel Castro and Ernesto Guevara, taken during their period of incarceration in the Mexican Interior Ministry's Miguel Schultz detention centre, in the summer of 1956.

Guns held aloft, the half-starved rebels of the *Granma* wade ashore after the boat beached on a sandbank some way from land. Within days both men would narrowly avoid losing their lives: only a dozen men survived when the group was attacked by the Cuban army.

Fidel and his rebel army captains pose near their base camp in the Sierra Maestra in 1957. Around Fidel, from right to left, are Juan Almeida, Jorge Sotus, Cresencio Pérez, Raúl Castro (crouching), Universo Sánchez, Che Guevara (in peaked cap), and Ramiro Valdés.

In late 1957 Fidel meets a group of peasants in the Sierra. To his right is Celia Sánchez, his much cherished secretary, personal aide, and lover.

A now far more confident Che poses with a group of guerrilla leaders in December 1958, shortly after agreeing a unity pact among the disjointed rebel forces in the central plains region of the island under his control. Pictured are members of the Directorio Revolucionario, a rival rebel group.

Fidel waves to the crowd from a Jeep on January 1, 1959 – victory day – at the start of his week-long caravan from Santiago to Havana, immediately after the close of the revolutionary war.

There was much about the U.S. that Castro admired. Here he stands before the Abraham Lincoln Memorial in Washington, D.C. during his visit to the North American capital in April 1959. Castro had excitedly discussed President Franklin D. Roosevelt's New Deal policies just months before, while fighting in the Cuban mountains.

Che undertakes voluntary labour at a construction site in Cuba. Voluntary labour schemes were central to his economic thinking while serving as Minister for Industries: it was something to which he gave almost all his spare time.

Fidel gets to work in *his* natural sphere – Havana's vast Plaza de la Revolución – during his first Declaration of Havana speech in September 1960. During the speech Fidel publicly tore up the Mutual Aid Treaty, signed by Cuba and the United States in 1952.

Brothers in Arms. Fidel speaks intimately with Che shortly after the rebel victory against Batista. Che still wears a sling about his shoulder after injuring his arm falling off a building during the decisive battle for Santa Clara.

with new clothes, shoes, a large bottle of French perfume, and a pretty bathing suit to replace her French Bikini, which infuriated him'. All this was clearly an enjoyable diversion at the time, but he must have known that any relationship was ultimately doomed. For Fidel, nothing came before the revolution.

* * *

On a Sunday afternoon in late October, Fidel learned that his father had died after an intestinal complication. 'Papa Castro is dead!' went the word in Oriente as the old Galician's body was carried through the streets. At the time Fidel was busy resolving a dispute between Ñico Lopez and María Antonia, which had caused María Antonia to run off in a fury. There is no record of his response to the news, or whether it even affected him very much. Raúl was upset when Fidel telephoned to inform him, and the two of them sent messages of condolence to their brothers in Cuba and to their sisters, Emma and Agustina, who had brought Fidelito over earlier in the month. Fidel and Raúl would not be attending the funeral, of course, although that did not keep people from coming for fear that they might.

It was another death in those weeks that really caught Fidel's attention, however: that of the chief of Batista's secret police, the SIM, Antonio Blanco Rico – a man he had regularly criticised and whose death he had reason to fear being blamed for. Rico was murdered as he was leaving the gaudy Montmartre nightclub – that 'magnet for Batista's top brass' – in the early hours of the morning. Fidel found out a few hours later, after he had been up all night writing an accompanying letter to Miguel Ángel Quevedo, the editor of *Bohemia*, for an article he had just written – 'The Nation and the Revolution in Danger' – denouncing Batista and the Dominican dictator Rafael Trujillo for being in cahoots with one another. In the article Fidel 'outed' a series of Trujillist agents, supplying all the incriminating documents with his habitual relish of the private detective, just as he had done years before against Prío. 'It is important to publish this,' he wrote, demonstrating that mentally he was already in the Sierra and was aware that the coming battle would be political as much as physical, 'you will not want them to attack us in the back when we are fighting'. On hearing of the assassination of Blanco Rico, Fidel wrote: 'I just found out now, having finished the article, about the attacks last night . . . . I am very sorry for the hard days that all Cubans will [now] suffer . . . . A state of psychological desperation is being created, [but also] of the absence of fear that precedes the great struggles.'

Fidel gave his last interview in Mexico in mid-November to the *Bohemia* journalist Mario García del Cueto. The journalist apologised on behalf of his editor that Fidel's tract had not been published. Fidel was furious, but Cueto explained the reasons. The tension back in Havana was at fever pitch. Following the assassination of Antonio Blanco Rico, another Batista front man, Brigadier Salas Cañizares, had also been murdered. As rumours of various other plots circulated, anyone under suspicion was liable to be arrested, media censorship was in place, and additional arms sales to Batista were rushed through from the USA.

The panic soon spread to Mexico. During the interview, someone approached Fidel and whispered in his ear the news that their colleague Pedro Miret had just been arrested and an arms cache uncovered. Fidel apologised to Cueto that he would have to cut the interview short. It then emerged that Teresa Casuso, in the house next door to Prieto, Fidel's old school friend and the Movement's arms expert, had also been arrested. If Fidel had been waiting for a reason to set the departure in motion, this was it.

Fidel now initiated the movement of men and arms to the port of Tuxpán, where the yacht he had recently purchased and had refitted, the *Granma*, was stationed. That night Che was back at the flat with Hilda and Little Mao to tell her that this time he really had to leave, as it seemed the police were on to them again. Picking up the last of his things, Che left with a kiss and a hug but no fuss and no lingering farewell.

By the end of the week everything for the men's departure was set, just as the whole careful organisation began falling down around them. In mid-November two of the newer recruits, Francisco Damas and Reynaldo Hevia, took off unexpectedly with some of the group's weapons and headed for the United States. Now, too, Rafael del Pino suddenly disappeared, leading Fidel to assume that yet more information about their plans would fall into the hands of the enemy.

It was with a sense of great urgency, therefore, that Fidel arrived at Che's safe house unannounced that Friday evening. The weather outside was turning. Fidel asked for Che, but Bauer Paíz's wife, not recognising him and sticking to the story, said there was no such person there. 'Yes, there is,' Fidel replied, in no mood to suffer his own deceptions as he jabbed his foot into the door before brushing past her and up to the attic where Che was hidden. He had just finished writing a final letter to his mother: 'To avoid pre-mortem patheticisms, this card will only arrive when the potatoes are really burning, and then you will know that your son, in some sunny American country, will be kicking himself for not having studied medicine a little more.' But medicine, he told her, now came second to 'Saint Karl' as he referred to Marx. His endlessly juggled medical career was put aside, rather in the manner of his favourite poem of all, 'If' by Rudyard Kipling. 'If the windmills don't break my nut, I will write later,' he concluded his last letter home for a while.

The very next night, as a storm blew in and the rain set to a permanent drizzle, Fidel's men descended on Tuxpán and for Ernesto Guevara it was time to find out where Saint Karl, or rather his immediate proxy Fidel Castro, would lead him. In a life that must have seemed a long way away, Ernesto had come here just a year before to present a paper on allergies at a scientific conference. Now he was putting all his trust in Fidel, and Fidel in turn was putting his trust in their leaving undetected and in Frank País's being able to create a sufficient diversion to cover their arrival. But fate, as ever, seemed to smile upon him. When the Federal Security chief Gutiérrez-Barrios – to whom Fidel paid one last visit before he himself left Mexico City for the coast – began receiving reports that Cubans were congregating in Tuxpán, he delayed acting on them. It would give Fidel and his men enough time, just, to make good their departure aboard the *Granma*.

7. MUD AND ASHES

TWO WEEKS AFTER the *Granma* beached off the muddy swamps of Las Coloradas, on Cuba's south-eastern coast, and despite the occasional Molotov cocktail still being thrown at government buildings in Santiago, the Cuban people had no clear idea what had become of the rebels who disembarked with Fidel. The government had promptly released the names of the dead – including Ñico and Juan Manuel Márquez – though it also glossed over the often cold-blooded circumstances of their death. The 'whereabouts [of] Castro and other members landing group', however, '[remained] unclear'.

Some even thought the rumour that a small troop of armed men under the leadership of the lawyer and former Ortodoxo party candidate, Fidel Castro, had staged an armed landing, was no more than an elaborate hoax. But Batista, who had received good intelligence from Mexico, was not one of them. Within just five days of the landing his troops had ambushed and decimated the exhausted band of rebels as they lay resting in a small clearing named Alegría del Pío. Fidel, firing his rifle and bellowing commands that, in the mayhem, no one could quite hear, tried to organise all the men into the relative safety of a nearby cane-field. He had little success. As he rushed across the clearing towards it, Che himself was shot in the neck. The man running with him, a rebel named Albentosa, was caught in the same rake of fire. '[T]hey've killed me!' Albentosa screamed, wheeling madly as he fired off his rifle in all directions.

In the midst of what soon began to look like a massacre – their 'baptism of fire', he would later call it – Che found himself lying on the ground, bleeding from the neck. He called out to Faustino Pérez who was crouching nearby. 'I'm fucked,' he said in muted anguish. Faustino glanced down. 'It's nothing,' he replied, which would turn out to be true (the bullet had merely grazed him), though his face initially suggested otherwise. As the rest of the men crawled or scrambled off, some of them also wounded, Che hauled himself up against a tree and, with the stark reality of war unfolding all around him – the flare of bullets strafing the rebels from attack planes, an overweight *compañero* seeking cover behind a sugarcane stalk, men babbling incomprehensible things – sat down to die. Then two comrades appeared and dragged him away. Those who could do so quickly fled, leaving behind 'columns of flame and smoke' and screams of 'fire!' as the army began to burn out a group of survivors hidden in the canefield.

Life in war is lived like this. It is an intense, cloying experience, and it would leave its mark upon both Fidel and Che. 'The war revolutionised us,' a much-changed Guevara would later explain, 'not the isolated act of killing, or of carrying a rifle, or of undertaking a struggle of this or that type [but] the totality of the war itself.' Though he never said so directly, the coming war would ultimately forge a deeper, more profound relationship between himself and Fidel Castro.

Initially, however, Fidel's treatment of Che was as up and down as the inhospitable terrain, the comradely affection of their days in jail together now consigned to the past. Fidel upbraided Che for his failings one minute, only to uphold him for his stellar qualities the next. He did this with everyone; it was his way of keeping subordinates on their toes. But he did it most of all with Che, perhaps because he already realised he could be made more of than the others.

Such trials as are waged in the restricted freedom of war raise temperatures, however, and before the first year of fighting was over Che's growing frustration with what he perceived to be

Fidel's erratic behaviour would bring about the first major disagreement between them. Che's anger was not born solely of Fidel's seeming indecision, however. It also stemmed from his own vision of the rebels' mission and from his growing sense of the importance of his position alongside Fidel.

*   *   *

'Tactically,' wrote an observer at the US consulate in nearby Santiago, reflecting upon the local terrain – perhaps the most desolate in Cuba – it was 'almost impossible to land forces in sufficient numbers and with equipment to defeat the Cuban army [here]'. Since their early rout at Alegría del Pío, confronting the army with a well-equipped force of sufficient numbers was not something Fidel Castro had much to worry about, however. The would-be revolutionaries had by now been reduced to just a handful of men, isolated from one another and most without weapons, while Batista's soldiers busied themselves ferreting out the last of the 'terrorists', as he referred to them.

Should they be separated in this way, the rebels had a prearranged plan to regroup at the farmhouse of Mongo Pérez, a first stop in the small but well-organised clandestine network of peasant sympathisers that Fidel's representatives on the island had been putting together while he was in Mexico. It would be several days before small bands of survivors began to arrive, however, travelling by night to avoid the lowlands near the coast where they were vulnerable to spotter planes and army patrols. It was just sixteen members of the *Granma*'s original eighty-two-man crew who finally regrouped at the Pérez farm, and they had just seven rifles among them.

Fidel had spent the initial period after the landing and dispersal hidden in a canefield with Faustino and Universo, until after a few days' walking they found themselves, sodden with rain, at the hut of a peasant into whose hands they took the risk of placing themselves to be guided, through stinking drainage culverts that ran beneath the roads, the rest of the way to the safe house. Che had stumbled along nearer the coast with Ramiro Valdés, Juan Almeida and Camilo Cienfuegos. Camilo was one of the recruits to have most recently joined up in Mexico and he would become Che's right-hand man over the following two years of the war. Eventually they too were taken in by a sympathetic peasant household to be carefully shepherded between safe houses to the Pérez farm. Fidel was relieved to see Che's group arrive, but furious when he learned they had left their rifles behind in order to be able to disguise themselves as peasants. 'You pay with your life for such stupidity,' he shouted, grabbing Che's pistol from him and giving it to Cresencio Pérez, Mongo's brother.

The first weeks and months of the war were hard on all the men. All day they struggled to open up paths through the undergrowth with their machetes as they headed east towards the sanctuary of the higher mountains of the Sierra Maestra, and at night they gorged on their occasional rations of sausages and condensed milk as though they were 'great banquets'. The diaries of Che and Raúl Castro both capture the experiences of the still somewhat novice guerrillas during the first days of the march eastwards. Che's dry humour seems to have kept him going as he regularly mocked their ungainly progress through the heavy jungle. He too had a lot to learn, however, proposing one day that he cook some beef *asado*-style, as if he were at his wedding still instead of preparing a practical supper. Raúl wrote dourly of this 'experiment' which left their meat rations for the following days either leathery or green and worm-infested. Fidel continued to drive them onwards in a determined march towards the misted peaks of the Sierra. A few of the local peasants joined up and as many left, usually with the cold, harrowed faces that those who stuck it out termed the 'hunted look'. But gradually they began to adapt to this life of 'dirt, the lack of water, food, shelter, and security'; a life of constant vigil amid snatches of sleep and rather more persistent cold from the altitude and hunger.

Conscious that he needed to undertake some action to remind

the outside world that they had survived and regrouped, albeit with a force of still no more than a few dozen men, in mid-January Fidel ordered their first attack on an army post. It was a brief and nervy skirmish, but the rebels successfully took some prisoners before rushing back into the mountains towards the heights of Palma Mocha. It was a minuscule first victory – an attack on a camp that most people would not have known existed, and that could have been taken down and moved on in a fraction of the time it took to over-run it. But it set the scene for all that followed: lightning raids by fleet of foot, followed by a life-or-death dash back into the sanctuary of the impenetrable forest, some parts of which lacked even horse-tracks, let alone roads.

When Che wrote to Hilda shortly afterwards – it would be his last letter to her for a long time – he noted, with satisfaction, a gun by his side and a new addition, a cigar in his mouth. The men had now proved, so he told her, that they could 'slip through [the army's] hands like soap'. Much to Batista's chagrin the rebels would continue to do so, taking on ever larger targets as their experience and store of stolen weapons grew. Meanwhile, Fidel and Che were shortly to face and overcome their first principal challenges of the war. For Che, this would centre upon a death and the enforced isolation that followed; for Fidel, it was a meeting and his acceptance, for now at least, that he could not control the entire movement while focusing on survival in the Sierra.

* * *

Throughout all the ups and downs of the war Fidel did not for one moment stop being a politician. And it was very much as a politician that, early in the morning one day in mid-February 1957 – just a couple of months after their landing, he left Che and the others at their camp and trekked down to the lower slopes of the Sierra for his first and most crucial meeting with an American newspaperman, the *New York Times*'s Herbert

157

Matthews. Since December Batista had affected a tone of disinterest with respect to the rebels. The 'would-be trouble-makers' lacked organisation and plans and afforded 'the possibility of [not] even the slightest skirmish', he had said in a press statement before Christmas. News censorship had confined knowledge about the guerrillas' survival to rumours that circulated by word of mouth. As Fidel well knew, that was not at all in the rebels' interest, and he was hopeful that the meeting with Matthews would change that.

'With these rifles, we can pick them off at 1000 yards,' Fidel said in demonstrative greeting as he strode into the clearing where Matthews, who had been brought up during the night from Havana, was waiting. A veteran reporter who had covered the Spanish Civil War, the American was a 'tall man, thin, half bald, a simple dresser, silent as a tomb, precise as a Swiss watch'. He more than anyone ought to have been accustomed to weighing the competing claims of official and revolutionary groups. But Fidel, always supremely skilled at propaganda, put a lot of effort into making sure that Matthews left with just the right impression. What seem to have won Matthews over, however, were Fidel's sheer physicality and exuberance, both of which seeped through into the first of three articles based upon his interview with Fidel, which was published on Sunday, 24 February.

The first article caused a sensation. Here was proof that Fidel Castro was still alive – contrary to what the Cuban regime had been claiming – and here too was it claimed that he was now leading a well-armed, well-organised and effective fighting force in the Sierra. For those who doubted it, Matthews had got Fidel to sign his notes. It was a massive blow to the credibility of the Batistiano press, who until now had strenuously denied such reports, and it left many seasoned observers with the view that the rebels were already 'making monkeys of the forces sent against them'. After the initial rout in Alegría del Pío, Fidel was back in the business of revolution.

When Matthews left at around nine that morning Fidel's work

for the day was only just beginning, however. Frank País – Fidel's 'Chief of Action and Sabotage' in Oriente province – and other members of 26 July underground movement had also trudged up through the thick mud and knotty vegetation to reach the Sierra that day. País was at this point rather more in the driving seat of the rebel movement's revolutionary plans than Fidel himself, who had spent the last few weeks focusing principally on surviving in the mountains. The city-based underground wing of the move-ment that he represented, the Llano, under the leadership of a National Directorate was the other half of the rebel forces: the guerrillas' supply chain and also their political wing.

One might almost have got the impression from the tenor of this meeting that Fidel's forces were but a sideshow in the more important business of urban-based insurrectionary politics. Some of the leaders of the underground movement who had come up with País – Faustino Pérez, who after arriving on the *Granma* had headed out on his own to make contact with the cities and was now leading the movement in Havana, Armando Hart and Haydée Santamaría – certainly hoped to convince Fidel to abandon the war, now that he had made his point. They wanted him to go and launch a political campaign from exile. But nothing could have been further from Fidel's thoughts, especially after the meeting with Matthews that morning, and a division that would soon rock the rebel forces to the core became discernible for the first time. Fidel had not been in Cuba for nearly two years. In his absence a lot had changed, and now that he was back the complex network of individuals that had been put together were not entirely convinced that guerrilla war in the mountains was the best route to power.

After two days of intense negotiations between these two sides of the rebel movement, the Llano returned to the cities with orders both to build up the urban underground movement and to supply the guerrillas with everything that was needed to maintain the war in the mountains. So too were they to begin organising support among middle-class professionals for a programme of national civil resistance and to organise the working class in preparation for a 'general revolutionary strike as the capstone of the struggle'. All these points were contained in Fidel's 'Appeal to the Cuban People', his first document from the Sierra, which he gave to his Llano comrades to circulate. When he read it, Che strongly approved, though it must have grated with him a little that he had not had much of a hand in drafting it. Why had he been so mute?

The most probable explanation was his hand in the recently concluded summary trial for one of their guides, Eutimio Guerra, who had betrayed the rebels' location to the army on several occasions. Fidel sat in judgement and pronounced the death penalty himself, only to turn and walk away from where Eutimio remained kneeling, his hands tied at his back. Nobody appeared to want to carry out the execution, and the dark moment stretched on. Eventually, Che could take it no more. 'The situation was uncomfortable for the people and for [Eutimio] so I ended the problem giving him a shot with a .32 pistol in the right side of the brain.' In his unpublished diaries he elaborated on the morbid scene as Eutimio slumped before him: 'He lay there gasping a little while and was dead. Upon proceeding to remove his belongings I couldn't get the watch tied by a chain to his belt, and then he told me in a steady voice farther away than fear: "Yank it off, boy, what does it matter. . . ."' What was clearly a hallucination strongly suggests that Che was more shaken by his summary act than he let on: an impact more than sufficient, in fact, to explain his lack of involvement in the Llano meeting, the most important event of the war to date. Indeed, having carried out this execution Che suffered an asthma attack. Of that night he recorded bleakly: 'We slept badly, wet and I with something of asthma.'

The consequences of Che's bad impression of the Llano would reverberate throughout the war, and within just a few months would see him throw down the gauntlet to Fidel. But it was a further, even more severe asthma attack in March that forced a period of isolation upon him. Unable to keep up with the troops at a critical time as they trekked through territory in which the peasants would have nothing to do with them (caught by now between the rebels' insistence on loyalty and the army's murdering of 'traitors' who protected the rebels), Che was left behind as Fidel took the rest of the men up into the sanctuary of the higher mountains.

The weeks that followed were, for Che, the lowest point of the war. His asthma would not shift and he passed dark, wretched days in a semi-existence. When he had to move in order to stay hidden at times he did so on his hands and knees and at other times he was carried by a stout comrade assigned to look after him. When he finally rejoined the main column, with a group of new recruits from the cities whom he had been asked to bring with him, and who had been led up to the mountains by a rebel named Jorge Sotús, it was as if he had washed up on some other shore. Few biographers appear to have picked up on the significance of the moment, but it is there in the writings that poured from him afterwards. Something fundamental had changed. As he put it in the rebel's own clandestine newspaper *El Cubano Libre* some months later, the 'timid stage of the revolution' was now at an end.

If it was with renewed enthusiasm that Che finally met up once more with Fidel, then the dressing down he received for the way he had failed to take full control of the troops led by Jorge Sotús, must have been doubly felt. 'At that time I still had my foreigners' complex and did not want to take things too far,' he later recalled – but Fidel was furious that a man relatively unknown to either of them had been in effective charge of a troop that vastly outnumbered the main rebel column of eighteen men.

Characteristically, Che simply resolved to make amends. His chance came in July, when Fidel ordered the rebels' major offensive in the war to date, a daytime attack on the military barracks at El Uvero on the coast. During the attack, Che struck out on his own with a group of four men. Afterwards, he stayed behind near the garrison with the wounded and a couple of volunteers. As he bound the chest of one of the men they had to leave behind, comrade Silleros, Che comforted him that they had the garrison doctor's word of honour that the wounded would not be harmed. Silleros replied with a sad smile to the effect that he knew it was over for him anyway. Che must have caught his eye for a moment to have noted it, but such moments are fleeting; their significance registered always afterwards. In the instant, it was an unflinching Che who returned the condemned man's gaze. When the transport that the rest of the men were waiting for failed to show up, Che took command of the group and headed back into the forest to catch up with the main column led by Fidel.

As Che manoeuvred his men over the next few weeks he began to show something of the pragmatic strand that he so admired in Fidel: making alliances with those he might once have denounced as enemies, establishing points of contact and support from the local peasants and regularly allowing those wishing to leave the chance to do so. His asthma continued to plague him, however, rendering him at times 'almost as immobile as the wounded', and the dried flowers he resorted to smoking in order to alleviate his chest scarcely helped. When they picked up recruits he was also often highly suspicious of their motives, in a way that Fidel never was. As if to test their allegiance he called them shit-eaters – one imagines to their faces – and he constantly goaded the others.

But his confidence was soaring when his small troop of men finally returned to Fidel's camp, and Che marked the occasion with an immediate statement of intent. One of the new recruits, Julio Martínez Paez, was a medic who had been involved in the urban underground in Havana. When he was introduced to Che, the latter handed over the small box of instruments he had been carrying. 'Listen, now you've arrived and from today I'm no longer a doctor. You're the doctor and no one else, so you can take all these things,' he said, handing over the rest of his equipment.

Che was pleased at what he saw back at camp. In his absence the rebel army had grown to around two hundred men – never mind that at least half of them wore straw hats instead of military caps, and ported cartridge belts about their shoulders as if they were *bandoleros* in some Cantinflas film. In fact they were scarcely even that: some carried no more than an ageing pistol, while others would have to wear their work trousers until the women in the cities could stitch together uniforms for them at night and send them up to the Sierra. But all the same, these men were better organised and better equipped than before. More importantly, they appeared to control the area immediately surrounding Mount Turquino, the highest point of the Sierra. For all these advances, Che was practically apoplectic to hear that Fidel had recently been visited by representatives of Cuba's civil opposition – Eduardo Chibás' younger brother Raúl, and Felipe Pazos. These 'middle-of-the-road' turncoats whom Che so despised whenever he had met them on his travels, had signed with Fidel a document that would become known as the Sierra Manifesto.

Clearly, in his absence, Fidel too had been busy. Frank País had been arrested shortly after returning from that first meeting in the Sierra in February and detained for a number of weeks. But since his release País had been instrumental in working with Fidel to push forward the 26 July's aims. So central was País, in fact, that Fidel had not even known that a group of civil opposition leaders were coming to see him until they arrived; País had simply sent up the letter explaining it all with one of the politicians themselves. The impetus behind the Manifesto had thus not been Fidel's at all: as so often, he had merely seen the possibilities and taken advantage, for it put civil society at the heart of any discussion of transition and in so doing placed pressure on institutions such as the labour movements and the political parties to move beyond their pacifist positions. The Sierra Manifesto also forced other political leaders in Cuba to begin to take sides in Fidel's struggle with Batista: 'the abandonment of the [Ortodoxo] party' by Raúl Chibás 'appears to doom it as a unified and nationally effective force', US intelligence commented on Chibás' signing of the Manifesto.

But to the recently returned Che it looked as if it was Fidel who was taking sides – and with the underground leaders whom Che so distrusted. Aware of his comrade's suspicions, Fidel appears to have deliberately chosen this moment to promote Che to second-in-command after himself. The moment has all too often been rendered as the triumphant veneration of Che Guevara for his military success at El Uvero. But in a letter that Fidel wrote recounting the attack there is no specific mention of Che's supposed feats in this operation. It seems rather more likely that the promotion was less a retrospective award and more a prospective fillip for the man whom Fidel now needed to lead his second front. Raúl had not yet acquired the confidence of his brother in organisational or military matters. Almeida was diligent and dutiful but offered Fidel none of the verve that Che did, and Camilo was still proving his worth as a commander drawn from the ranks. Fidel was ever a remarkable judge of character, and in selecting Che he had calculated well: Che's loyalty would only be boosted by such an award. 'There is a bit of vanity hiding somewhere within every one of us,' Che wrote later. 'It made me feel like the proudest man on earth that day.'

With the award of the star that would adorn his beret and become part of the later symbol, Ernesto Guevara was now Comandante Che Guevara to all but his closest of friends. And Fidel had given Che a task at which he knew he would excel. He was to go on the attack, hunting down the man who had most troubled the rebels to date – the army's head of operations, Colonel Sánchez Mosquera, who was leading his own troop of men within the Sierra – and the bandits who were riding the rebels' coat-tails and spreading mayhem throughout the region. Fidel knew he could trust Che with this task completely. He also knew that Che's politics could be a hindrance to the diplomatic web that he was spinning and wanted to continue elaborating on from the rebel's main base.

* * *

By the beginning of August, however, events had forced a change in both men's priorities and especially Fidel's. Frank País had been gunned down by the SIM at the end of July near his Santiago home. 'It is hard to believe the news,' a hugely disappointed Fidel wrote to Celia Sánchez, who would now become his effective chief liaison with the Llano, the following day. 'I cannot convey to you the bitterness, the indignation, the infinite pain that confronts us. What barbarians! They hunted him down in the street like cowards . . . What monsters!' What was to be done to fill the gap? In a letter to Fidel, reporting on his inauguration as Comandante in a battle near the village of Bueycito – 'a success from the point of view of being a victory but a disaster in terms of organisation', as he put it to Fidel – Che touched on the 'painful' subject of Frank and offered his own thoughts on the matter.

> I believe you [should] take a strong stand and send as chief of Santiago a person who would be both a good organiser and have a history in the Sierra. In my view, this person ought to be Raúl or Almeida, or in the worse case, Ramirito or I (which I say without false modesty but also without the slightest desire for it to be me the chosen one). I insist in the issue because I know the moral and intellectual character of the would-be leaders who will try to replace Frank.

Fidel had no intention of appointing Che to such a delicate post, of course, but in the absence of such a compelling figure as País to represent the interests of the Llano to Fidel, his thinking about the future course of the war, and the role of the two halves of the movement, would now come to be shaped much more strongly by Che's increasing successes as commander of the western front. There was a need to consolidate the breach in the mountains before thinking of other fronts, Fidel wrote to tell País's deputy, René Ramos Latour. The motto ought to be 'All guns, all bullets, all resources to the Sierra!' Fidel said, adding, 'I would prefer a spy who comes with a gun than a sympathiser who comes unarmed.'

While Che now began to earn his reputation as a fierce disciplinarian – he not only initiated a disciplinary committee, but enforced its codes so rigidly that even the man he assigned to lead it found himself regularly noting its excesses in his own diary – Fidel focused his attention on the politics of war. His primary concern was to build an alliance with the civic movements that would give the 26 July political support and prestige, even if those movements were not yet prepared to denounce Batista publicly. But first he had to repair relations with the Llano wing of his own movement. Since the death of País and Fidel's haranguing of the newly constituted National Directorate that had replaced País (for what he saw as their criminal failure to provide sufficient support to the Sierra fighters) these relations had deteriorated substantially. To that end, Latour, País's replacement as head of the National Directorate, ventured up into the mountains for a lengthy stay in early October. But while Latour and Fidel discussed the future political strategy of the Movement, Fidel's representatives in exile – Felipe Pazos, the exiled former Head of the National Bank and, as a man flexing his own political ambitions, a curious and always rather loose representative of the 26 July, and Léster Rodríguez, a long-time comrade of País, sprung an unpleasant surprise. Fidel had sent them to obtain whatever short-term tactical alliances were needed in order to keep the Sierra supplied while he patched things up with the Llano, but they overstepped the mark considerably by signing the Miami Pact, a wide-reaching agreement that tied the 26 July into a number of commitments that Fidel did not want at all.

He was distraught. The constant conspiring, tentative meetings, expressions of hope for mutual service and letters of positions that the opposition had engaged in prior to the Miami Pact were nothing new. Each of the opposition groups had been on the scene for a long time, and Fidel had had dealings with most of them in his own way. What was frustrating for him about the Miami Pact was its timing. His own representatives had signed it just at the point when the 26 July had finally begun to emerge as by far the most convincing of the opposition groups.

When drafting the Sierra Manifesto three months earlier Fidel had also deliberately asserted that the 26 July would not participate in any provisional government that might be formed if and when Batista fell, which, among other things, the Miami Pact now appeared to suggest was a possibility. But worst of all, the Pact foresaw that, after the war, the revolutionary forces would be subsumed within the standing army. As Fidel waged a daily life-and-death struggle against the planes strafing the forests and against the well-equipped army with its bazookas, this in particular was not something he could possibly countenance. He was, as Latour reported after his eighteen-day stay with Fidel in the mountains during October, 'thousands of leagues away from accepting proposals like those that Pazos and Léster accepted'.

But Fidel was rarely precipitate – in this he differed strongly from the impulsive Che – and instead of rejecting the Pact outright, or even alerting his Sierra colleagues to it, he played a waiting game. As Fidel saw things – for now at least – the guerrilla forces in the mountains should keep applying pressure on the government, while the Llano began to 'concentrate its terror' in the cities and prepare them for a mass strike, coordinated by urban militias, that would bring the government to its knees.

* * *

In command now of his own zone of operations, Che Guevara was setting out a very different vision for the role of the rebel army. He may have struck out principally to 'justify' Fidel's hopes in his command, but in the process he had gone somewhat further.

Receiving regular orders from his Comandante, but free to fulfil them as he saw fit, Che had moved decisively from a strategy of 'hit and run', as he put it, 'to a combat of positions, which must resist enemy attacks so as to defend rebel territory, in which a new reality is being built'. Fidel, preoccupied with the constant barrage of political and administrative duties of one incapable of delegating, had achieved nothing like Che had. By the end of the year Che had in fact done rather more than simply justify his own command. He had notably shifted the strategic aims of the war.

As winter set in, and the rebels approached the end of the first full year of fighting, Che's zone – centred upon the base camp of El Hombrito – had become a hive of small industry. What had begun with a bread oven and a simple armaments factory extended to a hydro-electric plant, put together by a group of volunteers from Havana University. Che, meanwhile, had person-ally produced the first edition of the rebels' own news-sheet. If it began on a scale hardly greater than that of *Tackle*, the rugby magazine from his Córdoba days – inked out on a vintage mimeo-graph machine hauled up into the mountains – it would soon become a pivotal element of the rebels' infrastructure and, until Radio Rebelde began broadcasting in a couple of months' time, the voice of Ernesto 'Che' Guevara's war. Che wrote to Fidel about all this with some pride at the end of November. The plan, he said, in case Fidel was considering ordering him otherwise, was to make this a well-defended spot and not to let it go at all.

By the end of November, Che would be required to do just that and he broke off halfway through a letter to Fidel as reports of enemy troop movements started filtering in. 'News arrives with a cinematographic sequence,' he continued his letter a few moments later. 'Now [Mosquera's troops] are in Mar Verde we are heading there at full speed. The continuation of this interesting history you will read later.' Che's next message was fired off in the midst of heavy fighting. 'Rapid help with 30–06s and .45 automatics would be most timely,' he said. When things had calmed down, Che resumed his letter once more. 'Now we wait for them again in El Hombrito, ready to fight again but with different tactics.' But Che's beloved El Hombrito was over-run, and in the next attack he himself was wounded by a bullet in the foot. Fidel had long since warned him to be a little more careful. 'I am very sorry not to have listened to your advice,' he then wrote Fidel, from where he was laid up in a sympathising peasant's house, 'but the morale of the men was quite down . . . and I considered it necessary to be present in the front line of fire.' He would always maintain this position, being much less willing than Fidel to suffer a temporary retreat, even if that could be turned to a tactical advantage later.

He was also far more easily caught up in the moment and it is little wonder that, immersed in the war as he had been, he had but scant time to address the political events taking place in Miami. Fidel had kept him out of the loop at the beginning, but now he wrote to Raúl and Che for their thoughts on the latest documents Hart had sent from Miami. Raúl scoffed, branding Hart a traitor. Che was, if anything, even more boisterous. With his foot up and time for once to mull things over, he now turned to deal with the issue that had most been troubling him since February. But first he received a letter from Latour, who had left his several-week stay with Fidel confident of the commander-in-chief's support for the Llano's strategy. Che was convinced that Latour was trying to cut him down to size, and his response was furious. The long-simmering power struggle between the guerilla wing of the 26 July and the Llano now erupted into a full-fledged power struggle between Che and Latour over who had the ear of Fidel.

Che knew that many of the Llano leadership were staunchly anti-communist. Perhaps this was why, against his inclinations, he had on the whole kept his political beliefs out of the war until now. But he harboured the impression that the National Directorate had been undermining him by refusing to supply the weapons and supplies that he needed. In truth, Fidel was suffering from the same problems, and if there were no weapons it was because the Llano itself could not obtain them. But Che was convinced it was deliberate sabotage and he fired back a typical sweeping response.

But before he wrote to Latour and the rest of the Llano leaders, Che wrote a letter to Fidel in which he set out precisely how he saw things and presented a rather extraordinary *fait accompli*.

> Fidel, If we see each other, or if I have the opportunity to write at greater length I have to give you my complaints against the Directorate, because I have reason to believe that there is an attempt to sabotage this column, and more directly, myself. I consider that, in light of this situation, there are only two solutions: [either you allow me to] act severely to prevent actions of this sort or I shall retire on grounds of physical incapacity or whatever seems best to you.

The Sierra provided a fraught and confusing setting in which to veer on to the sort of dangerous territory Che was launching himself at by pulling rank in this way. Correspondence in the mountains was a difficult and often roundabout process. Letters went astray, runners could be captured. A crucial piece of information might leave one rebel stronghold in good time to arrive at another, but get waylaid en route. Fidel's response to Che did not arrive until four days later, on 13 December. The letter has never been made public or even accessible by the Cuban authorities, but on the basis of Che's subsequent reply one can speculate as to its content. Above all, Fidel seems to have been at pains to reassure Che of his personal support for him, as Che replied: 'I must confess that together with the note from Celia, it filled me with tranquility and happiness. Not because of any personal question, but for what this step signifies for the revolution. You know well that I have not the slightest confidence in the National Directorate, neither as leaders or as revolutionaries. But neither did I believe that they would end up betraying you in such an open manner.'

Fidel knew there had never been any question of treachery however. In all likelihood, with the 26 July now in the ascendancy, he had merely been waiting to see if they could consolidate their position before burning their bridges with those other signatories of the Miami Pact. But he also must have set out some programmatic statement for the future of the revolution and this was most probably about the fact that he saw the army (increasingly Che's as much as his own domain of control) as playing a fundamental political as well as military role in the future of the rebel movement.

Che was relieved but unrelenting, and continued to press Fidel to clamp down on the Miami debacle: 'I believe that your attitude of silence is not the most advisable right now,' he wrote him on the 15th. By then Che had already responded to Latour. With his faith in his 'ardent prophet' Fidel now fully restored and 'for the good of the revolution' he argued with Latour that what had happened in Miami was a 'betrayal', and he lambasted the National Directorate for their political weakness and ideological blindness. It was an intriguing letter, part confession of his momentary loss of faith in Fidel, part declaration of the new direction he was assured they were both now taking. But no matter, he seemed to suggest: the revolution was set on a more radical course as of now – of that, Fidel and he were in accord.

If Frank País had feared in July that, despite the Movement's growing strengths, it still lacked a coherent philosophical vision, here it was beginning to be put into place and at the very point where a much deeper personal bond was forming between Fidel and Che. Latour noticed it immediately and, aware that the ideological direction of the entire revolution was now at stake, made sure that Fidel was copied in on his response, also written, so he said, 'for the record'. How dare Che accuse them of being traitors or saboteurs, Latour fumed back: dying when trying to get hold of the Movement's arms was no easier a thing than dying when firing them in the Sierra.

'Now is not the moment to discuss "where is the salvation of the world"', he went on, turning to the heart of the issue. What the peoples of our countries want is 'a strong America, in charge of its own destiny, an America that confronts haughtily the US, Russia, China or whatever other power attempts to commit outrages against its economic and political independence. . . . Contrary to this, those with your ideological formation think that the solution to our problems lies in liberating ourselves from a noxious Yankee domination in exchange for the no less noxious Soviet domination.'

Reading this note and Che's accompanying correspondence, Fidel had before him the two different routes along which his revolution might proceed from this point, each rendered to their essence and convincingly argued. It was a quarrel that Latour was not in a position to win. On the basis of personal loyalty and the sense that, at heart, they were of the same mind, Fidel chose the direction that Che was proposing. On the same day that he wrote to assure Che of his personal support, Fidel broke his damaging silence on the Miami Pact in such a way as to relegate the Llano firmly to second place. 'Perhaps more in irony than in a coincidence of destiny,' he wrote in a stern letter to the opposition leaders in Miami, news of the Pact arrived the same day that we needed arms to fight 'the most intensive offensive the tyranny has launched against us yet.' He accused them of 'lukewarm patriotism and cowardice' and of keeping the leaders and combatants in the mountains (deliberately and symbolically he hitched all three terms together) in the dark. In a rhetorical confirmation of which side he had come down in support of, he then despatched his letter denouncing the Miami Pact to Che for him to print as many copies as he could.

Che was delighted with this affirmation of solidarity: 'One thing is clear', he gushed somewhat in reply as he pushed Fidel's formula even further, 'the 26 July, the Sierra Maestra and yourself are three individuals with one single true God.' In a conspiratorial tone he went on, 'I await your news of new victories and with lots of belli-cose material. My foot is perfectly scarred but I still can't raise it.

The morale of the troop is magnificent. A sincere and emotional hug, Che.' With each man now investing in the relationship something of his own particular political aspirations, the two had ventured into new terrain together. They were a far more equal pairing than they had been in Mexico, when Che had been very much in thrall still to Fidel. In the process, the creative brilliance of the one and the tactical genius of the other began to resonate.

* * *

'How much the world resembles Cuba!' Che wrote in *El Cubano Libre* in January, 1958, unable to contain the sparkle he had regained along with his faith in Fidel and under his old nickname of 'Sniper'. Writing of the massacre of twenty-three rebels by the government, taken from their prison cells and shot where they were released in the foothills of the Sierra, 'carrying out activities', he revealed a new and more confident side that must have stood at odds with the still, 'almost childlike face' that an Argentine journalist saw in him at this time. 'It is the same everywhere,' he declared, when a group of patriots is murdered '[a]fter a "ferocious struggle", [in which] they fall under the guns of the oppressors. No prisoners are taken because all witnesses are killed. The government never suffers any casualties, which is sometimes true – since murdering defenseless individuals is not particularly dangerous . . . But everywhere, as in Cuba, the people are standing up to brutal force and injustice. And it is they who will have the last word: that of victory.'

With the restraint of one who knows perhaps that his time will come, Che was just about keeping a lid on his communist sympathies. His publicly known ideological leanings would soon be useful to Fidel, but for now they remained a constant headache. His strategy since Moncada had been to rely on history, not ideology, as the glue for the 26 July Movement. That was beginning to change, but Fidel was ever wary of being tied down. He was furious, therefore, when he received a note from Raúl about some radio broadcasts concerning communist influences upon the rebels. On his way back from a meeting with Fidel to deal with the political disputes of December, Armando Hart had been arrested with a copy of another 'for the record' letter about the Movement's ideological direction and the government had sought to wring whatever capital they could from such evidence of Guevara's and Raúl's communist credentials. 'They attacked me personally, as well as Che,' Raúl said. 'Of you, however, they say that they do not believe you are a communist.' It did not mollify Fidel one bit. 'I don't care if he's my brother, I'll kill him,' he said. But there is no record of him having launched a similar tirade against Che.

Through dint of his own hard work, and his unstinting loyalty to Fidel, Che had become the one whom Fidel now needed most of all. But there was another reason too. If the failure to launch a strike in December had revealed that Fidel had perhaps no clear strategy for taking power, what Che was demonstrating in his zone of operations was, at the very least, the best alternative. This may be why, when Fidel and Che – and it was invariably the two of them who first drew up the plans for such attacks – finally launched the next offensive in February, he asked Che to hold back: 'Che, if everything depends on the attack, from this side, without the support from Camilo and Guillermo, I do not think anything suicidal should be done. . . . You yourself are not to take part in the fighting. That is a strict order.'

It was Camilo – perhaps the rebel leader closest to the two of them in those months – who recognised what was happening in April, when Fidel went one stage further and removed Che from all combat activity in order for him to direct the new military training school for new recruits at Minas del Frío. 'Che, my soul brother,' Camilo wrote, his head nestled as usual under his *guajiro*'s [peasant's] straw hat. 'I see Fidel has put you in charge of the Military School, which makes me very happy because now we can count on having first-class soldiers in the future . . . . You've played a very principal role in this showdown and if we need you in this insurrectional stage, Cuba needs you even more when the war ends, so the Giant does a good thing in looking after you. . . . Your eternal *chicharrón*, Camilo.' But Che was having none of this, and his own response to Fidel appears to have been to return the favour. Three days later Fidel received a letter, signed with all the rebel captains' names, insisting that he too henceforth refrain from active combat. At the top of the list was signed 'Che Guevara, Comandante'.

Fidel was also now beginning to turn his thoughts to the future. 'Yes!' Fidel responded to Karl Meyer of *Reporter* magazine when asked if he favoured a Roosevelt-style New Deal for Cuba; but when a visiting Spanish journalist, Enrique Meneses, told Fidel, as they sat about the campfire one evening, of Nasser's agrarian reform programme in Egypt and Nehru's great state-led schemes in India, Fidel was equally enthralled, chewing his cigar and nodding in consent. It was clear to all that Fidel's utopia was still very much in his mind. And as far as many outside observers were concerned – and they were by now, increasingly concerned – that meant that he was susceptible to communism.

This was news to which the Americans, of course, were especially sensitive. 'My staff and I were all Fidelistas,' the head of the Cuba sector back at CIA headquarters in Langley recalled of the first few months of the war. But the CIA had begun to turn a cold shoulder, and the growing influence of Che Guevara upon Fidel Castro was one reason why. They asked the next American reporter to spend time with Fidel, Homer Bigart, to press him on certain issues, and Bigart duly reported on his encounters with the two acknowledged guerrilla leaders. When he had asked Fidel why he was relying so much on a communist from Argentina who was so heavily against the USA, Fidel dissimulated, telling Bigart that 'in reality Guevara's political convictions did not matter.'

Fidel could at least point to the fact that by now Raúl and Juan Almeida had branched out with two new columns of troops that soon took control of the mountains to the east and north of Santiago (effectively ensuring rebel control of much of the whole eastern region of the island). That left Che and himself in more immediate contact in and around the original rebel strongholds of the central Sierra Maestra. And with more time to share ideas, it began to become clear that something of Che's enthusiasm for the Soviet Union was rubbing off on Fidel. Looking up at the sky one night, Fidel pointed the Spanish journalist Enrique Meneses to a break in the forest canopy and said to him in awe, referring to the dog which the Soviets had just put into orbit, 'Can you imagine that somewhere up there is a dog named Laika!'

* * *

Not everything was going well, though. Engrossed in their comradely life and the 'little details' of war, and flattered too perhaps by the regular visits from the world's press, by March 1958, now over a year into the war, Fidel and Che had become dangerously out of touch with the national situation. Since the rebels' showdown in December, the Llano had operated as an almost parallel structure. Witnessing Batista's ruthlessness in the cities close up, the Llano leaders had become increasingly convinced that it was the right time to organise a decisive national strike against the regime. 'We find ourselves compelled to take action,' Latour wrote to Bebo Hidalgo, a comrade of his from the Santiago militia: 'We cannot vacillate for one minute.' Fidel and the rest of the Sierra leadership, Latour had now decided, would simply have to go along with them.

The die that Che had cast in December was now revealing its numbers for Fidel. Aside from quibbling that it should be his now much more spread out fighters who dealt with the other rebel groups that might pose a threat to the plans for a national strike, Fidel found that he was no longer able to break down the Llano's insistence. His stand of comradely loyalty alongside his friend was returning to cost him politically. 'What a surprise!' Celia Sánchez wrote in her diary on hearing of the final negotiations that were called for March. 'I tell Fidel that this meeting with representatives from the labour movement and Civic Resistance strikes me as reaching definitive plans . . . . They have always regarded the struggle here as something symbolic of our Revolution and not as a decisive factor of this war.'

Che too was utterly opposed to the idea: 'In no way can one underestimate mass struggle,' he wrote to Calixto García at the end of March. Partly in order to mollify his more radical wing, and no doubt Che in particular, Fidel disseminated a Manifesto of Twenty-One Points that sought to broach a middle ground with the organised worker groups rather than proceeding over their heads. 'I don't think Fidel's last manifesto clarifies every point, but it does fix a bit the worker problem, the one that frightens me most of all,' Che grumbled when he read it. It was an indication of how strongly opposed the two wings of Fidel's Movement were that what did not go nearly far enough for the likes of Che and Raúl went over like 'an atomic bomb' with the Llano's National Directorate in Havana. But the wheels were now in motion for an all-or-nothing assault on the regime to be carried out across the country within the next few days. And Fidel could do nothing to stop it.

Che too looked to the forthcoming events with some anxiety. He had worked hard to earn Fidel's respect as an equal. But from the moment Fidel committed to going ahead with the strike, either Che would be proved wrong and his newly won position as Fidel's second-in-command become untenable, or, if he was right, the strike would fail and the centre of power in the 26 July would shift decisively towards the guerillas in the Sierra. Both men watched and awaited the outcome, therefore, with considerable concern.

8. TOTAL WAR

YET ONE MORE 'tragic' chapter in the 'dark and bloody history' of Cuba was the *New York Times*'s verdict on the climactic moment of the war, the national strike of 9 April 1958. The strike was to herald also a new stage in the relationship between Fidel Castro and Che Guevara. It marked the beginning of a period in which Che's military successes would lead him almost to outshine his commander-in-chief, who would spend much of the rest of the war at his command headquarters of La Plata wrapped up in the minutiae of political negotiations and away from the intensity of the front lines. But once the rebels themselves were firmly on the attack, Che's growing public persona – and in particular concerns about his communist affiliations – also provided Fidel with a perfect foil for the political work he was by then undertaking in preparation for the moment the rebels took power. With this, the pattern to which the rest of their lives would conform was to be set.

All this began with the strike. Fidel had first acquiesced to, then supported, and finally urged with a desperate, wild-eyed frustration the revolutionary violence that was unleashed in Havana and elsewhere in Cuba on the morning of 9 April 1958 to mark the beginning of a nationwide revolt. '[B]ands of armed youths entered the CMQ and Progresso radio station at about 10 a.m.' one report stated, '[and] forced the operators to broadcast records calling on the people to strike.' By then, rebel militias had taken to the streets and sabotage units in the cities worked to cut off electricity supplies. Meanwhile, assassination groups had swung into action at various points around the country. Fidel had been delighted when he heard such initial reports in his mountain retreat, but he would soon regret having been, for once, persuaded to act against his instincts.

Within just a few hours government forces had moved 'with rapidity, precision and death-dealing effectiveness' to respond. It soon became clear that the Batista regime was all too well prepared for such a half-hearted attempt to oust it via a popular uprising, particularly one so fatally flawed by the disorder and factional splits that had come to characterise the rebel movement. By the following day, forty rebels had been reported dead in Havana alone and the pro-Batista Confederation of Cuban Workers could assert triumphantly: 'There is no general strike and all workers are at their jobs as usual.'

Fidel was furious. In the crackdown that followed, almost all the rebel safe houses in the cities were wiped out and the three bullet-riddled bodies that appeared by a road outside Havana, near the writer Ernest Hemingway's retreat, were but a few of the corpses to appear in the following days. When a 26 July attorney went to a police station to enquire about the fate of two comrades from propaganda, he too was taken in, tortured, and then beaten to death along with the two activists.

The fall-out from this precipitate lunge for power resulted in an internal shake-up within the 26 July. Such utter failure had revealed at a stroke that the Movement had neither the organisational competence nor, most of all, enough arms yet to undertake a nationwide rebellion. Having been let down, as he saw it, by the Llano who had insisted on the strike, Fidel's response was to look exclusively to the rebel army for salvation, and he seemed to find a sympathy for Che's constant complaints against the Llano that he had never voiced before.

This was not because their interpretation of events coincided, however. In fact, Fidel and Che understood the strike in decidedly different terms. But their responses did closely mirror one another's in one crucial respect: Che came away convinced that the problem would have been avoided altogether if more power had been vested in the person of Fidel from the start, while Fidel decided that henceforth he would be better off placing his faith in the hands of his most trusted fighters. And after his achievements of the last few months, it was Che Guevara of course who stood at the very top of that list.

On overcoming his initial anger at the failure of the strike, Fidel called an emergency meeting with the entire rebel leadership. The meeting was to take place on 3 May in the house of a peasant collaborator in the foothills of the Sierra. Those who didn't come, he warned, would be shot: the rebel army leaders wanted explanations, if not scalps. 'Let's talk for once with revolutionary sincerity!!' Raúl, who was unable to attend because, since the strike, he was having to deal with a resurgence of attacks in the more vulnerable sector of the Sierra Cristal under his command, weighed in with his brother beforehand. 'Who are the guilty ones?' he demanded to know.

What angered Fidel almost as much as the threat of likely retaliation, however, was that against his better instincts he had trusted his colleagues in the underground and had gone along with their assurances that the strike would prevail. If their intelligence and strategy were not to be trusted, then the guerrillas themselves were more vulnerable than he cared to imagine. 'I am the leader of this Movement and I have to assume the historic responsibility for the stupidities of others, and I'm just a shit who can't make a decision about anything,' Fidel had written to Celia Sánchez shortly afterwards. 'With the pretext of avoiding *caudillismo* [charismatic but strong-arm leadership centred in one person], everyone is doing whatever he pleases. I'm not stupid enough not to realise this, nor am I a man prone to visions or ghosts. I am not going to give up my critical spirit and intuition about things, which has helped me so much to understand situations, especially now when I have more responsibilities than ever before in my life . . . From now on I am going to take care of our problems.'

Che had no such fear of *caudillismo* – or, rather, he saw it as something that Fidel was more than able to transcend. For all that he loved rules, he cared for exceptions most of all; and in an agenda whose ferocity would have been all that caught the National Directorate by surprise, for he had long since made his case, Che sought to play kingmaker at the meeting. Indeed, this time he had consulted closely with Fidel beforehand. Four days after the failed strike, on 13 April, Fidel called Che over from the recruits' school at Minas del Frío, writing later to Celia to inform her that 'Che will go over there with me to take charge of a series of questions of much interest.'

Obtaining answers to those questions became, in the words of one historian, a 'bloodletting' that lasted for two days (actually, eighteen hours) of ceaseless argument. As had probably been decided beforehand, Che played the role of prosecutor as all present were put on the spot – though, one imagines, some more than others – and each individual's contributions and failings drawn out of them. Directing the turns of this mass expurgation with his unstinting disregard for the Llano, Che seems not to have disappointed. Seeking to undermine again and again the Llano's grip on power within the movement, he declared that the strike was evidence of the malign influence of 'rightist' elements in the underground. Che emerged from the meeting as Fidel's undisputed right-hand man and, thanks to the short work that Che made of the Llano, Fidel in turn emerged the undisputed leader of the Movement.

So, when he returned to rebel headquarters at the well-protected camp of La Plata, Fidel had even more complete authority over all areas of the 26 July Movement, as its general secretary and commander-in-chief of the rebel army, thereafter his preferred title. A new Executive replaced the more civil-oriented and moderate National Directorate of the Llano. The militias were to be dissolved or simply broken down and absorbed into the rebel army columns, and the former leaders of the National Directorate – Faustino Pérez, René Ramos Latour and David Salvador – would now join with the guerrillas in the Sierra, where Fidel could keep an eye on them. As Che noted satisfactorily in his diary, 'The line of the Sierra would be followed, that of direct armed struggle, extending it to other regions and thereby taking control of the country.'

No sooner had Fidel and Che emerged as the two clear victors from this reorganisation of power than the government began amassing troops for an all-out offensive on the rebel strongholds. Thousands of conscripts were called up, the navy and air force were put on alert and Batista's most trusted and ruthless generals were placed in charge of an 'encirclement and annihilation' operation codenamed Fin de Fidel (End of Fidel). As the army slowly drew the noose tighter around the Sierra, the rebels could do nothing but prepare themselves. In a daily stream of letters Fidel sought to coordinate these preparations, constantly imploring his captains to conserve ammunition and to hone their equipment as if it were priceless gold and not second-rate rifles hauled up into the mountains by mules or the home-made bombs cooked up by Che in the munitions factory at his own new camp at La Mesa.

But even on the eve of what would be a major defensive battle, politically Fidel continued on the attack. He hoped to exploit some recent divisions in Batista's army (which Batista himself had created by taking control of the eastern sector of Oriente away from General Eulogio Cantillo, who was leading the attack, and giving it as a kickback to Colonel del Río Chaviano, Fidel's nemesis from Moncada). Fidel also wanted to establish the position of the reorganised 26 July Movement more firmly and broadly within the opposition. To this end he was careful to present the Movement in a moderate light to the other opposition movements, both inside the country and in exile, and continued to seek a unity agreement with the other opposition parties in exile in particular. The fact that he did this with precious little intention of being bound by such an agreement has long given historians cause to suspect that he had other ideas in mind. But in fact he was thinking about some further internal realignments of policy – realignments that Che would be interested to hear about.

That Che was now his undisputed second-in-command was clear to all. 'If I'm not around try to respond to me via Che,' Fidel would say before picking up his telescopic rifle and cap and stalking out of the camp. And Che too kept Fidel informed of seemingly everything. They compared notes on the smallest of technical details – 'We've just solved the problems with the electric fuses,' Fidel wrote to Che excitedly, like a scientist basking in a breakthrough, 'use it with the five-battery current, directly, without the coil' – or on finances and, increasingly now, on political matters too. Fidel even seemed more distant from Celia Sánchez, finishing a particularly scolding letter to her: 'Hopes that you will understand me? None! Because when I have written you with the greatest clarity you have chosen to understand what has seemed most appropriate to you.'

This was more than a little unfair on his unstintingly loyal *compañera*. Celia had become used to being Fidel's first mate: his confidante, lover and guide rolled into one. During the previous year, when he had felt so isolated, it was to her that Fidel had turned. 'And you, why don't you make a short trip here?' he had written the previous summer, before she came up to join him permanently at the end of the year. 'Think about it, and do so in the next few days. A Big hug.'

Celia was Cuban, a staunch nationalist, Ortodoxo – everything that Fidel was familiar with and known for. She had responded to his call with an almost motherly affection and by moving up into the mountains full-time. Fidel, all the while, had continued with his time-honoured platform: the next-generation Chibás. But now, when for the first time he was considering in concrete terms what might come afterwards, it was to Che that he turned as his confidant and it was some of Che's ideas that appeared to be holding sway over him. Before the end of the month Fidel wrote to Che that he wanted to see him, just for seeing's sake. 'It's been too many days since we spoke,' he said. And that, he went on to add, was now 'a matter of necessity between us. Tomorrow I will make sure I am in the Mompié house to speak to you.'

In such meetings, by night and day and for the remainder of the war, Fidel and Che worked closely together. Even as the government troops closed in (and Che at times would almost stumble into them on his way back to his own headquarters from visiting Fidel) they sat in a fug of cigar smoke poring over documents and charts of the area, deciding on the tactics that they would pursue not only now, but in the future, come the revolution. It was the beginning of a closely woven partnership and the basis for a blossoming personal and political double act which contained the seeds of their great strength as a pairing, as well as the fundamental differences that would in time pull them apart. But there were more practical problems to deal with first. Towards the end of May Che and Fidel attended an assembly of a few hundred local peasants about the coffee harvest. It was the first of many such meetings at which the rebel army played the role of facilitators. But as Fidel stood up to close the event with a speech, planes started machine-gunning nearby. The long awaited government offensive had begun.

* * *

Batista's forces planned to take no chances. 'Either we must go there, or they will come here,' the Cuban Foreign Minister, Gonzalo Güell, had warned the Americans at the start of April as he jockeyed implicitly for their support in the offensive. Listening carefully to Güell at his office in Havana, Ambassador Smith no doubt nodded and smiled and maintained the official policy of neutrality. But these were not his thoughts once the Cuban had left. As he confided in his report to the State Department that evening, Smith saw both Batista *and* Castro as 'tigers' whom the Cuban people were being forced to ride and, so far as he saw it, 'Exchanging tigers is no solution.' So the Americans too now began their own quiet moves to head off the growing possibility that the rebels might actually defeat the government.

The onslaught lasted for seventy-six days, until the vastly outnumbered rebels had somehow managed to beat the army back to the foothills. Fidel and Che were both active in the fighting – their earlier attempts to sideline each other from the action now appeared a wanton luxury when all hands were needed. For most of the government attack Fidel was stationed in his head-quarters, making occasional sorties to scout out troop movements. While La Plata itself was shelled from the air and the sea, Fidel set about orchestrating the rebels' defence, using the field telephone they had just installed and relying upon his hard-won knowledge of the complex terrain to give him the upper hand over government commanders trained in classrooms far removed from the tangle of forest that was the Sierra Maestra theatre. 'Fidel knew the area better than I did and I lived here since a kid,' one of the peasant recruits recalled – and he sought to turn it to their advantage. His strategy, however, was always simple: to fight in defence, ambushing and laying mines to scatter the raw and unseasoned recruits before hunting them down. Even the Santiago chief of police, Salas Cañizares – that 'extremely uncouth' man who drank and whored and spat frequently on to the floor – openly acknowledged that in such an ambush the soldiers were inevitably done for. It was feral and thuggish, but it represented the rebels' only chance.

Amidst this 'chaos and disorder' of full-scale war, Fidel and Che kept up a constant flow of messages; their letters revealing how they were beginning to work together with an implicit sense of the other's activity. 'Send me this, I will be there,' one would say. 'I cannot read this, translate it and send me the answer over there.' Like dancers, they anticipated their partner's steps. 'P.S., be careful with the wounded and the bullets that remain on the other side!' Fidel finished a lengthy series of orders to Che on 1 June, seeming to know exactly where he was headed. Two days later, he made a brief excursion from his headquarters to visit Che at the recruits' school, writing later to tell his friend how pleased he was with what he had seen of it. He did so with a certain brotherly pride. In terms of preparation they now had it all. As to the rest, that was 'all a question of a bit of luck', he acknowledged. Putting this thought to one side, he then returned to the more mundane but ever important matter of rationing bullets.

Though the army offensive began tentatively – the large number of new army recruits were wary of venturing into the densely forested mountains – by mid-June Fidel's own rearguard position had been beaten right back to the long hill-top crest of La Plata by sheer force of numbers. Consumed by the immediate need to defend his own now precariously held camp, Fidel delegated – seemingly without hesitation or equivocation – effective decision-making power to Che. 'Although you left the code here I can't decipher the message because I haven't the slightest idea. I am sending you the code and the message so that you can try to decipher it and make some sort of response,' as he said at one point, and 'I am sending you the papers; resolve this however necessary' at another.

Che's response was revealing. He clearly did not see the defer-ment of power as simply a procedural affair, the authority vested in him to be carefully tended but not used. Though he was well apprised of Fidel's precarious current situation and was intent on doing all he could to resolve it, he none the less had no inten-tion of allowing his leader's immediate needs to compromise those of the army as a whole. And when Fidel began to fire off more and more desperate requests for reinforcements to all of his captains, against his own usual strategic good sense, Che stepped in to ensure that the bigger picture was adhered to. 'As of yet I am not sending the men, even though they have arrived here. I refer to the men that you ask for Santo Domingo,' he replied calmly, adding with a certain insouciance that none other of the rebel commanders would have got away with, 'If there is a detonator, I need it over here.'

As Che sought to remind Fidel, they were all up against it. And even after Celia had been despatched to get the men – usually a guarantee that something would be done with immediate effect – Fidel continued to feel the brunt of Che's refusal to act, as he would have done, on instinct rather than evidence. Che held out, and things in La Plata became increasingly desperate. The army attacked from the south, intending to push the rebels down the northern slopes of the Sierra into the waiting army on the northern flank. With a patience he extended to almost no one else, and despite the abject nature of the situation, Fidel showed that yet again he was prepared to humour Che more than the others. 'Send to Che the complete message that Pedrito sent so that he understands the situation here,' Fidel ordered Celia, before writing directly to Che with the rather more plaintive: 'Send help. Mortar shells are exploding near us.'

The situation had become critical elsewhere, too. In the Sierra Cristal, Raúl had been taking such a beating from the planes that he had resorted to kidnapping a number of American sugar workers to prevent any further attacks. They were lost at that point, as his future wife Vilma Espín, an underground operative from Santiago who had joined him in the Sierra Cristal earlier in the year, recalled. It was far from universally unpopular, though. The local population themselves referred to the Americans as their 'Anti-aircraft battery'.

But by mid-July, even as the government offensive switched to concentrate its efforts on Fidel's own principal flank to the south, the tide had begun to turn and Fidel's spirits lifted. 'Today we bombed the guardias!' he wrote to Che, explaining how his men had managed to trick the army into bombing one of its own positions by means of a hoax radio transmission. Fidel took special pleasure in ordering the rebel making the broadcast to 'sound like a real goat' as he gave the hoax orders to the government planes to open fire, just for authenticity. Revealing his characteristic ability to be able to fight battles on many different levels at once, Fidel also now secured an agreement with a useful tranche of the opposition in a new opposition political document, the Caracas Pact. It was signed on the same day that he took four hundred soldiers hostage after trapping them in a ravine and starving them out during a week-long siege. Much broader-based than the Miami Pact, which it replaced, the Caracas Pact also contained very little by way of concrete commitments. Now that they were getting more than enough weapons from captured government troops, Fidel knew he no longer needed to make such promises. What the Pact did provide, however, was an umbrella under which Fidel and Che could work as they set about creating a more radical platform for the revolution.

* * *

The government forces made their last push at the rebels' weakest point, Santo Domingo, at the end of July. But by the first week of August it was all over. The army whimpered back to the foothills, 'its spine broken', as Che put it, truly satisfied, to 'try and figure out a new strategy'. Fidel knew he had won in the Sierra: his 'fanatical, hardcore' rebels had proved too agile, too well supported by the local population and, in the final analysis, too committed to be defeated by the increasingly unwilling forces that Batista had all too carelessly pushed forward to confront them. But the war was far from over yet, and in order to push his advantage Fidel now needed to take it down on to the plains as far as Las Villas province, the narrow belt of land that forms the middle of the country. The strategy of total war that had failed in terms of the strike would now be given a rather more literal twist.

For this most important of missions Che and Camilo were Fidel's obvious choices, but for Che it carried a two-fold responsibility. He was to act as military governor of all the territories he passed through, and was tasked with negotiating relations with each and every group, 26 July or otherwise, that he encountered. By pushing west he was to seal off the eastern end of the country while Fidel himself dealt the *coup de grâce* to the major towns in Oriente. Throughout August, Che selected and prepared the men he would take with him. Half their number ought to expect not to survive, he told them, shortly before they crept down on to the plains. A bitter hurricane struck them as soon as they were out of the mountains, though, making almost all roads impassable and immediately forcing them to give up on the limited transport they had managed to obtain.

For the next six weeks they could only trudge on by foot through the worst that the wet season could throw at them. They forded 'streams that had become rivers', fought against the ravages of mosquito swarms, and drank water 'from swampy rivers, or simply from swamps'. Che hounded them constantly the whole way. After a week most were walking barefoot, their feet lacerated and swollen with pus, and once the first skirmishes with the army had begun they abandoned even the few horses they had with them because they made the rebels easier to spot from the air. The men spent some nights in standing water up to their belts, and ate once every two days. As Camilo's group had set off first shortly before Che's, they had the added disadvantage that the army were waiting for them.

It was a poignant moment for Che to strike out on his own. In the midst of the fighting of the previous months, and the mayhem of the army onslaught, he had received a letter from his mother shortly after one of the few phone conversations they had had in the five years since he had left Buenos Aires.

'Dear Teté: I was so overcome to hear your voice after so much time,' she wrote. 'I didn't recognise it – you seemed to be another person. Maybe the line was bad or maybe you have changed. Only when you said "old lady" did it seem like the voice of old.' She was now alone, she told him, and much of the letter conveyed her pride in all of her children and their exploits. Che would surely have been moved to hear how his sister was winning architectural prizes, while Robertico was now a father of two beautiful blonde little girls. Little else could convey the difference between the life he was now leading and the one he had left behind. But Celia finished the letter on a dejected note, one that, despite the immediacy of the war all around him and his complete immersion in it, must have touched him deeply. 'I don't know how to write to you, or even what to say to you,' she said, fearing that she had 'lost the measure' of him for good. 'So many things I wanted to say my dear. I am afraid to let them out. I leave them to your imagination.'

She had once been the most important person in his life, and had always been his most intimate confidante. It is impossible that a man as sensitive as he would not, as he read this letter in the semi-privacy of his hammock, feel some catch of nostalgia, some lump of emotion at the frankness of her words. But since he was a man in the ascendance, with enormous demands on his time and facing death each and every day, it is unlikely that any such sentiment would have detained his thoughts for long. But that was in many ways the proof of Celia's point. It does not take more than a few moments' snatched conversation for a mother to recognise such things. She had immediately noticed the presence of a new man within her son, and the time away from Fidel, who had become the strongest influence on him, was to provide the requisite space for this other figure to more fully emerge.

* * *

'Fidel, I write you from the open plains,' Che began his first report on 3 September, sending a somewhat nostalgic embrace as he looked back to the peaks of the Sierra which now appeared as little more than a blue tint on the horizon. By the 8th he had reached Camaguey, and was in a more upbeat mood. The planes that had so troubled his forces as they moved across the plains seemed to him now like 'inoffensive doves', though he confessed he was fearful at the thought of what might happen if they needed to retreat with so many inexperienced recruits, and commented ruefully that his attempt to impose a tax in Leonero, a small town they had passed through, had 'got nowhere'.

'The Fidelisms I've had to engage in just so we can arrive with the shells in good condition are straight out of the movies,' he wrote Fidel, suggesting he hadn't quite left his comrade's influence behind. He added, in another message, five days later, 'There are many other questions I would like to raise with you,' but this was just before he moved his troops on from Camaguey: alas, he said, 'time is not on my side and I must leave'. Doubtless some of those questions concerned what he ought to do about the way he was being painted a communist 'rat' by the government. Since the army had picked up a series of documents which the rebels had left behind after a skirmish on 20 September, 'Wanted' posters for him and Camilo had been put up, with a hammer and sickle hovering over them.

It was a moot point, and one that was even less clear-cut at Fidel's Comandancia. The Cuban Communist Party (PSP) had first made contact with the rebels, via Che, in the autumn of 1957. While still a political freelance at university, Fidel had largely kept away from the PSP (unlike his brother Raúl, who was a member and who, like Che when he subsequently joined, kept his membership a secret from Fidel). The simple fact was that the so-called Popular Socialist Party was not nearly popular enough for Fidel. And even in Mexico – where Fidel held highly secret meetings with representatives of the Cuban Communist Party just prior to his departure – they too seemed to think little of his putschist strategy, feeling that his appeal was limited to the lower middle classes and the young. The war had changed all that now. Fidel was the major threat to their position as an opposition movement, while at the same time their organisational capacities and their influence on the working class made the PSP of strategic interest to Fidel. That and the fact that, thanks to Che, he was also becoming more interested in their ideas.

It was with Che's support that one of the PSP's leaders, the goatee-bearded Carlos Rafael Rodríguez – a senior figure who would none the less soon have a lot to do with the young rebels – first came up to the Sierra in 1957. When Che left for Las Villas with Camilo, Rodríguez remained in the rebel camp (he sent Che off with a book of Mao as a gift), though the reception from others in the Comandancia then cooled somewhat: the staunchly anti-communist view of most of the Llano leaders prevailed up in the Sierra too. Rodríguez departed about a month later, but as the Americans noted, some communist officials, as well as many other 'Johnny come latelys', were still holed up in one of the camps there, La Vega de Jibacoa: present, but 'not permitted to take an active part in the 26th of July Movement'. This was not quite right. Isolated they may have been, but they were certainly not ostracised by Fidel, and it was ultimately his views that counted. When asked why he risked United States public opinion by 'surrounding himself with communists' Fidel replied, doubtless aware that his words would be reported elsewhere and knowing full well the main source of people's concerns, that he considered Che to be 'his most able Lieutenant', adding for effect, 'especially in sabotage'.

All this flak that Che was drawing made him ideally suited to the mission Fidel had given him. In public Fidel continued to reject any such accusations of 'communist infiltration'. When interviewed on the radio by the *Chicago Tribune* journalist Jules Dubois from Venezuela, he responded indignantly. 'The only person interested in accusing our movement of being communist is Batista, so as to continue obtaining arms from the US who, by so doing, are marking themselves with the blood of murdered Cubans.' But in private he knew all too well that, come the victory of his rebel forces, he would need the sort of organisational capacities that were only available to him via the PSP. That was why there were communists in Fidel's camp, and that was why Che, with Fidel's approval, had been incorporating members of the PSP into his own column since the previous summer. When

Raúl Chibás paid his own visit to see Fidel during those weeks, he recalls that they spoke of just about everything *but* communism. Given Fidel's modus operandi, that makes it rather likely that this was precisely what Fidel by then had in mind.

Whatever political strategies Fidel was lining up, it all hinged, as well he knew, on military success. He was therefore ecstatic when he heard confirmation from Che in October that he had made it to the Escambray Mountains marking the half-way point to Havana. 'Che is extraordinary!' he enthused. 'Really extraordinary!'

* * *

On 5 November, around fifteen minutes after a silver-white Air Cubana DC-3 had taken off late from Manzanillo, en route to Holguin, five gunmen aboard donned 'dark green uniforms' and 'M26 armbands' before quickly commandeering the plane and redirecting it to deliver a secret stash of ammunition to one of the Territorio Libre areas under rebel control. But, empty of fuel on what was supposed to have been just a quick hop, the plane crashed into the sea before it could deliver its booty to Raúl's area as planned. Writing shortly afterwards, the US Consul in Santiago, Park Wollam, observed the inevitable: '[T]here are very definitely problems between the rebels and United States interests whether or not the rebels are officially ignored,' he said. 'Problems' was by then putting it somewhat mildly.

It had been a bad month for rebel incursions against US interests. Just a few days before the hi-jacking, the Texaco refinery in Santiago was held up and the last two of seven Jeeps which the rebels had been slowly taking from their owner, Mr Dodge, were requisitioned. But it had been a good month for the constant stream of pretenders to the throne that the US embassy officials had been having round for coffee and candid discussions as they looked for alternatives to back to prevent Castro coming to power: groups like Eusebio Mujal's powerful Confederation of Cuban

Workers (CTC), representatives of Carlos Prío, and 'close associates' of any number of disaffected generals angling for a United States-sponsored military coup. And all these groups knew what buttons to press. As one of their number put it to the Americans: the communists were 'not up in the hills reading the bible'.

As the Americans cast their net wider for information, they dredged up more and more that they disliked about Fidel Castro and those around him. They had been relieved by what the hostages debriefed in June had told them – that the rebels would 'rather be called sons of bitches than commies.' But in October they had spoken with a former teacher of Fidel's, then a PPL presidential candidate, Márquez Sterling. The Americans were informed that Fidel and Raúl were 'mentally unbalanced' and that there had been talk, when he was at university, that Raúl was homosexual. Lawless elements were now joining up and 'seeking sanctuary' in the July 26 Movement, of whom 'between 80 and 85% . . . are communists'.

By now the Americans wanted to find out all they could about the rebel leadership. But their attempts appear to have been confused by the different roles played by Fidel and Che. Of Fidel, they assembled a picture of a wild card. He was 'not a communist and well-intentioned but . . . he acts often on inspiration', as one informant put it to them. But of Che, they saw only red. 'This seems to me as authoritative a statement we have re. the communist proclivities of "Che" Guevara', a note appended to a report by the Argentine Foreign Minister read. 'I would doubt his being equally informed regarding the Castros.'

For now at least, Fidel was still considered a 'good Cuban at heart'. All the while that Che was putting the central region of Las Villas to the torch as he passed through it en route to Havana, it was easier for Fidel to maintain this more favourable image with the Americans, who, as Batista's government crumbled, would come more and more to be the principal authority that Fidel confronted on the island.

A government summary report of the situation at the end of

the month was even more hysterical in the picture it painted of Che: 'Rebels, commanded by Camilo Cienfuegos in North and Che Guevara in South, were only ostensibly under direction Fidel Castro, actually taking orders directly from Juan Marinello and other Communist leaders. Communist cells were being quickly organised in villages, Communist pamphlets and literature distrib- uted and other methods typical of Communist guerrillas were being seen.' This was not even remotely accurate as to the real communist activities of Che Guevara at this moment, but as to the impact that his campaign in the region was having, it said all that needed to be said. If only for his string of military skir- mishes, for many Che was fast becoming the prominent figure of the revolution.

This was a rather different way of drawing attention from himself that Fidel had altogether less patience for. By then, he had been holed up in La Plata seeking to keep a rein on his commanders for too long. As early as June he had moaned to Celia of those who now surrounded him: 'These people bore me. I'm tired of being an overseer, of going back and forth without a minute's rest. I miss those early days when I was really a soldier. I felt much happier than I do now. This struggle has become for me a miserable, petty-bureaucratic job.' Deciding that the time had come for him to re-enter the field of operations, Fidel now assembled the greater part of his forces to begin a series of attacks that, he hoped, would gradually over-run the smaller towns of Oriente so as to encircle Santiago in a final and decisive offen- sive that he himself would lead. All other matters he would now deal with on the go. It was to become his working style for many years.

By the time Fidel laid siege to the city of Guisa in November, Che had already put into action his general plan of assault on Las Villas. Resistance had been sporadic. The soldiers had fled the barracks at Jiquima, a key objective, before Fidel's troops even got there, giving the rebels control of the central mountain range of the Sierra de Escambray from the Agabama river in the west to the Sancti Spiritus–Trinidad highway in the east. After these initial successes the government forces launched a stinging counter-attack, forcing Camilo and Che to regroup in order to present sufficient strength in numbers. The province was by now in a state of utter chaos. Rebel units were marching around in all directions, burning bridges and smashing government posts. In the streets people were either cheering or packing up their bags. Whenever they could predict the enemy's movements government warplanes bombed and strafed the larger rebel columns and, across the plains, plumes of smoke rose from countless skirmishes between the two forces.

This was the context in which Che had to deal with the existing political factions of the region. There was an urgent need for some form of order to be imposed, and in the absence of Fidel that order inevitably bore his own imprint. Che's arguments with the Llano had not subsided and the two sides were as uncompromising as ever. But, meeting them more often face to face, he now seemed to win a certain grudging respect from some of them. As Marcelo Fernandez, the 26 July coordinator in the region, said on leaving a heated late night discussion between himself and Che: 'In spite of everything, one can't help admiring him. He knows what he wants better than we do. And he lives entirely for it.'

Che had grown more assured in these last few months. His asthma did not once recur and he looked lean and a good deal more mature. His hair was down now almost to his shoulders, and he wore what would soon become an iconic black beret with its single commander's star pinned to the front. The beret framed and accentuated the distinctive heavy, protruding brow. Another 26 July leader in Las Villas, Enrique Oltuski, a young engineering student and former Shell employee before he began working full time as a revolutionary, was one of many whose first encounter with Guevara, the man of myth from the hills, was shaped by what he had already heard about him through the grapevine, or Radio Bemba as it is known in Cuba. When Oltuski came to find

Che for the first time he was standing with his men around a campfire, a black cape hanging over an open shirt. The way that the light from the fire made the shadows from his moustache fall about his mouth caused Oltuski to think he bore a striking resemblance to Genghis Khan.

Che had lived two years of life-and-death struggle, and it had left him with a tendency to take things literally. His already natural impatience was now tested further by the intensity with which the grandest and most mundane decisions alike had to be taken. For the weeks he operated at the head of the army in Las Villas this was quite literally the case, as he waged a relentless series of minor battles – Güinía de Miranda, Banao and Fomento – before returning to his camp, wherever that was, and seeing those who had been waiting all day to speak to him.

As Che returned to camp at the end of one such evening his Jeep pulled up near a pretty young girl who was sitting on the edge of the pavement. Aleida March had been an underground operative for the 26 July, often bringing messages and money to Guevara's headquarters from Llano leaders around the province. She was undoubtedly brave – having planned sabotage missions and even carried bombs under her fashionable bulbed skirts – and she was wanted by the government. A principal go-between for the shaky alliance between Che's rebel forces and the Llano, she had returned from one mission to find her cover blown and been forced to stay on in Che's column. It was a far from desirable situation for either party. She found the leader, like so many others who encountered him during those months, hard to get on with, not to mention 'skinny and dirty'. She in turn carried the insuperable blemish of being a member of the Llano.

When Che pulled up that night he asked her what she was doing there; she replied that she couldn't sleep. When he told her he was on his way to attack the town of Cabaiguán, and asked if she would like to come along – this was a revolution, after all – she hopped in alongside him. Driving through the night, they had greater opportunity to discover that their mutual reservations had cause to go much further. She was an anti-communist from a well-to-do family. He was every bit as rough and intransigent as she had observed him to be while stationed in his unit over the previous weeks. But if he was brusque, he was no more so than she, and what appears in one glance to be alien and distasteful can very quickly become fresh, exciting and desirable. They were an instant match, and for the rest of the war they rarely left each other's side.

* * *

In contrast to the blossoming romance with Aleida, in December reports began to emerge of 'a growing rift between Che Guevara and Fidel Castro.' 'Castro is becoming increasingly annoyed at Guevara's growing independence of action and adoption of a leftist position in disregard of Castro's disciplinary orders for a more moderate position and Castro's recent instructions that all policy statements will be made only be Fidel Castro himself from rebel headquarters.' This was proof, if any was needed, that their little double act was working. The report went on: 'Castro destroyed a communication from Guevara before Guevara's messenger' and 'otherwise told the messenger of his ire'. One can imagine, given Fidel's temper, what that might have involved. The source of the report, a Cuban exile named Carlos Piad, suggests the interpretation may have been a little over-enthusiastic: Fidel and Che had in fact delivered such mixed messages that the opposition in exile was not at all sure where Fidel stood. But the plain truth was that Fidel had every confidence in Che, even if on a personal level – and here there was doubtless some truth in the scene – he may have been piqued by all the attention that Che was getting in his campaign in Las Villas. If it had been latent before, a certain competitiveness now edged into their relationship.

As the year drew to a close, however, everything seemed to be going the rebels' way. By 15 December, government troops had relinquished control of much of Oriente and were either laying down their arms or joining the rebels. Since the end of November, the two commanders had been in the thick of the war and at opposite ends of the country. The economy had been strangled – 'Sugar, of all things, is short in Manzanillo,' stated one report – and the rebels' ongoing sabotage of the transport system meant that many products had to be laboriously shipped around the country. Victory seemed tantalisingly close. In Oriente, having won an important battle at the town of Guisa on the 6th, Fidel was laying siege to the town of Maffo. The affair had been dragging on for some days and he was growing restless. Juan Almeida's column was getting ever closer to Santiago, while the so-called sixth column, under Raúl, was pinning the army down seemingly across half the province. Fidel felt left behind. 'I'm so pissed off with these people in Maffo,' he wrote his brother, 'it will be a miracle if I don't shoot them all when they surrender.'

He wrote to Che at the same time, 'The war is won. We have ten thousand soldiers bottled up in Oriente', before warning him, in a way that suggests he did not know quite how well Che was dealing with the political elements of his role, 'It's essential for you to realise that the political aspect of the battle at Las Villas is fundamental.' Fidel was by now well aware that the only thing not going the rebels' way was their relationship with the United States. As the Americans desperately sought to patch together some sort of military junta, Fidel scrambled to head them off.

For that reason he was furious when Che revealed he had finally dragged a signed unity pact out of the intransigent and bickering local opposition groups of Las Villas. It may have been the only way to do it, but written accords were the last thing Fidel wanted now that the momentum was so strongly in their favour. Batista's forces were crumbling by the day, only the two crucial provincial capitals of Santiago in Oriente and Santa Clara in Las Villas remained, and Fidel and Che were poised outside of each respectively. While they waited to launch the final strike, Fidel had returned to his preferred strategy of keeping all doors open and all potential opposition guessing.

On the 29th Che's forces struck at Santa Clara, a city with a population of 150,000 augmented by all the reinforcements Batista could afford: a force totalling some 3500 men. The engagement lasted for three days, with the guerrillas advancing through the streets against tanks and artillery and with civilians occasionally joining in the fighting. It was the one real pitched battle of the war and cost a large number of lives on both sides. When a rebel contingent took the railway station, and some of the defending soldiers tried to escape in an armoured train along a track that Che had wisely ordered to be dug up, the carriages twisted up and folded over in front of some nearby houses. A fat sergeant got off with a Thompson machine gun in his hands and, with all the bravado he could muster, told the rebels they were kidding themselves with their attack. Tanks were already on the way, he warned them. But he was answered with Molotov cocktails that soon turned the train into an oven, and the soldiers had no choice but to jump out and surrender. It was the making of Che Guevara: a simple but effective attack to be later adorned with legend.

In these last few days of the war Fidel's life could not have looked more different from that of Che, the leader at the head of his troops, his arm even cradled in a sling after a fall. In contrast, on Christmas Eve Fidel dined, for the first time in many years, at the family ranch in Birán, he and Celia joining his mother and brother Ramón. After dinner Fidel puffed away contentedly at a cigar before Celia called the somewhat incongruous evening to a close, driving him off to what would be a crucial meeting with General Cantillo, Batista's chief of armed forces. Cantillo flew in to the nearby Sugar Central América by helicopter the following morning, bringing brandy, cigars and the firm message that the army no longer wished to fight. While Fidel turned his attention to the siege of Santiago, Cantillo took advantage of Batista's flight into exile on New Year's Eve to lead a junta that would take control of the government. But Cantillo's scheme was no more successful than the many others being hatched by the various opposition groups who wanted to keep Fidel from power. All of a sudden, Fidel knew that political as well as military victory was now just a hair's breadth away.

*　*　*

On 1 January 1959, Cubans awoke to the news that Batista had fled, 'gone in the night', and for some time the streets of the cities remained quiet. Then, as Che ordered the surrender of Santa Clara, and Fidel drew his troops around Santiago to demand the same, gradually the hubbub began. It was over. The rebels had won. 'Night falls as we, the *barbudos* [bearded ones], come down from the mountains looking like the saints of old,' one of the rebels, Carlos Franqui, recalled. 'People rush out to meet us. They are wild.' Another, the future author Reinaldo Arenas, noted, 'The rebels kept coming, with crucifixes hanging from chains made of seeds; these were the heroes. Some, in fact, had joined the rebels only four or five months earlier, but most of the women, and also many of the men, went wild over these hairy fellows.'

Fidel ordered Che and Camilo to push on to Havana and take command of the military headquarters there. Then he called for a national strike before marching into Santiago himself to soak up the atmosphere and adulation. The following day, the first rebel columns marched into Havana. People clambered up street lamps, or stood atop their Plymouths and Chevrolets, to see them. They were jubilant scenes. Pistols fired off victory reports among the crowds that thronged the streets, cheering wildly, if just a little bit nervously as well.

As they sat on the cusp of a new phase in their lives, one whose dimensions they could not yet begin to fathom, Fidel Castro in Santiago and Che Guevara in Havana had little time to reflect on the fact that the war was over. But it had forged a bond between them that was as deeply ingrained as the dirt on their clothes and the adrenaline in their veins. But without that link, what would they do? Che had never promised that he would stay longer than he was needed. As his own column approached the capital on the 3rd he turned all of a sudden to Núñez Jiménez, one of the revolution's future leaders, and said, 'My mission, my commitment to Fidel ends here, with our entry into Havana.'

PART 3

9. A HUG AND A
LONG KISS OF YEARS

THE CUBAN REVOLUTION was a creeping, tentative affair at first. This was not Russia in October 1917, much less was it Paris in 1789. The people stormed no Bastille or Winter Palace to seal the rebels victory; the soldiers did not rise up in revolt but instead remained quietly in their barracks. People ventured on to the streets that first day, called only by the shouts of the newspaper sellers and driven by the news on the radio. They were curious to see what, after all these years of civil war, the revolution was going to look like.

At first it did not look like much at all. In Havana, El Principe prison was smashed open and the prisoners released while the printing presses of a newspaper owned by one of Batista's cronies, Rolando Masferrer, were destroyed. A few casinos and hotels and the homes of some former government officials were also sacked and looted. But within hours M26 militia with their red and black armbands began to take control around the city and a surprising degree of order was restored.

As Che arrived in Havana and installed himself on Fidel's orders in the La Cabaña garrison in the heart of the city, there was rather more inner confusion in his mind than there was on the streets around him. His confusion mirrored that of Fidel's. Che Guevara, alongside him in the Sierra, was of undoubted value for Fidel. But Che was, after all, an Argentine in a fiercely nationalistic country, and he had been painted brightly by the press in the colours of international communism. He thus represented at the very least an implicit threat to Fidel's realisation of such a straightforwardly nationalist revolution – and Fidel was already coming under pressure, as all new heads of state in Latin America did on inauguration, to take a stand against communism. It was the burning political question of the day.

From the moment Fidel appeared on a podium in Santiago, flanked by his old guardian angel, Archbishop Pérez Serrantes – the man who had helped ensure his safety during the Moncada trial – and his new choice for president, the Cuban lawyer and long-time supporter of the 26 July Movement, Manuel Urrutia, he appeared to make it clear that his own deeply felt nationalism was to be the platform upon which consensus for his revolution would be built: 'The revolution begins now. . . . It will not be like 1898, when the North Americans came and made themselves masters of our country,' he said to cheers and whistles from the crowd. 'What greater glory than the love of the people? What greater prize than these thousands of waving arms, so full of hope, faith and affection towards us?' The world saw the beards and rifles, but here was the 'great avalanche' of people that came behind them.

Fidel was lionised in Santiago – 'The man whose very name is a banner' and 'the most outstanding figure of this historic event', so they said – and he could not help but add to the spectacle as he toured the length of the country towards Havana. Travelling at first by Jeep, mobbed by euphoric crowds, he was on the road for five days, inching along and stopping all the while. As if on some royal progress of old, Fidel took full advantage of those first, expectant days to show himself personally to the people, laying claim to their adulation as he did so.

It was the moment he had worked for all his life. It made the years in prison, the bitter endurance of exile and the hard months of living hand to mouth during the war, with its constant struggle waged just to stay alive, all worth while. The people found his mere presence reassuring. In the person of Fidel the revolution became real; things really had changed. And as he headed west he himself became convinced of one thing above all others: that it was his own personality that would be the key to consolidating the rebels' coming to power.

On the night of his arrival in Havana, Fidel delivered the first of the oratorical marathons he would become famous for. The atmosphere was as incandescent as the spotlights that tracked around the former military barracks, illuminating the crowd around the podium with its M26 banners and Cuban national flag draped about it. The crowd were ecstatic throughout, responding to their new leader's every rhetorical question in a kind of eager duet. Towards the end of the speech, one of the spotlights picked up two doves that fluttered down to rest for a moment on Fidel's shoulders. Symbolism being close to truth in the heavily religious and superstitious Cuba, the moment touched off a gasp and then a roar of 'Fidel! . . . Fidel! . . . Fidel!' 'How am I doing?' Fidel asked Camilo. 'You are doing alright, Fidel,' Camilo replied with his oaken smile, coining a new revolutionary slogan in the process.

Well away from public view in those early days, Che did not get to meet up with Fidel immediately upon his arrival in Havana: hardly anybody could get near the popularly anointed 'Maximum leader' at that stage. Conchita Fernández, Eddy Chibás' old secretary who would now serve Fidel remembers the moment she saw him for the first time in a long while, strolling out of a lift, bodyguards and general clamour on either side, and his rifle slung from his shoulder. 'I've been looking for you since I came down from the Sierra,' he said. While Fidel spent most days in front of a microphone, speaking sometimes until three or four in the morning, Che spent his days quietly organising affairs at the La Cabaña garrison, perhaps with the radio tuned to Fidel's ever-present voice, while he installed the group of loyal and dedicated assistants that had flocked to him during the campaign in Las Villas. He devoted much of his time to writing up his recent experiences of war. It was as if he was back from one of his lengthy periods of travel and wanted to set down the gist of it all while things were still fresh in his mind. But now, of course, he was no longer organising his thoughts just for his own private reflections. Che worked hard to become, and he would remain, the revolution's principal voice of reflection for the rest of his time in Cuba.

Without ever quite explicitly addressing the question, then, it had soon become clear in the way that both Fidel and Che threw themselves into the work of building the revolution that for them the war would continue; indeed, a war of some sorts *had* to continue if they were to sustain that partnership they had established in the mountains. They needed the constant flux of danger and possibility, the sleepless nights and the struggle that demanded all of their time. It was the saturation of their lives by this all-encompassing fight that their relationship was now based upon.

Whatever question marks had hung over Che's continued stay in Cuba certainly appeared to have been solved by 9 February, when Fidel passed a law making him a naturalised Cuban citizen. The law applied to all people who had fought against Batista for more than two years and who had held the rank of Comandante for one: in effect, none but Che himself. Fidel then also enabled them both to take ministerial rank in the government by lowering the minimum age from thirty-five to thirty. It was a clear indication of how Fidel saw the shape and nature of the revolution's leadership and the guerilla's role in it.

To some extent, it was also a recognition of reality. When Prime Minister Miro Cardona resigned after realising he was getting nowhere in a spat with Fidel over the closing of Havana's brothels and casinos (Fidel maintained they must stay open for the time being), Fidel, who until now had held no official post beyond commander-in-chief of the rebel army, moved in seamlessly to fill the gap. It was 'an inevitable step', as Teresa Casuso, his helper from the Mexico days and, now that she was repatriated, his media secretary, put it. It was inevitable 'because . . . the government did nothing. It did nothing because it had no authority. Despite Fidel's insistence that people go to the constituted government authorities with their problems and projects, it was to him that they came, because it was widely known that even President Urrutia and his cabinet ministers did nothing without first consulting the man who had given them their posts and who was the acclaimed idol of the entire population.'

There was another reason that the government did nothing, one that had everything to do with the terms upon which Fidel had convinced Che to stay around. Because of their personal intimacy, but also because of his great competence, his ability just to get on and to do things, Fidel had already decided to make full use of Che's not inconsiderable skills. But he knew only too well that Che would be committed to nothing less than a full and uncompromising revolutionary programme, and he rightly calculated that Che would only stay on the promise that there would be a radical turn some time soon.

What Fidel proposed to Che was therefore formulated in this context. But it was not within the official government that he now asked Che to work. Instead, he was to work within two secret groups whose existence was not known outside Fidel's innermost circle. Fidel was all too aware of what Martí had called 'the scorn of our formidable neighbour who does not know us' and he wanted, for now at least, to maintain a more moderate front by keeping the well-known firebrand, Che, away from the official government headed by Urrutia.

The first of the two groups in which Che was to play a central role was the Office of Revolutionary Plans and Coordination, where he worked with Fidel's old and well-trusted friend Alfredo Guevara, Raúl Castro and Raúl's new wife Vilma Espín, Oscar Pino Santos and Antonio Núñez Jiménez. Their task was to draw up a more radical platform for the revolution. Second, Che was to be present, along with Fidel and Camilo principally, but also with Ramiro Valdés – Che's former deputy from the Sierra – and again Raúl when he could make it from Santiago, at a series of negotiations with the top leadership of the PSP, the Cuban Communist Party.

The PSP leadership was represented by Blas Roca, Carlos Rafael Rodríguez and Aníbal Escalante, all drawn from the party's Executive Bureau. They were at least ten years older than the young rebels, Rodríguez somewhat more, but they shared a not dissimilar history. The PSP had been formed in an anti-imperialist mould in 1925 and immediately declared illegal; its leaders had been persecuted under the Machado government, with one, Julio Mella, assassinated in Mexico and another, Carlos Baliño, in Cuba. Now, at this seminal moment in Cuban history, the leadership of both sides shared a culture of secrecy that would keep these meetings out of the public eye.

So secret was the arrangement that not even President Urrutia was aware of these two groups, and the full details of their activities would not become known anywhere for decades. None the less, in these two organisations – executive bodies completely unfettered by the dictates of public office – the future of the new Cuba was being drawn up. In due course they would be merged with governmental positions, but until then this was where real power was located. As Fidel had already confessed in a private comment to Alfredo: 'We are going to take the cake, and turn it upside down', making the appropriate gesture as he did so. It was just a matter of time.

But the revolutionary leaders who formed part of these groups had a daunting task. The Moncada manifesto, the 1940 constitution, the more radical, essentially communist platform Che had pushed for in the Sierra – all had to be rendered down into a workable shape for Cuba. The first step was to draw up an agrarian reform law that would soon become Fidel's principal instrument of unchecked power. But the PSPs principal allegiance was to Moscow and, schooled in its Marxist dogmas, as far as they were concerned, Fidel, Che, Raúl and the rest of the revolutionary leadership were already-numbered elements in a bigger puzzle, members of the radical bourgeoisie whose use to the PSP was in guiding the proletariat along the right path. The PSP held their sentiments in check during these first meetings, but they would gradually begin to bring into the revolution a labyrinthine and dangerous maze of doctrinal politics. Meanwhile, the façade of a liberal government continued, with Fidel directing both fronts – at times almost literally the one by day and the other by night.

In February, suffering from the strain of the various demands now being made upon him, coming as they did on the back of his exhausting campaign in Las Villas, Che was ordered to rest. One wonders if he had even noticed the state he was in, so accustomed was he to pushing onwards when his body collapsed on him, as it often did with his asthma. In fact he was so ill, said one of his aides, 'he wouldn't have lasted three more months had the war continued'. From then on, the meetings of the Office of Revolutionary Plans and Coordination took place at Che's new villa in Tarará, just outside Havana, where he would spend several weeks recovering. Che bristled at the idea of being put up in a former Batista official's luxury villa, as one newspaper editor who tried to accuse him of taking a government perk found to his cost when Che fired off a snarling public response to him. But his illness in fact provided the perfect cover for their meetings.

The meetings with the PSP, on the other hand, continued to take place at Fidel's nearby hilltop villa in Cojímar, a peaceful setting with views of the sea. For the meetings with the PSP Raúl would fly up by helicopter from his governorship in Santiago and Fidel would stop by after agreeing the day's official government business with Urrutia in Havana. 'Shit, now we're the government and still we have to go on meeting illegally,' Fidel commented drily during these initial weeks. But he was enjoying the conspiracy of it all. So was Che. 'Yes, things have really changed. Now we have an agenda,' he added ironically. For all his sardonism, Che had been pushing ahead with that agenda more than most. In his first major speech before he was taken ill, which he had given on 27 January at a PSP-sponsored forum in Havana, Che had argued that a true and 'simple' agrarian reform programme was required, more than had begun to be carried out in the Sierra in those lands the rebels controlled during the war. Little

211

wonder, then, that the Americans continued to see Che as the 'evil courtier' at Castro's back, who had 'practically monopolised his [Castro's] attention'.

If not quite up to the stirring oratory of Fidel's constant speeches on television or to the cheering masses in the newly renamed Revolutionary Plaza, Che's speech was none the less a crucial indicator of future revolutionary policies because by 'simple' he meant that constitutional impediments to such a reform would need to be waived. They would merely slow things up, and the revolution had a freshly cut debt to pay to the peasants on whose backs it had been fought. He set out a similarly bold line on countless other occasions during the first months of the revolution.

In terms of their physical appearance the two could scarcely have made themselves more different. For a start, their posture and body language were at opposite ends of the spectrum. Fidel exuded nervous energy with the constant swishing of his arms, the baying head, the way he would take the little finger of his right hand and twist it between the fingers of his left: Che stood much more solidly, with eyes that pivoted about. His movements were in general far less emphatic – but the meaning of his words was no less so. Indeed, the content of Che's speeches was invariably far more radical.

To appreciate the ways in which these radical-sounding declarations were of a piece with what Fidel was thinking, and not – as many of the embassies and intelligence gatherers wrongly concluded at the time – in contradiction to it, one needs not only to know of the existence and function of Fidel's parallel government but to have the benefit of hindsight as well. Fidel and Che's comments dovetail in a pattern that is only comprehensible over time: ideas that Che would invariably express first, and only in bold outline – ideas that Fidel would often contradict to begin with – would later be given shape in a more moderate-seeming form by Fidel himself. When Che raised the prospect of nationalisation, for example, Fidel did almost the opposite: he gave an assurance that the government would not confiscate foreign owned property. The effect was to throw everyone off guard: precisely the conditions needed to button down the revolution.

In peacetime, as in war, a rather useful division of labour had thus been established between Fidel and Che; one that turned their very differences – and the very different ways they were received – into an asset. Where Fidel spoke to the people Che worked behind the scenes, delivering speeches to the main revolutionary institutions. Indeed, it was an approach to peace that looked very much like their approach to war, the one laying out the more radical programme as a decoy and the other running around picking off the opposition when they stuck their heads up to protest. Cuba was an 'armed democracy', Che had told the PSP meeting in January, and indeed that was how, between them, they now set about running it: a series of feints and dodges, deliberate retreats and sudden counter-strikes. Instead of laying ambushes with weapons, now they did so with words. In so doing they carved out also what would become their natural constituencies. Fidel's real constituency was the masses, the undifferentiated throng, while Che addressed himself more to the administrators and the fighters, as he sought to try to mould the two together.

＊　＊　＊

These two approaches came to a head in late spring over one of the most controversial issues of the time; one whose resolution would see Che despatched from Cuba for several months by Fidel. In his capacity as commander of La Cabaña, and because Fidel trusted that he would do the job thoroughly, Che oversaw the process of swift revolutionary justice – tribunals and executions – applied to members of the former regime. Since early January he had personally pored over each of the cases before him while by night the sound of gunshots rang out across the bay. The executions were tolerated on the whole by the Cubans; but they drew a storm of protest from foreign governments and the international press.

It was at this time that Che's family, who had not seen him since that snowy day in Buenos Aires some six years before, arrived in Havana. Camilo had found them a place on a plane repatriating exiles from Argentina, telling Che only at the last minute. If Che would not himself have brought them over just yet – there was the business of government to be seen to now, after all – he was none the less delighted to see his father, his sister Celia, his youngest brother Juan Martín and, above all, his mother. He gave them what time he could, installing them in a suite a few floors beneath Fidel's own rooms in the Havana Hilton: a spearmint-coloured wedge of a building that had become Fidel's centre of operations and would soon be renamed the Habana Libre. But they had to accept that the business of revolution – not always the most pleasant – had to go on. Che's father in particular was shocked at the harsh disciplinarian his son had become.

They were not the only ones. Fidel was besieged with questions about the executions from foreign journalists as he returned to his rooms at the Hilton one day. 'If the Americans don't like what's happening in Cuba,' he told them, 'they can land Marines and then there will be two hundred thousand gringos dead.' It was an off-the-cuff remark, but it made headlines around the world and revealed his deep-seated fears about what the Americans might yet do to derail his revolution.

In the United States, where the memory of blacklists and McCarthyism was still fresh, Fidel had become a figure of great interest. But United States officials were still rather unsure what to make of him. Certainly the man they found 'voluble, garroulous [sic] and impatient' had, since coming to power, done enough to rub the Eisenhower administration the wrong way – having demanded that it withdraw its military mission and set out a programme of land reform likely to upset the significant US interests on the island. The revolutionary policies that were coming into effect – there would be almost one thousand new pieces of legislation by the end of the year – may have been met with great applause from the working class in Cuba, but they were viewed with growing dislike by the foreign and landed interests on the island: tariffs were imposed on luxury goods, and rents were lowered by 50 per cent in March. For all his bluster Fidel was not yet an outlaw though, and the first trip that he would make to the United States, in April, held out the promise that he might yet be able to charm them as he had his own people.

To soften the Americans up Fidel had already sent his most popular commander, Camilo Cienfuegos, on a 'good will tour' announced at the last minute. The 'soft spoken' Camilo, looking 'every inch the frontiersman' according to the *Washington Post* – did a great job. 'We won the peace,' he said, 'and we're going to keep it.' But the press delighted in headlines about the rebels who 'roamed' through the capital, their long hair down almost to the shoulders of their green zippered jackets. It was the perfect preparation for Fidel's trip: all of the colour and romance of the war, and nothing of the firing squad or the garrotte.

But it could not persuade them to see Fidel as anything other than a new and unpredictable force in the political relationship between North and South America. Behind the scenes, the officials at the US embassy in Havana had chafed at the way Camilo's trip had been organised by the newly empowered rebels: 'more out of ignorance than malice aforethought and is another example of the direct, oversimplified (Sierra Maestra) way of doing things'. And there was more than a twinge of chagrin in their despatch: the embassy was used to being kept fully abreast of matters but the new ambassador, Philip Bonsal, would meet Fidel only a handful of times in more than a year.

Again and again the reports that did reach American ears painted a picture of Fidel as a truculent child in need of reining in: 'Irritated by delays and counsels of caution, and notably sensitive to criticism,' said one, while another, the managing director of the Grace Line of passenger ships who had long and profitably ferried wealthier Americans down for the sex and salsa in Cuba, confessed that he, like other businessmen, was going through some 'soul searching' regarding Castro, not least 'because of the political immaturity he has demonstrated'. In reality, however, Fidel was going on his US trip in reasonably good faith: it was only fair that Cubans should live well, he said to his media secretary Teresa Casuso, shortly before they left and as they looked out across the beautiful view of Havana from the terrace of her office, 'because after all, we have made enough sacrifices'.

Fidel was aware that he needed to build some bridges, at least for now, and the aim of his visit was to present a good image of the revolution. 'Smiles, lots of smiles,' the American PR firm he had hired counselled him. When asked difficult questions in Washington he responded with just the right answers: 'We are not communists' and 'Laws and constitutions should go hand in hand,' he said when doorstopped by journalists at the Jefferson Memorial. He was demure and charming at the receptions laid on for him, allowing himself just a few hours of 'Fidelisms' when he left the rigmarole of the official circuit to eat in a downtown Chinese restaurant. With his small entourage, he stayed there late into the night, debating with some students.

But it did not all go his way. The response from the US government was decidedly colder. The Cuban economy was 'going to the devil', one official said. Castro 'has gone haywire' and was being stuffed full of benzedrine to keep going, claimed another. Because Castro had not received an official invitation Eisenhower decided to be away playing golf, and the hastily arranged meeting with Vice-President Nixon in the draughty chambers of the Capitol on a Sunday afternoon was 'notable for an absolute lack of mutual understanding'. Instead, the two men passed a difficult two hours maintaining the taut veneer of mutual respect. The trip had been a public relations success, but it was clear that Fidel was being given the cold shoulder from the government. So when Raúl put a call through to tell him the word in Cuba was that he was selling out to the Americans, he practically flung the telephone out of the window in fury. Casuso recalled that he 'almost wept'.

Fidel extended his foreign tour to accept an invitation from Brazilian President Juscelino Kubitshek to visit his new capital,

Brasilia, and to attend an economic conference in Buenos Aires sponsored by the OAS. But in a gesture that was indicative of a descending cloud, Casuso, who had been in charge of organising the trip until then, was unceremoniously left out. In the course of the tour she had become engaged to an American reporter, who had asked Fidel to transfer her to a job with the United Nations. Fidel took it as a betrayal and scarcely looked at her again; politics was always personal for him. So, as Fidel flew on to South America, Casuso returned to Cuba on a commercial flight and packed her bags to leave.

Once over the Mexican border Fidel was back on more comfortable terrain – speaking his own language, for a start – and he went to great lengths to position himself where he had always wanted to be: a twentieth-century pan-American leader in the tradition of Bolívar and Martí. He would open his country's doors to exiles – sheltering them just as Mexico had once sheltered him – but of course the implicit message was much stronger. Where Cuba had gone, others might follow.

In Buenos Aires Fidel 'suggested' that the USA make $30 billion of aid available to Latin America. This idea was met with some derision in Washington, of course, but he could later content himself with the thought that it bore a remarkable similarity to the $25 billion Alliance for Progress package that President Kennedy would announce just two years later. Castro had already begun canvassing for the role of Latin American statesman: he 'looks upon Cuba as a sacrificial lamb with which . . . to wreck the inter-American system, and to move on from there to be the Liberator of all of Latin America', as one observer put it. Though there was some truth to the comment insofar as Fidel did indeed have almost Bolívarian ambitions for his future role in Latin American affairs, it was also couched in the usual presumptions of American authority in its 'backyard' that so angered Fidel and other nationalist leaders like him. Ever since the establishment of the Monroe Doctrine in 1823 the United States had professed a moral right to safeguard the 'interests' of the nations of all the

Americas. But it was a policy that the increasing tensions of the Cold War were pushing once more to the fore. Fidel was touching raw nerves both north and south of the Mexican border.

While Fidel toured the Americas and the polarising effect of the Cuban revolution began to be felt abroad, Che had been quietly consolidating his position within the revolution, working on the agrarian reform law, giving speeches, and beginning the quiet work of communist education within those areas of the revolutionary government over which he had control. He had also been dealing with a difficult personal situation. In January, Hilda had descended upon Havana with their now three-year-old daughter, Hildita. If she was hoping for a rapprochement, she was to be bitterly disappointed by the presence of Aleida in Che's life. They settled on an amicable divorce, as she wrote in her memoirs, but she was determined to stay and would soon be working in the same building in which Aleida served her husband as his secretary: a situation that caused not inconsiderable resentment among all three of them.

* * *

Shortly after his return to Havana, Fidel launched the agrarian reform law. He grandly announced it from his former headquarters at La Plata in the Sierra and took on the role of president of The National Agrarian Reform Institute (INRA) in addition to his position as Prime Minister and commander-in-chief of the army. Before the summer was out Fidel was installed at its new offices, the tall city hall built by Batista overlooking the great civic square now renamed the Plaza de la Revolución. Over the next few months INRA officials would gradually be assigned to posts in the regular ministries until such time as this secondary seat of power, the parallel government, became indistinguishable from the actual government. Che was always there, along with Celia Sánchez who saw that some order at least existed. By now there was a constant cycling of personnel as the true extent of the changes became apparent. Exiles of the previous regime began to return, while others realised it was time for them to leave – such as the taxi driver who had himself fought for the rebels during the war and who bellowed at an American diplomat who was taking the political temperature on the streets: 'Tell that SOB Castro I don't like it, not one little bit.'

But what 'it' was had become increasingly unclear as official bodies and movements that just a few weeks earlier had been heralded as the new seats of authority seemed all of a sudden to be defunct. INRA was not just a means of taking over the 'official' government of Urrutia and his cabinet from the inside. It was also a means of 'diluting' – as Fidel's old school friend and gun-runner from the Sierra, Pedro Miret, put it – the 26 July Movement itself. Fidel needed a new platform now, and throughout the summer he realigned the balance of the revolutionary forces themselves. In June, he replaced the pro-American Foreign Minister Roberto Agramonte with the far more radical Raúl Roa. Then, in a welter of theatrics in July, he forced Urrutia out by resigning in protest when Urrutia blocked the passing of revolutionary laws and then had himself called back to duty by the masses of peasants trucked in to celebrate the 26 July anniversary.

When Fidel decided that month to send Che abroad for an extended goodwill trip many tongues wagged that he too was being sidelined in the drive towards a predominantly Fidelista-controlled state. Indeed, there were rumours of 'significant changes [to be] made in top governmental positions'. The timing was certainly inauspicious for Che. He and Aleida had only just married. A photo of the couple on their wedding day shows Che looking pleased but bemused at the spectacle, his tunic clean but not tidy. Aleida looks beautiful and stern at the same time, and around them are a strange bunch: Raúl and his wife Vilma, good friends both, Che's pilot and his bodyguard Alberto Castellanos among others. Fidel suggested that Che should take his new bride with him, but Che of course refused.

Part of the reason was possibly that Che's trip included a secret component: he was to make contact with the Soviets. Fidel was not therefore demoting Che, but responding to a distinct sense that it was Che who was growing impatient with the slow pace of reform. There is circumstantial evidence to suggest Fidel had reason to be. Che had once again threatened to leave during his visit to the USA when both he and Raúl had been angered by what they saw as his grandstanding among the moderates. Fidel was at pains to give Che a clear message that he was now ready to usher in 'a new phase' of the revolution.

On the day of Che's departure, Fidel came to see his 'trusted lieutenant' off at the airport. They sat for a good hour at the end of a table, drinking and chatting. Aleida hovered near by. When Che's flight was called, Aleida, wearing a spotted print dress, clung to him amidst a crowd of reporters, her hair scrunched and her smile radiant. He looked proud – as if, for that moment at least, he sensed that he belonged somewhere. As ever, the sensation only dawned just as he was leaving. But now, just a few months after Fidel's own foreign trip, Che was to be the official face of the Cuban revolution abroad.

Travel had always liberated Che's mind, and the thoughts he had been gestating since January appeared now to find release. Wherever they went, he pressed national leaders on what they were doing about agrarian reform – clearly that was on his mind. But so too was his role as one who was now in a position to devise and implement such policies. As his plane lifted out of Havana Che was embarking on the great odyssey he had always wanted: a three-month trip that would take in the most important members of what would soon be designated the non-aligned countries, and, to Che's mind, some of the more exotic places on earth: Cairo, Delhi, Jakarta, Tokyo, Beijing, Colombo, Rabat. During this trip he seems to have come to terms with his position and his responsibilities and, as Castro had done, to have reached an important decision. 'I am the same old loner trying to find his way,' he wrote in a letter to his mother . . . but I now have a sense of my historical duty. I have neither home, nor wife, nor children, nor parents, nor brothers. My friends are friends as long as they think politically as I do – and yet I am happy.' Within just their first few months in power both men had set out the ways in which they would proceed for the rest of their lives.

Che dated this letter 'approximately July 2', as if time did not matter, and the use of the word 'happy' was curiously vague. Perhaps he was just tired with the routine and out of sorts because of jet-lag. 'Take it for what it is,' he said, 'a letter written on a stormy night, above the skies of India, far from my homelands and my loved ones.' But there is enough of the yearning tone of his earlier letters to warrant a second look. 'My dream of visiting all these countries has come true in such a way as to thwart all my happiness,' he goes on in a rather more melancholy frame of mind. 'Instead, I talk of economic and political problems; throw parties where the only thing lacking for me is to put on a penguin suit, and I forsake untainted pleasures like dreaming in the shade of a pyramid or over the tomb of Tutankhamun.' This was a curious message from a thirty-year-old man who, to most observers, would appear to have the world at his feet. No less curious was his signature: Ernesto. He took a delight bordering on the vain in his most recent nickname, Che: he signed official documents with a flourish, his hand leaving the page before the word was quite formed on the page. To have reverted to Ernesto was a clear signal of how he wished his letter to be read: as one written from a stormy present, far from the past.

During his trip Che tried his best to put on another identity, that of the diplomat. He flew in, shook hands, picked politely at the buffets laid on for him and toured the sites of interest: Agra and the Red Fort, the Suez Canal, the snows of Fuji-san. He posed for photographs (though he was far more interested in taking his own) and declared his meetings 'satisfactory', expressing his 'hopes' for diplomatic relations, whatever his privately voiced comments as to some of the antics and habits of the world's political elite. It must have been a strange trip in many ways; his first opportunity to stop and to gather his thoughts after three years of living on the edge. It afforded him also the chance to meet or to get very close to some of his greatest heroes, and yet he did so almost as someone else.

As countless anecdotes reveal, this diplomatic life was not for him, and not just because of the sort of reception he was given by the Yugoslavs in Zagreb, who were apparently far from impressed by his 'beatnik' appearance. He had awaited the meeting with Nehru nervously, allowing himself the quip, as he dressed in his finest, that he was at least sufficiently well attired to dine with the Prime Minister of the poorest country in the world. Sitting between the Indian leader and his daughter Indira, playing first lady, Che smiled and did his best to stand on ceremony, fussing with the food and the formal conversation. When he finally asked Nehru what he thought of communist China, his question fell on deaf ears: 'I am pleased that you have liked the apples' was the response from the man whom, as a youth, he had idolised as a fighter and man of conviction. At another point Che upbraided the Egyptian President on his insufficiently radical land reform, and by way of reply Nasser confided that he was surprised at the vehemence of Guevara's anti-American 'grudge'. When Che pushed his point, Nasser retorted that he was 'liquidating the privileges of a class but not the individuals of that class'. Che was out of his depth with a statesman of Nasser's standing, but he did at least pick up something of the art of dissimulation that Fidel excelled in: when asked in Sri Lanka whether Castro was a communist he replied that Castro would say no, but Eisenhower would say yes.

All these disappointments were of a sort that he seemed to have been encountering since the end of the war, as if nothing from now on could capture the intensity of those days and as if even his once greatest ambitions proved underwhelming when finally realised. He returned from his trip ready to throw all his energies at the revolution once more, but unsettled within himself about the course his life should now take. His letter to his mother had been just like those of old: adamant in its pronouncement of his new-found conviction, but utterly devoid of any sense of where that conviction should take him.

Fidel, meanwhile, had kept a close eye on Che's trip, phoning him and on not a few occasions asking Che to let Aleida join him. Che stubbornly refused. The secret aspect of his mission – to establish a dialogue with the Soviets – was now in full swing and he wanted nothing to jeopardise it. Che's tour was in fact yet another example of the artful collaboration between the two rebel leaders. In preparation for Che's anticipated first meeting with the Soviets, in Egypt, as soon as he had flown out of Havana – doubtless this is what they spoke about at the airport – Fidel had immediately and publicly demanded that the Americans increase their quota of Cuban sugar imports from 3 million tonnes to 8 million. The demand was, of course, immediately rejected by the Americans, but it had given notice that Cuba's sugar was now available for others to buy. Che's meeting with the Soviet commercial attaché in Cairo was crucial to ensuring that the Soviets stepped in where the Americans had bowed out, and it was followed up by various prearranged meetings with Soviet embassy staff dotted across the countries he visited.

During his trip, Che's delegation had been much derided for lacking the requisite diplomatic savoir-faire. The Americans had demanded the 'fullest coverage practicable' from their diplomats in each of the cities Che was to visit, and that was what they got. A typical comment from Rangoon in Burma derided the visitors as 'not inconspicuous (wearing uniforms including caps during tea in hotel lounge)'. But while the snoops in every capital he visited watched his curious appearance closely, they missed the fact that Che had sustained a continual dialogue with the Soviets right under their noses. It was a subtle first step in a tentative dance with the Soviets and it went almost completely unnoticed. Fidel's conspiratorial side would have been enjoying all this. Perhaps it was best that Aleida had not gone after all. Che too was pleased. His diplomatic duties discharged, he treated himself on the return flight to a new Leica and a Minox, having not been able to choose between the two cameras during their three-hour stopover in Hong Kong.

While Che was away Fidel had finally spent some time with the American ambassador, Philip Bonsal, at a dinner hosted by Fidel's new Foreign Minister, Raúl Roa and his wife. After dinner the men set about talking politics. Bonsal told Castro about some of the anti-American statements Che had been making on his trip. Fidel was not amused, but not because he disagreed with Che – it was more likely that he was beginning strongly to dislike being told what to do, above all by the American ambassador. Fidel suggested that Che was just young and exuberant. Bonsal was not unaware of this, and despite the way he was increasingly sidelined in Havana – not to mention the fact that Che's staunch anti-Americanism kept him from ever making a courtesy call – he was close enough to observe that Che was one of the few who stood independently around Fidel.

But what was really revealing itself in that first year of the revolution was a partnership based upon substantively different approaches to work, mutually supporting talents and a common commitment to completing tasks together. The last of these demonstrated the effect of each upon the other, for Che had formerly been incapable of completing anything, while Fidel, in turn, had rarely been prepared to start a dialogue that he did not intend to control throughout. In power, their differences had thus become rather complementary. Out front it was Fidel who led the people. But behind the scenes it was Che who helped shape them in such a way that they were prepared to be led and were ready to jump whichever way Fidel pointed. Fidel's acclaimed dialogues with the masses included Che as the silent orator of the dress rehearsal. Bonsal was one of those beginning to notice this.

* * *

By December 1959, the second step of Cuba's shift from American to Soviet patronage was well under way. With it had come Fidel's own shift to the left. When Che arrived back in Havana, he was both surprised and pleased at the speed of change while he had been gone. His debriefing at the Foreign Ministry was with one of the new faces, Raúl Roa, and with the changes in key positions that Fidel had effected over the summer it had become clear that a more radical pull was being exerted on the course of the revolution.

While Che was away – as always, the absence of his more dogmatic friend gave Fidel greater freedom of movement – Fidel had dealt head on with the growing political rivalries that had carried over from the Sierra and simmered away ever since and which had come to the boil with the formation of INRA and the launching of the agrarian reform law. The moderates saw it as going too far, and the radical left, the communists of the PSP, were outraged that they had been a part of neither its design nor its execution. Though he had legalised the Communist party (partly as a result of Che's and Raúl's insistence) Fidel had otherwise blown hot and cold over the communists since January. At that point, it had seemed to everyone that Fidel felt he was best allied to his own loyal rebels who had proved their worth during the war. He had then gone so far as to declare the communists heathen, leading PSP secretary-general Blas Roca to warn the party at its May Plenum, 'We are now in a critical moment for the revolution.' At that point the communists even feared possible 'excommunication'. But things change quickly in a revolution, and Che had arrived home just in time to witness Fidel turning against some of his own 26 July officers in favour of the more radical groups jockeying for position, above all the PSP.

Huber Matos was one of Fidel's most trusted and high-ranking soldiers. During the war he had flown in arms to the Sierra and stayed on to lead his own column of men. In January, he had been Fidel's first choice for governor of Camaguey province. But in October he resigned his post in protest at the communist influences on Fidel, who had just promoted his communist brother Raúl to head of the armed forces. Fourteen other officers resigned with him. Fidel could not accept what he saw as high treason and sent Camilo to Camaguey to arrest him. In protest, the moderate Felipe Pazos, who had returned from Miami, resigned from the post he had taken up as head of the National Bank, touching off a dispute that split the entire government. Old debates reared their heads again as Faustino Pérez, Enrique Oltuski and Manuel Ray – former representatives of the more bourgeois Llano – also stood up for Matos. They too would soon be removed from their positions in a purging of the right that ripped through the government in the second half of the year.

To make matters worse, while all this was playing out Fidel's former air force captain and personal pilot, Pedro Díaz Lanz, who had gone into exile earlier in the summer, returned to drop anti-Castro propaganda leaflets which fluttered down to warn of the growing communist threat. Matos, whose fate was probably determined by also being a friend of Díaz Lanz, was put on trial in December and sentenced to twenty years. Revolutionary unity would now be policed by the watchword of counter-revolution with which Fidel would whip the crowds into a frenzy, using his vast mandate to weed out much of the bourgeois and liberal elements within the government ranks, and allowing, in turn, the formation of popular militias operating across the country.

Fidel emerged from this initial swamp of disagreement and the more aggressive belligerent tone it effected among the people much stronger. The revolutionary courts were reimposed towards the end of 1959 (Matos narrowly escaping them for a twenty-year prison sentence) and he tightened his grip on the press. Those papers that survived did so by following the government line. Some of Havana's wags now jokingly referred to *Revolución*, one of the official papers of the new government, as 'Bonjour Tristesse' for its negative and aggressive tone.

Far from being the one seeking a middle path between the future represented by Che and that of his own more moderate supporters, Fidel was now the one pushing things forward. By November he had finally managed to get the affable American

ambassador Bonsal to snap. Fidel was seeking to worsen relations, he claimed, finger right on the button. But no sooner had
Bonsal said this than Fidel had Roá his Foreign Minister, jump
on him with an indignant letter accusing Washington of
supporting the counter-revolutionaries. It was rather as if Fidel
had sent out the setters to startle the game into his waiting sights.
Signalling his growing closeness to the PSP, an editorial in the
communist newspaper *Hoy* confirmed that this was no 'adolescent haughtiness' on the government's part. It was merely saying
what needed to be said.

The Matos affair caused Fidel to lose one other of his most
trusted men but one close to Che above all. Returning to Havana
from his mission to Camaguey, Camilo's Cessna disappeared.
Despite a week-long search, in which Che and Fidel took part
personally, no trace of Camilo's plane was ever found.

Che, who of the two had perhaps been closest to Camilo,
seethed with a pent-up frustration he did not yet have a channel
for. The enemy had killed Camilo, he fumed, 'because we have
no safe planes, because our pilots cannot acquire the experience
they need, because, overloaded with work, he wanted to be in
Havana in [just] a few hours. . . .'

But Che himself seemed almost to seek out such levels of work
as he complained beset Camilo. Since his return in the summer,
Fidel had made him minister for all nationalised industries, a
growing portfolio that encompassed an eclectic and not easily
managed mix of businesses and institutions. He was also
appointed the new head of the National Bank, to replace the
recently departed Pazos. 'All this is enough to satisfy my thirst
for adventure,' Che wrote to his parents, 'it's all here; an ideal for
which to fight coupled with the responsibility of setting an example
that doesn't depart from it. We're not men, but work machines,
fighting against time in difficult and brilliant circumstances.'

Between them, as they did all this, Fidel and Che were creating
not just a political but also a personal environment in which
they, but perhaps not too many others, could thrive. Either Fidel

was 'busy with Che Guevara and under no circumstances could he see anyone until later', or he was listening intently to what he said. A little later in the year Fidel had a meeting in Havana with President Sukarno of Indonesia. Sukarno was telling Fidel of the inextricable link between Cuba and the United States when Che entered, noticed Fidel 'nervously chewing his beard', and asked for an explanation. When told what Sukarno had said, Che sarcastically remarked, 'It appears we have nothing more to do with this man since it is evident he is also a "latifundista" [landowner].' With little further ado, the Indonesian leader's visit was cut short.

An old Argentine friend of Che's, Gustavo Roco, recalled that during a visit to Cuba in 1959 he looked for Che but failed to find him; then Che and Fidel turned up at his hotel room late at night. 'They stayed until nine in the morning, questioning me about Argentina. Specifically, they were speculating about the pro-Cuban neutrality of Mexico and the anti-Cuban neutrality of Argentina.' His account captures the nature of the life they lived. It was the guerrilla way to keep the hours that the job demanded; to govern as if they were indeed still at war. Already, the revolution was self-selecting and it was not only to do with ideology. Either you were passionate, and could make the meeting on fish stocks at four in the morning, or you were out.

* * *

Fidel, meanwhile, continued to try to draw in the Soviets by pushing an aggressive line with the Americans. By the autumn he certainly had their attention, but because of his more committed record it was Che whom the Soviets chose to approach first. They did so via a young KGB agent named Alexandr Alexiev who was sent to Cuba under cover of being a correspondent for the Soviet news agency TASS. It was a reminder of Che's continued worth to him, then, when Fidel received a personal note from

Che informing him he had just had a meeting with a Soviet 'TASS correspondent' who had some interesting things to say. Fidel must have been ecstatic, just as he had been during the war on hearing that Che had reached the Escambray; now Che seemed to have found a way to reach this other, much greater shore.

At the end of January 1960, after weeks of careful and secretive negotiations, a Soviet trade fair that had been touring the United States and Mexico descended upon Havana. After meeting with Alexiev himself, Fidel had agreed that this would be the best first step to take towards establishing diplomatic relations between Cuba and the Soviet Union. The fair was both a highly incongruous sight and a big hit, though more for the replica of Sputnik, the Soviet spacecraft – which Fidel had now, in a way, succeeded in bringing down to Cuba from where he had gazed up at it in the sky above the Sierra – than for the show homes and industrial equipment that were its more usual stock in trade. The American correspondent Ruby Hart Philips noted that the Coke and Pepsi machines had attracted perhaps the most interest of all. And the fair also, of course, provided the pretext for a series of behind-the-scenes meetings between the two governments. Fidel and Che both led the meetings with Soviet Deputy Premier Anastas Mikoyan who was, as had been planned, accompanying the fair.

Meanwhile, Che kept up his work at the National Bank, the informal clothes he insisted on wearing deceptive as to the nature of his work ethic. He arrived mid-morning and left in the early hours of the following day. Che had become renowned for his boldness, recklessness even, during the war, and he would prove no less so as a minister.

Above all, Che – who would never be much of a bank manager – insisted that political considerations came before economics. One can, as his biographer Jorge Castañeda does, read the severity (if not the initiative) of the issues that would soon see Cuba arc towards the Soviets as due, at least in part, to Che's unwillingness to compromise on such things under his control as the sugar quota, arms deals, the expropriation of American assets and his insistence that Western oil companies refine the Soviet oil that now began to arive at Cuba's ports. By such means he wielded the Cuban economy as his stick for beating Fidel towards a more radical path.

The following month, the Americans made one last overture to Fidel to supply him with limited arms. But, confident now of the Soviets' likely support in the event of an outright break with Washington, Fidel rejected their offer. Not long afterwards, Fidel gave his second May Day speech before the assembled masses. It was a hot day, the militias marched, the crowd chanted, and his lengthy oratory, going round in circles as ever, touched down again and again on the spectre of threats from abroad before finally he announced that on 8 May diplomatic relations with Moscow would be established.

If the beginning of the Soviets' 'warm organic' embrace was marked in an unofficial way by Mikoyan's visit and the extension of credits and agreements to purchase some of Cuba's sugar, then the moment of the Americans' departure was perhaps also encapsulated by the explosion of the French freighter *La Coubre*, which ripped through Havana harbour in March. The cause of the explosion of the ship supplying Belgian arms to Cuba was never determined but Fidel was convinced the CIA were behind it. With this, and the arrival of the first Soviet oil in the bowels of the *Andrey Vishinsky* and as US warplanes throttled past the city on demonstrative sorties, Fidel might have felt justly pleased, however, that his revolution was getting the sort of recognition he thought it deserved.

The French philosophers Jean-Paul Sartre and Simone de Beauvoir, who were visiting the country to experience the revolution, certainly thought so. Observing the international stand-off, they stood in awe. '"It's the honeymoon of the revolution," Sartre said to me [de Beauvoir]. No machinery, no bureaucracy, but a direct contact between leaders and people, and a mass of seething and slightly confused hopes. It wouldn't last forever but it was a comforting sight. For the first time in our lives we were witnessing happiness that had been attained by violence.'

Speaking just a few days after the taking of that most extraordinary photograph of him, with hair billowing against a grey sky and eyes set to the distance, Che addressed the nation on television in a more belligerent tone as if to give substance to de Beauvoir's words. 'To conquer something,' he said, speaking of the fact that redistribution and equalisation came at a cost, 'we have to take it from someone.' And in doing that, he added, '[i]t is just as well to speak clearly [about this] instead of hiding behind concepts that can be misinterpreted'.

Here was the by now usual coded warning from Che that would soon be followed up by action from Fidel. But Che was also laying down the gauntlet to those who were content simply to stand and wait. Che's ultimate view of intellectuals such as Sartre and de Beauvoir was the same one that he conveyed to a group of journalists who came to take photos of him doing voluntary labour one day. Were they here to work, he asked them, because if so they should hang up their cameras and get on with it. In case anyone had missed the point, the revolution would be toughening up from here on. At the end of the day, words were simply not enough.

But Che knew that words have their uses in revolution too, and he also spent much time hunched over his writing desk churning out a constant stream of articles: treatises on the problems of trade in primary products, an excoriation of Harry Truman, a critique of the infringement of national sovereignty by American U-2 spy plane over-flights – many of these published in the column he began writing that April in the magazine *Verde Olivo*. Che always wrote with a wider audience in mind. Occasionally jocular, but invariably combative, his writing had but one aim: to reveal the bigger picture to those who might grasp at its features but not know what to call it. It lacked the sharpness of Fidel's insights and Fidel's ability to simplify issues, but it did all the work needed to round out what Fidel proposed. And above all it contained the same unbending rigidity of purpose, the same derision of any shade of grey that was driving them both onwards with unrelenting conviction. The future towards which it was driving them was not yet clearly defined, but they were feeling their way by the same instinct and that, for now, was enough.

By July, Soviet personnel had begun to filter into Cuba and there was an atmosphere of defiant tension. Revolutionary chants and slogans filled the air. Gone were most of the holidaymakers and the late night revellers and in their place were arm-banded militias. Relations with the United States went into terminal decline amid an increasingly bitter tit-for-tat of recriminations. 'I just hope to Christ the United States doesn't cut the sugar quota,' Ernest Hemingway said at the time. 'That would really tear it. It will make Cuba a gift to the Russians.' Indeed such an action, Fidel had already warned, would cost the Americans 'down to the nails in their shoes'. This was not bluster. In an ingenious move Fidel had fixed the system of compensation payments for expropriated American land to income generated from the continued US sugar quota, so that he would in fact be paying Americans with American money.

But President Eisenhower would not be cowed by an upstart like Fidel. That July, Congress responded to the wave of nationalisations that Fidel had unleashed in June by ordering Cuba's sugar quota to be cut. It was just as Hemingway had feared and the value of Che's trip from the previous year, and the secret conversations with Mikoyan, now became clear as on 20 July Khrushchev, the Soviet leader, immediately stepped in to buy up the remaining 700,000 tonnes of the US quota for that year.

After a long year and a half of growing recriminations, Cuba had now finally switched allegiance to the Soviets in all but name. At different points along the way Fidel and Che had been the driving force behind this move, the final achievement being conceivable really only as a result of their mutual efforts. In so doing, however, they had set a new course for Cuba, one that would lead ultimately to the dramatic showdown of the missile crisis and, in its wake, to a showdown between themselves.

10. REVOLUTIONARY ANATOMY

HAVANA WAS ALIGHT that summer of 1960, and not just because of the international stand-off. For once, the rumours that Fidel was seriously ill – there had already been several health scares – were true. By the end of July his body had finally succumbed to the punishing routine to which he subjected himself (though if the reports of his having been brought home at times 'roaring drunk' were accurate, that wouldn't have helped). His personal physician begged the public to allow him the 'absolute physical and mental rest' he needed and Fidel withdrew to his hilltop villa at Cojímar, scene of Hemingway's novel *The Old Man and the Sea*. Earlier it had been suggested that Fidel should go to a top clinic in Boston or Moscow, but Fidel himself ruled that out 'for obvious political reasons'. Cojímar would have to do.

Fidel's 'uncertain illness' was not the 'malignant condition' that some within the US administration had hoped for but an early manifestation of the bowel trouble that would ultimately see him retire from active politics many decades later. It was certainly not, as the more hysterical reports had it, that he had been brainwashed under psychiatric treatment at the hands of the communists who, so it was said, were plying him with 'sedatives and drugs'. Far from losing his marbles, Fidel was intent upon not showing any weakness at all at what was a critical stage of the revolution.

With Che's assistance, if not partly as a result of his direct lobbying, Fidel had by that summer managed a complete radicalisation of what had begun as a bourgeois liberal revolution. One of the last things the two of them had done together before Fidel fell ill was to draft the so-called 'machete law' which, in retaliation at the recent American reduction in the all-important Cuban sugar quota, expropriated almost all remaining US property. They had worked on it together for three days and nights at Fidel's office in the vast INRA building. Between them they had also managed that year to drive the last of the remaining moderates from their positions of authority: Rufo López-Fresquet, the Finance Minister who had accompanied Fidel on his first trip to the Unites States, resigned in March, Marcelo Fernández and Enrique Oltuski left their posts in July, and Raúl Chibás joined the growing flood of those leaving for Miami before the summer was out, fleeing with his family in a motorboat from the 'Red indoctrination' he saw everywhere.

To the Americans it all looked rather too much as though the two principal architects of the revolution were being allowed to get their wicked way. *Time* magazine played up Che's role especially, running him as its cover story and declaring him 'Castro's brain' (Raúl was sketched as Castro's 'fist', while Fidel himself was the 'heart' of the revolution). *Time* also declared Che one of the principal 'reds' exerting a malignant influence on Castro. To emphasise the point, on the cover they set images of 'Mr K' [Khrushchev] and Mao into a red wash behind Che's portrait.

The Americans had never cared much for Che, given his communist sympathies, but they were reluctant to lose Fidel to the other side too. They would have been particularly piqued to learn, then, and 'from excellent sources close to Fidel Castro' (in fact, the information was conveyed via Raúl Roa's sister-in-law, who had had enough by now and was herself leaving for America with her husband), that Fidel was 'perfectly delighted with the course of events'. And as regards the severity of the sugar quota cut in particular, Eisenhower was informed that Fidel was 'doubly pleased'. The American sugar quota provided Cuba with a guaranteed sale of a large proportion of its annual sugar crop. Any change to the basic quota would make the Americans extremely unpopular. 'Castro thought that it would be limited only to the distribution of the deficit. The fact that it cut deep into the basic quota meant that he could charge economic aggression all the more effectively.'

In late August Eisenhower gave Fidel further pretext to radicalise the revolution. At that month's meeting of the Organisation of American States in San José, a declaration was signed that condemned 'energetically' the 'intervention or the threat of inter-vention, even when conditional, by an extra-continental power in the affairs of the American republics'. The Mexicans, who wanted to maintain relations with both countries, stated for the record that the America-led initiative was not directed at Cuba, but everyone knew that really it was. The Cuban Foreign Minister, Raúl Roa, certainly thought so and he stormed out even before the vote was taken, saying, with not a little diplomatic chutzpah, 'I am going and with me go the people of Latin America.'

Fidel himself voiced the official Cuban response within the week. He called for as large a crowd as possible to assemble in the *Plaza de la Revolución*. It was a hot afternoon; one of those days when everything seemed to stand still. Che himself almost missed the proceedings, however, and had to rush across the city after transport had been shut down with his bodyguards trailing, desperately worried that he might be swallowed up in the throng. But Che knew that this would be a performance worth catching.

After he had spoken of the country's treatment at the hands of its enemies, Fidel produced a copy of the Mutual Aid Treaty of 1952, signed by Presidents Truman and Prío. 'Let those here who believe the treaty should be annulled right now raise their hands,' he ordered. The crowd cheered, at which Fidel tore the document clean down the middle: 'We shall save it for history, torn as it is.' It was a wonderful act of theatre. The crowd were ecstatic. Then he went on to read from his own declaration, what would become known as the Declaration of Havana. In the face of the shifts and changes of that summer it was to be Fidel's anchoring point, his affirmation that 'the people of Cuba have acted with free and absolute self-determination' and that they were not acting at the behest of the Soviet Union or of China. They merely welcomed such support as was on offer.

Fidel went on to launch a virulent attack on the Yankee aggressor to the north, decrying everything from racist bigotry to the execution of the Rosenbergs for spying for the Soviets and citing Martí on the slow-drip 'poison of the loans, the canals, the railroads', by which means foreign capital dripped into the veins of prostrate countries as if it was the harbinger of death itself. His speech climaxed with a call to duty and revolutionary arms that would ring in people's ears for days:

> The duty of peasants, workers, intellectuals, Negroes, Indians, young and old, and women, [is] to fight for their economic, political and social claims; the duty of oppressed and exploited nations [is] to fight for their liberation; the duty of each nation [is] to make common cause with all the oppressed, colonised, exploited or attacked peoples, regardless of their location in the world or the geographical distance that may separate them. All the peoples of the world are brothers!

This was not just affirmation of his new revolutionary platform, however. It was also 'a speech within a speech', a nod of future intent to the communists around him to indicate that he was ready. Afterwards, once the crowds had dispersed and the revolutionary leadership could begin to digest the significance of the speech, Aníbal Escalante and Carlos Rafael Rodríguez, two of the principal leaders of the PSP, harped gleefully to Alexiev, the KGB man, of their growing influence on Fidel and of their confidence that the revolution would soon be taking a more overtly communist direction. Escalante was particularly excited. He was an ambitious man with plans for wielding his own power in Cuba. An arch-Machiavellian by nature, and therefore not unlike Fidel, Escalante was a hard-line communist who knew better than either

Fidel or Che how to play the communist party game that they were inviting upon themselves. Before long Escalante's designs on power would threaten to come between the two comandantes. For now, though, it was clear that they were set fair upon moving the revolution towards the Soviet camp as fast as possible.

* * *

Shortly after making his most defiant revolutionary call to arms yet, Fidel touched down at New York's Idlewild airport for the twenty-fifth meeting of the United Nations General Assembly. Among his papers was the recently torn treaty that he had brought along for effect. 'More key world figures than ever before assembled,' intoned Ed Herlihy's monotone voice on Universal–International News. But it was the arrival of the many 'red satellite chieftains' that was of most interest to the American public. Now classed as one of them, Fidel was attuned to both the dangers and the possibilities of his trip. Perhaps this explains his surprisingly nervy arrival speech on the steps of his DC-10. His brow was visibly furrowed as he cursed at his own unsteady English and he cut his comments surprisingly short. This shaky start notwithstanding, Fidel had arrived in a spirited mood. Though he suspected that there were plans to assassinate him, he was confident too that the Americans would not risk trying to achieve this on home soil. All the same, the situation was 'red hot', as one of his entourage put it.

Fidel's party were staying in the upmarket Hotel Shelburne just off Park Avenue. There, the usual chaotic scenes of the Cuban roadshow unfolded: 'the place where the Cuban delegation arrived, was where the greatest disorder I have ever seen would be installed', Carlos Rafael Rodríguez observed after having made many such trips with Fidel. 'We could even bring disorder to the Palace of Versailles.' None of this – the cigar ash on the floor, the hammocks strung up between bedposts, the endless queues, the chattering and the late-night convocations – were to the tastes of the hotel manager. And he let his displeasure be known to any newsman who cared to listen.

Furious with the way he felt they were being treated, Fidel paid a visit to UN Secretary-General Dag Hammarskjöld to protest before storming out of the Shelburne and relocating his entire delegation across town in the run-down Hotel Theresa in Harlem: 'I will be honoured to lunch with the poor, humble people of Harlem,' Fidel said in his soft-spoken way. 'I belong to the poor, humble people.' The action was a media sensation. Together with Khrushchev's later antics – this was the year of the famous shoe-banging incident – it would ensure that this year's Assembly was the biggest ruckus in United Nations history.

Run down though the Hotel Theresa had begun to look (the neon sign outside read 'HOTEL THE—'), it throbbed with an energy all of its own. Malcolm X, Duke Ellington and Joe Louis had all stayed here, and though it might resemble 'something of a bordello', as one of his own delegates put it, Fidel was enamoured of the place immediately. He treated the eleven-storey hotel's black workers to dinner and was only too happy to receive, among many other well-wishers who came to see him, the springy-haired radical 'beat' poet Alan Ginsberg.

For the next few days, chants of solidarity with Fidel and the recently murdered African independence leader Patrice Lumumba could be heard coming from the crowd outside. They were ecstatic when the Soviet Premier himself paid an eager and what looked like spontaneous visit to Fidel. By some measure the taller man, Fidel squashed Khrushchev's face right up against his chest in an enthusiastic and soon famous bear hug.

If Fidel grasped the Soviet leader with a little too much enthusiasm, it was because he had been waiting for the moment for some weeks. 'It will be the first time that I attend such an Assembly,' he had confessed to Khrushchev via the new Soviet ambassador, Sergei Kudriatsev, a few weeks earlier in a private meeting, 'and I do not know yet which way to carry myself. That's why Khrushchev's advice will be very useful for me. I would like to know how I can meet with Khrushchev in a situation where there would be a possibility to discuss all Cuban issues. It is not absolutely clear to me personally', continued a rather novice-sounding Fidel, 'where such contacts among heads of delegations and delegations themselves are conducted.' Stepping back into character somewhat more, he then went on to describe how the speech he was preparing would draw attention to the limitations of movement that the US authorities were imposing on them both. 'These actions will turn against the Americans,' he promised Khrushchev.

When Fidel returned Khrushchev's visit in New York by dropping by at the Soviet embassy, he managed, for all that he was eager to please, to keep his host waiting for half an hour. He apologised profusely on arrival, but Khrushchev was unperturbed: 'Don't worry about it,' he reassured Fidel. 'Protocol has no importance.' In fraternal greeting, the Soviets then plied the Cubans with three-pepper vodka. Fearful of so much alcohol, though he was a solid enough drinker when need be, Fidel parried with Cuban cigars whose rich, velvety smoke soon turned the Soviets pale. Undetered by the required tastes of their respective cultures, the two delegations joked and drank toasts. It was the highlight of the trip for both leaders.

Not long after his arrival in New York the authorities had seized Fidel's plane at Idlewild airport in recompense for his expropriation of American property in Cuba earlier in the year. As Fidel boarded a Soviet Ilyushin 18 that Khrushchev had lent him to get the Cuban delegation home, he pitched one last riposte to his reluctant American hosts, the complexities of what was now happening summed up in one simple phrase. 'Here you took our planes,' he said in faltering but passable English before sweeping up the steps. 'Soviets give us planes.'

* * *

While Fidel had spent the summer recuperating at his villa in Cojímar and preparing for his visit to the United Nations, Che had been cracking on at his usual pace with his own projects. The two men had now settled into a routine of harmonious co-operation, one upon which Che modelled his whole view of working relations. Such relations, 'cordial, harmonious, [and based on] mutual cooperation', ought to be at the heart of all revolutionary workplaces, he would later urge.

Che and Aleida had moved house again that summer, this time to the well-to-do district of Miramar, with its svelte lawns and tree-lined roads off the long central boulevard that cut through this part of town. It meant he was no longer so near Fidel's head-quarters in Vedado – not that Fidel was there much anyway. Both before and after his illness, life for Fidel was a constant blur. But for Che at least things had begun to settle down, and one or two figures from his former life had reappeared. Most prominent was Alberto Granado, the incorrigible sidekick who had accompanied him on his first trek around Latin America, and who had turned up at the National Bank one day in July to see how 'Fuser' was getting on.

But it was Fidel's return from New York that would signal the opening of the next phase of the revolution for Che. Fidel had arrived back in Havana pleased with the personal bond he had established with Khrushchev, and immediately wanted to extend it. He continued to view Che as his most dependable comrade, and it seemed natural to entrust him with the task of developing relations with the Soviets so he asked Che to go to Moscow for the anniversary of the Bolshevik revolution. On behalf of Fidel, Che was to take a petition that set out what the Cubans hoped for in substantive agreements with the socialist camp. Fidel himself had not been able to prise any firm financial commitments from the Soviets in New York, and was hopeful that Che might be able to do a little better.

Che flew into Moscow on 22 October. He had travelled in his capacity as a minister, but was welcomed very much as a hero. Cuba was a beacon for world socialism, he was told. A perform-ance at the Bolshoi was laid on for him, and he was treated to a tour of the Moscow subway and visits to factories. The high-light of all this hospitality came when he was asked to stand atop Lenin's Mausoleum as Khrushchev's honoured guest. This was the realisation of a long-standing dream for Che, and while many other socialist leaders were present – Ho Chi Minh, Gomulka, Novotny – they were all somewhat displaced by Che during the thundering military parade across Red Square. In pride of place next to Khrushchev, Che gazed across the great space with a 'satisfied, radiant, happy' look.

Khrushchev was pleased too, knowing that he had beside him the second most important figure in the revolution. Raúl Castro and Antonio Núñez Jiménez had both made behind-the-scenes trips over the summer, but had received no such honours. Rumour even had it that Che and Raúl had had a big row before Che left, perhaps about Fidel's sending Che rather than his own brother. But Khrushchev was simply intrigued to know more about this Cuban of Argentine origin.

He kept Che permanently by his side at a feast laid on that night in the Kremlin. Bowls of fruit and delicacies adorned the tables, while copious amounts of Georgian champagne were served to the throng of military men in their carefully pressed uniforms studded with ribbons and stars. Standing alongside them were writers and figures of note in Soviet society. As the night wore on 'and the champagne took effect', recalled one of the Cuban press delegation, Khrushchev ordered a microphone to be brought to him. Then he began a never-ending series of toasts, downing his glass in one gulp only to have it refilled by a scrupulously attentive waiter. Among Khrushchev's first toasts was one to Fidel and to the 'brave and glorious' Comandante Guevara at his side. Che, when he later responded, managed what was more goad than heartfelt thanks, praising the value of the 'invisible armour' that the Soviet Union offered Cuba. The Soviets, of course, had not yet done more than merely promise support. The older members of the Soviet leadership, such as Khrushchev and Mikoyan, still looked at Cuba's track towards socialism with a fond nostalgia for their own revolutionary days but with little sense of urgency. They did not realise quite how serious a matter it was for the Cubans, who now felt under constant threat from the Americans.

The only other Cuban allowed access to the inner sanctum around the Soviet leader was PSP representative Aníbal Escalante. He was Moscow's ear to the ground in Havana, and his task was to introduce Che to what one of the delegation aptly described as the 'thick world of Russian officialdom'. Escalante seemed almost to feel more at home in the tight-lipped world of intrigue that Moscow offered than in Havana. For once Che too seemed to be at ease with all the hospitality that was being laid on. But when an orchestra started up with the popular song 'Moscow Nights', and everyone, Khrushchev included, started to dance, Che decided he had had enough and began inclining his head towards the door. On the way out, as he and his entourage waited to catch an ancient-looking elevator, a guard motioned to them that they were not allowed. 'This is only for members of the Comintern,' Escalante quickly explained. Che shot back an ironic look. 'Yes, already I see there are as many privileges here as in capitalist countries.' And with that, rather as Fidel had done in New York, he took the stairs.

Fidel was well informed about the positive reception Che had received in Moscow. Perhaps it was to make sure that his comrade did not steal *all* the limelight, therefore, that later that same night, after attending the equivalent anniversary celebration at the Soviet embassy in one of the leafy suburbs of Havana, Fidel headed back across town to the offices of the communist newspaper *Hoy*. To an audience that consisted of little more than the night shift – a few journalists and the typesetters whom Fidel knew would none the less spread word of what he was saying back to Moscow quicker than any official despatch – Fidel declared that he had been a Marxist since his student days. Once he had warmed to his theme – how he used to visit the small Marxist library on Carlos III Street, his longstanding connections with communists such as Alfredo Guevara – Fidel's 'impromptu' speech did not finish until nine in the morning. For all the modesty of the surroundings in which it was delivered it was a monumental statement and, just as Fidel had predicted, its content was immediately transmitted to the leadership in Moscow.

This rather stunning news was met with some trepidation there. 'We were uneasy because it put more pressure on the Soviet Union,' Khrushchev's son Sergei recalled. But this was precisely what Fidel intended, and with Che's delegation then heading on via North Korea to the other *madre patria* of world socialism, China, Khrushchev was afforded a reminder of just why he might want to usher in Fidel under Moscow's wing. The tensions that would soon erupt into the Sino–Soviet conflict were already becoming apparent. Nikolai Leonov, Che's old friend from Moscow and now working for the KGB as the Cubans' translator on this important state visit, was prevented by the Chinese from accompanying Che any further than North Korea.

Perhaps almost as much as he had wanted to visit Moscow, Che had long harboured a desire to meet the great Mao; he may have hoped to share with him some of his anecdotes of the war and to tell him how Mao's own writings had inspired him. So it would have been all the more disappointing to him that his asthma, which clung to him throughout the trip, hit him particularly hard the day the two men met. His travelling companions recall him getting up at least three or four times during the night, clambering to the bathroom and locking himself in with his inhaler until the worst of the attack passed and he could return to bed.

Whatever his physical state, Che encountered considerable good-will towards the Cubans from Mao and his government. As far as the Chinese were concerned, the Cuban revolution proved the validity of their doctrine of armed insurrection over Khrushchev's mantra of peaceful coexistence and Che returned with a $60 million loan. It didn't need to be repaid, Prime Minister Chou En-lai assured him. Che was more impressed with China than he had been with the Soviet Union. 'Truly, China is one of those countries where you realise that the Cuban revolution is not a unique event,' he declared on his return. With his habitual disregard for protocol, not to mention his characteristic tactlessness, he had even commented that Mao's China was more revolutionary. 'That did not exactly do him any favours,' recalled Sergei Khrushchev.

While in China Che heard that Aleida had given birth to his second daughter, this one named, as had been his first with Hilda, after her mother: Aleidita. He took no time off on his return to enjoy the moment, however, but immediately conveyed his thoughts on his trip in a lengthy television appearance. He spoke as if he were the island's correspondent bringing back news from some distant place. The Cuban people were connected to that place, he told them, relaying with some pride the agreements he had secured. This would involve some hardship, of course, but then he went on to say that what would make it all worth while was the 'humanitarian spirit' these countries had themselves shown in going out of their way to support Cuba in the absence of any real economic incentive for so doing. This was where the future lay: 'with countries who fight for world peace and justice distributed amongst all'.

It was true that Che was swayed by the sense of a community of nations that the countries he had visited had been at pains to show him. But he had also caught a glimpse of much that he did not like and, away from the rhetoric of the public stage, had issued Fidel with a private warning. Unimpressed by the luxury and division, as well as the bureaucracy and the dogma of technological determinism that he had seen, he told him, 'The construction of socialism in Cuba has to avoid this mechanicism [sic] like the plague.' Ever more sanguine than his idealistic friend, Fidel chose to ignore this advice for the time being. He had become convinced that there was much he could learn from the Soviets, particularly with regard to fighting off the constant threat of attack from abroad and counter-revolutionary dissent at home. As Fidel saw it, the Soviets could help him to consolidate his position. This difference between what the two men saw when they looked at the Soviet Union was entirely logical within the frame of their characters. But it was one whose effects would, in time, prove deleterious to both and to their own plans in Cuba.

At the start of 1961, just a few weeks after Che's return, Cuba was, in many respects, well on the way towards that future. Russian technicians, those 'droves of pink-faced, fair-haired burly young men', as one correspondent put it, had begun arriving with their families. Their Spanish was even worse than that of the Americans, who had now all but left, and their customs and dress were a source of endless fascination for the Cubans. And of course, they were but the more visible side of a series of changes now afoot in Cuban society.

A quieter, but for Fidel and Che more dangerous development was also at work however. Before Che had returned from his trip the PSP, and Aníbal Escalante in particular, had used Fidel's desire to foster much closer relations with the Soviets to obtain a greater influence with Fidel, as indeed they had predicted they would over the summer. And in Che's absence, Escalante had in particular been encouraging Fidel to deal far more forcefully with the counter-revolutionaries whose groups still roamed the countryside. He had also overseen the formation of the Committees for the Defence of the Revolution, one of the more notorious elements of the Cuban regime, whose presence in every neighbourhood soon gave the government eyes and ears on everything. Worried at this time by the counter-revolutionary bands operating in the Escambray region in particular, Fidel was evidently swayed by such measures. 'Only the old communists and the Soviets know anything about communism,' Fidel said in a private conversation with Carlos Franqui, the editor of *Revolución* before the end of the year. 'We must be patient and learn from them.'

* * *

On New Year's Eve the US chargé d'affaires, Daniel Braddock, attended the annual reception for the diplomatic corps and foreign dignitaries in Havana. He did so with considerable reluctance. He was only going, he cabled back to Washington, 'lest absence [of] US representatives give[s] colour to charges of "imminent Yankee aggression"'. He need not have worried, for the Cubans were no longer very interested in diplomacy with the Americans. Tellingly, neither Fidel nor Che was present. Fidel had been spending his time with a Soviet youth delegation, accompanying them on visits to farms and to a gathering of some ten thousand in his home town of Mayarí. When they asked if he was going to visit the Soviet Union Fidel replied that he would love to, 'but not with an official visit,' he said, 'just without receptions and meetings. That would be great.' Above all, he hoped to go hunting, with just a rifle and some friends. 'Is it possible to hunt?'

The final straw for the Americans came, just two days after the reception that Braddock had reluctantly attended, on the anniversary of the victory of Cuba's own revolution. This year, in true Soviet style, Fidel presided over a vast crowd and mobilisation of the armaments that had by then finally come Cuba's way, no doubt thanks to Che's goading in Moscow. In his speech Fidel demanded that the Americans withdraw all their embassy staff down to the last eleven – the same number Cuba had in Washington. Eisenhower was furious. 'That did it!' he fumed, and diplomatic relations were promptly severed.

Khrushchev was delighted at this latest turn of events. Cuba's 'sincere and disinterested friends' would never abandon her, the TASS news agency crowed. With President Kennedy's inauguration just a few weeks later, on 20 January, two key foreign developments now came together to shape the choices that would confront Fidel and Che over the following years. Kennedy had won the election of the previous year by the smallest of margins and had inherited not only the presidential office but plans, now well advanced, to launch an attack on Castro. As underground attacks increased in Cuba (the exclusive El Encanto department store, where Aleida had picked up her wedding dress, was torched in

April), a troubled year on both sides of the Florida Straits was under way.

* * *

By April Fidel was aware that some sort of US-sponsored attack was imminent. He spent the night of the 14th alert and in his command post: preliminary orders for defence had been given to Che, Raúl and Juan Almeida, who were each charged with guarding different sectors of the country, Che taking the western sector of Havana and Pinar del Río province. News of what would soon turn out to have been diversionary assaults had by then begun to filter in but it was not until the following day that the scale of the invasion became clear.

The previous afternoon Fidel, enraged at the casualties already sustained, took a group of journalists out to an air force base that had been attacked. The walls were pockmarked with bullet holes and the windows had been blown out. 'Inside, one of the offices was a large pool of blood – that of a young militiaman mortally wounded in the attack. Before he died, he had written a single word on the cream-coloured door with his own blood – "Fidel".' The door would later be kept in a private museum for posterity, but a response was prepared immediately.

Fidel had decided the time was right to declare, officially, the socialist nature of the revolution. He had been planning to make a declaration to this effect a couple of weeks later, in his annual May Day speech. But the American attacks had provided an even better pretext. Later that day he gave a speech 'as angry as the sun was hot' at the Colón cemetery, site of his clandestine activities prior to Moncada. As Fidel spoke out he could see Chinese-made Coleman lanterns held aloft by the thousands of workers in the darkness, the people holding them as they sat down on the black asphalt, exhausted by their journey from outlying parts, immobile, and listening to Fidel's voice. Fidel recalled the explosion of the *La Coubre* the year before and the constant attempts by counter-revolutionaries to set fire to the canefields since. Then, thriving as ever on the spontaneity of the moment, he let it out as if inadvertently: 'The imperialists,' he said, 'cannot forgive us for making a socialist revolution in the very nostrils of the United States.' It was now official, and as the invasion began in the early hours of the following day, centred on the swampy beaches around the Bay of Pigs, the soldiers and militia with the task of defending the country would know for certain what it was they were defending.

The invasion, by well over a thousand Cuban exiles and mercenary fighters, lasted three days. Che, who had injured himself when he dropped his own revolver – it fired a bullet that grazed his face – played little role in the affair. He suffered a violent reaction to the anti-tetanus injection and was laid up in a medical centre, where Aleida was despatched to look after him. Their nanny, Sofia, and the baby Aleidita whom Che had nicknamed Aliusha, were then taken to Fidel's headquarters in nearby Vedado, his operations hub under the charge of Celia Sánchez who was busy relaying communications.

Fidel, however, was fully involved in events. Though he crashed out one night next to where Sofia and Aliushá were sleeping, he was alert and involved almost the entire time. He oversaw the strategy of the defence himself and visited the front lines on several occasions. At one point he even commandeered one of his own tanks and ordered it towards the front line to head off an enemy detachment. Clearly he was relishing the chance to take part in the fighting himself. But according to his then bodyguard who travelled in the tank with him, he still fought like a politician: on this occasion he worked inside the tank by flashlight on the speech he would give once they had subdued the attackers.

The attack ended in a resounding victory for Fidel, with several hundred prisoners taken captive. Fidel conducted the interrogations of the men himself. Seeking to maximise the theatre of it all, he did so in public, at Havana's sports stadium, the captured men eventually being released in exchange for $53 million worth of medicines. Then he appeared on television to explain to the people what had happened and why it was they had triumphed.

* * *

The invasion, and their successful defeat of it, left both Fidel and Che with a sense of invincibility and confidence. The Soviet Union was courting them; the Americans had tried, and failed, to oust them. Both men followed up the Bay of Pigs victory with a battery of words. They used every opportunity to keep a running log of all acts of aggression, every loss of life, every achievement, decision or event. Whatever cinema it was that was burned, whichever villager caught in counter-revolutionary actions, all were recorded. In the process the revolution was daily enumerated and disseminated, the experience of it made common to all and the different aspects of its complex machinery overhauled piece by piece.

All this must have been intoxicating for two men only just reaching their mid-thirties, and it was an experience which they could really only share with each other. If one was to select the moment at which they stood closest together then it was perhaps this one, as the crowds cheered and the nation seemed to be marching in step, united in its progress towards a free and independent future.

Yet it was apparent that they now also had somewhat different views of what that future should look like. Certainly both seemed to have taken the Bay of Pigs as marking the end of an era. But for Che it was the consolidation of the revolution, the end of the struggle that had begun with the voyage of the *Granma*. Impatient as ever, he now set out on what he saw as the next phase: putting into place everything that would be necessary to ensure a wholesale transition to a socialist society. For Fidel, on the other hand, it now became imperative to overhaul his entire government and security apparatus. Nothing like what had just happened could be allowed to happen again.

'Castro is not a communist but you can make him one,'

Khrushchev warned Kennedy at their summit meeting in Vienna that summer. But the Bay of Pigs had already pushed Fidel in that direction. The future, as he saw it, lay not with his old and loyal comrades of the Sierra but with the efficiency offered by the PSP, whose power and position he ensured when he merged them with his own 26 July and the third main opposition group to have retained any real identity since the end of the war, the Revolutionary Directorate, to form a new body called the Integrated Revolutionary Organisations or ORI. The new men of influence within this umbrella organisation were the sort of men who would get things done – men like Fabio Grobart, Lazaro Peña, Severo Aguirre, Blas Roca and Aníbal Escalante – which was what he needed right now. What Fidel had not sufficiently counted on, however, was that some of these men were more loyal to Moscow than to himself.

In forming the ORI, Fidel unwittingly sparked off yet another power struggle similar to that which had been waged between the Llano and the Sierra during the war. In many ways, this was inevitable. With his own rather sudden announcement that the revolution was to be a Marxist–Leninist one, Fidel found himself in need of a party structure. But where usually such a party would have been in the vanguard of the struggle itself, Fidel had come to power at the head of a far more diffuse and overlapping set of interests, cut into numerous revolutionary groupings, and without any overall coherence. Converting this informal and somewhat heterodox structure into a unified party format (the ORI) was a crucial task, but it smacked of long, arduous and unexciting work. This was not for him, and it was not for Che either. Fidel therefore devolved most of the responsibility to Escalante.

Escalante was delighted at this turn of events and lost no time in using his new position to develop a personal powerbase of PSP supporters within the party structure that Fidel had asked him to build. All of a sudden, heads of government institutions and organisations who had thought their positions safely ensconced within the existing organisation found themselves being first 'advised' – as the euphemism had it – then swiftly replaced by Escalante's communists. All the while, Escalante exerted pressure on Fidel to adopt a more conformist Soviet line on various matters. This included pushing the party line into areas he had not previously dared to touch, including the freedom of the press. This Fidel curtailed at a strange and unpleasant 'hearing' in the reading room of the National Library, where the anxieties that had beset him personally were assuaged at the cost of Cuba's once lively alternative press. Henceforth a highly diaphanous line would separate critique from treachery. As if to push home the point, at the annual 26 July event Fidel began speaking heatedly of defenders and slanderers, of revolutionary truth and imperial lies, and of the revolution's moral authority to combat the counter-revolution and the traitors.

There is nothing on record as to what Che made of all this, but undoubtedly he would have had an opinion – whether voiced to Fidel or not. In any case, the crucial difference between them was already marked. The American ambassador might have been overstating it when he reported that 'Castro was cynical re basic goodness of man', but there was some truth to his words. Fidel always wanted to channel an individual's capacity, and to do so he was prepared to entertain the full range of means at his disposal; Che's efforts were invariably geared towards harnessing individual capacity. It was a subtle but important distinction. When Fidel spoke of revolutionary responsibility he meant obedience; Che used the same term to refer to a more creative task, one that he now began to explore somewhat apart from Fidel in his new role as Minister for Industries.

* * *

Che's office at the Ministry of Industries, where he began work in February 1961, bore all the usual hallmarks of the spaces he inhabited, with its spartan furniture and cluttered desk. His workload there was immense, and he would pass long days hunched over reports before bounding out to berate or congratulate those who had produced them. Though Raúl often stopped by to see him, Fidel did so rather less. With the move to the Soviet Union publicly affirmed, it seemed that the two men had entered a new phase in their relationship. Che no longer praised Fidel publicly and hectored him privately; for now the two seemed prepared to explore their own avenues alone, content for the time being with the general direction they were heading in.

Fidel did call at the Ministry one day, though, entering by the front door just as Che's bodyguard was leaving. 'Hey, you! What are you doing here?' Fidel snapped. The bodyguard had been assigned to Fidel until just a week before, and explained that he was now working with Che. 'How come I don't know about this?' Fidel demanded. 'Where's Che?' The bodyguard told him he was meeting a Mexican delegation, but Fidel told the man to fetch him anyway. When Che was told of all this, he said he would come in a minute. When he did, he found his staff getting an earful from Fidel, so Che asked what was the matter. 'What's the matter,' Fidel replied, 'is that I came here and I find that these people are working for you and nobody asked me!' But the Ministry was Che's domain and his anger at discovering his body-guard had moved over to it, reinforces the extent to which Fidel – who interfered in almost everyone else's affairs – recognised this.

It was certainly at the Ministry that the always somewhat 'ascetic' Che found his true niche. He spent more and more time there with his closest aides, people like Orlando Borrego (whom he nicknamed 'Vinegar', quite approvingly, for his sour demeanour) and Enrique Oltuski, whom Che had taken on after he was demoted during the Matos affair. 'Maybe you are not such a son of a bitch as I was told,' Che joked with him on his arrival. Now, the two would often stay up playing chess late into the night. When it was hot, Che would open the windows to the night air, take off his shirt and lie on the floor smoking a cigar and giving full vent to his romantic side: they would take good care of the world, they promised each other.

The Ministry was in that sense Che's perfect home – one he could always be sure he was passing through. Aleida was often there in her capacity as her husband's secretary. And then there was Emmita, Che's 'bashful' typist. Tactfully, Hilda had not been employed this time, but little Hildita was a regular sight. Visitors coming to see the new Minister for Industries might arrive to see her swinging from Núñez Jiménez's long arms. Outside of this, Che had precious little life to speak of during these intense days. Occasionally he went to the cinema with Aleida, or passed a Sunday afternoon playing with his children and his German shepherd dog Muralla (wall). But most of their socialising was limited to the late-night reception of visitors at the Ministry,

Fidel too had been striving for a more harmonious personal life. But while Che had been able to re-create something of the atmosphere he had grown up with in Argentina, Fidel found this rather more difficult. His most consistent shell since the beginning of the revolution had been his car, as it carried him from whichever residence he was using to whatever function, event or meeting he was attending. That year in particular he had devoted much of his time to a literacy campaign: it was to be his greatest contribution and bulwark of his government for many years.

But it was through the literacy campaign that Fidel met his future wife, Dalia Soto del Valle, 'Lala', a schoolteacher from the city of Trinidad in central Cuba. For Fidel, who had driven away the women who loved him the moment they came between him and the revolution, this was his great chance to keep some small part of himself separate from his life's work. For that reason, of the life that Fidel lived subsequently with Lala, of his five children with her and of his more personal side, we know nothing more of substance.

* * *

That August, as Minister of Industries, Che attended an economic conference at Punta del Este in Uruguay. The venue was a luxurious beach resort, the St Tropez of South America. Despite Che's title he was not, as he made sure to point out to the delegations from the other South American states, there on purely economic grounds. Che began his speech to the opening plenary by listing all the recent attacks against Cuba. Such attacks, he said, were the reason he did not in all honesty feel he could 'talk technical matters at this assembly of illustrious technicians'.

'Whoever speaks of economic union, speaks of political union,' Che went on, this time citing Martí. And as far as he was concerned this economic conference was political twice over: first because it is impossible to talk of economic measures that will shape the future of humble men and pretend that it is not a political act, and second because it was conceived in opposition to Cuba. Che was referring to the 'technical' report of the conference, which had made a passing reference to Cuba as an 'imminent danger' in the continent. He was also alerting the delegates to why he too would now frame a political response. He catalogued the exercise of imperialism around the world, listed the attacks that had taken place against Cuban sugar, arms and personnel, and pointed out that a month after Kennedy had made his famous speech announcing the Alliance for Progress – the terms of which they were here to debate – he had also unleashed the Bay of Pigs invasion.

Before long the speaker interrupted and asked Che to refrain from making such wild accusations. But Che did not much care what the speaker, nor any of his immediate audience, thought. He was speaking over their heads to others. Had the delegates really thought about what they were getting from the Alliance for Progress? 'Don't you get the slight impression they are pulling your hair?' he asked them. 'They give dollars to build motorways, they give dollars to construct roads, they give dollars to make the gutters,' he said, before asking with some exasperation, "Señors, with what are you [actually] going to make the gutters? You don't have to be a genius to see it. Why don't they give dollars for equipment, dollars for machinists, dollars so that our under-developed countries, all of them, can convert themselves into industrial countries, agricultural countries, in one go? Really, it's sad.'

Che's speech was notable if only as a measure of his understanding of the bigger picture. In his writings and speeches the previous year he had begun to update his understanding of political and economic problems from the Central American context to the continental scale. Now he was wielding those arguments in an analysis that spanned the globe. To look at Cuba in isolation from the world was sheer foolishness, he was saying: 'Cuba is part of a world in tension.' Look beyond Cuba, to Berlin and look further still, to Laos, the Congo – and about the Congo he pulled no punches in declaring that it was imperialism that had assassinated Lumumba – look further still to Vietnam, divided, to Korea, divided, look to Algeria and to Tunisia.

Had anyone cared to consider the details behind the rhetoric they might have come to the conclusion that Che had been looking very carefully at each of these places. During his travels the previous year he had caught a glimpse of the wave of national independence movements, and he was bringing what he had learned to the table in Uruguay. If it had not been clear before, it was clear now that Latin America was being confronted by two main choices at that moment: the path represented by the Americans, or the path represented by Cuba. Cuba would have a higher gross domestic product than the USA by 1980, Che promised. So which was the siren path?

* * *

On the surface of things, all was going well for the Cuban revolution. The literacy campaign to which Fidel had been devoting most of his energies all year was proving a major success, and domestic opposition to the revolution had grown a little quieter. None the less by the end of the year, Fidel, who was 'always imagining, always thinking, always developing plans', was growing uneasy. The foreign governments with embassies in

Havana tried to find out what was wrong. Reasons were sought and found: 'absenteeism and job slowdowns', the growing queues for basic foodstuffs, the rise of the *bandidos* – the counter-revolutionary groups roaming the countryside, Cuba's expulsion from the OAS. But none of these was really the issue.

Fidel was aware that the country was facing major economic shortages and he had not yet secured the full support of the Soviet Union. At the end of the year, and trusting in his personal rapport with Khrushchev, he had tried to resolve this by publicly declaring himself personally committed to Marxism–Leninism for life. Once again he was taking a calculated gamble: could he, by making such an overt declaration, force the Soviets to extend greater support to his government? But Khrushchev would prove to be a reluctant patron: the Soviet press covered Fidel's statement 'without comment', and when at the start of 1962 Khrushchev congratulated Fidel on the third anniversary of the revolution he did not mention the matter. 'This absence of comment on Castro's open profession of faith is interesting,' observed the British embassy. Even those on the left across the continent saw it variously as 'an act of political stupidity', a sign of his growing difficulties, even 'treason'.

The real problem was not this somewhat lukewarm response from the Soviets but a much more genuine crisis closer to home. What really intrigued the embassy watchers were reports of a silent 'creeping coup d'état' within Fidel's own government. Escalante's drive to instil the PSP in every position of authority had undermined Fidel's own control of crucial state organisations, and his seeming willingness to let it happen led some to believe that he was losing the solid grip on power that he had always held until now.

The US government continued to consider Che the *éminence grise* behind Fidel, but the real secret puppeteer was Escalante. Plenty of individuals complained of Escalante's activities, but Fidel refused to take any action. Perhaps he was not wanting to give Moscow any further reason to delay the country's full and open acceptance into the socialist bloc. But whatever the reason, by the end of the year Escalante was quite possibly the second most powerful man in the revolution.

Tongues immediately started to wag. 'The up till now indispensable Fidel Castro . . . is becoming less essential as the party machine takes over,' the British embassy reported early in January, scarcely believing it themselves. 'Is his hand still firmly on the tiller?' the Canadian ambassador wanted to know as he openly speculated, along with many others, as to whether Castro's Faustian pact with the communists had left him looking like little more than their 'stalking horse'. From out of nowhere what might have been described as the unthinkable – were it not that all the diplomats were thinking it – appeared to be happening. All of a sudden it looked as though Fidel could be on the brink of being ousted from power.

11. HANGMAN'S NOOSE

IN THIS MOMENT of greatest danger, it was to Che that Fidel instinctively turned, knowing that his comrade would be there and trusting in his loyalty above that of all others. It was true that Che had become somewhat marginalised towards the end of 1961, at least from the party political process; and Fidel had certainly been aware of this. But Che never cared particularly for political position, and in any case he had devoted himself for most of the year to his work at the Ministry. Like all those who enjoyed Fidel's greatest confidence Che accepted the constant flux of isolation and embrace. So when Fidel now called him to head up a commission of inquiry into Escalante's activities Che responded without hesitation: with Fidel under threat, the revolution too was at stake and Che would move to defend either at the slightest provocation. As he understood it, the two could not be separated.

Che had his own reasons to be rid of Escalante. Through his efforts at the Ministry of Industries, Che's own plans for the way the socialist revolution in Cuba ought to look had been projected more and more on to factories, mills and offices across the island. The workplace had in many ways become Che's natural constituency, a quiet but none the less powerful counterpart to Fidel's constituency of the plaza. But this was precisely where Escalante had himself been shoehorning PSP members into positions of authority. With Fidel's summons, a silent, secretive struggle now began to unfold as, with his own considerable reach into these places, Che set to work compiling the information that would indict not just Escalante but the very practice of bureaucratic entrenchment he was promoting.

Meanwhile, Fidel tried to settle issues with the Soviets, gently at first because he still desperately needed their support. But he had no intention of suffering in silence Escalante's drive to replace his own supporters with PSP men of his own choosing. It did not help, however, that Fidel loathed the Soviet ambassador, Kudriatsev, a pompous man who insisted on wearing a bullet-proof vest wherever he went. Steeling himself, in mid-February Fidel called Kudriatsev round for a private discussion. He tried to drop a few hints about his dilemma and his refusal to suffer it quietly for much longer. Cuba was the vanguard of all the Americas, Fidel reminded the ambassador, hoping that this might in turn remind Moscow of the importance of looking after it. But then he went on to warn him about the revolutionary vanguard in this part of the world. The leaders of the Latin American communist parties, Fidel said, 'are often prisoners of old dogmas and do not listen to young voices'. The arrogant and disdainful Kudriatsev would not have appreciated such presumptuous talk from a man who just months before had confessed to only having read the first few chapters of *Das Kapital*.

Just a few days later, and unaware that Fidel's recent conversation might affect his own plans, Escalante too paid a visit to Kudriatsev. Keeping Moscow informed on Fidel's activities, as he had been doing since the previous summer, Escalante reported that his task was nearing completion. The formation of the new Integrated Revolutionary Organisations that he had been over-seeing was almost complete. And the reports that he offered to the ambassador on Fidel's weakening physical health he perhaps relished as a foretaste of his weakening political health. 'He practically cannot sleep and some of his chronic pains have sharpened,' Escalante said. Fidel was soon to be relieved of dealing with everyday issues, he added, 'so that he can concentrate on dealing with the main problems in internal and foreign affairs'. This was the sort of meeting Kudriatsev preferred: reports of work done according to predetermined doctrinal guidelines. Escalante was a plotter and a man of dangerous ambition, but he was ruthlessly efficient and was certainly no liar. When the list of the new ORI leadership was unveiled in early March there were indeed relatively few members who were loyal first and foremost to Fidel. By then, however, Che had supplied Fidel with the evidence he required and Fidel was ready to strike.

* * *

Fidel launched his bloodless counter-coup on the night of 26 March. First, he appeared on television to deliver a sermon on what he termed 'sectarianism', the offence with which Escalante and almost anyone he had put in power would now be brought down. Fidel did not shy from including among that list Escalante's principal patron, the Soviet ambassador himself: 'Those gentlemen who want to force their ideas on others are almost indistinguishable from Batista and his henchmen!' But Fidel did not want an overt spat with the Soviets and for that reason the following day Escalante quietly disappeared, flying to Prague for an 'extended vacation'. Then, even more quietly, Kudriatsev was placed under close observation until such time as the Cubans and Soviets could agree to his being even more inconspicuously replaced.

The following day the PSP leadership convened at Kudriatsev's flat, licking their wounds somewhat. The self-abnegation with which they applauded Fidel's decision suggests they realised they were now being bugged. Fidel's resolute response had certainly dealt a 'heavy blow to the party' and to Moscow's attempt to assert its control over the Cuban leadership without supplying substantive military or financial support. 'We [will] have to work hard to overcome this dissatisfaction,' Blas Roca – one of the PSP old guard, and no stranger to Moscow – fretted to Kudriatsev in late April.

Roca's comment laid bare what was really going on: the Soviet leadership, while welcoming the Cubans with open arms, also wanted to keep them under firm control. It was how they dealt with satellite nations. But these were their first dealings with Fidel, and before the month was out all plans for an integrated party structure that had been intended to serve as a stepping stone towards a more traditional communist political system were shelved. Instead Fidel had in place a new, six-man party secretariat of those he trusted most: Raúl, Che, President Dorticós, Emilio Aragonés and just one representative of the PSP, Blas Roca. Once more, Fidel had brought back into the heart of government the core of the revolutionary movement that he had begun with in the Sierra and in whom he had complete confidence. 'Sectarianism, dogmatism, clanism' were 'vicious methods', he said in a private conversation with a Soviet official, Nikolai Andreevich Belous. This was not how things would be handled in his country. 'The tactics of the game have changed,' he told Belous.

Aware of the potentially damaging line that Fidel was taking with these sorts of comments, Carlos Rafael Rodríguez, who was without doubt the PSP leader personally most loyal to Fidel – indeed, he would later become something of a mentor to him – tried to put a gloss on Fidel's words. 'Fidel Castro is a very impulsive person, he wants to do something good for the people as fast as possible. As a result, he sometimes suggests solutions that are not suitable . . .' he said to Khrushchev before his departure. Moscow was less concerned with what Fidel did in Cuba, however, than it was with how his actions fitted into the bigger picture. The reason they had wanted PSP representatives in Cuba in the first place was in part to counter-balance the influence of those around Fidel who wanted him to follow a more proactive line abroad.

In this regard they watched the rise of Che's star once more with care. Although Fidel himself never quite admitted the influence Che had on him – certainly never in the way that Che so openly declared his admiration for Fidel – it was there and

Moscow knew enough about both men to recognise the synergy between them. Fidel had in fact given no little confirmation of the realignment of his position with Che's in February, when he delivered his Second Declaration of Havana: a speech that breathed pure defiance and allowed back into public discourse more than a little of Che's brand of revolutionary adventurism. With the revolution becoming ever more consolidated at home, the two leaders' thoughts were beginning to turn towards contributing something more than the ad hoc support for other revolutionary movements around the continent that Cuba had provided to date.

Fidel and Che were both capable, given half a chance, of looking forward and seeing things on a vast and as yet unmarked plain. And when Fidel spoke as he did in his Second Declaration of Havana he articulated better than Che the reasons why they wanted to make the revolution on a continental scale. But it was a constant presence in both their thoughts. How else, without some larger plan to draw them on, to help them make sense of the multitude of decisions required each day, could they have progressed this far already? Increasingly, as they confronted an international situation that was becoming more and more fraught, they would cherish and nurture this view as an antidote to the only other available option for a small country such as theirs, siding with one camp or the other in the Cold War.

* * *

Che's implicit critique of Soviet socialism was not limited to the question of what made the right conditions for revolution, however. He was also formulating his own views on socialism itself. None of these 'unorthodox' ideas was yet an overt criticism of the Soviet model – they were more generously intentioned than that – but the Kremlin may well have seen before Che where his critique was headed and they were concerned that he might just take Fidel along with him.

On 30 April, the day before International Labour Day, Che spoke to a gathering convened to award prizes to workers selected by the Ministry of Industries. '*Compañeros*, all of you,' he began, 'I must tell you that this is an emotional moment for me.' Che felt himself humbled before those, he said, who 'made history day by day, through work and daily struggle'. But he was not there to pat backs. 'Socialism,' he said, 'is productivity', and through working together to secure that productivity it was dignity. Here were the two great themes – dignity and production – at the centre of everything he held dear about the Cuban revolution.

By now, Che's theorising of revolution had been compacted down into a set of ideas about what he called the 'new man'. He would never write out at length exactly what these thoughts were, but there is enough to give a sense of what he had in mind. He had first used the term the previous summer. 'How does one actually carry out a work of social welfare?' Che asked. 'How does one unite individual endeavour with the needs of society?' These were age-old revolutionary questions, but Che wanted to put his own spin on them. Productivity could be leveraged by moral as opposed to simply material incentives, such as increased salaries or perks, and those incentives needed to be worked into the fibre of every member of the labour force. This 'new man' 'should be satisfied with the absolute reward of doing his duty,' he said one night to Llovio-Menéndez, a bureaucrat with whom he had occasional dealings, his shirt unbuttoned halfway to his chest and his feet propped up on a small table. Individuals, Che said, putting it more succinctly 'must disappear'.

Here was the nub of what Che would dedicate the rest of his life to. And here too, amidst this view, lurked the unnamed yet distinctively recognisable shadow of Fidel Castro. In so many of his speeches and writings on the theme of what makes a revolutionary (as opposed to just an amorphous figure wildly wreaking revolution) it is the figure of Fidel Castro that emerges. Sometimes, as in an article he wrote for the magazine *Verde Olivo* in April examining whether Cuba was the historical exception or the vanguard of a much wider anti-colonial struggle, this was explicit. It was a methodical piece: he weighed the evidence for and against, concluding that what made Cuba the exception was, in the end, the unique figure of Fidel Castro. 'He is a great leader,' he said, which, added to his qualities of 'audacity, strength and valour' and his 'extraordinary eagerness to examine and divine the will of the people', made him, Che, certain that Fidel had done more than anyone else to build the formidable structure of the revolution from nothing. It was a reminder of the extent to which the revolutionary ideas that were being developed so often gelled about their friendship. But that structure, not to mention the friendship between Fidel and Che, was about to be severely tested in the greatest moment of danger yet to confront the young revolutionaries.

* * *

In May 1962, what for Che had been a long-expected event co-incided with some entirely unexpected news. Since learning it was to be a boy, Che had awaited the birth of his first son with growing excitement and anticipation. Finally, on the 20th, Aleida gave birth to Camilo Guevara, named after his father's great friend from the Sierra. It was a momentous occasion for Che. But on the very day that the child was born, Che was called by Fidel to leave Aleida's side. When he arrived at the revolutionary palace the two of them were joined by just the four other members of the new governmental secretariat: Raúl, Dorticós, Aragonés and Roca. The news was stunning. Khrushchev had responded to their constant demands for greater arms, and he had done so in a way that committed the Soviet Union to Cuba unequivocally.

Over the winter, Khrushchev had learned from his rocket men in their Siberian caves that the new generation of Soviet missiles were not good enough to mount any sort of response to an American first strike. The Chinese were openly criticising his weak leadership and he wanted a way of gaining leverage over the new and very young American President, John F. Kennedy, who for all his own weaknesses, as Khrushchev saw it, appeared infuriatingly buttressed by his brother Robert and a surprisingly hawkish team of aides. With all these mounting problems on his mind Khrushchev had come to the conclusion, as he looked out of the window during a train journey back to Moscow from Bulgaria, that he could perhaps deal with the lot in one single, bold counter-strike: the installation of nuclear missiles in Cuba. It is not impossible, either, that his decision was in part a response to the temporary lack of trust between the Cuban and Soviet governments after the Escalante affair.

Given those recent events, Khrushchev certainly could not be sure how the Cubans would respond. He had therefore sent Alexiev – who since Kudriatsev's fall from grace had been promoted to ambassador – to sound Fidel out. Alexiev was met at the airport in Havana by Raúl, who was immediately informed that with Alexiev, in disguise, was the leader of the Soviet missile squadron and that they needed an audience with Fidel right away. By the time Che arrived the following day, Fidel had made his own mind up about the matter. Fidel knew well that, in politics, 'things often hang on a thread, a detail, an accident'. But, like Khrushchev, he was a natural gambler, and his instinct was to defend by going on the attack. Che, who was if anything even more strategically aggressive than Fidel, fully supported his decision.

All those who gathered that day to take the final decision firmly believed that Cuba's interests would be well served by accepting the missiles. Though they had doubts as to how such a feat might be achieved in practice, these were offset by their still apparent awe of the Soviet Union. The parades that thundered through Red Square, the sometimes crucial intelligence the Soviets had been sharing with the Cubans, all left their mark. Had they not stood alongside Yuri Gagarin, the first man in space, at a celebration in Havana just the year before? Crucially, therefore, they all believed, or at least they wanted to believe, that the USSR could mount the scale of deception that would be required to deliver the missiles, the machinery and the accompanying hordes of technicians undetected from one side of the planet to the other.

When Khrushchev heard of the Cubans' unequivocal support for the plan he was delighted, and immediately wrote Fidel a complimentary letter to tell him so personally. Fidel appreciated such gestures – he took considerable pride in the growing personal relations between himself and the leader of the socialist world. The relationship seemed fitting to him. But, as in the previous summer when he had been careful to state explicitly and on television that the Soviet offer of protection was entirely 'spontaneous', what Fidel wanted to ensure above all else – he practically made his acceptance conditional upon it – was that this was a move to strengthen the socialist camp in general, not a protective arm around just Cuba. Khrushchev concurred. It would help the broader strategic ambitions of the Soviet bloc, or the 'greater success of our general affairs' as he rather more elliptically put it.

Fidel sent Raúl to Moscow in July to secure a formal agreement concerning the missiles. Once there, Raúl was taken aback at the ease with which the whole affair was concluded, so rumour has it, on the top of a grand piano in a protocol house somewhere in Moscow. His nerves must have shown, because an aide was asked to stay and sit through a good few slugs of Armenian cognac with him afterwards. Raúl was pleased with the draft, but Fidel saw that his concerns had not been fully addressed. 'While the people of Cuba would approve of your draft,' he said, 'in its present form it could be useful to reactionary propaganda.' The preamble said the *Cubans* had asked for the missiles to be stationed in their country. Fidel wanted that to be changed, and for the mutual nature of the agreement to be public. 'We are not outlaws,' he said, 'we have every right to be doing what we are doing.' Fidel, though he trusted they could pull it off, would rather the Soviets not try to install the missiles in secret. But

Khrushchev wanted to spring a surprise on Kennedy and make public the missiles' existence only after they were installed.

* * *

Throughout that summer Operation Anadyr, as it was misleadingly named after a Siberian river, proceeded apace. The final details of the political agreement about the missiles, their purpose and who had officially asked whom to put them there in the first place were not yet even finalised. So at the end of August Fidel sent Che to Moscow to try to improve the terms of the agreement that Raúl had earlier brought home. The Cubans were received warmly, but Khrushchev still would not be persuaded to make the agreement public until after the missiles were installed. What if the whole operation were discovered? Che had asked. It was the same question, the *only* question, that Fidel had asked Raúl to put to Khrushchev earlier in the year. Khrushchev reassured him there was no need to worry. 'If there is a problem, we will send the Baltic fleet,' was his reply. The Soviet leader was now set on this plan for his own, only partially disclosed reasons, and would not budge.

While Che was still in Moscow, Kennedy received ever more incontrovertible proof as to what was afoot 90 miles off the Florida coast. In response, he put 150,000 reservists on standby. Three days later, Khrushchev adjusted his own tack. He advanced the deployment of smaller, tactical nuclear weapons and beefed up the flotilla of forces that would accompany transport of the main nuclear missiles. By the time Che returned to Havana from Moscow, the situation had already become tense. A break in the weather had allowed the American U-2 spy planes finally to get to work, and the CIA had obtained the definitive proof they needed in order to lobby Kennedy to respond. The incriminating wheel tracks scarred into the Cuban soil, the hastily dug in compounds, all told the seasoned eye, even from a photograph taken at several thousand feet, of missile emplacements under construction.

The response of the American administration was at least in

part framed by the failure to comprehend what was happening in Cuba. The British suffered from the same malaise. 'Even after five weeks in Oriente Province,' the new British consul wrote home from Santiago that summer, '. . . it is difficult to shake off the feeling of being an Alice in an especially crazy wonderland.' Such a place, of course, was not somewhere that any self-respecting superpower was going to allow the nuclear missiles of another to be based. Through his own personal fascination with the island, Khrushchev had overlooked the peculiar qualities of the place itself, not to mention its proximity to the US mainland, to raise passions and fears alike. The stage was set for the most dangerous showdown of the twentieth century.

* * *

In the early evening of Monday 22 October, Kennedy began his famous televised address about the 'secret, swift and extraordinary build-up of Communist missiles' in Cuba. Just hours before, in Moscow, Khrushchev had convened a meeting of his Presidium to address the fact that the Americans had discovered what was going on. Immediately after that meeting he sent Fidel a personal letter, informing him that the Soviets were 'ready for combat'. It was what Fidel had wanted to hear. He enjoyed these moments of readying the troops. 'Well, things are clear, things are clear,' he said to himself. In Havana, an eerie calm then descended and remained all week as events edged ever closer to the brink and the world looked on, fearful of a countdown to nuclear war. The tension steadily mounted. First, Kennedy imposed a naval embargo. Then Khrushchev ordered his ships to keep steaming regardless and, unbeknownst to either, Soviet submarines surfaced dangerously close to US warships, unaware of the situation because they had been out of radio contact.

Playing out likely scenarios in his mind, Fidel was convinced that the outcome of the continued escalation would be another land invasion of Cuba. All summer he had been overseeing a large increase in his intelligence service and cultivating personal relationships with as many of the agents as possible. Confident in his views, as with the Bay of Pigs just the year before, he planned his response carefully. Fidel was determined to outfox the Americans once more. But Kennedy's imposition of a blockade as opposed to the pre-emptive strike he had been expecting took him completely by surprise. When the blockade then failed, as Khrushchev's ships ploughed on, Fidel became genuinely fearful that an attack would take place any minute. On the Friday evening he called Che and Raúl and his other military top command for a crisis meeting before despatching them to their defence posts. Then, in the early hours of Saturday morning and too agitated to sleep, he asked to be driven over to Alexiev's residence.

All week, Fidel had been growing frustrated with Khrushchev's continued refusal to admit publicly the existence of the missile sites in Cuba – even though it was obvious that the game was up. Now, as the climax looked like being just hours away, he was more convinced than ever that the Kremlin was losing control. An attack of some sort by the United States was 'inevitable', he kept telling Alexiev. Finally, he said that he wanted him to take down a personal letter for Khrushchev. Fidel had always prided himself on finding the right words for the occasion. When composing his speeches he kneaded his words until they fitted exactly what he wanted to say, beginning with some rough template of an idea, often ending, via circular reasoning, in a specific policy or concrete plan. But now, as he wrote to Khrushchev, with each of his words being weighed in human life, he was at a loss. Exhausted after a long day and the unbearable tensions of the week, each time he tried to say what he meant he failed. He kept reading through the drafts and discarding them. Finally, Alexiev interjected: 'Do you wish to say that we should be the first to launch a nuclear strike on the enemy?'

* * *

On the morning of Sunday, 28 October, Alexiev would have his answer. And so too would Fidel. What Fidel wrote had, in the end, stretched the bounds of diplomatic language to the extreme. But the Soviet Premier prided himself on reading between the lines, and what he read in Fidel's letter had struck fear into his heart. 'Dear Comrade Khrushchev,' the final draft of Fidel's late-night missive began, 'the danger that the aggressive policy [of US invasion] poses for humanity is so great that following that event the Soviet Union must never allow the circumstances in which the imperialists could launch the first nuclear strike against it.' Before receiving this letter – which was so ambiguous that he would have had to read it several times to get the sense of it – Khrushchev had already made up his own mind to defuse the situation, to cut the 'knot of war', as he put it. What Fidel seemed to be proposing could not have been further from his thoughts. Had this young man lost his mind? Had he not understood that the whole point of the exercise had been to force Kennedy's hand, and not to go to war with him? Khrushchev was ever adept at turning around his original intentions and recasting earlier decisions as the now mistaken thinking of others. Fidel would be dealt with by such means in due course.

Meanwhile, Fidel would learn over the radio of Khrushchev's secret promise to Kennedy that he would 'remove the missiles that you find offensive' if Kennedy promised not to invade Cuba. When he heard this Fidel flew into a rage kicking the wall and smashing a mirror as he hurled a 'string of obscenities' in Khrushchev's direction. If Khrushchev ever came to Cuba, he would later say, he would 'box his ears'.

Anticipating such a response, Khrushchev sent a personal letter to Fidel to try to soften the blow. The outcome 'allows for the question to be settled in your favour', Khrushchev assured Fidel, wary of his acute nationalist sensibilities, before going on to 'recommend', with a complete disregard for Fidel's character, that he 'not be carried away by sentiment and ... show firmness'. Khrushchev was alarmed by the fact that one of the American U-2's had just been shot down. But his far from diplomatic letter merely infuriated Fidel even more, Fidel responded to the Soviet

Premier in kind: he conveyed an official answer over the airwaves, while sending also a private letter just as Khrushchev had done to him. Not shooting down the plane, Fidel now replied somewhat bitterly, would have weakened them not only militarily, but morally too.

Engrossed in his own responsibilities, Che had been curiously absent from all of this. He had been stationed in his command post controlling Pinar del Río province, where he had been joined by one of his guerrilla units who were just then completing their training. But he was present at the meeting Fidel called at two o'clock on the Sunday afternoon after hearing that the Soviets were backing down. Fidel had by then regained sufficient composure to put a positive spin on what was evidently a disastrous outcome for them all. 'Cuba will not lose anything by the removal of the missiles, because she has already gained so much,' he declared defiantly. But behind the scenes, Fidel was feeling vulnerable. Alexiev visited him on 29 October, reporting afterwards to Moscow that he had never seen him look so depressed and irritated. In truth Fidel felt abandoned by Moscow to some future savaging at the hands of the Americans. 'It is not that some Cubans cannot understand the Soviet decision to dismantle the missiles,' he told him, 'but all Cubans.' This betrayal, as he saw it, touched on all of his personal anxieties. A foreign official who saw Fidel soon after the event described him as looking 'sallow, haggard and thin, mentally and physically deflated'. Alexiev might have said the same about Che, who was equally enraged.

* * *

All this worried Khrushchev greatly. He was perfectly aware that if he lost Fidel he might well lose Cuba to the Chinese and the USSR's not insignificant investment in the island's revolution would have been wasted. Such was his concern at Fidel's response that he ordered none other than his favourite envoy and Senior

Presidium member Anastas Mikoyan, Cuba's 'friend in Moscow', to fly there immediately after concluding negotiations with the Americans in Washington. Mikoyan arrived to find an angry Fidel. 'We do not understand why we are being asked to do this,' Fidel had just berated U Thant, the UN Secretary-General, about the need for inspections of the missile sites, '. . . we have no intention of reporting to, or consulting, the Senate or the House [of Representatives] of the United States on the question of what weapons we may consider advisable to acquire, and the measures we may take to defend our country accordingly.'

Khrushchev knew that if anyone could talk Fidel round it would be Mikoyan, but it would not be an easy task. Fidel was too aware of his country's history to avoid the obvious comparisons with the Treaty of Paris, in which, after helping the Cubans to fight off the Spanish during the War of Independence (1895–8), the American delegation had determined Cuba's future sovereignty without really consulting the Cubans at all. But Mikoyan's mission was further hampered by the continuing and bitter exchange of letters between Khrushchev and Fidel. Khrushchev's next letter to Fidel, delivered after talks with Mikoyan had begun, laid out a much sterner line. He reminded Fidel, condescendingly, that what had just happened had been a 'clash of two superpowers'. Khrushchev went on, 'We feel that the aggressor came out the loser . . . He made preparations to attack Cuba but we stopped him and forced him to recognise before world public opinion that he won't do it at the current stage.'

But Fidel thought it was Khrushchev who had been both the aggressor and the ultimate loser, and was inclined to tell him so in his next reply. From the 'most endangered trenches' of the Cold War Fidel wrote back, reminding him what a pivotal moment had just passed. 'Danger has been hanging over our country for a long time now and in a certain way we have grown used to it.' Fidel alluded to the fact that there had been considerable popular support in Cuba for the idea that Cubans might fight alongside the Soviet troops stationed there. The 'surprising, sudden and practically unconditional decision' to withdraw the missiles brought tears to these brave men's eyes, he said indignantly.

He then addressed what for him, personally, had been the most hurtful part of the whole affair. 'We knew, and do not presume that we ignored it, that we would have been annihilated, as you insinuate in your letter, in the event of nuclear war.' Fidel was growing tired of foreign governments and their condescending views of Alice in Wonderland and the Latin temperament. Despite that chance of annihilation, he went on, 'that didn't prompt us to ask you to withdraw the missiles, that didn't prompt us to ask you to yield. Do you believe that we wanted that war? But how could we prevent it if the invasion finally took place? The fact is that this event was possible, that imperialism was obstructing every solution and that its demands were, from our point of view, impossible for the USSR and Cuba to accept. . . . You may be able to convince me that I was wrong,' Fidel told him, 'but you can't tell me that I am wrong without convincing me.'

'We mustn't underestimate the diplomatic means of struggle,' Mikoyan reminded Fidel at one of their meetings. The irony of Mikoyan – who had always opposed the plan – offering the Cubans an autopsy of the correctness of Soviet actions was an object lesson in socialist relations that Fidel had only now, but rather too late, begun properly to note. And Mikoyan's comment was a well-intentioned but ultimately misunderstanding inter-jection too many. Fidel flew into a range. The Soviet Deputy Premier could not understand it. Had not disaster been averted?

It was Che who stepped in to try to defuse the situation. He referred to Fidel's own comment: 'The USA wanted to destroy us physically, but the Soviet Union with Khrushchev's letter destroyed us legally he said.' 'But . . . we did everything so that Cuba would not be destroyed,' Mikoyan replied, at a loss as to how to get through to these people. 'You offended our feelings by not consulting us,' Che shot back, and what was more, 'you effectively recognised the right of the USA to violate interna-tional law. . . .' It was this that worried Che the most. 'It may

cause difficulties for maintaining the unity of the socialist countries. It seems to us that there are already cracks in the unity of
the socialist camp,' he said pointedly.

Later, when he was in the mood for such things again, Che
would make a joke of this: 'Kennedy and Khrushchev are playing
chess. The situation is complicated. It's Khrushchev's turn and
he doesn't know what to do. At this moment Khrushchev sees
the vision of Capablanca who says: "Sacrifice the Knight".'* But
right then he too, like Fidel, was still furious.

By now, Khrushchev himself had had enough. It was all just
'shouting and unreasonable', he himself shouted at a Presidium
meeting on the 16th, even before hearing the outcome of
Mikoyan's final report. 'If the Cuban comrades do not wish to
work with us on this matter and do not want to take steps together
with us to resolve this crisis, then, clearly, our presence there is
of no utility to our friends', Khrushchev cabled to Mikoyan.
Before leaving, Mikoyan himself turned to Che and said: 'When
I return to Moscow I should have the right to say that I understood the Cubans, but I am afraid that when I return I will say
that I don't know them, and in fact I will not know them.'

* * *

By the end of the year, Moscow and Washington were eager to
move on from that frightful moment when they had stepped close
to the brink. But Fidel and Che still felt deeply the bitterness
of Khrushchev's betrayal, and *Revolución* continued to carry
anti-Soviet speeches. For Che there was just one lesson to be
drawn from the whole affair: that the unimpeachable solidarity
he knew and felt at Fidel's side and among his comrades in Cuba
had not been matched by the Soviets. They had not stood by
them 'to the last' as the Cubans had hoped. 'I will never forgive

*Capablanca was a former Cuban World Champion Chess player and one of Fidel's
nicknames in the early years of the revolution was 'el caballo' (the horse, or knight).

Khrushchev,' Che later confided to a friend. And to another he said, 'Our only hope is to not give up even one iota of our principles,' pinching his thumb and forefinger together in emphasis.

Fidel was not yet capable of articulating his anger. He had scarcely undertaken any government work throughout November, and his 'pointed' absence from public view was noted by foreign observers and intelligence posts, most of whom suspected a major government shake-up or policy decision was imminent. In fact his absence was not pointed at all. It was simply the result of the physical and mental exhaustion engendered by recent events. But Fidel was drawing a very different lesson from Che, bitter and unpleasant, but inescapable all the same. Fidel knew that Cuba had no option but to acknowledge Soviet authority for now. As ever, he needed to talk himself round to believing what his head told him was true. He began passing by the University to hold impromptu gatherings with students, debating with them and trying out his thoughts. Observing Fidel from the comfort of his own home, which afforded him a view of these events in the leafy university quarter of Havana, the British ambassador wrote: 'I do not . . . see these somewhat unorthodox excursions as a clear indication that Castro is going out of his mind, as some of my colleagues do. He is immensely tough and resilient and his capacity for survival seems unlimited.'

The ambassador appeared to have penetrated Fidel's inner thoughts rather more successfully than had either Mikoyan or even Che himself in the long and painful post mortem that followed on from the Missile Crisis. Though outwardly he was at that moment the more distraught of the two, once reconciled to his own choice Fidel would come to terms with the situation much more quickly than Che. And when he did, it would carry him forward in a direction that Che, least of all, was expecting.

12. DROWNING OUT OF COURTESY

THE MISSILE CRISIS changed everything for Fidel and Che. 'Our right to live is something which cannot be discussed by anyone,' Fidel had declared afterwards. 'But if our right to live is made conditional upon an obligation to fall to our knees, our reply once again is that we will not accept it.' This line, forthright and defiant, was one that Che supported wholeheartedly. He too believed that the Cuban people had reached a zenith, an almost ecstatic willingness to sacrifice themselves for the greater good of a socialist future.

But for all that the Missile Crisis and, for the Cubans, its painful, drawn-out aftermath had seen the two comrades stand firmly side by side as they each drew different lessons from the experience. Fidel's primary concern, it soon became clear, was to consolidate the revolution's past achievements. Che was more deeply troubled by the prospect that, as he put it, thanks to Khrushchev's *volte face* on Cuba, 'we can now expect the decline of the revolutionary movement in [all of] Latin America'. The Missile Crisis had revealed to both men where their true priorities lay.

These different responses were almost entirely driven by their characters: Che's dogmatic and resolute, Fidel's much more pragmatic, flexible even. Such differences had for a long time now played out against the backdrop of Cuba's gradual arc from American to Soviet patronage. And if anything they had provided the Cuban leadership with a useful means of negotiating that difficult transition. In the aftermath of the Missile Crisis, however, the principal issue confronting Fidel and Che would be the question of Cuba's position *within* the socialist camp itself as the increasingly fratricidal split between the Soviet and Chinese leadership opened up what was almost a second front in the Cold War. Played out against this next set of events, their differences would prove altogether less helpful.

* * *

Initially, Che responded to the blow that the Soviet Union had dealt them in October the only way he knew how. He threw himself into an almost maniacal programme of work, living to a rigidly enforced schedule that he also piled on to those around him. 'He kept giving me new tasks without ever removing the old,' one former colleague recalled. Above all, Che was now determined to see how far he could push his ideas on promoting moral incentives – a task that he saw as being at the heart of his mission to create a new socialist society – while at the same time wrestling with the bureaucracy that had begun to engulf the country. These were Herculean tasks but, as he saw it, the failure to address them was what had started the rot in the Soviet Union in the first place. Cuba would have to be different and, to make sure of it, Che worked ever harder at the Ministry. He wanted to prove that the form of socialism they were developing in Cuba was superior to that in the Soviet Union, and he would keep at his desk until the early hours. Sleep during these months was brief and heavy – though he drank little, which helped. In the mornings, Aleida would fix him a short, sweet black coffee.

Usually, Che was never happier than when immersed in work like this. But it was clear he was pushing himself to the limit. When Oltuski – 'the little Polack', as Che called him, for his parents were of Polish origin – made some criticism of his writing one day, Che turned to him and said: 'I am Minister of Industries, head of the western army, international conspirator, and author. You are a simple vice minister, and all you do is criticise me.' Those who knew him best simply let him be. Raúl commented to Alexiev in February, 'if a day comes when Guevara realises that he did something dishonest in relation to the revolution, he would blow out his brains'. When he heard of this Che pulled one of his ironic faces as he contemplated the image and observed with a rueful laugh: 'scruples are sometimes harmful for government figures'.

By February, however, the extent to which Che – driven by his pent-up frustration – was throwing himself at his work gave those closest to him cause for concern. 'Rumour in Havana had it that he had gone crazy, that he wasn't just doing voluntary work anymore, that he wanted to cut all the cane by himself,' his good friend Haydée Santamaría recalled. During his voluntary labour expeditions each weekend he was trying to break a new cane-cutting record. At the end of it, his energy finally spent, he gave in: this was 'exhausting' work, he said. '[T]he canebrake never ends!' At that, the workers jumped to their feet applauding. They knew only too well that the canebrake never ended. But Che did not do voluntary work for symbolic effect. For him, it was not only the way to deal with the worst of the country's problems of poor machinery and inefficient output, it was also a means of instilling a revolutionary ethic. It was about inculcation.

This was made acutely clear one day when Che took over a reading class for workers. He was impatient and unkind with one worker who was struggling hard with the basics: 'Well, if you keep studying, maybe you'll get to be as smart as an ox in twenty years,' he told him. Later, after some prompting from Regino Boti, the Economic Minister who was with him, he apologised, but it was indicative of his curious paradoxical relationship with people: on the one hand eminently capable of empathy, on the other distant and cold. He was, in short, rather better at giving than taking, at learning by himself than at being taught. But to

Che all this was just part of what he called the 'strange and moving drama of the building of socialism'.

* * *

Fidel's response to the Missile Crisis could not have been more different. In January 1963 he received a letter from Khrushchev, inviting him to come and spend some time in the Soviet Union; he could take the opportunity to get to know real socialism, Khrushchev said. Still furious with the way he had been treated, Fidel initially declined. His health, in any case, was still not up to it, and as he emerged from the black mood into which he had slumped he sensed the need to secure his own position in Cuba. Fidel did not think it a good time to be making a prolonged trip abroad. As ever, his instincts had not let him down. Plans to topple him – shelved to some degree after the Bay of Pigs fiasco – were indeed being reviewed once more in Washington.

But as the weeks went by and Fidel continued to pick and snipe at Moscow in his speeches, Alexiev was eventually tasked with sounding him out. The Soviet ambassador broached the issue indirectly at first, via Emilio Aragonés, Che's deputy. Aragonés told him that the continued sore feelings over the Missile Crisis were problems of 'form, not substance', but that the Soviet leadership's insistence on publishing its side of events was not warming them to Fidel: it 'arouses the reaction of Cuban leaders', Aragonés put it, as diplomatically as he could.

In fact, Fidel was buying time. He knew that he would have to go to Moscow to settle the issue. But he also knew that this would involve confronting head on the nature of Cuba's relationship with the Soviet Union, and that when he returned it could only be with a clear sense of which way Cuba was heading. For that he needed to be prepared. All that spring, therefore, while Che worked himself into the ground, Fidel took to the podium and in a succession of speeches sought to harry his people into a vigorously defiant state of mind, creating new enemies at home and abroad and stoking the threat of counter-revolution to ensure that, whichever way Cuba was going, Cuba would be going as one.

In February, Fidel finally felt ready to address the whole issue of the Missile Crisis. He began by confiding personally to Alexiev his thoughts on the Soviets' foreign policy line. Unlike in their previous conversation, this time it was he who was sounding out the likely response. 'With regard to the policy of peaceful co-existence, I am generally not against it,' Fidel told him carefully, before clarifying, 'as in the cases of those countries, like Italy and France, where the peaceful path to socialism is possible . . . . But in general in Latin America there aren't the necessary conditions for such an approach.'

On the surface it looked as though Fidel was sticking to his guns, but those who knew his indirect manner of working – and Alexiev was one of them – would have realised that he was in fact gradually working himself towards the reconciliation that he knew was inevitable. And slowly but surely, Fidel tuned his speeches to the line. Speaking at Havana's Chaplin Theatre in February to a meeting of the United Party of the Socialist Revolution (PURS) the latest umbrella organisation for the different revolutionary groupings that included Fidel's own dominant 26 July, along with the PSP and the Revolutionary Directorate, and with a large painting of Marx behind him Fidel insisted that four years of struggle had 'purified' the revolution but that people should not dwell on the past. 'The present is for struggle [but] we must work for the future. Revolutionaries have their eyes to the future.'

Nobody could fail to understand that what Fidel was calling for in these speeches was unity: unity of local government with national government, unity of revolutionaries against the counter-revolutionaries, and unity of the nation, united with the Soviet Union, against the imperialists. His platform established, Fidel was ready for what would now be publicly billed as a reconciliation trip to Moscow. Privately, however, and, before he would

281

actually consider any sort of reconciliation, Fidel intended to find out all he could about the events of the previous October.

* * *

At the end of March, after a long, bone-shaking flight via Iceland in a converted TU-114 bomber, Fidel touched down at Murmansk in the Soviet Union. He had never travelled outside of the Americas before and, bristling with excitement, as the plane came in to land he was standing up in the cockpit like a young boy. The weather in this north-westerly Russian outpost was atrocious, and with Fidel returned to his seat, the pilot was forced to go for a blind landing in the thick fog that clung to the valleyed terrain. The plane failed to land on the first two attempts, but once it was finally on Soviet soil Fidel, dressed in trenchcoat and fox fur hat, was greeted by Mikoyan before being put through on a crackly telephone line to Khrushchev.

When he arrived in Moscow, the well-prepared Muscovites who turned up in droves 'whistled, cheered and stamped their feet'. But genuine excitement and fascination *was* aroused by this colourful and imposing figure who seemed so much more alive than the clayed men in drab suits they were used to hearing mumble through their speeches. Against all custom and procedure Fidel smoked in front of Khrushchev and he spoke to the people as if they were his own, bringing his improvisational approach to a country dogged by routine.

In everything he did as he travelled through the Soviet Union, from Tashkent to Tbilisi to Krasnoyarsk and Kiev, Fidel seemed to be aware that he was in a class of his own. In Volgograd, the former Stalingrad, which had withstood the Nazi invasion some twenty years earlier, he practically brought the house down, speaking to the crowd as if he knew them well, reminding them of their history and of the lesson they held up to the world. As his speech built in intensity the editor of the transcript being produced by the Soviet news agency TASS scrambled for superlatives.

'[Applause]' soon gave way to '[stormy applause]'. These duly added, his speech was printed the following day in *Pravda*.

One evening a concert was held in Fidel's honour at the Palace of Meetings in the Kremlin. In the audience was a young girl, the daughter of a Politburo member who had gone in her father's place as he was unable to attend. Her seat, she soon realised with a rush of excitement, was near to where Fidel would be sitting at the front. On his arrival, Fidel was ushered in down the main aisle to the first row. Once seated, just a little way in front of her, he turned to the audience and waved. The audience immediately rose to their feet and clapped. Then the concert began. Muslim Magomaev, at one of his first performances in Moscow (he would become an almost instant star after that night), started up with '*Cuba Libre*' in Russian and soon the whole audience had joined in. During the interval Fidel stayed near the front, talking with people. He did not notice the young girl standing behind him and holding on to his sleeve. 'I just wanted to touch him,' she recalled.

Fidel had caught their imagination, of that there could be no doubt. But their response had left a profound impression upon him too. Master of propaganda that he was, he must have realised that to some extent all this was staged. But there was more than a little truth to his words when he declared that 'Leningrad was too beautiful to completely remember; too warm in its sentiments and deeds, for the traveller and visitor to leave without feeling sad', while in Irkutsk he was moved to reflect on the 'fellow-feeling and love for us' that he sensed there.

Khrushchev had intended Fidel to feel welcome. But so too did he want Fidel to know that he had stuck his neck out far enough on Cuba's behalf the previous year. If he smarted at that, Fidel kept silent. It was not until a brief stop that Fidel made with Khrushchev at his dacha in the hills outside Moscow – the Soviet Premier had specifically requested that Fidel be kept as busy as possible – that the two leaders finally addressed their real concerns. Fidel, of course, was not in the least bit tired by the pounding schedule, and once he had settled down with Khrushchev he forced the Soviet leader to pore through months of telegrams, reading out each one to him with a translator as Fidel, no less patient, cross-examined them all. He was determined to get to the bottom of it. 'Had the Americans agreed to withdraw their missiles from Italy as well as Turkey?' he asked Foreign Minister Gromyko at one point. 'Turkey yes, but not Italy,' was Gromyko's reply, and it stuck to the official line. But as he went through the letters and Fidel bombarded him with laboriously interpreted questions, for neither spoke the other's language, Khrushchev, Fidel noted, had said yes to both. Immediately his ears pricked up. Removing missiles from Italy had nothing to do with defending Cuban interests. 'Come again please?' Khrushchev knew he had made a slip. He repeated it. All he could do was smile his mischievous smile and all Fidel could do was acquiesce. He knew the terms upon which Moscow's continued support of his revolution rested.

Back in Cuba, Che was less willing for any great rapprochement with the Soviets, however. As he now saw it, to replace one foreign imperial power with another was to make the same mistake twice. When Alexiev had asked him if he wanted to come to Moscow too, he had simply shrugged the suggestion away with a laugh. He knew he was seen in Moscow as the 'troublemaker', he said, and sabotaging Fidel's plans was the farthest thing from his mind. Better to let Fidel go on his own, Che urged, before adding in an affectionate tone that the offer had seemed to revive Fidel. In a recent meeting of the national leadership, Che recalled, Fidel had been asking 'if there was a tradition of speeches being made from the Lenin Mausoleum, and whether Soviet friends would let him speak during the demonstration'. Alexiev had been pleased to hear this – it being one of the first signs that Fidel might actually go – but he denied that Che was seen as a troublemaker. 'In my country you are appreciated precisely for your honesty and sincerity, your firmness in defending your ideas, even though they are sometimes wrong, and for your courage in recognising your mistakes; and a certain taste for troublemaking is not a defect in our eyes' was his rather official-sounding reply.

Che's laughter at Alexiev's cleaving to the party line hid his true feelings. It was no secret that Che had, for some time, been growing increasingly sceptical of the Soviet Union and if he had refrained from being more explicit thus far it must have been largely out of respect for Fidel. He could not resist the occasional dig, however. In an article he wrote at this time Che acknowledged that the Cuban revolutionaries might have begun as bungling amateurs. He was certainly quick to lampoon the 'primitive epoch of our management of the government,' even citing their naïve reliance on 'guerrilla tactics as a form of state administration'. But he was equally sure that 'attempting to destroy "guerrillaism" without sufficient administrative experience' had resulted in 'general chaos'. It was criticism pitched as critique, but neither were words that Moscow wanted to hear.

* * *

When Fidel returned to Havana, he was glowing. His stance could not have been more different than it had been at the start of the year. The Soviet system was 'invincible' and an example of 'a communism which is based on the mandate of man' he began saying right away. And as for where Cuba stood in relation to this grandeur: 'We are communists and our fate is bound with that of the entire communist camp. We are on the right way.' Fidel even went so far as to assure the Soviet leadership that Cuba would restrain its previously vocal support of armed revolutionary uprisings across the South American continent.

Moscow had a particular interest in securing such a commitment from Fidel in light of the growing Sino–Soviet conflict that was beginning to undermine the unity of the socialist bloc. Mao's China had, by the late 1950s, come to rival the Soviet Union in many respects and Mao was increasingly prepared to show his disapproval of the policies Khrushchev had implemented since taking over from Stalin. Above all the Chinese were in favour of the idea of armed insurrection as the appropriate means of spreading the socialist creed while the Soviet leadership under Khrushchev had ventured on to the path of 'peaceful coexistence'. Such peaceful coexistence did not preclude the occasional rattling of sabres, as Khrushchev had intended by installing missiles in Cuba. But it did mean that socialism was to be exported to other countries via party channels and political influence rather than through revolutionary uprisings. Above all, Moscow wanted no more flashpoints that might jeopardise its relatively fragile peace with the Americans. The Chinese simply viewed this as weak-kneed and defeatist.

The Cuban leadership had always been somewhere in between these two positions. They knew more about, were more comfortable with, and so had perhaps inevitably first developed close relations with the Soviets. At the same time, their own revolutionary history, based upon a war in the countryside rather than upon urban insurrections, had more in common with the Chinese experience. Cuba's revolutionary government had always supported other leftist insurrectionary groups, and did not just confine their support to Latin America. They had also taken a stand of militant solidarity alongside the revolutionary movements in Algeria and Vietnam.

This was partly a case of the solidarity of the small, but Cuba had fired imaginations across the socialist camp and, in ideological terms, what the Cubans did mattered greatly, even to the lumbering powers of the Soviet Union and China. But as the additional price for his reconciliation with Moscow, Fidel had been forced to take a stand on the dispute and he committed Cuba to the Soviet line.

Khrushchev was pleased. This greatly boosted Soviet prestige vis-à-vis the Chinese. But the Kremlin might have guessed that Fidel would be more reluctant than he might let on to give up his plans of fomenting revolution elsewhere. Evidently aware of the need to reinforce what they had made clear to Fidel, at the time of his return to Cuba the Soviets sent a coded warning to those who would take the revolutionary process into their own hands. Latin American communists 'would be wrong to pin all their hopes on the armed struggle', the arch-Stalinist Mikhail Suslov conveyed, in a sufficiently open manner that the CIA also had no trouble picking up on it. 'Revolution cannot be accelerated or made to measure, nor can it be appropriated from abroad.' Of all the people Suslov wanted to convey this to, above all for his position alongside Fidel, Che was foremost in his mind.

Suslov, it seemed, knew whereof he spoke. Before the end of the month Fidel had despatched Che on a brief trip to Algeria. Ostensibly Che was there to represent Cuba at the first anniversary of Algeria's own revolution under Ahmed Ben Bella, but he was also there to obtain Ben Bella's support for some of Cuba's most secret revolutionary initiatives, ones that Moscow above all was not to be privy to. Cuba had been fingered as the place from where a good deal of arms were finding their way into Latin America and, now that he was not supposed to be supporting such ventures any more, Fidel needed an alternative base from which to channel them. Strategically, using Algeria as such a base was a brilliant move at a time when the great rivalries of the Cold War were beginning to smother what little room for manoeuvre smaller countries such as Cuba had to enjoy in international affairs. But Fidel's continued commitment to supporting revolutionary movements in defiance of the Soviet Union had the potential to become a very dangerous game indeed.

* * *

Che's revolutionary ideas also expanded that year to take greater account of the international scene. And while he was in Algeria he was also furthering some plans that he had been developing more or less independently of late. Above all, a guerrilla unit that Che had selected and begun to train the year before was now stationed in Algeria en route to its destination posting.

Its members included two Argentines, journalist Jorge Masetti, a close friend of Che, who would lead the mission, and the painter Ciro Roberto Bustos, who was to provide logistical support.

Che had tasked this group with developing a guerrilla insurgency in Argentina, in the Salta region to the north, near the border with Bolivia. Che intended that, once they were established, he would come to lead the group himself in what he hoped would be the beginning of a series of guerrilla flashpoints across Latin America, a great revolutionary dynamo that would ignite not just one country but the entire region.

The Salta expedition was the means by which Che hoped to put his own brand of revolutionary internationalism into action. But the ideas themselves – the beliefs, even, that were shaping his every action more and more – were contained in his major treatise to date, *Guerrilla Warfare: A Method*, which was published shortly after his return from Algiers, in September 1963. The manual was a follow-up to his already widely known book, published the previous year: *Guerrilla War*. The previous work was marked by the tension of a government minister writing as a rebel at heart. This new piece was far less obviously constrained: it seemed that the rebel in him was winning out. Indeed, just as Fidel had talked himself into a major decision earlier in the year in his marathon run of speeches on the theme of unity, so now did it become clear that Che had been writing himself into clarifying *his* own thoughts.

'We shall begin from this basis,' Fidel had written of the consciousness-raising experience of abject poverty and the imminent crisis of imperialism that he foresaw would result, 'to analyse the whole matter of guerrilla warfare in Latin America.' These words were from Fidel's Second Declaration of Havana, and Che used them as the preface to his own much more applied work. Che wrote *Guerrilla Warfare* as if Fidel was his active and willing co-author, but it was only the more bellicose parts of Fidel's declaration that he incorporated into his own text.

In large measure Fidel was perfectly of a mind with Che's

ideas. However, he understood that guerrilla warfare was but one tactic among many and it revealed a basic character difference between them: Fidel wanted to strategise, Che wanted to act. Che also felt that the times required a clearer, more absolute response from Fidel and he used his friend's own words as both springboard and guide to make the case, teasing more and more from Fidel's insights until they suggested to him what he wanted to hear: namely that ideals were there to be acted upon. No impediments to the revolution should be allowed to exist; all must be swept away. 'The duty of revolutionaries, of Latin American revolutionaries', Che quoted Fidel back to himself as saying, 'is not to wait for the change in the correlation of forces to produce a miracle of social revolutions in Latin America, but to take full advantage of everything that is favourable to the revolutionary movement – and to make revolution!'

There was more going on here than just the rendering of a first draft of Che's *own* revolutionary manifesto, a sort of 'third' declaration of Havana. Che was fully aware of the pressures being put upon Fidel to relinquish their plans for guerrilla operations, and he wanted to make the case for the continued relevance of that strategy. And, just as he had fought for Fidel's heart with René Ramos Latour at the end of the first year of war in the Sierra, so was Che going to fight it out with the Soviets over Fidel's revolutionary plans now. *Guerrilla Warfare* was just a more elaborate means of doing so. Che had been inspired again by Fidel's Second Declaration: it was as if Fidel had broken the locks and was handing out rifles once more. And Che saw it as his revolutionary duty to guide Fidel's insights towards what he thought was their appropriate end.

The Soviets were less concerned with the subtleties of what Che might have been doing in this text than with its overall tenor, however. Moscow was outraged, the Soviet embassy in Havana branding it 'ultrarevolutionary bordering on adventurism'. And – perhaps as Che had planned – Fidel certainly felt a little compromised. Having his differences with the Soviets being pointed out was at this moment the very last thing he wanted. It was the same as when Che had declared his Marxism while Fidel was trying to convince people of just the opposite during their time in detention in Mexico.

But despite Fidel's unwillingness to break from the official Soviet line when the publication of *Guerrilla Warfare* gave him every opportunity to do so, Che would none the less achieve rather more than he might have hoped for with the book, which very soon became required reading for aspiring liberation groups around the world. And it must have brought both a wry smile to his lips and the flicker of an idea, when later in the year Raúl Roa, who was then in Europe, sent him an English copy of *Guerrilla Warfare*, adding, conspiratorially, 'If you want, I can use my good standing with Mao so that 600 million copies can be published in the language of Lao-Tse.'

* * *

It was temperament and not ideology that lay behind these gradually sharpening differences. 'Fidel would agree in principle with anything', but Che, increasingly, did nothing except *out* of principle. Increasingly now, their characters had begun to drive their respective visions of the revolution in different directions. Always the more patient of the two, Fidel had come to accept that the advancement of the revolution internationally would take much longer. He was not of Che's view that Latin America in particular was ripe for revolution, at least not in every country. Fidel was more inclined to see a series of waves of revolution around the world as providing the necessary first steps to tilting the balance of forces in favour of anti-colonial nationalists such as themselves, and he looked in the first place to Algeria as being the next country to carry the baton for a while. So apparent was his enthusiasm for Ben Bella's revolution that one newspaper was prompted to run a cartoon of Fidel being carried in Ben Bella's arms like a Middle

Eastern bride with the caption, 'Let me take you to the Casbah' written underneath.

Che, by contrast, was always that man standing impatiently before a map that a group of Argentine compatriots found one night on entering his office at the Ministry. On receiving his visitors, Che brought out some maté and they sat there sipping it and sharing tales until Che said suddenly, 'Revolution can be made at any given moment anywhere in the world.' 'Anywhere?' someone enquired. 'Even in Argentina or La Paz?' Che proceeded to place his finger on his own home town on the map. 'Even in Córdoba there can be revolution,' he proclaimed.

When not extolling the virtues of Ben Bella's new Republic Fidel, by contrast, would be more commonly seen in these days at work with the figures and trends of his own revolution. He would go on ceaselessly enumerating them throughout his life: literacy rates going up, infectious diseases coming down, sugar productivity veering around as he imposed his increasingly different views from Che upon the yearly cycle. Fidel was, on the whole, content to watch these figures rise or fall, to impart shape to them, to explain their trajectory. He who had travelled so little, was always content with the journey. Che, however, wanted more. He wanted to arrive. So far as Fidel saw it, that could be counterproductive.

While Che was hectoring Fidel over his international commitments that summer, trying to drag him towards what he believed was the right path, Fidel began to question some of Che's approaches to domestic affairs more openly. Shortly after returning from the Soviet Union, and framing his words in the long, ambling and decidedly inverse manner that preceded his criticisms, Fidel had weighed in with a critique of much of what Che had been striving so hard to achieve through his various appointments as head of the National Bank and, more recently, as the Minister of Industries: 'There are institutions like that famous national bank which has 1,097 employees and half of them are not needed,' Fidel said. Then he began to chuckle. 'Why are you all looking at Che, it is not Che's fault for any of this. He was in the national bank but he did not place any bureaucrats there or anything like that. [What] he has not done clearly is to say: "Let's throw these people out."' Che had been the key architect of the Cuban economy for over two years but now, Fidel appeared to be saying, the country's industrial and economic development was an area that he was going to have a say in too.

Che's response was voiced privately in a conversation with his Soviet minder, Oleg Daroussenkov. 'Fidel's recent speeches regarding boosting agriculture,' he confided, 'have a great importance. However, it doesn't mean that Cuba has changed its development orientation towards agriculture .... Agriculture [ultimately] hinders the development of our country.' These differences of opinion as to what needed to be prioritised cut across almost everything. Both agreed on the need for more steel, for example. But when Che thought of steel he was not thinking, as was Fidel, of the tractors or cane cutting machines that might assist agricultural production. His mind saw ahead to ships – 'our trade is maritime and we have virtually no shipping fleet ourselves,' he had complained before now.

Fidel was growing more sceptical about such grand schemes for rapid industrialisation. He was concerned by the shortages of things and, though he sometimes sat on the fence while Che engaged in his endless arguments with colleagues such as Regino Boti and Carlos Rafael Rodríguez about the nature of socialist work, he was, on the whole, happy to offer *whatever* incentives – material, moral or otherwise – would get people to work towards the goals he saw were necessary. 'Who is in the vanguard?' Fidel had asked a group of Uruguayan communists in an interview the previous year. 'What revolutionary goals can be sacrificed? What does the proletariat gain if the struggle is left in the hands of the bourgeoisie, who then consolidate their position? What can be given up, and what not? This is a question of tactics. It is necessary to try to unite a number of different segments without sacrificing the fundamental objectives of the revolution.' Frank

País, Fidel and Che's city-based comrade from the Sierra days and until his murder the head of the 26 July underground movement, had once remarked that 'tactics in politics and tactics in revolution are not the same'. It seemed now that País's view was proving itself to be true. Albeit in the name of what he saw as safeguarding the revolution, Fidel had reverted to the tactics of politics; Che held fast to those of revolution.

* * *

Throughout 1963 the two revolutionary leaders seemed to be veering off in different directions as Fidel sought to safeguard the revolution's achievements and Che continued to put everything at risk in the pursuit of an ever purer revolution reaching out to ever more people. By the end of the year however, they would each suffer a setback that would heighten these tensions at the same time as it suggested their solution.

A blow to Fidel's gradual consolidation of authority occurred when President Kennedy was assassinated in November. With Kennedy went a secret back channel to Washington that Fidel had been trying to engineer even before his reconciliation trip to Moscow. The negotiations had been couched in no formal agreement, just on the word of the President. Indeed, the idea of a back-channel had not been something that Fidel had foreseen until a chance encounter came his way and, as ever with Fidel, a new path, once opened, was embarked upon at speed.

On 22 April he had granted an interview to the American television journalist Lisa Howard. An actress and former soap star, and the first woman to anchor her own news show, Howard was a 'slight, trim woman with a husky voice [and] enormous dark eyes'. She had made her name by scooping an interview with Khrushchev during the Vienna summit in 1961. Now it was Fidel's turn. Their first meeting, which began after midnight in the lobby bar of Havana's Hotel Riviera, went on until 5.30 in the morning. Howard wore a low-cut cocktail dress for the meeting and Fidel toyed with a scotch and soda thoughout. She did most of the talking, telling him what she thought of his revolution (nothing especially positive), and asking him for free access to go where she liked to pull together a report, telling him she had no time to be sent to jail.

In short, for all her criticisms of his revolution, Lisa Howard was Fidel's sort of woman. But even this 'pushy Clairol blonde' was caught off guard by the astonishing listener that Fidel proved to be. As he had done with Naty years before, he charmed her with his literary small talk – this time he spoke of Albert Camus. Unlike Naty, who seemed to take everything Fidel said at face value, Lisa was more than a match for his verbal pirouettes. Camus, she pointed out, had broken with communism in 1955. For the televised interview itself, in her hotel room, she made the questions deliberately tough. Fidel commented on it afterwards, though he seemed to have enjoyed it more than anything. 'Did you really tell him that?' Raúl Roa asked at a cocktail party afterwards when she told him of the criticisms she had voiced to Fidel. 'I am glad.'

But in between these conversations the rather more serious idea of a back channel to Washington had been touted, considered and finally agreed upon. When Howard returned to Washington she had a meeting with a representative of the CIA and told him that Fidel wanted to talk. 'Liza [sic] Howard definitely wants to impress the US Government with two facts: that Castro is ready to discuss rapprochement and she herself is ready to discuss it with him if asked to do so by the US Government'. With the idea implanted Fidel was soon thinking further ahead than Washington might have suspected, though. Knowing full well the likely outcome of his trip to Moscow, such a back channel might be his one hope of engineering a political counter-balance to the otherwise inexorable process of Sovietisation that would be the price of his own political security. By the time of Kennedy's assassination on 22 November 1963, plans had progressed as far as a proposed meeting between representatives of both sides. In fact, the message confirming this from the Cubans was delivered to Kennedy's desk just as the President was riding in the ill-fated motorcade in Dallas.

The abrupt closing of the Castro-Kennedy back channel as the fatally wounded Kennedy slumped forward in his presidential limousine, was perhaps *the* missed opportunity for Cuban–American relations. But more personally for Fidel, it meant an end to his hopes of retaining some room for manoeuvre with the Soviets. And that had implications for the current situation with Che, whose continued and vocal insistence all that year on the need to support armed uprisings wherever they might occur had constantly led to accusations of being pro-Chinese. To be labelled such a thing at a time when Cuba was, by Fidel's own doing, determinedly supporting the Soviets made for a serious problem between the two of them.

By the end of 1963, Che had begun to find himself ostracised by some of his comrades in the Cuban leadership. Raúl, with whom he had once been close, had taken up a dogmatic position in support of the Soviet camp and was quite prepared to accuse Che of cleaving to the opposite side, as he did at that year's New Year's Eve party in front of much of the revolutionary leadership. 'I assured him we did not think such things,' Che's minder Daroussenkov wrote in a report of a conversation with Che in December. But Che did not believe him. 'A label is not an argument,' was all he said by way of reply.

But labels have a way of sticking when others want them to, and Che now became an easy target for those who wanted to curry favour with Moscow. Representatives in Havana of many of the smaller Soviet satellite states tried to take advantage of Che's suddenly vulnerable position. Pavlicek, the Czech ambassador, kept reporting to Moscow that 'Some members of National leadership are influenced by this propaganda, Ernesto Che Guevara in the first place.' And Siurus, the chargé d'affaires at the Polish embassy, was equally busy stirring trouble for Che: 'Chinese propaganda falls on fertile soil not only among middle and lower class workers, but also among a part of the National leadership,' he said to Anikin, the deputy head of Moscow's Latin America Department in a deliberate nod towards Che.

Che, not oblivious to all this, was not 'pro-Chinese' in any sense other than that he found Mao, personally, an inspiring example. He knew perfectly well that just a few choice words would calm Moscow's nerves and quell the speculation. But he was so disappointed by the presence of such a split within the socialist camp in the first place that he could not bring himself to utter them. In this he had responded very differently from Fidel, who had been confronted by the same choice in Moscow earlier in the year. Fidel had needed not a moment to take the politically more expedient path whatever his personal view.

Fidel's own choice was confirmed in January 1964 when he accompanied Politburo member Nikolai Podgorny, who had made a brief stopover in Havana, back to Moscow for his second visit to the country in less than a year. A photo taken during this trip shows him visiting Khrushchev at his dacha in the Caucusus, a beautiful spot, seemingly far from the vicissitudes of international politics, on a former meadow with a little marsh nearby. Here Khrushchev would sit on Sundays reading his documents and newspapers at a wicker table.

This time he delighted in showing Fidel his experimental minifarm, with its clusters of red berries and rows of vegetables – squashes and cucumbers and lettuces – that he personally tended. Perhaps this was fitting, for it was an agricultural trade agreement – specifically to finalise a new sugar deal for Cuba – that the two leaders signed before Fidel's return. The deal would ensure Fidel's security for some years to come. It would also finally give the Soviet Union the claws on the revolution that it wanted: a lifeline that could be withheld if ever the leadership strayed too far from the party line.

Fidel had now completed the task that Che had begun, leading the Cubans full circle from the American sugar quota to a Soviet deal that likewise agreed to buy Cuban sugar at above world prices. But for Che, the focus of whose work at the Ministry had been getting the country industrialised, this would come as a major setback to his own plans for building socialism in Cuba. For Che, sugar was slavery. It was as simple as that. And as for the material incentives that Fidel, like everyone else, appeared to favour, for Che that was just a way of 'letting capitalism in through the back door'. Very suddenly, the world of seemingly infinite possibilities they had set alight with the unlikely success of their revolution in 1959, had been narrowed down and the two men found that different paths were opening up before them: paths from which it would prove extremely difficult for either of them to deviate.

PART 4

13. NEW ALIGNMENTS

IT HAD LONG been on the cards. 'There's an altiplano, in South America,' Che had said to Alfredo Menéndez, a colleague who accompanied him on his first tour as Fidel's emissary back in 1959. '[T]here in Bolivia, in Paraguay, an area bordering Brazil, Uruguay, Peru and Argentina', he went on, listing further possibilities, 'where if we insert a guerrilla force, we could spread the revolution all over America.' He was thinking above all of an area near to a scene he could recall from his travels with Calica, a spot they had holed up in for two days while his asthma abated and where the image of two flags facing one another had caught a young traveller's eye.

Perhaps it was the sense of being back on the road again during the first summer of the revolution that had taken him back to the earlier moment with a different ambition in mind, one formed from his current duties as a figurehead for the revolution and after two years of war. Menéndez recalls that he 'never associated it with a real plan', at least not until later. There is no reason why he should have, of course. It was just one of those conversations between two men a long way from home, reminiscing and sharing their hopes for the future. But all the same it is quite possible, if not probable, that Che had decided even then that there would come a time when he returned to his homeland once more to fight. For now, at the beginning of 1964, Masetti's Salta expedition, which was then establishing itself in the north of

Argentina in anticipation of Che's joining them, was still his best hope of doing so.

Whatever he had been saying to the Soviets recently, Fidel was far from averse to such talk. From as early as 1960 he had supported any number of small-scale insurgency movements across the continent, and a large part of his secret services was devoted to just this task. 'Ever since he wrote "History Will Absolve Me", his chief intelligence operator, Manuel Piñeiro, recalled many years later, 'Fidel had made clear that this revolution was seeking the liberation and integration of Latin America . . . . In Che, Fidel found someone who shared this same determination.'

But Fidel also saw that the role of leaders in any revolution was to be wise: to stay alive and to lead. True, he had leaped eagerly into battle at Girón, but that was a few years ago now. He had no wish to play the *guerrillero* himself any more. In any case, he was in no position to do so. During a late-night conversational session with foreign journalists over cups of strong coffee at Havana's 21 Club the previous year, Fidel had been asked to comment on the comparison between himself and the great South American liberator Simon Bolívar. 'It's not the century of Bolívars. It's the century of the masses,' he had replied. 'There was so much Bolívar can do. There is so little I can do.'

Fidel was speaking just at the moment when he was beginning to feel his hands being tied by the Soviets. As he paused between sips to reflect on his answers that night – and if not then, it was certainly some time around then – he might well have hit upon a possible solution to the twin problems then confronting him: his increasingly constrained freedom of movement abroad with respect to the Soviet Union, and his increasingly intractable differences with Che Guevara at home. With such constraints, and acting as one man, there certainly was little that Fidel could do as compared to Bolívar. But if he and Che could work something out between the two of them, it might yet be possible to pursue the revolution abroad while striking at least a nominal pose in favour of peaceful coexistence at home. What was more, it was a solution that held out the promise of salvaging their personal relations despite their growing political differences. But how would Che view such an idea?

* * *

Che's asthma was as bad as ever that year. He had resorted, not for the first time, to horse doctor remedies, often using adrenaline, which tended to intoxicate him and gave him stomach pains. He was also still reeling from the double shock of the Soviets' betrayal of the Cubans during the Missile Crisis and of what looked like Fidel's apparent willingness to accept it. As the year progressed he continued waging the same battles as before. But now, when he tried voluntary labour to cheer himself up, for the first time he came away utterly deflated by it. As he said during a meeting at the Ministry after one such trip: 'I kept looking at my watch every fifteen minutes to see when my hours would be up . . . because it didn't make any sense.'

It was a further sign that he felt under attack when he resorted to mocking the bureaucracy and the endless circular debates at the Ministry and at JUCEPLAN, the Central Planning Board. In February he wrote to the economist Regino Boti, with whom he had now been cracking heads for over half a year about the issue of worker incentives and who embodied for Che much of the spirit of the stifling bureaucracy that prevented any of them from getting anything done: 'I greet you, Comrade Minister, with the JUCEPLAN war cry: Long live the letter-writing war! Down with productive work!'

In February he wrote to another correspondent, José Medero Mestre, in an equally ironic, if more acerbic, tone. 'Unfortunately, . . . apologies for the [current] system seem more forthcoming than [proper] analysis of it . . . For that reason – because you *think* – I thank you for your letter,' he wrote to Medero in response to his criticisms of the industrial-scale bureaucracy, adding, 'It's only a shame we don't agree [about what to do].' He then let slip a revealing insight into a tired mind that was burning bright with possibilities. It was late as he wrote and his thoughts were evidently wandering. 'In this world it is you who knows me and I who may not remember your name; it could have been the reverse, and then I would have to write to you from some remote region of the world where my Andean bones had carried me for I was not born here.'

Whether Che was at that moment wondering about the progress of the Salta expedition which he had checked on as its members completed their training in Algeria, or whether he was thinking about when (or even if, given his commitments in Cuba) he himself might be able to join it, we do not know. We do know that he had in mind his pride at having worked by Fidel's side 'in the difficult moments of the Cuban revolution and in some of the most tragic and glorious moments of the history of a world that is fighting for its liberty', because he said so in his letter. But Che needed some way of reconciling his personal loyalty to Fidel and his growing disappointment with the way some aspects of the revolution were proceeding.

When the opportunity came to escape the island for a while to represent Cuba at the first United Nations Conference on Trade and Development in Geneva that March, he took it gladly. The UNCTAD conference – heralded as a 'new era of international cooperation' – represented the first major step by the UN to deal with trade as a development issue.

The speech that Che gave in Geneva was one of the few that really did justice to the thorny issues such a conference needed to address, perhaps because he was not afraid to call a spade a spade: he expressed his hope that the conference would expose 'the imperialistic policy of robbing weak countries'. The ideas behind his speech were typically forthright and they were not what the majority of the assembled delegates wanted to hear. George W. Ball, the US representative in Geneva, reported to the State Department on the 'considerable restraint' shown in general by the socialist countries at the conference, adding that: 'Che

Guevara, on the other hand, delivered a 1½-hour tirade. His speech might have been effective had it been short, but, in the end, it bored the delegates and a number expressed their gratitude to us for not taking Guevara on and making the Conference an East–West donnybrook.'

Che would probably have been the first to remind Ball that the conference had been convened to discuss north–south issues, not east–west concerns, but it was true that he was not optimistic about UNCTAD's prospects and Ball probably rightly detected that Che was spoiling for a fight. At that moment in fact, Che's position was steadily becoming less agreeable. First of all, he was finding that his attempts at the conference to contact other comrades from the socialist bloc countries were treated with caution, if not outright rebuffed. It was as if, all of a sudden, he was the *persona non grata* of the socialist camp. But what really blackened Che's mood was the news that his Salta expedition in Argentina had failed. Though they had successfully established a base on the Argentine–Bolivian border, Masetti's group were soon infiltrated by Argentine government agents. Masetti himself was lost in the high mountains, his body never found. Most of the rest were captured and imprisoned. Che's long-cherished plans to join them would have to be dropped. Of his reaction to this one delegate left a glimpse: he reported having seen Che sitting by the shore of Lake Geneva staring out across the water towards Mont Salève, utterly lost in thought.

If Che had hoped that, when the time came for him to join this mission, he might escape the increasingly difficult situation in Cuba he was to be disappointed. That particular way out was now closed to him, and Che left Geneva knowing that he would have to return and resolve things properly with Fidel one way or the other.

* * *

On his return to Havana, Che first of all took up the issue of his treatment in Geneva by the representatives of the other socialist countries with his minder and some-time chess partner, Daroussenkov. One wonders if this was not just a way of redirecting some of his growing frustration with Fidel. He asked why the socialists were coming to see him as an enemy. 'This is a big mistake. I never used to be your enemy. I am just a difficult friend who always says what he thinks; a friend that will never be a puppet, just like Fidel. You tend to consider me pro-Chinese as some of my ideas objectively coincide with those of the Chinese. But I'm only honest about it. I did not conceal it even in conversation with Khrushchev.' And as to which side was right, he added, 'Convince me, prove to me that you are right and I will change my opinion on the issues in question.'

In May Che made a speech to the Young Communist members in his own Ministry – a place he now referred to as 'a den of meticulous bureaucrats and hatchetmen'. Once again it raised hackles in Moscow. Che had been implying that the Soviet party structure was perhaps not quite what Cuba needed, and that inveterate snoop Belous was tasked with finding out whether 'the thoughts expressed by Guevara reflect the National leadership position or his personal views'. This time Belous asked Fabio Grobart, who pointed out that in fact Fidel and Che *both* tended to make announcements that did not necessarily represent the 'collective opinion' of the government. 'Their speeches are not prepared beforehand, are not discussed and are often mere improvisation,' Grobart responded.

Grobart seemed to be concerned by the same thing as the Soviets. In his speeches, Fidel was yet again talking of armed insurrections and the possibility of the death of the leadership, none of which Grobart found any more amenable than Che's sabre-rattling and all of which was of great concern to Moscow. Had Che been speaking to Fidel already? Certainly Fidel seemed once more to be 'under the influence of emotions', as Grobart put it.

In fact Grobart was hopeful, or so he told the Soviets, that, for fear of breaking the unity of the national leadership, Fidel was simply waiting for the right moment to condemn the Chinese model of supporting revolutionary uprisings. But since this conversation took place in May, it makes Grobart's speculation as to Fidel's duplicity unlikely. By then Fidel had little reason to tread carefully. In March he had orchestrated yet another shake-up of allegiances within the revolutionary ranks by means of a show trial which he used to damp down the resurgence of disagreements between the old communists of the PSP and the new communists, the Fidelistas, within the government. As he consolidated his own authority once again, as ever, Fidel had his eye to the long awaited but now imminent formation of a formalised party structure. Confident finally that the right men would be elected to the right positions, Fidel was now happy to let the PURS (the United Party of the Socialist Revolution) go the way of the ORI as it made way, this time, for an official Communist Party structure of government.

*   *   *

Such political manoeuvering was something Che had little time for and the differences between the two over the future direction that should be taken by the revolution in Cuba began to come to a head that summer as the dogma of 'party unity' that Fidel was insisting upon – and which was contrary to Che's personal wishes – appeared to have reached even Che's closest aides. 'It is hard for the middle classes to identify with Marxism–Leninism and moreover to firmly stand on its grounds,' said Aragonés, now party secretary of the PURS, in a private conversation with Daroussenkov. Che could hardly be accused of being one of those opposed to the old communists, though he had his doubts about some of them. But the Soviets were determined to keep a close eye on Che at this particularly sensitive time while the new party structure was being put into place and even his most innocuous activities did not escape their prying eyes.

For some time, Che had been attending classes on political

economy at the University of Havana along with a sizeable portion of the rest of the revolutionary leadership: Carlos Rafael Rodríguez, Augusto Martínez-Sánchez, and, though they had given up on the classes by now, Raúl Castro, Osvaldo Dorticós and Faure Chomón. In May an attaché at the Soviet embassy, Pronsky, was asked to drop in on the teacher of this rather unusual class – Anastasio Cruz Mansilla, a Spaniard who had taught in the Soviet Union – to find out a little more about Che's current tendencies. Che was the brightest in the class, Mansilla assured Pronsky; he would regularly stay behind to debate further the points discussed. But it was also clear from Pronsky's conversation with Mansilla that Che tended to be reluctant when asked to 'accentuate the positive' about the USSR.

For all their growing differences, Fidel knew rather better than to worry about such reports when they filtered through to him. He knew that Che was a perfectionist who could accept no deviation from what he saw as the right path, and he greatly valued that aspect of his character. But as Fidel sought to put together a more formalised party structure modelled upon that of the Soviet Union he needed people like Dorticós – someone who 'listens carefully, generally agrees but rarely expresses his own opinion', as Professor Mansilla put it – rather more than he needed Che's well-intentioned but invariably troublesome 'scruples'.

Quietly, then, and without the excess of argument that one might imagine the climax of a revolutionary dispute to entail, the two of them had finally reached their impasse. Each was preventing the other from moving forward as he would like. They were confronted, as a result, with the choice between loyalty to one another, which would entail one or other of them compromising on their revolutionary beliefs, or loyalty to those beliefs, which would entail the severance of their political relationship. Wilful to the last, they both refused, in the end, to make that choice. Which left only one available option: the long and dangerous path of permanent revolution. Only if Che were to

During the first eighteen months of the revolution, Fidel and Che worked closely together, both in public *and* in secret. Here they are seen leaving Havana's famous 1830 restaurant in 1963. By then both were beginning to formulate different ideas on the future of the revolution.

Fidel and Che converse after landing at a rural airstrip in 1960. After gaining a pilot's license Che would regularly fly himself and his close acquaintances around the country.

Che in rustic straw hat looks toward the stage during a 'manifestation' in the early 1960s. In the background, Fidel barrel-laughs at the photographer.

Che is showered with confetti during his visit to China in late 1960, on his first tour of the socialist bloc. He was to become increasingly drawn to the Chinese model of socialism as opposed to that offered in the USSR; something that would increasingly cause friction between himself and Fidel.

Fidel enjoys a stroll in the countryside near one of Khrushchev's dachas on the outskirts of Moscow during *his* first visit to the USSR in April 1963. From right to left are Khrushchev, Nikolai Leonov (KGB interpreter and old friend of Che and Raúl from their Mexico days), two bodyguards and, wearing thick spectacles, Soviet Ambassador to Cuba – Alexandr Alexiev.

Fidel holds forth with Soviet cosmonauts on January 20, 1964, during his second visit to the USSR. Yuri Gagarin is sitting next to Castro, on his right. Fidel enjoyed his visits to the USSR far more than Che.

In Havana, Che relaxes with a cigar and a recent issue of the popular magazine *Bohemia*, featuring Fidel on its front cover. A natural division of labour developed between them: Fidel would tend to be on the cover of journals and magazines and quoted therein, Che was more likely to write for them.

Just prior to his first visit to the USSR in 1963, Fidel met with US television journalist, Lisa Howard. Howard would become a central figure in a secret back-channel of communication that began to develop between Castro and the Kennedy administration before John F. Kennedy's assassination later that year in Dallas.

Fidel speaks to aides and journalists in a hotel room in 1963. Fidel could rarely stay in one place for long. Hotel rooms were often as likely a place for a meeting as any government office. Che kept rather more ordered, though no less intensive working hours.

In 1964 Fidel took decisive measures to consolidate his personal vision of the revolution. Here he relaxes by pitching a few balls, but more complex, dangerous games were afoot behind the scenes.

Shortly before his clandestine journey to Tanzania, Che submits to the painful process of being disguised. Prostheses and hair-plucking were a standard technique used by the Cuban secret services.

The disguise completed. Similar treatments would see him travel through Moscow, Paris and Rio de Janeiro completely unnoticed. These were the years Che lived his life very much in the shadows.

Che (third from right) poses for a photo with the men who agreed to fight with him in Bolivia in late 1966, all of them having arrived from Cuba like him, in disguise. This final campaign, planned during the long months of hiding in Prague and Cuba after the failure of his mission to the Congo, would end with his death in October 1967.

Fidel surfaces after a dive near one of his beachside ranches outside of Havana. Diving was one of Fidel's favourite escapes. During 1966 and 1967 he had considerable need to escape: he bore the brunt of soviet anger at Che's actions in Bolivia.

July 13, 1997. Che Guevara's remains are repatriated to Cuba after years of mystery surrounding the fate of his body in Bolivia. Fidel looks on, deep in thought, with his brother Raúl and Che's close friend, Interior Minister Ramiro Valdés to his right.

leave Cuba and continue to fight elsewhere could their partnership continue. The idea had its attractions. It would fulfil Che's desire to fight for socialism as a broad ideal, unfettered by the political realities which chipped away at that structure and tarnished its gleam, and it would enable Fidel to pursue the more aggressive foreign policy line to which he was personally committed but which, in the current climate of the Cold War, he was in no position, officially, to support.

If Fidel was in any doubt about embarking on such a path, then the defection that June of his sister Juana probably confirmed his decision. Though she had once helped her younger brother by raising funds abroad for the 26 July Movement, Juana did not share his more radical views and latterly she had become quite vocal in opposition to the revolutionary government. As early as 1960 the US embassy had reported that 'neither she nor her mother are in any way intimates of Fidel', adding that '[I]n general relations between them are poor'. By 1964, Juana had decided she could stand what was happening in Cuba no more and left to visit her sister Emma in Mexico on 20 June, never to return.

No sooner had Juana arrived in Mexico than she called a press conference to denounce her brother's regime. Fidel made no comment about the event for almost a fortnight until he was cornered by journalists at a reception at the Canadian embassy in Havana. 'I knew you were going to ask me this question,' he told them. 'But I prefer to write my response, because I would rather they be transmitted textually.' As when he had felt betrayed by Mirta during his time in prison, Fidel was stung by Juana's actions. But he had no intention of letting this show, of course. And there were political points to be scored. 'These declarations were made in the American embassy in Mexico. They contain all the infamy that imperialism has devised against the Cuban revolution.' He described his sister's defection as a low and repugnant act and added, 'If I had been one of those governors who makes millionaires of his family I would not have suffered this problem. This fact, for me personally, is very bitter and profoundly painful. But I understand that this is the price of being communist.' Outwardly, Fidel presented himself as uncompromising and implacable. Privately, however, Juana's defection was a timely reminder to him that there are times when it is best just to let people go.

* * *

Before the end of the summer, Fidel was already preparing for Che's exit from the scene. He now placed in positions of authority those who were more amenable to working within a party structure, one of the most noticeable changes indeed being the installation of Dorticós as Minister of the Economy and Director of the State Planning Board, effectively setting him up as a counterweight to Che's authority over economic affairs. At the same time, some of those advisers who were closest to Che were also moved; they included his closest aide, Orlando Borrego, who would head up a new sugar industry that would now operate outside of Che's control.

Che was a proud man, and despite his plans to leave, albeit still only privately floated with just Fidel, he must have viewed with regret these changes going on about him. But no comments on his thoughts crop up in any of the private memoranda of his conversations from this period. It seems a strong indication that he had some compelling reason to keep quiet. That autumn Che struck up a rather unlikely-seeming correspondence with the Spanish poet Leon Felipe that would endure throughout his last troubled months in Cuba and that sheds some light on what he, and by extension Fidel, might then have been thinking. Writing to Felipe in August of that year, Che recounted that when he had recently addressed a crowd of workers there had been 'an atmosphere of the new man in the air', he said, as if he could smell it.

For some reason a line of one of Felipe's poems had then come into his head and he had recited it to the audience. 'No one has been able to dig the rhythm of the sun, . . . no one has yet cut an ear of corn with love and grace.' It was a revealing choice. Felipe's line was a lament for the impossibility of reconciling the most human virtues with the brute fact of toiling to survive, and vice versa, but Che had recited it because he felt that such toil in Cuba now did have a point and was a life-affirming activity. Man in Cuba had rediscovered his way, Che said in his letter to Felipe afterwards. But the sudden change in both Che's and Fidel's demeanour that autumn; the seeming patience, stillness almost of those months, suggest rather that these two men in particular had rediscovered their way as a new path had opened up for them. But as time would tell, it was not one that would lead them out of the maze of Cold War politics, so much as deeper into it.

*　*　*

In November it was Che whom Fidel asked to go as his envoy to the Soviet Union. Their faith in one another was evidently by now restored. 'We sent the person closest to us,' Fidel said, making it apparent that his recent moves to downsize Che's official positions represented a change of plan more than it did a change of heart. By then, the international landscape had itself shifted again. An increasingly marginalised Khrushchev had been ousted that October of 1964 in a conspiracy led by Leonid Brezhnev, and the Soviet Union had subsequently, and drastically, scaled back its ambitions for Latin America. Fidel and Che, who had just settled upon the notion of working together to spread the revolution elsewhere on the continent therefore needed to know right away where the new Soviet leadership stood with regard to such a plan.

There was a lot going through Che's mind therefore as he stood in Red Square once more that November next to Lenin's remains (though no longer Stalin's, Khrushchev having succeeded before his own fall in having the latter removed from the mausoleum and placed into the gritty mass of the Kremlin's walls). A certain clue as to the tenor of his thoughts, however, comes from some of the notes he had taken that year when reading Lenin's *Complete Works*. 'Here he confuses two terms,' Che wrote disparagingly beneath a series of quotations taken from the book, 'dictatorship of the proletariat and the Russian revolution; they are not the same. One encompasses the other, but is much richer. . . .' The 'pigsty', as Che now called the Soviet Union, clearly no longer fooled him. But perhaps it might yet be useful.

During his visit, while he endured the pleasantries and the protocol of his official status, Che made sure to meet with Yuri Andropov, then head of the Central Committee's International Department, and Vitali Korionov, who was responsible for the communist parties in Latin American states. Che did not prevaricate. He wanted to know, straight up, whether there would be support from Moscow and from the communist parties in Latin America for his and Fidel's vision of a continent-wide revolution. The answer was a flat no.

Che returned swiftly to Cuba. During the few days that he was back before leaving again, this time bound for New York, Fidel hosted a 'highly secret extraordinary conference' of leaders of the Latin American communist parties at which Che was present. In light of the splitting of certain Latin American communist parties, notably the Peruvian one, into pro-Soviet and pro-Chinese factions, Fidel's task was ostensibly to try to thrash out a common stance to be taken at a forthcoming international meeting in Moscow. Fidel was expected to ensure unity and support for the Soviet side at the meeting.

Fidel set the right tone, picking a fight on the first day with the Peruvian communists – perhaps the most divided group of all – that would presumably do no harm to his image in Moscow's eyes. The issue that dominated proceedings however, was Cuba's sponsorship of guerrilla forces around the continent. The majority of the Latin American communist parties, accustomed to patronage and support from the Soviet Union, were fiercely loyal to Moscow and to its line of 'peaceful coexistence' and they did not take kindly to the constant sabre-rattling of the

Cuban leadership in Havana, much less their actual support for revolutionary projects in their own countries.

But Fidel was never one to shy away from a confrontation and he immediately took the slavish majority to task, as one of the few available reports of this meeting testifies. 'We have learned from reliable sources,' said the East German ambassador, 'that Comrade Fidel Castro initially accused several Latin American parties of not being sufficiently aggressive: they should make the revolution, not wait for it.' Few took kindly to that, and they responded 'vehemently' that Cuban interference in their affairs 'had led, at times, to tragic consequences'.

Fidel had a more secret agenda at the meeting, however. Just as Che had done in Moscow, he was gauging the level of support they might expect in their plans for a continent-wide revolutionary front and whether they might, at the end of the day, be able to prise some of those parties from Moscow's grip. As Victorio Codovilla, the Argentine communist party representative, reported, Fidel and Che apparently set out to 'ask each speaker many questions and throw phrases in that . . . sometimes contain dislike towards the Soviet Union and the fear of total dependence on the USSR'. For the moment, at least, it seemed that there was precious little support available for any such plans.

Before he left for the United Nations General Assembly in New York, Che touched base once more with the Soviets. As ever, the minders needed to be kept informed. Che told Daroussenkov all about the plans for his upcoming speech at the conference; he even opened up a document wallet stuffed with 'materials and photos' of American acts of aggression against the island, most of it coming from the naval base at Guantánamo Bay that the Americans had held since the 1903 Cuban–American Treaty. So far as his pending official diplomatic tasks went, Che gave the impression of being quite open with Daroussenkov. But he was demonstratively unforthcoming about anything else. He said nothing further about his plans in New York nor indeed of exactly where he was going or what he was planning to do (he would be away for a full three months). Daroussenkov was being given, in effect, a coded *fait accompli*. Henceforth, the Soviet leadership might consider itself welcome to know what the Cuban leadership were up to, but only when they were up to it and not a moment before.

If Fidel and Che seemed very much more back in step together, there is a sense that they too scarcely knew what they were up to. Such plans as they had for the future were being put together off the cuff and, while they seemed to have established the general outline of a plan that was very soon to see Che leave Cuba for good, they had not as yet been able to work out the detail. Instead, they had opted for a way forward sufficiently broad in scope that it might somehow swallow the differences between them. In doing so, they had found a way to keep their relationship on track, but so too had they raised the stakes considerably. 'They internationalised the blockade,' Fidel would say later of American foreign policy towards Cuba, before adding somewhat more candidly: 'we internationalised guerrilla warfare'.

14. STRAIGHT TALKING

CHE'S VISIT TO New York in December 1964 was replete with all the customary drama of his international appearances: 'Massed pickets brandished placards (INVADE CUBA NOW) and jeered at Communist-bloc delegates'. A 'knife-toting woman tried to claw her way inside' to attack Che, while another group of exiles were detained after launching a 9-lb bazooka shell at the 'sleek, glass-skinned' UN Building. Despite all the mayhem, Che seemed utterly undeterred, nonplussed almost. Asked about it by a reporter during a stopover in Ireland a few days later – 'He lives a very dangerous life, is he worried about this?' – Che smiled patiently through the translation before replying, 'If only all dangers were of that sort.'

Despite the assassination attempts, Che did not even bother with extra security in New York. Instead, he passed the evenings playing chess with the standard detail New York City police guards stationed outside his hotel room on East Sixty-seventh street. If Che was unconcerned, however, it was because he was focused on the considerable task at hand. He had come to deliver a withering attack on colonialism at the United Nations General Assembly and to lay out his manifesto for war.

In a statement more of his own views than those of Fidel or of official Cuban government policy, Che made it very clear during his major speech in that vast marble-clad hall why he thought the whole idea of 'peaceful coexistence' was flawed.

Cambodia, he said, was being attacked because it had been neutral over Vietnam, and in the Congo people were suffering while the West just squabbled over its resources. 'This philosophy of despoilment,' he said, '. . . is stronger than ever' and there was nothing 'peaceful' about it. Peaceful coexistence in reality meant little more than apathy, and apathy was a form of betrayal. He gestured to the Western powers' acquiescence in the 1961 murder of Patrice Lumumba, the short-lived independence leader of the Republic of the Congo, to sharpen his point. 'But the scales have fallen from our eyes and they now open upon new horizons,' Che went on. 'We can see what yesterday, in our conditions of colonial servitude, we could not see – that "Western Civilisation" disguises under its showy front a scene of hyenas and jackals. That is the only name that can be applied to those who have gone to fulfil "humanitarian" tasks in the Congo. Bloodthirsty butchers who feed on helpless people!'

Not surprisingly, a good few of those countries implicated in Che's tirade responded with their own, directed in person at him. Che was in an argumentative frame of mind, though, and he returned to the podium to reply to their criticisms, harranguing Costa Rica, Nicaragua, Venezuela, Colombia, Panama and the USA in particular. To the Nicaraguan representative, who had made a quip about his accent, Che replied, 'I hope he did not find an American accent in my statement, because that would be dangerous! It may be that I have a trace of Argentine,' Che went on, with his eyebrows working the irony heavily. 'After all, I was born there and it is no secret to anyone. But I am a Cuban as well as an Argentine. I hope you will not be offended if I say that I feel I am a patriot in any Latin American country.'

His performance at the podium having kicked up quite a stir, the following day Che went on *Face the Nation*, where he was questioned by Paul Niven and Richard Hottelet of CBS and Tad Szulc of the *New York Times*. 'Dr Guevara,' Hottelet asked him, 'Washington has said that there are two political conditions for the establishment of normal relations between the United States and Cuba. One is the abandonment of your military commitment to the Soviet Union. The other is the abandonment of your policy of exporting revolution to Latin America. Do you see any chance of a change in either of these two points?'

Che's response was both witty and wise. 'We place absolutely no conditions of any kind on the United States. We don't ask that it change its system. We don't ask that racial discrimination cease in the United States. We place no conditions on the establishment of relations, but neither do we accept conditions.' After the show was over Che stayed on talking to Szulc, chatting for several hours about Cuba and the Third World.

In Havana, although his words were not exactly off the party hymn sheet, Fidel was pleased with the response Che had generated. Perhaps he was smarting still from President Lyndon Johnson's rebuff to his tentative offer of an olive branch the year before. Probably also he hoped it might just jolt some of the Latin American communist parties out of their own mire of inertia. Certainly it was with some satisfaction that he observed 'the imperialists were so surprised when they heard the statements made by Major Ernesto Guevara at the United Nations on behalf of the Revolutionary Government of Cuba'. Apparently they did not know 'the firm and militant position of Cuba with regard to imperialism'. Well, he concluded, 'Now they know.'

Before Che left New York, he agreed to a secret meeting with Senator Eugene McCarthy. They met during a drinks party that Fidel's sympathetic envoy Lisa Howard had laid on at a friend's downtown apartment in the hope of rekindling the back channel between Washington and Havana. Howard had tried, without success, to persuade a senior respresentative of the US government to meet Che, but the broadly sympathetic McCarthy was the best she had been able to do. Che was not in any case in much of a mood to open new lines of dialogue with the Americans either. In the somewhat forced conversation with McCarthy, Che appeared not the least bit interested in hiding Cuba's subversive activities nor the fact that they were training revolutionaries 'and would continue to do so'. It was clear that, in Che's mind, the time for reconciliation had passed. From New York Che set off for Africa on what would end up being a three-month tour of thirteen African countries with a detour to Communist China and yet another turning point in his life.

* * *

It was Fidel who had first grasped the significance of the events taking place in Africa at this time. In March 1963, when visiting Khrushchev, he had tried to persuade the Soviet Premier of the importance of supporting the Algerian President, Ben Bella. Khrushchev had asked him not to go for security reasons and it was Che, already familiar with that 'Afro–Asian Balcony' from his diplomatic tour of the non-aligned countries in 1959, whom Fidel had sent in his place.

Though nothing had then been decided, Fidel and Che were impressed by what they saw as the revolutionary potential of the African continent. In 1964, Che had even shared with a group of visiting Africans his thoughts of leading a Soviet- and Chinese-sponsored anti-imperialist war there. Perhaps somewhat optimistically, he thought it might be a way to ease the Sino–Soviet conflict. Though that initiative came to nothing, with the need now to find somewhere for Che to go, and with the possibilities of leading any sort of mission in Latin America for the moment severely limited – given the lack of support from the region's communist parties – Africa offered the most likely setting for a venture that would allow both him and Fidel to develop their plans for an international revolutionary front. As Fidel wrote to Che while he was in New York in December 1964:

Che: Sergio [del Valle] has just met me and described in detail how everything is going. There does not seem to be any difficulty in carrying the programme through to the end. Diocles [Torralba] will give you a detailed verbal account.

We will make the final decision on the formula before you return. To be able to choose among the possible alternatives, it is necessary to know the opinions of our friend [Ahmed Ben Bella]. Try to keep us informed by secure means.

Che's first stop, then, was to be Algeria where he spent a week making further preparations, away from the media circus he had only too happily left behind in New York. From Algeria he travelled on to Mali, the Congo, Guinea and Ghana before returning late in January to Algiers. The ever more fractious politics of the Cold War were never far behind him, however, and Che was obliged to fly to Beijing in February to smooth relations with the Chinese which had cooled since Fidel's more overt support of the Soviet line. The Chinese had sent Carlos Rafael Rodríguez packing on a recent visit, and for all the personal sympathy that Che commanded in China, he too was left hanging around as a sign of the Chinese government's displeasure. He and Fidel really were on their own.

Back in Africa once more, Che visited President Nasser in Cairo, where they spoke at length about the regional situation. Che's first meeting with Nasser, during his 1959 trip, had been strained. Previously, 'President Nasser tended to dismiss them as a bunch of Errol Flynns,' Nasser's chief assistant, Mohamed Heikal, recalled. This time they got along rather better. Nasser thought that Che looked troubled, and asked him how things were in Cuba. Was everything all right between him and Castro? He evidently perceived Che to be in something of a crisis.

'[Che] had so many questions to which he could not find an answer. He said Cuba was faced with tremendous problems and there were no quick answers.' Che appeared to acknowledge the difficulty of the task: 'I used to talk a lot about social transformation and then I was given the task of supervising that transformation.' It had not gone as well as he had hoped, he implied. But now he was embarking on a new challenge, one whose details he did not divulge to Nasser, and it required him to make a concerted, if time-pressed, analysis of the regional situation.

Now that Che had been, in effect, spurned by both the socialist superpowers, he was able to work at this task relatively unfettered by the demands of realpolitik. The aides who accompanied him were military ones, and back in Havana it was already being joked that Cuba had no better way of emphasising its 'neutrality' than having Che represent it. Over the next two months he pushed through a great number of clandestine meetings with resistance groups and anti-colonial leaders from a number of African countries.

But if he was hoping for an immediate reaching out of brotherly arms from the African revolutionaries, he was to be disappointed. 'We talked, we debated,' Lúcio Lara, leader of the Congolese Popular Movement for the Liberation of Angola (MPLA) recalled much later and somewhat non-committally. '[T]hey were not very happy after speaking with Che,' Lara's wife ventured. One can imagine why. Who was Che to these leaders, much less their own people? Che found a similar response in Dar-es-Salaam in Tanzania – that 'haven for exiles from the rest of Africa' – where most of the liberation movement leaders he met were equally suspicious of his motives.

* * *

Throughout Che's trip, Fidel too was busy. While Che was promoting the public face of Cuban solidarity with the African independence movements (and at the same time putting into place rather more effective, clandestine means of conveying that solidarity), Fidel set to work providing him with the diplomatic cover needed to keep Moscow – watching Che as closely as the Americans now – off both their backs. On 2 January 1965, in a speech to celebrate the sixth anniversary of the revolution, he sent a clear message to the Soviets to the effect that countries ought to be allowed to develop and to pursue their affairs in their own way. Fidel was then in the midst of negotiating a new aid package with Moscow and the Soviets were not – as Che had repeatedly warned him – as beneficent as he had hoped.

It was this very theme that Che spoke to at the end of February at an otherwise unremarkable plenary conference, the Seminar on Economic Policy in Afro–Asian Nations, in Algeria. But, feeling himself now to be freer than he had been for years to speak his mind, he went very much further than Fidel. 'We discussed his speech all night,' said Algeria's Ben Bella many years later, 'he was fully aware of what he was going to say.' Che knew also that Fidel was not going to like the speech he was about to give – one that would secretly be referred to in Cuba for a long time afterwards as the 'last bullet' from the man who was nicknamed 'Sniper'.

Che began harmlessly enough, castigating monopoly capital and urging greater solidarity among nations. But then he turned on his masters. 'How can it be "mutually beneficial",' he asked rhetorically, 'to sell at world market prices the raw materials that cost the underdeveloped countries immeasurable sweat and suffering, and to buy at world market prices the machinery produced in today's big automated factories?' The socialist countries were 'accomplices of imperialist exploitation' and they had a 'moral duty to put an end to their tacit complicity with the exploiting countries of the West'. Che was, in effect, demanding the Soviets subsidise the underdeveloped world with interest-free loans.

The speech struck an immediate chord with his audience and the final resolution of the conference reflected, as the Americans noted with regret, 'many of the more extreme proposals' that had been tabled by Che. But his speech caused even greater consternation in the corridors of power around the socialist world, and within days his 'discordant note' was being excitedly talked about everywhere from the Kremlin to Hartford, Connecticut. And for all that Fidel had more than a little personal sympathy with Che's arguments, there could be no doubting from the moment he stood down from the platform that his tenure as a government official in Cuba was now finally over. It was simply not possible to suggest that failures in the communist countries 'would lead to a return to capitalism' as Che had done and expect to remain one of the principal leaders of a satellite state. Whatever his personal thoughts, Fidel would not only never be caught saying such a thing, he would never allow himself to be seen even approving of the idea.

* * *

On Che's return to Havana, his plane was forced to prolong its refuelling stop in Ireland to undertake some necessary repairs. Whereas just a few months earlier he had been mobbed by television journalists, this time the Cuban delegation kept largely out of sight. The best account of their two-day stopover comes from the Cuban poet Roberto Fernández Retamar. Retamar knew Che from before, but they were acquaintances rather than friends. He was himself returning from Paris, and Che ribbed him about the comfortable, bourgeois lifestyle of Parisiens before confessing he too had once longed to study there. Che was in a mood to talk.

To begin with, all Che wanted to discuss was Africa – the two of them even spoke of setting up a literary journal, free of the constraints of promoting this or that party line, that would allow Cuban works to be better known on that continent. Retamar proposed to Che that they could do with such a journal in Cuba. 'Yes, edited by some unwitting fool,' Che replied, smiling as he thought of the likely bureaucratic mountain that would be placed in such a journal's way. 'Something like that,' Retamar chuckled. Then Che asked him why he thought the Soviet Union had 'gone to shit', as he put it. Retamar was taken aback, and dissimulated. Che answered for him: it was Lenin's New Economic Policy, he thought. That and his own premature death which prevented him from correcting it. As much as anything else, Che believed that leaders owed the people a duty to recognise and correct their own errors. That was part of the unstated reason that he was embarking on this new path still known only to very few people beyond Fidel and himself.

On the second day Che, Retamar and the other Cubans from their plane simply had to get out of the small airport in which they were holed up. They caught a bus into Shannon – the green army fatigues of half the group winning scarcely a glance from the locals – where they headed for the sea and, as one does in Ireland, retired to a nearby 'modest pub'. In fact it was the Marine Hotel, where a young artist was earning his keep pulling a few pints behind the bar. Che's entrance had such an effect on him – 'Castro, Guevara, and Camilo Cienfuegos – they were my heroes,' he later recalled. He could scarcely believe that here was one of them in his local pub.

The Cubans ordered beer and took up a small table in the corner. Che had just been speaking of how crazy his life had been over the last few years, with not a day's rest, and his mind was floating on the possibilities when his thoughts were inter-rupted by one of the Cubans knocking the table and spilling his beer on his uniform. Che said nothing, but got up, using what was left in his glass to fling back a couple of red pills – which, given his self-medication, could have been for anything – then headed out for a brisk walk around the block. He was grown-up enough to be on his own, he told his companions, when they tried to stop him for security reasons. And whether it was Ireland, or the beer, they acquiesced and Che headed out to take in the sea air alone.

* * *

When their plane finally touched down in Havana, Fidel was waiting for Che at the airport along with Aleida – who had just given birth to another baby boy, Ernesto. Che's principal polit-ical opponents, Raúl and President Dorticós, were also there. As to what transpired next, a whole plethora of conspiracies, rumour and gossip – some of it plausible, much of it not – has surfaced in the years since, though most sources point to two days' worth of heated discussions. For his part, Fidel has never spoken about it and nor have any of those who were present or even close, including Aleida, despite countless entreaties to do so.

To the extent that it may be plausible, the most detailed account of the 'huge argument between *el Fifo* [Fidel] and *el Che*' involves an ear pressed to a door to catch Che saying to Fidel, 'All right, the only alternative left me is to leave here for wherever the hell, and please, if you can help me in any way in what I intend to do, do so immediately; and if not, tell me so I can see who can.' Another account, this time by a Soviet official, has Fidel accusing Che of not following the party line in his speeches throughout his tour, only for Che to respond that Fidel had not exactly been following the party line in his own recent speeches. There is a ring of truth to this latter account. Just a few days before Che's return – and certainly well after he knew all about Che's speech in Algeria and the responses to it in Moscow – Fidel himself made an impassioned speech about Vietnam, saying, '[A]ll socialist countries have the inexcusable duty to support it [Vietnam].' This too was a goading of Moscow's non-interventionist line, if not as blunt as Che's.

Whatever transpired during those two days, it is inconceivable that strong words were not spoken. Che's speech in Algeria in particular had been a major breach of protocol; Raúl had been in Moscow at the time, and knew from first-hand experience just how badly the Soviets had responded to it. But Fidel's anger stemmed not from his disagreeing with the general thrust of Che's comments so much as the undiplomatic way in which he had, as ever, gone about making them.

In fact Fidel had followed Che's progress in Africa with great interest. And while Che had been meeting African revolutionary leaders to establish how, when and where a Cuban force might be deployed in the region, Fidel had been overseeing the selection and training of that very force, visiting the men regularly at their secret training camps in Pinar del Río. Fidel had been propagandising the cause in his speeches, too. Just a few days before Che returned he had spoken of the Congo and Vietnam together, making an explicit connection between the two. The ignominy of imperialist aggression around the world required the unity of the socialist camp to confront it, he said in yet another implied criticism of both the Soviets and the Chinese. Such divisions as existed in the socialist camp at this moment were merely encouraging the imperialists in their adventurism and putting small or impoverished countries, like Cuba, the Congo and Vietnam, in danger. There had been enough talking, he was saying. Now it was time to act.

These were not the words of a man diametrically opposed to Che's position, and they undermine the more vociferous rumours of some great split between them. So too does Che's agreeing to the publication, just a few weeks later, of a laudatory account of Fidel as an example of that venerated figure of the 'New Man'. So while the two-day 'show-down' may have begun with raised voices, it seems far more likely that most of the time was spent digesting the results of Che's trip and planning what they were going to do next, together.

* * *

Che had landed at Havana airport in such a rush that he had not been able to return a book of poetry that Retamar had lent him for the flight back from Shannon. While Che was packing up in the Ministry, Retamar – who had been rather affected by the time they had spent together – called in to ask Che if he could work for him. Che himself was busy, but Manresa, his secretary, returned the book. He confided to Retamar that Che had asked him to copy out one of the poems for him. 'Which one,' Retamar asked, at which point Che emerged from his office. Che had just a little time to talk, but Retamar got the answer to his question on the way out: it was 'Farewell', by Pablo Neruda.

The day that Che left his well-worn and much-loved office at the Ministry he got his own dose of symbolic irony, however. It was in the early hours when, finally having packed up what he wanted to, he called for his dog Muralla and headed down in the escalator to the basement car park. Fidel had been speaking with him in his office and left just beforehand. It was a normal hour for him to be working. In the basement Che's assistant, Gravalosa, and his driver and bodyguard, Cárdenas, were waiting there for him, passing the time listening to their boss's car stereo. His car then was a Chevrolet, 'a 1960,' Gravalosa recalls, with moulded panelling and great wings sticking out at the back. Cárdenas had turned the music right up to listen to a tango that was playing. Gravalosa warned him, 'Listen, you turn that up and the battery's going to go flat.' When all of a sudden Che appeared with Muralla, Cárdenas expected to get an ear-bashing and quickly switched off the radio. But Che shouted at him instead for turning it off. 'Shit, kid, turn the music back on!' It was his favourite tango of all, 'Adios Muchachos' by Carlos Gardel. And with that he left the Ministry – to cut cane, so he said.

In fact after a last 'hectic round of bittersweet farewells' he went to a safe house near El Laguito where the group of fighters that had been assembled by Fidel and trained over the previous weeks were waiting for him. The last few days that he would spend in Cuba for a long time were passed here, engrossed in the intense preparation needed to head up this military expedition to Africa. Che would be busy writing one minute, then jumping up to do press-ups the next. But first he had a surprise for his new comrades-in-arms who would accompany him on this next adventure.

'You OK, Dreke?' said the man with short hair, glasses and strange-looking teeth, who had just been introduced as Ramón to Víctor Dreke, the leader of the Cuban fighters at the safe house. 'You don't know him yet?' Osmany Cienfuegos, the brother of Che's old 'lion' Camilo, asked Dreke. Osmany was then Minister of Construction, but he was also part of the planning committee for this mission. 'Stop fucking around and just tell him,' said the man with the glasses. And then it hit Dreke that Ramón was in fact Che trying on the disguise that would have to get him to Africa and that they were about to depart on the mission that Fidel had had them training for.

When Osmany returned to the camp just a couple of days later, Fidel was with him. The two comrades were to part company for now, but if all went well they would remain in touch, secretly at least. Che knew the script that he wanted such an occasion to conform to. When he had heard of the death of his Guatemalan friend Julio Caceres, El Patojo – whom Che had seen off on a mission not unlike the one he himself was now embarking on – Che had written: 'With what right, could I have asked him not to go?' All El Patojo had expected, and all that Che asked for now from Fidel, was a 'warm handshake' and words of encouragement to take with him into the battles ahead. In return, he left behind a heartfelt letter that he had scribbled on an old pad of lined paper and the half-cock plan that the two of them had been dreaming up together.

Fidel:

At this moment I remember many things: when I met you in Mària Antonia's house, when you proposed I come along, all the tensions involved in the preparations.

One day they came by and asked who should be notified in case of death, and the real possibility of it struck us all. Later we knew it was true, that in a revolution one wins or dies (if it is a real one). Many comrades fell along the way to victory.

Today everything has a less dramatic tone, because we are more mature, but the event repeats itself. I feel that I have fulfilled the part of my duty that tied me to the Cuban revolution in its territory, and I say farewell to you, to the comrades, to your people, who now are mine.

I formally resign my positions in the leadership of the party, my post as minister, my rank of commander, and my

Cuban citizenship. Nothing legal binds me to Cuba. The only ties are of another nature – those that cannot be broken as can appointments to posts.

Reviewing my past life, I believe I have worked with sufficient integrity and dedication to consolidate the revolutionary triumph. My only serious failing was not having had more confidence in you from the first moments in the Sierra Maestra, and not having understood quickly enough your qualities as a leader and a revolutionary. I have lived magnificent days, and at your side I felt the pride of belonging to our people in the sad but luminous days of the Caribbean [Missile] crisis. Seldom has a statesman been more brilliant as you were in those days. I am also proud of having followed you without hesitation, of having identified with your way of thinking and of seeing and appraising dangers and principles.

Other nations of the world summon my modest efforts of assistance. I can do that which is denied you due to your responsibility as the head of Cuba, and the time has come for us to part.

I want it known that I do so with mixed feelings of joy and sorrow. I leave here the purest of my hopes as a builder and the dearest of those I hold dear. And I leave a people who received me as a son. That wounds a part of my spirit. I carry to new battlefronts the faith that you taught me, the revolutionary spirit of my people, the feeling of fulfilling the most sacred of duties: to fight against imperialism wherever it may be. This comforts and heals the deepest of wounds.

As Fidel left the safe house, he took Dreke and Tamayo to one side. 'Look after Che,' he urged them before he jumped into his black sedan for the drive back to Havana. The following morning Che, alias Ramón, eased himself into Cienfuegos' car with a new group of comrades alongside him as he too left the safe house, en route to the airport.

When he had first met Fidel, Che had been seeking to free

himself of the mindless anonymity of constant travel. Now he was returning to a series of rather different journeys as the assured and purposeful clandestine operator. The public face of the revolution he had ceded to Fidel, who returned to his own daily preoccupations a little unburdened for not having Che around with his scruples and a little emptier for the same reason. They had each changed in the last two years, and they had been drawn steadily apart by their different views of the revolutionary life. A new phase was now opening up in their relationship and in their respective pursuit of a revolutionary future. But they had time still to rebuild their friendship around those changed circumstances, as indeed they had rebuilt it before; to reinvent it in whichever way might allow them best to fulfil the one thing they would always hold in common: the revolution.

15. RED LETTER DAY

WITH NO WARNING, much less any explanation, one of the most recognisable political leaders in the world simply vanished. For the Cuban secret services who had helped accomplish the feat it was a significant coup: just a few months before, in New York, US Under-Secretary of State George Ball had commented on how difficult it was to arrange any sort of private meeting with Che because the man could not go anywhere without people knowing. The full story of what happened over the following year was kept, as one historian has put it, 'under lock and key . . . invisible to all but the most trusted supporters of the Cuban government' for the next thirty years. It constitutes a fascinating, almost unprecedented saga of a friendship lived from one side in the full glare of public scrutiny, and from the other in utter, impenetrable secrecy.

'The most difficult thing of all – the official disconnection – has already been done,' Fidel wrote to Che conspiratorially more than a year after his disappearance, though not, he confessed, 'without paying a price in the form of slander, intrigues and so on'. By then Che was coming towards the end of a four-month period of hiding in Prague, where he had travelled in secrecy at the end of his entry and subsequent exit from a vortex of events in Central Africa. The rumour mill that Fidel referred to, as he assessed the impact of the Houdini act they had pulled off in making Che 'disappear', had by then churned mercilessly for more than a year. Che was said to be in neighbouring Santo Domingo, where a leftist uprising had recently drawn President Johnson into despatching marines. He was in a mental asylum in Cuba, or under house arrest, madly dashing off letters to Fidel about their revolutionary differences. In the first few months after his disappearance, many even insisted that he was dead.

None of these, of course, would turn out to be the truth. But there remains a considerable lack of information pertaining to 'the year that Che was a shadow'. Fidel let Alexiev know, but most of the rank-and-file Soviets – and to his chagrin that included Comrade Belous – were as much in the dark as anyone else. What we do now know is that Che's clandestine departure for the Congo signalled not the end of his partnership with Fidel, as has often been argued, but the beginning of a new and very close collaboration with him. 'It is likely that no more than three men made the decision to send troops to Zaire [former Congo]: Fidel, Che and Raúl Castro,' writes the pre-eminent historian of this period in Cuba's foreign policy. And of these, Raúl was not privy to the political aspects of the mission. This was indeed, then, a venture conceived of between Fidel and Che themselves. Moreover, it was their first step in a far more ambitious plan: the clandestine export of the Cuban revolution proper.

Fulfilling his part of the bargain, almost as soon as Che left Cuba Fidel began firing up the tone of his public announcements. In his May Day speech he railed against the notion of 'peaceful coexistence' – just as Che had done in New York – and in affirming his conviction that the Dominican people would have the support of the socialist camp against the US Marines, he added that they would also have that of the non-aligned countries. This was all important groundwork for Che's clandestine efforts in the Congo. Providing such cover was henceforth to be Fidel's principal role.

But the Cuban leader also wasted no time in adjusting to life after Che. As Alexiev was told by one of Fidel's right-hand men, Carlos Rafael Rodríguez, later that year when he tried to get to the bottom of Che's disappearance, 'Guevara's absence in the leadership has made it easier for Fidel Castro to reorganise central bodies, to get rid of incidental elements.' He also assured Alexiev that Fidel was 'very satisfied' with Che's suggestion that he leave all his positions in the party and government and switch to fulfilling special tasks. 'On the surface Castro showed that he approves of Guevara's suggestion, but in fact he is mainly glad that he can get rid of Guevara's influence this way. At the moment Castro is forming a small circle of people who are whole-heartedly devoted to him and have demonstrated great organisational skills.' Rodríguez was deliberately telling the Soviets what they wanted to hear. All the same, those who were now among that circle included the staunch Fidelistas José 'Pepín' Naranjo, Armando Hart (who would displace Che's aide Emilio Aragonés) and Osmany Cienfuegos.

Quick to read this as evidence of the break in relations between Che and Fidel, many have interpreted the speed with which Fidel made these changes after Che's departure as evidence that he had been plotting all along to be rid of him. But a revolutionary partnership is different from most other political double acts. Fidel and Che had long fed off the wax and wane of fortunes between them and knew how to turn whatever individual loss they suffered into a collective advantage. And these shifts in personnel were to positions of somewhat 'unspecified' work, much of which was to enable Fidel to keep in touch with what Rodríguez himself acknowledged was a priority for Fidel: the 'support [of] liberation movements, especially in Africa'. When a group of journalists cornered him about Che in May, he was emphatic that 'the relationship between us is friendly – in fact, it has never been better'. This time he was not lying.

But the changes in ministerial positions did now officially confirm the end of Che's influence on various aspects of Cuban government policy. In his 26 July speech, Fidel even went so far as to rubbish Che's idea that individuals alone could bring about revolutionary advances, and the centralisation that Che had worked so hard to perfect he put down to inexperience: it was the people acting together that made real progress, Fidel countered. Henceforth, excessive centralisation was to be 'heatedly denounced'. If a dog shits in the street, Fidel said graphically, you don't want to have to call the central authorities to come and remove the mess.

Such changes as Fidel made to the effects of Che's hard work were, as ever, the result of differences of personality as much as differences of ideology. Che had based five years of economic policy on finding the right way to drive people forward. Fidel, who sparked people into action all around him without effort, believed the solution lay more in letting them go. Che set goals; Fidel got them moving. He had watched with restrained frustration for years as he had let Che try his own way forward. But now he was doing things his way. 'In real life at present we cannot think of that,' Fidel went on with regard to the issue of centralisation, 'but we will be able to think that way as the new generations of our country become trained.' That man be morally motivated was a nice idea to bear in mind, Fidel was saying, but he knew the Cuban people, and it wasn't going to do the trick just now.

Fidel's position seemed for the first time now to be strong and secure. Afraid that any activity they undertook might jeopardise the prospects for détente with the Soviets, the Americans had backed off somewhat, while in the Escambray the last of the counter-revolutionary *bandidos* had now been rounded up. By the summer of 1965, even McGeorge Bundy the United States National Security Advisor acknowledged that 'we had spent some months in searching for ways to hurt Castro without hurting ourselves more and had not found them', and support to dissident groups was being wound down: it had become decidedly more difficult to recruit agents willing to risk working against Fidel's now well-entrenched regime.

It was an exuberant and confident Fidel Castro that the American journalist Lee Lockwood found that summer when he was invited to join the Cuban leader at his summer retreat on the Isle of Pines. Lockwood had been pestering Fidel's aide René Vallejo for an interview for months, and indeed Fidel had promised it, but only now had the opportunity arisen. Lockwood was immediately bundled into a car and driven to the house Fidel was staying in at the time. Fidel was waiting for him there, playing with his German shepherd dog, Guardian, a large charcoal-grey beast with all the energy of its master. 'I got him as a puppy and raised him myself,' Fidel beamed as the dog charged about. Then Lockwood, Fidel and the dog squeezed into the back of a car that would take them to the coast. Fidel piloted them across to the Isle of Pines in a high-speed launch: 'We could get to Florida in three hours,' he boasted.

Evening was falling by the time they arrived at Fidel's house, an old L-shaped white-painted wooden ranch set amidst thickets of trees a little way inland. It was a peaceful place, adorned with rocking chairs and surrounded by a well-kept lawn and tropical shrubs. It was here that Fidel liked to read, to catch up on his study of all manner of subjects technical and arcane. It was not at all unlike one of Khrushchev's retreats. 'I want to do some hunting and fishing [and] I have a great pile of books to read,' he had told Lockwood. But no sooner had Fidel sat down on the veranda to tape the first interview than, as ever, he began to get carried away. What was intended to be a series of short inter-views turned into a week of conversation.

From the picture Lockwood assembled Fidel seemed happy, but he seemed rather more alone now too. Wherever he went he was permanently protected behind a wall of bodyguards and armour plating, and if relations with his immediate entourage – with Vallejo, Chomi, Pepín, Celia Sánchez and Núñez Jiménez – were informal and familiar they were not in every case intimate. When they sat down to eat there was certainly no protocol, though however they arranged themselves Fidel would always find his way to the middle, but life for Fidel had not the intensity, nor could it offer the comradeship, of the Sierra. One night, as the group reminisced about those days, Celia sighed: 'Oh, but they were the happiest times, weren't they? *Really*. We will never be so happy again, will we?'

After several days of ceaseless conversation with Lockwood,

working late into the night and starting early the next morning, Fidel took off after lunch one afternoon to go skin-diving. 'Fine,' the heavily overworked aide Vallejo pronounced and, having calculated the time that Fidel might be gone, went to bed. Fidel returned by helicopter some hours later, fully revitalised. 'His beard was still damp, and he was panting slightly,' Lockwood recalled. '"Four hundred and six pounds of fish," [Fidel] announced, tapping my chest with his forefinger.' He was exuberant all that week – all summer, in fact. It was as if he had found himself. Or rather that he had simply reconciled himself to how things would now have to be.

At one point Lockwood asked Fidel about Che's future role in the administration of the country. Fidel refused to be drawn. 'At the present time I cannot answer that interrogation. What I can tell you is that there has been absolutely no problem in the relations of friendship and the fraternal relations, the identification that has always existed between him and us. I can affirm that categorically.' It was somewhat distanced language. Lockwood tried again, but again Fidel dodged. To answer, he replied, 'would be digging up the mystery' and so he simply couldn't. Fidel was giving nothing away.

* * *

Once he had arrived in Tanzania, en route to the Congo, things moved quickly for Che. After filtering into the country in groups of twos and threes, Che and his team of fourteen men were driven in Mercedes-Benz cars from Dar-es-Salaam to the town of Kigoma on the shores of Lake Tanganyika. From here they travelled by boat to the Congolese village of Kibamba, where they were met by members of the Congolese Liberation Army.

The situation in the Congo during the early 1960s was no less of an international preoccupation than the breakup of the former Yugoslavia in the 1990s, Patrice Lumumba, the left-wing prime minister of the newly independent Congo had asked in 1960 for

Soviet assistance, touching off a cascade of events pivoting around the central question of what political future – capitalist or communist – the Congo and other newly independent states, would have. Since his tour of Africa earlier in the year Che had clear views about this and he, like Fidel (with whom he had talked over the idea) believed that inserting a well-trained guerrilla force might just tip the balance in favour of socialism. The first indications were good. The camp was set among 'sudden escarpments, rushing rivers and twisting tracks'. It was, as Colonel 'Mad Mike' Hoare – a British mercenary – who formed part of the array of forces closing in on one another in the region recalled, 'the ideal terrain' for guerrilla operations. Che was heartened to note that the rebels who met them off the boat were heavily armed too: well supplied with everything from land mines and machine guns to 76-mm cannons and Chinese-made 'bamboo bazooka' rocket launchers.

Then things ground to a halt and Che immediately began to realise that what he had entered into was not at all what he had imagined. Cuban intelligence had told him to expect a plain that stretched six kilometres inland to the mountains. 'In reality,' Che observed ruefully on arrival, 'the lake is a kind of ravine and the mountains . . . begin right at the water's edge.' This was too severe, even for men with guerrilla training. Topography was to be the least of his worries, though. During the Cuban revolutionary war there had been a range of opposition movements with sometimes conflicting interests, but they had all been clearly arraigned against the government. The situation in the Congo was, as Che now found out, much more complex. Not least, he was completely taken aback by the presence of some four thousand Tutsis who had been driven out of their homeland in Rwanda and were helping the Congolese to man the defence of the Fizi-Baraka region of the Congo in the hope this would help them return later to their own country.

Ethnic tensions between the forces were but a part of the headache that confronted Che. He was soon forced to give up on his hope of 'political work', saving that for a constant stream of carefully tempered letters in which he sought alternately to cajole, mollify and corral into something resembling a unified front the numerous self-proclaimed leaders who headed the different strands of the Congolese revolution. In this he was to fail utterly. To make matters worse, that 'ideal terrain' in which Che had set up camp was itself now surrounded by Colonel Hoare's mercenaries.

Despite the immediately apparent difficulties, reinforcements from Cuba arrived throughout May, and from the camp they had established up in the hills Che sent his men out to conduct occasional ambushes along the road that led between the mercenary strongholds of Bendera, just to the west of Kibamba, and Albertville directly south. But Che was able to do very little more until his presence – which, even upon his arrival, he had kept secret from the Congo's opposition leaders – was formally acknowledged. When finally he confronted Chamaleso, the acting deputy of National Revolutionary Council, Laurent Kabila, with his true identity, the response was devastating. 'He kept talking of an "international scandal" and insisting that "no one must find out, please, no one must find out",' Che recalled.

While Che waited in this seemingly eternal limbo, he was informed that his mother had died in Buenos Aires. It was, as he recorded in his diary, 'for me, personally . . . the saddest news of the whole war'. For all his anguish, it is revealing that the news of his mother's death did not lead him to question even for one moment why he was there. Both he and Fidel believed that the struggle in Africa was the heart of the struggle against imperialism. And they both believed that Cuba ought to be able to exert considerable influence on the African political landscape. In one sense they were right, as the long history of Cuba's involvement in the continent would attest. But as Che was finding, the potential for guerrilla operations was, for the moment at least, rather limited.

A further setback to their plans now occurred. In Algeria –

through which both men and weapons travelled – President Ben Bella was overthrown in June. Algeria had been a fellow nation for Fidel, and it was through that country that the Cubans had been able to smuggle arms to Latin America. 'I will not speak in the language of a diplomat,' Fidel said in response to the news. 'I will speak as a revolutionary.' It was a revealing comment. For Fidel it was possible to be a calculating, pragmatic revolutionary. That, in Che's absence, he found it easier to be both was partly the source of his new-found energy. Che's being stationed abroad provided an outlet for Fidel's deepest and most bellicose instincts, while at the same time channelling them in such a way as not to compromise his more calculating ambitions at home in Cuba.

While for Fidel Che's departure signalled an easing of the tensions that had grown within him, for Che the departure merely accentuated a certain inner turmoil. For all that he sought to emulate Fidel's political skills, Che had never been a natural diplomat, much less was he any good at setting his beliefs to one side. But so keen was he to overcome what he recognised as his own natural cynicism that the initial reports he sent to Havana from the Congo largely glossed over the very real problems; and so hard did he try to put a positive spin on things that he ended up duping even himself. For Fidel, knowing Che always to be brutally honest and to be negative whenever the possibility arose, to receive even moderately optimistic reports was an indication that things were going particularly well. Despite the unfortunate events in Algeria, the impression Fidel got was that the rest of their 'programme' was proceeding to plan.

These reports were only confirmed when Fidel received Gaston Soumaliot in September. Soumaliot was the leader of the Congo's National Revolutionary Council – the body that sought to represent the coalition of resistance groups fighting in the country – and the figure to whom, nominally at least, Che was answerable. Soumaliot had just ousted Gbenye and was touring sympathetic capitals trying to drum up further support for the movement. There is some confusion over what was said between them, but on balance it appears that Fidel was still optimistic that Che's mission in the Congo could be a success. Certainly Soumaliot was roundly feted, and left with a promise from Fidel for a further fifty doctors to support the revolutionary movement. Enthused by Soumaliot's visit, Fidel kept up the reinforcements being sent to Che and granted special permission for two of his highest-ranking ministers – Aragonés and Cienfuegos – to visit him in September. It was as if half the Central Committee were being funnelled in secret into another continent.

※　※　※

The ongoing mystery as to the whereabouts of Che Guevara continued to haunt Fidel, however. In May he had returned to some of his old hideouts in the Sierra to commemorate the anniversary of the battle of Uvero. It was a 'bright, sunswept day' with 'a spanking breeze blowing off the sea.' There was everything there that Che disliked about such events. While the crowd waited, they were entertained by a small red biplane from which petals were thrown for them to catch; gymnastic displays, speeches, a pageant of schoolchildren and a brass band completed the warm-up act. Then Fidel arrived in a helicopter, followed by Raúl. It was Raúl's first time back to Uvero since the battle eight years before. 'I'm just trying to remember how everything happened,' he said to an American journalist standing nearby as the leader took to the podium. During his speech Fidel too appeared to be in the mood to reminisce, and he made glowing reference to Che as he recounted that bloodily fought battle. 'Comrade Guevara' was one of our best fighters, Fidel said, 'who at times' – he was interrupted by a burst of applause – 'who at times was a soldier, and when we did not have a doctor he was also a doctor.'

In June Fidel had spoken at length about the sugar harvest, and there again was mention of Che, with Camilo this time, rushing through the canebrake in the final days of the war. And when Fidel spoke to a gathering of the Interior Ministry the crowd once more broke into applause at the mention of Che's name. This time Fidel decided to address the issue. 'And now that I mention our comrade Major Ernesto Guevara [applause] – who is so deserving of this applause – you have probably heard the rumours circulated by the imperialists. They say that Comrade Ernesto Guevara does not appear in public, that he was not present on 1 May, that he was not present the week when the cane was cut . . . . Our people, however, are not concerned. They are acquainted with their own revolution and they know their men.'

But the people wanted to know about Che, and Fidel knew he could not keep silent for much longer. In October, in his very first speech to the newly formed and long-awaited Central Committee, Fidel finally broached the thorny issue. The new leadership structure was in most cases a straight transplanting of the former PURS on to a Central Committee model, with many of the key personnel simply being confirmed in their posts. But there was one conspicuous absence: Che. Adding to the intrigue, the only three former ministers excluded from the new Central Committee were also loyal supporters of Che: Luis Álvarez Rom (who had been with Che at the National Bank), Orlando Borrego (his close friend and aide at the Ministry), and Arturo Guzman (then acting Minister of Industries).

'There is an absence—' Fidel began in his speech to the Central Committee. He stopped mid-flow, and somewhat gingerly touched one of the microphones before him as a large draped curtain swayed in the draught behind 'of one who possessed all the merits and all the virtues, and to the greatest degree required, to belong to [this forum].' He might have been half expecting the eager cries and applause of the audiences who had cheered at every mention of Che in his speeches all that year. But this was an audience that knew how to behave. They merely looked up, rapt, as Fidel went on to survey the mire of speculation that had engulfed him over the previous months and then brought out the letter that Che had penned on the night of his departure. He had told Fidel then that the letter could be made public when it was most of benefit to the nation. And, confronted with the need to explain why Che – of all people – had no role in the Communist Party structure, Fidel had decided that the time was now.

An expectant silence befell the vast auditorium as Fidel read out the letter in full. Aleida was sitting to the side of the main audience, 'dressed in black and verging on tears'. The cameras were ready to capture the scene as they swept, Eisenstein-like, across the auditorium. At the mention of their missing comrade the newly crowned party faithful hung their heads in a concerted display of emotion, but once Fidel had finished reading the letter there were several minutes of applause from the auditorium.

It was a public airing of the issue rather than an explanation, of course. Fidel was hardly in a position to explain precisely where Che was or what he was up to. Some immediately questioned the letter's validity. It was too adulatory to be real, they said. They could not have read Che's far more extreme 'Ode to Fidel' written some years earlier. Others focused their speculation on what had happened to Che. Fidel ignored all the rumours, considered the matter dealt with and moved forward with his own plans as if oblivious to the clamour.

Throughout that winter, he continued to consolidate the importance accorded to his immediate entourage of loyal comrades within the party apparatus he had constructed around him. The elaborate pageant of the formation of the Central Committee was evidently little more than a sop to keep Moscow happy, and it would be another ten years before he held the first regular party congress. Keeping a close eye on him at this time were not only the Soviets but the East Germans, who seemed to have more than a few well-placed observers. The previous year they had observed that Fidel wanted 'to have the only say in deciding all important issues' and that he had 'evidently taken great pains to ensure that no one (not even his brother Raúl or a Party leadership committee) encroached upon his towering position on the inside or the outside'. But Fidel had not put Che from his mind.

At around the time he was convening the first plenary of new Central Committee, he sat down and wrote to Che at length.

* * *

José Ramón Machado Ventura, Fidel's trusted comrade and Minister of Public Health arrived over the crest of the hill that marked the last part of the journey up to Che's camp from Dar-es-Salaam. He had carried Fidel's letter with him, hidden beneath his undershirt, for almost a month. When he read it, however, Che was furious. Fidel appeared to be paying more attention to travelling emissaries, such as Soumaliot, who preferred 'whisky and women' to fighting and who were duping Fidel into taking decisions that were fast making a mockery of Che's situation. This was not how things ought to be if they were to succeed, and if Fidel thought that with Che far away and his disappearance explained he was free of the consequences of his comrade's scruples then he was mistaken. Che overlooked the fact that his own reports had been on the whole rather positive. He no longer believed that things were any good at all.

Che had been even less happy, though, when he heard on the radio that Fidel had read out his letter in public. One of the Cuban fighters recalled the moment: 'Che was near me. He became very serious, he lowered his head and began to smoke.' What Fidel had not seemed to notice, but Che realised instantly, was that the now public renunciation of his citizenship and his government posts undermined Che's authority over his men. Suddenly Che was the outsider again – 'a man from other climes', as he put it – just as he had been during those first few difficult months for him in the Sierra. When Machado Ventura left for Havana a few days later, he was carrying with him a rather more strongly worded letter to Fidel than the one that had just been read out to the Central Committee.

'I received your letter,' Che wrote Fidel, 'which has aroused contradictory feelings in me – for in the name of proletarian internationalism, we are committing mistakes that may prove very costly. . . .' Above all, Che was now at pains to point out – his short lived attempt to accentuate the positive vanishing with the cigar smoke that curled into the moist air as he listened over the radio to Fidel reading out his letter – 'Soumaliot and his partners have been leading you all right up the garden path.' He went on: '[W]e can't liberate by ourselves a country that does not want to fight; you've got to create a fighting spirit and look for soldiers with the torch of Diogenes and the spirit of Job – a task that becomes more difficult the more shits there are doing things along the way . . . . The business with the money is what hurts me most, after all the warnings I gave.' He then went on to criticise the way Fidel had been giving out money to figures like Soumaliot. 'Don't make the mistake again of dishing out money like that . . . . Trust my judgement a little and don't go by appearances . . . . I have tried to be explicit and objective, synthetic and truthful. Do you believe me?'

When he received Che's note Fidel accepted his comrade's criticism seemingly without comment. Machado Ventura must also have filled him in on the situation in the Congo. Immediately, Fidel changed his whole appraisal of the situation. He cabled Che to tell him that sustaining a guerrilla presence there did indeed look an impossible task. It had been a false start. They would have to think again. Fidel knew instinctively when not to push a bad position. 'We must do everything save for the absurd,' he wrote Che. 'If our presence is unjustifiable and not useful, we ought to think of retreating . . . .'

It was a sudden turnaround, and a belated recognition that the 'revolution' in the Congo had begun to die out even before Che had arrived. But it was a timely one none the less. By mid-November Che too was about ready to admit defeat. By then the advance base to which he had been more or less confined for the last few months had fallen without a fight. That same month Che received news from Pablo Ribalta, ambassador at the Cuban embassy in Tanzania that owing to a political settlement the

Tanzanians – who had so far provided Che's camp with a rear-guard base – were now definitively withdrawing their support as well. Tactical retreats were a part of guerrilla warfare, but now, for the first time in his life, Che was forced to beat a full and for him all too humiliating one.

As they passed through villages the peasants rushed out of their huts to join Che's retreating men, fearful of their impending fate in the rebels' absence. All around them were reminders of what that would be: 'peasants fleeing, smoke rising from the villages that were burned, villagers accusing them of not having armed them allowing their women to be taken away'. Then, when they reached the rendezvous point on the shore of Lake Tanganyika, the boats due to pick them up did not show: problems with the Tanzanian authorities, they were told. In desperation more than with any concrete plan in mind, Che ordered his Cuban aides quickly to select a crack troop that might stay on with him to the end. They managed to cobble together twenty or so who were willing to take their chances.

'The idea of staying around continued to circle about my head until the early hours of the morning,' he wrote afterwards, but Che knew he had no alternative but to proceed with the inglorious withdrawal across the lake. After receiving word that the boats were now on their way, he spent the final hours awaiting evacuation 'alone and perplexed.' The retreat itself was a 'desolate, sobering and inglorious spectacle . . . . I had to reject men who pleaded to be taken along', knowing full well the fate that awaited them at the hands of the mercenaries. To sobbing and entreaties by those being left behind that they be saved also, for they could not all fit aboard the boats, the three boats with the Cuban soldiers under Che's command headed back to Kigoma on the eastern shores of the lake.

Che felt this failure keenly, and a return to Cuba along with the rest of the Cuban forces was the last thing that he would now consider doing. When they reached the safety of the other side of the lake Che turned to three of his followers, Pombo,

Tuma and Papi, and said, 'Well, we carry on. Are you ready to continue?' 'Where?' Pombo asked. 'Wherever,' Che replied. Che knew that he was now a creature of the shadows, the 'roving incendiary' that the CIA had long painted him as being. And until the next destination was decided upon, he kept himself hidden in a small upstairs apartment in the Cuban embassy in Dar-es-Salaam.

* * *

In the embassy, his books stacked on a table and a mirror that he would later use to take a peculiarly reflective portrait leaning up against a wall, Che had all the time in the world to reflect on the bitter experience of the first setback to his and Fidel's grand vision of starting up an international revolutionary front. Here he spent several weeks in quiet contemplation – it was his 'vacation', as he wrote of it ironically. And while he waited he sucked on his maté gourd, and he thought, and he wrote.

First he wrote a book for Fidel and those revolutionary leaders who might put the experiences of his recent failure to good use. He worked on it for two months. 'This is the history of a failure,' he began on the first page. Then, having set down his thoughts on his own military failure, he wrote a critique of the Soviet *Manual of Political Economy* – Moscow's textbook summary of its vision of Marxism. It was '*muy fuerte* [very strong]', said one aide of the text.

In Havana, meanwhile, Fidel once again had to try to do something about Che, who could hardly remain holed up in an embassy for the rest of his life. But Latin America, where Fidel knew that Che really wanted to go, was not ready for another guerrilla front just yet. The conditions weren't right. But Che, of course, believed that they could be made – a belief he had picked up from Fidel in the first place. As Dreke, Che's second-in-command during the Congo mission, recalled, 'There was an ongoing struggle with Fidel to keep [Che] from going to Argentina and [make him]

345

come back to Cuba.' But Che was not interested. He wanted to go straight on to start all over again.

At a loss as to what to do, and feeling somewhat responsible himself, Fidel encouraged Aleida to visit Che in Tanzania. Perhaps he was hoping she might be able to talk him out of this idea he seemed so set upon. Perhaps Che might even be convinced to return to Cuba, even if only for a short time while they decided what to do next.

Early in January, after travelling halfway around the globe on false papers and in disguise (something she would have cause to do again), Aleida was brought to the embassy in Tanzania. When the car that had carried her from the airport stopped outside she was rushed upstairs and straight into the flat. On what was really the first and last occasion they ever spent much time alone together, Aleida and Che lived together in that small apartment for the next six weeks. Food was brought up to them by Ribalta on a tray, but aside from his presence they had no other human contact and not once were they allowed to leave the flat.

Aleida's visit can only have had the effect of reminding Che what he was denying her and himself. But as he had already written, 'The leaders of the revolution have . . . wives who must be part of the general sacrifice of their lives in order to take the revolution to its destiny. The circle of their friends is limited strictly to the circle of comrades in the revolution. There is no life outside it.'

Even with Aleida now in Tanzania Fidel continued to feel Che breathing down his neck. At the Tricontinental Conference held in Havana that January he began taking steps to find a way of moving his friend on. 'Revolutionaries in any corner of the world can count on the assistance of Cuban fighters,' he said to the assembled delegations. That included everyone from the newly formed Palestine Liberation Organisation (PLO) to the Vietcong and even a few representatives of the Black Power movement in the United States. Among the many groups and individuals attending was Ilyich Ramírez, the young Venezuelan who would later become better known as Carlos the Jackal.

The Tricontinental was the sort of event Fidel revelled in: on his home ground, he could charm the leaders of the radical left, give them his time, show them the fruits of revolutionary achievement in Cuba, and insert himself into their business. Uppermost in Fidel's mind was Che's insistence on finding somewhere quickly. Fidel appeared to be so concerned to find somewhere, in fact, that for once he abandoned his political judgement.

Though the conference had ostensibly been convened to declare support for the struggle in Vietnam, Fidel took the opportunity to renege on his promise, made to the other communist countries in their secret meeting of 1964, to refrain from open support for guerrilla insurgencies in Latin America. Now he called for insurgency across the continent. He ratcheted up the Cuban propaganda machine once more and the Latin American Solidarity Organisation, which the meeting founded, was charged with using 'all means available to support liberation movements.'

As the CIA noted, Fidel had until now always been 'canny enough . . . to keep his risks low' in such declarations, changing the form and extent of his efforts. Suddenly he seemed not to be so careful. The Soviets and the Chinese were both present at the conference in their role as 'observers', so Fidel can have been under no illusion that the Soviets would not have reacted strongly when he said. 'We believe that on this continent, in the case of all or almost all peoples, the battle will take on the most violent forms.' Che's secret, pent-up presence was almost tangible in the uncharacteristic urgency of Fidel's words.

* * *

The picture that, on behalf of his friend, Fidel began to put together of the revolutionary potential in different countries on the South American continent was not encouraging, though. Despite a simmering discontent from Guatemala to Peru, by the mid-1960s the Latin American stage was riven by infighting between the radical parties of the left which severely limited the possibility of developing a guerrilla force in most countries. About the only half-promising option – though the opposition parties there were as divided as anywhere – was Bolivia, and Fidel was immediately eager to explore it. At least Bolivia had a recent history of worker uprisings and he invited to Havana represent-atives of both the pro-Moscow orthodox Bolivian Communist Party (PCB) headed by Mario Monje and the Maoist Commu-nist Party headed by Oscar Zamorra.

Monje was more than a little suspicious when he arrived in Havana for the conference that Fidel had convened as a façade for his altogether more clandestine enquiries. He had been studying news reports carefully. 'Where is Che?' he was wondering. 'What is his role in all of this?' Monje was a sharp character who had regularly reported to the Soviets on his meetings with the Cuban leadership. The previous year he had been particularly lurid when reporting that Che had said to him of the Soviets, 'It is hard to believe in the sins of someone who you were brought up to respect.' Monje was also sharp-eyed enough not to have been taken in by the rumours of a split between Fidel and Che. He knew that, whatever their immediate differences, they were at heart loyal to one another. And he would soon find out precisely the extent to which he was right about Che's involvement in the ideas that were being quietly touted by Fidel's most trusted men at the conference. More so than Fidel, Che looked to Bolivia as the most fertile ground upon which he might develop a guerrilla insurgency that roamed not just across the highlands of one country – as he and Fidel had done in the Sierra Maestra – but across the territory of all the nations bordering Bolivia: Peru, Brazil, Paraguay, Chile, and above all, Argentina. Considered as against a geopolitical map – and Che must have pored over countless maps in Tanzania – the reasoning seemed sound enough. And Che's own memories of the country that he had travelled through with Calica Ferrer were of a nation in political ferment. Perhaps above all, Che knew that starting an insurgency somewhere in this Latin American borderland region would help take some of the heat off Fidel's position in Cuba for a change while also allowing him to stay true to his word and to keep fighting. If Bolivia was not the perfect destination to open up a new front of active fighting in the Cold War, it was certainly the least worst option and Che was desperate enough to take it.

As the year unfolded, Fidel continued to agitate for a new revolutionary consciousness. The Tricontinental was just one of several 'new indications' of Fidel's 'longstanding determination to spread revolutionary violence in Latin America'. On 12 March he 'repeated his thesis on violent revolution', and on 1 May he 'once again proclaimed his determination to "fulfill his duty of solidarity"' with revolutionaries around the world.

By now the CIA were paying special attention to Fidel's comments. They were pleased that, for all the rhetoric, there was as yet little evidence that Cuba had 'actually given meaningful support to such groups so far this year'. That was soon to change, however, with the re-emergence of Che Guevara on the Latin American scene. But first, Che was moved in March from Dar-es-Salaam to a safe house that had been prepared for him in Prague in Czechoslovakia. From there he was in a much better position to begin preparations for the next attempt to internationalise the revolution. Via a steady flow of messengers Che and Fidel kept up the conversation they had begun while Che was in Tanzania, with Che pushing things forward and Fidel asking him, without success, to wait.

In one of the many letters that Fidel wrote to Che in Prague in June he said, 'Events have overtaken my plans for a letter. I read in full the planned book on your experiences in the C. [Congo], and also again the manual on guerrilla warfare, with the aim of making the best possible analysis of these questions, especially bearing in mind the practical importance with regard

to plans in the land of Carlitos.'* Fidel was well aware that Che
was reluctant to return to Cuba, but, as he continued, 'on any
coolly objective analysis, this actually hinders your objectives;
worse, it puts them at risk. It is hard work to resign myself to
the idea that this is correct, or even that it can be justified from
a revolutionary point of view.'

By now Fidel could not understand Che's reluctance to return.
He would be making the trip in secret, and so Fidel could see no
political reasons not to do so. In fact, once he had taken to the
idea he had become increasingly insistent that his friend return.
In part he wanted to see him. But he also knew that in Prague,
Che was in no position to prepare himself properly for the next
stage. 'What is the reason for all this?' Fidel wrote Che. 'There
is no question of principle, honour or revolutionary morality that
prevents you making effective and thorough use of the facilities
on which you can depend to achieve your ends. It implies no fraud,
no deception, no tricking of the Cuban people or the world.' The
really unforgivable thing, Fidel argued in an older-brotherly tone,
would be not to take advantage of all the help that his comrades
in Cuba could offer. 'I hope that these lines will not annoy or
worry you. I know that if you analyse them seriously, your characteristic honesty will make you accept that I am right.'

But Che would not be made to wait. Fidel tried digging a little
deeper. 'Did Marx, Engels, Lenin, Bolívar and Martí not have to
endure sometimes waiting for decades?' he averred. 'We ourselves
had to invest 18 months in Mexico before returning here.' Che
would not even have to wait that long – everything could be put
into place in the minimum time necessary and while working
with the greatest speed, Fidel assured him.

Fidel would later say that the idea to go to fight in Bolivia was
Che's: 'The idea, the plan, everything were his alone.' But this is
not true. Fidel too was behind the idea – that the available evidence

*'Carlitos' was Carlos Gardel, one of Che's favourite Argentine tango singers. It was
code for Argentina.

suggests was taken at about this time – as his conversations with Monje and the Bolivian communists suggest. The final, fateful chapter in Che Guevara's life – and their friendship – was thus one that the two of them decided upon together. Fidel finished his letter imploring Che to come home, saying. 'I know you will be 38 on the 14th. Do you think perhaps that a man starts to be old at that age?' About to turn forty, it may well have been a question he was posing of himself too.

* * *

When Che did finally return, in June, it was as quietly as he had left and for scarcely any longer than during his last flying trip. No sooner had he arrived than he was taken to a farm called San Andrés de Caiguanabo, well out of view atop an inaccessible cliff-edged limestone formation in the beautiful mountainous region of Pinar del Río. There he and Fidel were reunited. But there was no time for elaborate reconciliations. The revolution was at stake, and they set to work immediately. Che was introduced to the new group of men that over the previous few months he and Fidel had hand-picked to accompany him on this second mission.

Fidel still did not believe that the conditions were right just yet for Che to lead the struggle. Perhaps asking his comrade to return so as to hasten his preparations was just a bluff to get him home so that he could speak to him face to face. If it was, then it did not work. Che would not be swayed. The months of forced confinement that he had endured had left him desperate to move on with the plan as soon as possible.

Already by the summer, as Che began a series of hikes and exercises with his new unit, Cuban agents on the ground in Bolivia had begun to prepare reports and establish a basic support network. They had even purchased a farm to be used as a rear-guard base. They all worked 'meticulously' hard, Fidel's chief spymaster Piñeiro recalled, 'because it involved Che'.

A few days before Che's departure Fidel laid on a lunch to which he invited Che, in the disguise he would be wearing when he left, along with a number of high-ranking members of the Central Committee. 'I told them I wanted them to meet a very interesting friend of mine. . . . But none of the people who were there realised it was Che.' To achieve the effect, Che had endured having the hairs on the top of his head plucked one at a time, to give the natural look of a balding man.

Che was also in disguise, again with the name Ramón, when it was arranged for him to see his children for the last time before leaving. But Aleida was only able to bring the youngest in the end – there was a risk that the older ones might recognise their father. Hildita, Che's 'Little Mao', now aged ten, was not even told her father was in the country. When the younger children arrived with Aleida, to visit the man introduced to them only as 'Uncle Ramón', they naturally clung to their mother. Che had already joked off one of these difficult moments, saying to Aleida, 'Enjoy them, because when they're older they're mine.' But when his six year-old daughter Aliusha hit her head and it was 'Uncle Ramón' who tended to her with infinite care, she ran straight back to Aleida saying, 'Mamá, I think that old man's in love with me.' Aleida would later recall how she struggled not to cry in front of the children.

Then, in the early hours of 22 October, Che prepared to leave Cuba again. Fidel had arrived with Raúl, Vilma and Piñeiro to say farewell. It was gone midnight as Fidel and Che peeled away from the main group, as they had done on the night that they met. Neither necessarily expected it to be the last farewell, but they knew there was a high probability that it would be. 'Fidel and Che talked together in low voices for a long time,' Piñeiro recalled much later. It was a 'simple farewell' – they stood up finally and embraced each other briefly. Che had written of such moments before: 'Always cold, always less than you expected, when you find yourself incapable of externalising a deep feeling.'

It is almost certainly true that Che was smiling, as Piñeiro recalled, because he always did smile when leaving everything that was known behind him. That was no indication that he found the moment easy. For his part, Fidel was adamant, firm, but ultimately still unsure: 'I [had] expressed my reservations [about the mission] to some of them,' he later recalled, though it was clear that he had kept up a strong face for Che, not wanting to disappoint his determined friend. Ominously, that was precisely how Che had deceived Fidel as to the real prospects they confronted in the Congo.

16. A LIFE AND DEATH FORETOLD

'TODAY BEGINS A new phase,' Che selected as the first lines in his unlikely-looking journal: an ugly desk diary he had picked up in Germany during his clandestine journey to Bolivia. He had travelled with Alberto 'Pacho' Fernández Montes de Oca, an old comrade from the Sierra, as his only company on a route that took them, on numerous passports and *noms de guerre*, to Moscow, Prague, Vienna, Frankfurt, Paris and Madrid before arriving in São Paulo, Brazil, and travelling overland to La Paz.

It was 7 November by the time they arrived at the farm which was to serve as the guerrillas' base camp, having driven the last part of the journey down from La Paz in separate Jeeps. For this final stage they had travelled on yet more false documents that one of Che's secret agents, 'Tania' – an East German of Argentine origin whose real name was Haydée Tamara Bunke Bider, and who had long been undercover in Bolivia preparing the ground – had provided in La Paz. Once at the farm they waited for the rest of the troop of several dozen men to assemble over the coming weeks.

Ñancahuasú, where the farm was located, was a forbidding region of black scree spotted with dense jungle. It was a far cry from the thin air of the high-altitude capital that Che had wandered about as a young man. Here, as they set up camp near the farm and made exploratory forays into the surrounding region, with their only enemies the *yaguasa* flies and the ticks, Che took time to write to Aleida. A little later he and his men would begin the study of Quechua, a local dialect though not one spoken in this region (suggesting the extent of Che's ambitions), while Che lectured and instructed the men on different aspects of the coming mission. But for now, during this time of preparation, there was time enough to reflect:

My only one:
  I'm taking advantage of the trip of a friend to send you these words. Of course, they could go by post, but the 'para-official' route always seems more intimate. I could tell you that I miss you to the point of losing sleep, but I know that you wouldn't believe me, so I'll refrain. Still, there are days when the nostalgia advances uncontrollably and takes possession of me.

Gradually the men started to arrive: Rodolfo Saldaña, who would serve as liaison with the city; and the young Eliseo Reyes Rodríguez (Capitan San Luis) and Antonio Sánchez Díaz (Marco), both of whom Che knew and trusted from the Sierra days and who were now members of the Central Committee of the Cuban Communist Party. More Cubans, Leonardo Tamayo (Urbano) and Juan Vitalio Acuña (Joaquín), came next, with the Bolivians Braulio and Ricardo arriving shortly afterwards. Seated on a tree trunk, Che had 'a cigar in his mouth, and was relishing the fragrance of the smoke,' as he greeted Inti Peredo, one of the next Bolivian volunteers to arrive. With the fighters camping nearby, the ranch was left to another Bolivian conspirator to run. This was Bigotes, who, when he was driving Che to the ranch for the first time, had nearly brought the whole affair to a premature end when he crashed into a ditch on hearing of Che's true identity behind the disguise of the professiorial-looking Alberto Mena. Che's presence could be a mixed blessing, after all.

Before long, the shipments of food supplies and weapons to the ranch roused the suspicions of some of the locals. Most of them simply assumed that the guerrillas were cocaine barons or cattle thieves: fair game for this part of the world. Those few neighbours with whom Che's men came into contact, they could usually buy off or, in the last resort, threaten. At the very least, they needed to remain undetected for long enough to complete their training and to consolidate a support network outside the zone of operations.

Bolivia is a vast and hauntingly beautiful country in the very heart of Latin America. Fidel and Che had chosen its south-eastern region because it was sparsely populated and ought to have allowed the guerrilla unit to develop relatively unnoticed until they were ready to begin operations. But Bolivia was marked by strong nationalist sentiments that would lead the peasants who were so vital to the support of such movements to treat the primarily Cuban force that Che had assembled with much suspicion. Moreover, many of the peasants in this region had been 'introduced' in the 1940s, after the Chaco war between Bolivia and Paraguay, making them the very opposite of the disgruntled and dispossessed peasants Che was expecting to find.

During the previous year, Fidel had worked hard to muster support for the mission that Che had dragged him into. He tried, above all, to obtain the support of Mario Monje, the leader of the Bolivian Communist Party, and seems to have thought he had succeeded. But when Monje visited Che at the ranch between Christmas and New Year it soon became clear that Monje had begun to have second thoughts. The Bolivian insisted that any support he might offer was conditional upon him being in charge of the mission himself. The one lesson that Che had brought back from the Congo was never again to allow any local political leader to assume control of an operation in which he, and his men, were putting their own lives on the line. He steadfastly refused even to consider it.

The people wouldn't follow a 'foreigner', Monje warned Che. The people would never believe that Che Guevara was following Mario Monje, Che retorted. This was true enough, but Monje's comment was not groundless and in the months to come the Bolivian army would indeed make considerable propaganda from the 'foreign' nature of the struggle. Of course, as far as Che was concerned there was no 'foreign' in Latin America. He would willingly fight in any country regardless of kith and kin, and he expected others to do likewise. Monje left the guerrillas' camp the following day, after cordial but strained toasts for the New Year that in the towns nearby was celebrated with firecrackers and ringing bells. From that point, Che knew he could no longer count on the support of the Bolivian communists.

Politics was not the only problem. The territory in which they had been advised to set up the guerrilla force – a 'hostile region characterised by innumerable deep and densely wooded ravines' – also caused them difficulties. The Ñacahuazú river had cut a jagged and viciously steep path bordered by sandy strips that would disappear all of a sudden, requiring the guerrillas to climb the steep canyon sides covered in rough vegetation. Sharp reeds, strangling vines and prickly little cacti formed a natural armoury here, so that anyone moving through it could 'count on leaving some flesh and clothing behind'.

✳ ✳ ✳

Their plan, as they had elaborated it back in Cuba at the ranch in San Andrés, had been for a mother column led by Che to establish itself firmly in the Bolivian zone, with further guerrilla columns breaking off from the main unit to fan out into the neighbouring countries of Argentina, Chile, Peru and Brazil, creating a continent-wide guerrilla front as they went. It was their bid to create what the young French revolutionary theorist Regis Debray, a student of Sartre whom Castro had taken to heart over the last year, described as a 'Revolution in the Revolution'. Debray's book of the same name was a self-conscious synthesis of Fidel's revolutionary internationalism and Che's theories on guerrilla warfare. On Fidel's orders the first print run in Cuba exceeded a hundred thousand, making it in effect the manifesto of the Castro–Guevara theory of revolution, a sort of 'third way' that cast aside the ossified dinosaurs of the Soviet Union and

China in favour of a more mobile, fleet of foot and fast-track approach to wholesale revolution.

Turning his attention to how best to support Che in Bolivia, it was this vision that Fidel began speaking about in December. 'We have all been disturbed by the bitter and maddening reports that the Yankee imperialists, in their escalation, have committed the crime of directly bombing the capital of the sister Vietnamese nation,' he said in a speech that looked like it was going to be purely about Vietnam until he turned to his rather more immediate interests. 'In the same measure in which Vietnam resists, the revolutionary liberation movement will grow in other parts of the world,' he went on. 'Other fronts of the struggle for liberation will open throughout the world in direct proportion to Vietnam's resistance.'

On the anniversary of the revolution in January, Fidel became more explicit still. In Bolivia, Che tuned in to the radio to hear him address the crowds in Havana. He had spent all that morning encoding a message to Fidel, informing him of recent events. But from the tone of Fidel's speech it seemed clear that Che's rearguard in Havana did not yet know of the break with the communists on the ground. In his speech, Fidel sent out a very public 'message of solidarity and encouragement' to revolutionary leaders across the continent, from Douglas Bravo in Venezuela, to Fabio Vázquez and the National Liberation Movement in Colombia, and to César Montes now in charge of the Rebel Armed Forces [FAR] in Peru. It was nothing less than a call to revolutionary arms, and in his next breath Fidel bowed to the man who might lead it.

'And our special, warm message,' Fidel said, 'for it comes from deep inside us, from the affection born in the heat of battle – our message, wherever in the world he may be, to Major Ernesto Guevara and his comrades.' The crowd were ecstatic, their applause stretching out for a good five minutes of palm-blistering solidarity. 'The imperialists have killed Che many times in many places,' Fidel went on, this time to sustained boos from the crowd.

Instinctively, he followed their lead. 'But what we hope – what we hope is that some day, where imperialism least expects, as it should be, Comandante Ernesto Guevara will rise from his ashes, a warrior and a guerrilla – and in good health!' The crowd once more broke into applause. 'Some day, we will again have some very concrete news about Che,' he finished.

In Bolivia, Che was gladdened by Fidel's public affirmation of his presence. The last the Cubans had heard of him had been the day Fidel read out his farewell letter over a year earlier. 'He talked about us in a way that made us feel even more committed, if that is possible,' Che wrote afterwards in his diary. It inspired him to demand even more discipline from his men: we must be a 'model nucleus', he told them shortly afterwards, 'one of steel'. But Che knew that alone would not be enough.

As he tried to point out to Fidel via the painfully slow means of a message deposited in a drop box in La Paz – a means of communication that made their system of runners in the Sierra look advanced by comparison – of greatest importance was the need to secure immediate, local support from the Bolivians.

Fidel seemed to get the point. On 25 January he replied, saying that he planned to see Jorge Kolle Cueto, the organisational secretary of the Bolivian Communist Party who, in the absence of Monje, was Fidel and Che's next best link to the Bolivian communists. He would pressure him to offer assistance, Fidel assured. A month later, Fidel updated Che on the situation. Kolle had claimed not to have been informed that the undertaking was to be on a *continental* scale and now, knowing that it would be so, he was more prepared to collaborate. Fidel perhaps ought to have been suspicious, but he told Che not to worry. He had sent Kolle back with instructions to present himself to Che and work out what might be done. But neither Kolle nor any of the other members of the PCB would ever make it to the camp. They all decided to hedge their bets; to wait and see how Che got on. It was 'the age of the guerrilla,' Fidel was constantly announcing. But just when it counted, it seemed he could not find any. 'Latin

America's Vietnams', as one perceptive journalist of the time put it, were suddenly 'short of guerrillas.'

* * *

'We now enter the era of the bird,' a tired and hungry Che wrote sardonically in his diary on 1 May. He was writing of the augmentation of their shrinking rations when one of the Bolivian guerrillas, Ñato, killed a small bird with a slingshot. His comment was equally a statement on the stark reality of the situation beginning to confront the guerrilla unit; a reality that stood in complete contrast to Fidel's high-flying rhetoric in Havana and perhaps also, he must now have begun to think, Fidel's own understanding of progress on the ground. But Che was not one for losing faith.

Things in Bolivia had begun to go wrong as early as January, when some of the men succumbed to malaria and the guerrillas' radio transmitter was rendered unserviceable by damp in the cave where it had been stored. Che had then taken the men on a two-month trek in which they roamed far to the north, suffering from hunger and exhaustion all the while and struggling with the impenetrable terrain. While they were gone, the ranch that served as their base camp was raided by the police at the same time as soldiers began moving into the area. All too soon Che's 'model nucleus' had proven to be nothing of the sort.

By March Che's plans gradually and carefully to continentalise the struggle were also proving unattainable. Few of the continent's other revolutionary leaders appeared to have heeded Fidel's call. During his prolonged absence from the ranch Che had sent the agent Tania to make contact with Ciro Bustos, the Argentine who had served as the urban coordinator on the Salta expedition, as well as to find some willing recruits to come and be trained by him first in Bolivia. By the time Che had returned from his 'breaking-in' trek Tania was waiting for him, along with Bustos and Regis Debray, Fidel's favoured high theoretician of revolutionary struggle. The fighters, however, had given up waiting and gone home. There would be no new additions this time.

Che was rather less taken by Debray than Fidel had been. The Frenchman told Che he wanted to join the struggle, but Che refused, asking him instead to help obtain external support. He had plans to write letters for him to deliver to Sartre and Bertrand Russell. Bustos was assigned the task of returning to help set up a new *foco*, or guerrilla focus, in Argentina. Che made plans at the same time for a third *foco* to begin operations in the Ayacucho region of Peru later in the year. On paper, it all looked promising. But documents that Tania had left behind in her Jeep as she brought the visitors to the camp were discovered by the authorities, and once the army had tracked down the guerrillas' base camp they were forced to leave the area in which they had established themselves. It pushed them, prematurely, into the active phase of operations.

Ironically, their first skirmish – an ambush of a small group of soldiers under the command of Major Hernán Plata – would turn out to be the guerrillas' major success of the operation. Pinning down the army in a ravine, and to cries of '*Viva la liberación nacional!*', the guerrillas raked the soldiers with fire from their positions on both sides. Major Plata, who was found cowering in a bush in the throes of a heart attack, was captured, along with fourteen others. Seven soldiers in all were killed. The guerrillas picked up weapons and interrogated the captured men, Plata and his second-in-command, Captain Silva. The two officers 'talked like parrots', and Che was able to establish that the army was advancing on their position from both sides. The guerrillas were about to be thrown into a full-scale war with but the barest of preparation. 'Everything gives the impression of utter chaos,' Che wrote in his diary on 20 March.

To maintain greater speed across the difficult terrain, and to allow him to drop off the 'visitors' – who had been stuck with the guerrillas since the discovery of their vehicle – in the nearby town of Muyupampa, Che had divided the group into two, giving command of the second unit to Joaquín, the oldest of the group and a stout fighter Che trusted. It was only intended to be for a few days, but the two halves would never quite manage to find one another again. On 20 April the army briefly pinpointed the position of Che's unit, and a few hours later Bolivian airforce planes came to bomb the house of a sympathetic peasant on whose land they were cooking food. One of the guerrillas was wounded by some shrapnel; the rest were lucky enough to be outside the building at the time.

A few days later, Che listened in to the May Day speeches from Havana. He was unaware that at that very moment his seven-year-old daughter was a guest of honour on the platform, standing between Fidel and President Dorticós. As they watched the Soviet-supplied MiGs do their acrobatics ahead, she concentrated on tugging their trouser legs. Che did pick up on a subtle message to him during his old comrade from the Sierra, Juan Almeida's speech, however, and commented on it in his diary that night: 'Almeida passed the mantle to me and the famous Bolivian guerrillas,' he wrote. But he was more than likely being ironic, for they were being talked about rather less than were the sizeable forces being sent in to find them. Counter-insurgency was the new buzzword and the media were as interested in the growing American presence in the region as they were in the guerrillas themselves. The guerrillas had succeeded by now in engaging the army in a few skirmishes, but for all Fidel's propagandising on their behalf the majority of the news centred upon the chase.

* * *

'This revolution will never be anyone's satellite or be subjected to anyone's conditions,' Fidel had declared in March, once more making it clear that he saw his domestic and especially his foreign policy as nobody's concern but his. By then, the socialist embassies in Havana and the Soviets themselves had begun to voice more prominently their concerns over what Fidel and Che were up to and Fidel was finding himself under siege politically in Cuba, just as Che was being surrounded by soldiers in Bolivia.

To keep things moving along, Fidel kept speaking of a new wave of revolutionary fervour. Vietnam was very much on his mind that year. Soviet Premier Kosygin had been in Hanoi as the bombs began falling on North Vietnam in February, but still the Soviets had stood idly by. After the Missile Crisis, Fidel could all too easily imagine the same happening to Cuba. But Vietnam contained another lesson for the revolutionary-minded: the Americans were struggling. Resistance was not futile. It was a red rag to a bull for Fidel who, true to form, drew one final political lesson from it all: that if the Soviets were worried they weren't looking supportive enough he would probably not find a better time, strategically, to push forward the plans he had with Che to develop a continent-wide revolutionary front.

But as Che had found, the Latin American communist leaders like Monje were now more interested in working within the system. '[T]he Cuban leadership,' read an East German report from the year before, was in danger 'of plunging headlong into unintentional self-isolation'. Fidel responded boldly to these sorts of attacks, hammering the socialists for all he was worth for their lack of solidarity. But no matter how great the provocation, the communist parties on the ground in Latin America would not be bent to his will. In March, the Venezuelan Communist Party rounded personally on Fidel. They accused him of 'playing the role of judge over revolutionary activities in Latin America, the role of the super-revolutionary who has already carried out the revolution in place of the Latin American Communists . . . . We categorically reject his claim to be the only one who decides what is and is not revolutionary in Latin America.' The new Soviet leader, Leonid Brezhnev, himself agreed: 'What right', he asked, did Fidel have to launch revolutions elsewhere?

Fidel and Che were becoming dangerously isolated, each in his own way, but Fidel's response to these latest accusations against him was so furious that even Che, preoccupied as he was by then, found time to comment on them. He noted especially Fidel's 'harsh attacks' on the position of the Soviet Union,

savouring – one presumes with a certain relish – the even more
ferocious arguments that might have taken place behind the
scenes. This was the most overt criticism Fidel had yet levelled
against the Soviets. It was as if he was, once more, following in
the ever blunter, sometimes bolder footsteps of Che. But the
criticisms of the other socialist parties were not entirely wrong,
and the more Fidel shouted from the podium the more he was
painting himself into a corner.

To the surprise of almost everyone, it was Che's voice that was
the next to be heard in this gradually escalating saga. In April, a
contribution by him was included in the first issue of a radical new
journal that followed on, and took the same name as, the Tricontinental meeting Fidel had convened the previous January. Titled
a 'Message to the Peoples of the World', Che's piece called for a
'second, third Vietnam'. If not quite written on the go as Lenin's
State and Revolution had been this was none the less equal in many
ways to that document for the way that it captured the growing
sense of the moment. As ever, Che was just a little ahead of things.
Vietnam must not be left alone, he said, condemning again the
current 'solidarity' of the socialist world and the people of Vietnam
as being that of the solidarity of the plebs with the Roman gladi-
ators. In his text Che exhorted, just as Fidel had been doing, the
need for another way forward for world communism, a third way.
Their lives could scarcely have looked more different at this moment,
and yet they were back in step together, calling with parallel voices
but in their own ways for the same revolutionary ends. Amidst the
timbre of chaos and war they had once again established a point
and counterpoint of revolutionary harmony.

* * *

In order to maintain the tempo of events Fidel set about walking
an incredibly fine line between overt criticism of the Soviets,
which entailed the real possibility of his banishment from the
socialist camp and the end of the Soviet economic lifeline that

his country had come to depend upon, and insufficient support for the still newborn guerrilla movement in Bolivia. He was forced to draw upon all of his diplomatic cunning, making major statements in public more regularly than he had done for some time, to maintain the careful balance, see-sawing this way and that as he steered as straight a path as possible though this political minefield. But with his continued glowing references to the 'heroic' struggle in Bolivia, the 'surprise visit' he received from Soviet Premier Kosygin on a baking hot day at the end of June would not have come as much of a surprise at all.

Kosygin had come straight from his meetings with President Lyndon Johnson at the Glassboro Summit in New Jersey, where Johnson had confronted the Soviet Premier with 'direct evidence of Cuba's encouragement of guerrilla operations in seven Latin American countries'. Kosygin had remained silent, which Johnson interpreted as suggestive of his being 'a little upset with Castro', though he was careful not to say so.

That Kosygin was upset was undoubtedly true. On the one occasion they had met, Che had found Kosygin a 'serious, thoughtful, clever leader who approaches problems without hurry, only after deep analysis'. But that was just one side of the man who had served more than a decade under Stalin. Though ostensibly now in Cuba to explain the recent Soviet stance in the Middle East crisis – a stance that Castro had been highly critical of – Kosygin was in fact 'in Cuba to reprimand Castro' and to present him with a 'virtual ultimatum' over his support for Che's activities in Bolivia.

In one of the relatively few and notably 'frank' discussions they had, 'Kosygin and Fidel talked for seven hours without a break'. The conversation became 'very hard' when 'Kosygin then asked Fidel to stop the support of liberation movements in Latin America. The Soviet Union, he said, did not approve of these activities. Above all, Fidel had to cease his support for Guevara's mission in Bolivia. On this the conversation was 'especially bitter'.

Fidel replied, again, that Che had gone to Bolivia under the same terms as when he had first come to Cuba. He added that

Cuba was helping him only indirectly, 'supporting the local party, through public statements'. This was only half true, of course. Fidel, pushing his position into uncharted terrain, then subjected Kosygin to a lengthy lecture on Latin American liberation traditions, touching on Bolívar and San Martín especially. Fidel was making it perfectly clear that he would not be told what to do in his own sphere of influence. Above all, he wanted the Soviets to understand the significance of the fact that, while they pontificated from afar, Cubans lived daily under the threat of American intervention from very near by.

Fidel had stood his ground. Kosygin left with no concessions and no send-off from Fidel, who continued to call for revolution. The guerrilla movement in Latin America was making 'excellent progress', he said when asked about it later that summer. But on this Fidel was being misled, disingenuous or deliberately misleading himself for by then little could have been further from the truth. There were times he could recall from the Sierra when the always-outnumbered guerrillas would go quiet and simply have to focus on survival. Fidel had stood his ground with Kosygin but he knew now he could not get any more involved than he already was. Che would have to try to reach the tipping point on his own.

* * *

By late summer, Che's guerrilla unit was looking terribly vulnerable. Not only were they still struggling with the Bolivian peasants – who were 'hard as rocks', Che complained – but the threadbare political network supporting the guerrillas had not grown in strength as it had in Cuba; rather, it had deteriorated in a cascade of treachery and ineptitude. Only a few hours after Che had dropped off Debray and Bustos in Muyupampa, the army picked them up. The two men, poorly disguised as journalists, would soon be subject to a very public trial which would greatly damage Che's chances of success. Without messengers or adequate radio equipment, the guerrillas now found themselves with almost no support as they confronted the disorganised but none the less waspish Bolivian army and their CIA trainers.

Since early spring the guerrillas had managed to bloody the army's nose on more than a few occasions. But now, as they arced forward and doubled back and sought desperately to stay one step ahead of the army, they were gradually being ground down. By this time the army was sitting on their rearguard camp from where it scatter-gunned across the region, slowly pinpointing the movements of the two guerrilla columns under Joaquín and Che as they sought desperately, without any means of communication, to find one another in the harsh terrain.

At the end of May Che's column smashed into the small town of Caraguataenda like curiously charitable brigands, confiscating two vehicles that belonged to a government-owned petroleum company – and that they would henceforth keep running by urinating into the radiators – breaking into a store to replenish their supplies and paying the townspeople handsomely for this treatment. As they left, Che wondered momentarily whether to drive south along a railway line that led towards Argentina. In the end he elected to keep heading north. He would never again be in a position to consider returning to his homeland.

By June they had to work hard at not bumping into unexpected army patrols, but even so they would still run into soldiers every few days. They soon had to abandon their trucks and, as supplies ran out and they began the cycle of fasts and gorging that left them sometimes incapable of moving, the troop began steadily to weaken. With each skirmish came the risk of further losses. Rolando had died in April, and Che's old comrade Tuma was killed in June. 'Still in one piece', Che wrote of himself on his birthday, 14 June. But by now they had strayed close to the large city of Santa Cruz. When they entered the outlying town of Samaipata, the men fanning through it in a desperate search for medicines for their now physically stricken leader, it alarmed the government, which put into immediate action another major offensive against the guerrillas.

In July, Fidel sent word that one of his agents in La Paz had made contact with the Workers' Revolutionary Party and that some of their members might be prepared to help the guerrillas. It was a beacon of hope for the beleaguered men. But there is no mention of it in Che's diary. It was now a battle of wills and, above all, of willpower. By August, however, his own reserves of strength were depleted. He no longer had any of his asthma medication and an injured foot had left him incapable of walking. He tried injecting himself with Novocaine, even an eyewash solution that had a trace of adrenaline in it, but all 'to no avail'. Che's body had reached its limit.

Encrusted in his own faeces and vomit from the lack of proper food or water, with his clothes torn to shreds, like those of all the others, from the rough terrain, he was forced to ride one of the pack mules they had obtained earlier in the month from some peasants. Soon food became the only thing the starving men spoke about, and the rest of the mules began to be slaughtered for it. Che kept listening in to Fidel on the radio. But even if there were coded messages from Havana in the shortwave broadcasts, he no longer had a book of ciphers to decode them. All that was left was to try to hang on and hope for a change in the course of events.

* * *

'The history of Cuba is the history of all Latin America,' proclaimed the banners at the conference of the Latin American Solidarity Organisation that opened on 4 August in Havana. The slogan 'fluttered in luminous letters on an immense banner' beneath portraits of Simón Bolívar, Máximo Gómez, José Martí and Che Guevara, recalled one of those who attended. Yet again there was an eerie sense of Che's imminent martyrdom, and Fidel did little to dispel the effect. He hailed Che an 'Honorary Citizen of [all] Latin America'.

But Fidel was doing something else too. He was holding his comrade up as an example in order to frame, two months after his visit, a stinging riposte to Kosygin's ultimatum. Cuba would go on making revolution and spreading revolution, Fidel insisted. This was communist heresy of the first order and Fidel knew it. But he would not be told what to do by the Soviets, above all when his own men's lives were on the line. There was an ideological war being fought between 'those who want to make the revolution and those who do not want to make it . . . , who want to curb it'. Fidel declared himself unequivocally on the side of the former.

Given the competing pressures from Havana and Moscow that most of those present were being subjected to, the conference was a modest success for Fidel. Before the delegates had departed Fidel had secured a resolution to the effect that guerrilla warfare was the fundamental path for the Latin American revolution and that *guerrilleros* were to fight under the banner of Marxism–Leninism. But Fidel had hoped for so much more. And he knew full well that it was the Soviets, digging in their heels, who were to blame. By now he realised that there was nothing more he could do for Che except to listen in to reports on his progress and wait, hoping to the last that he was able to reverse the tide.

On 13 August, Fidel headed out to the Isle of Pines. It was his forty-first birthday. At a birthday meal on his ranch, he was joined by some of his closest comrades – Papito Serguera, Juan Almeida and other high-ranking officers, and a journalist who had recently gained his trust and favour, the formidable Polish born, K. S. Karol. During the meal, Fidel brushed off a toast to his birthday that someone tried to make. He preferred to celebrate with some rather more applied reflection.

Above all, he mulled over the recent conference. He was surprised, he said, at the reticence of many of the delegates to support armed struggle. How could they fail to understand the reasons behind their constant internecine struggles? It was so obvious to him. He also announced that he had just read Isaac Deutscher's magnificent trilogy on Trotsky – a work that only Fidel could turn to for genuine relaxation – and it had got him wondering what might have happened had the Bolsheviks not signed the treaty of Brest-Litovsk extricating them from World

War I. Trotsky's ultimately doomed attempt to stall the treaty for long enough to precipitate an international worker uprising against the feuding European upper classes that had led them into war was certainly an object lesson in the interconnectedness of great power conflicts and revolutionary movements that held some currency still in the Cold War context of the 1960s.

'Yes, the more I think if it,' Fidel said as he stood up, 'the more I realise how right Marx was when he said that there can be no real revolution until there is a world revolution. We are not stupid enough to believe that we can build a brave little Communist state in splendid isolation.'

Fidel was interrupted only when a tropical storm that had been brewing finally broke. 'Very well,' he said in light of the horrors of Stalinism that the conversation had recently turned to, 'the Communist movement has a very long history . . . . But everything would have been quite different had communists everywhere come to one another's aid, just as Cuba is trying to do. Unfortunately the imperialists seem to be the only true internationalists left.' With that the thunder clapped. 'I wonder what sort of world we are living in!' With this off his chest, Fidel then sat down to finish his meal.

Despite his ruminations, Fidel appeared still to have complete confidence in what he and Che were doing. After the meal, he invited Karol to take a stroll with him. The journalist asked, in light of all he had just said, whether Cuba's reliance on the Soviet Union did not hamper the notion of its contributing to a wider Latin American advancement. Not at all, Fidel replied, adding conspiratorially, 'We are not building socialism in complete silence, as you may have come to think; we have our own way of explaining ourselves.' Fidel was clearly still banking on the promise of good news from Che.

* * *

In Bolivia, however, the news went from bad to very much worse. On 30 August Joaquín's column had been massacred as they crossed the Rio Grande at a point known as Vado del Yeso. A peasant had betrayed them. As the column crossed, guns held aloft, with Joaquín at the front and Tania in her white blouse and brown pants standing out at the rear, they were mown down with ease. She was one of the first to fall, along with Moisés Guevara and Braulio. Her body was carried downstream where it would be found several days later, bloated and disfigured.

Sensing the end, Bolivian President Barrientos now upped the ante against the intrusive Guevara, offering a bounty of 50,000 Bolivian pesos, around $4200, for Che's capture, dead or alive. By now he had the dedicated assistance of the CIA who were supplying him with men and arms and who had Che, above all, in their sights. In September, as the net tightened around the last remaining guerrillas under Che, the urban network finally caved in too. The government had gained so much information from the captured guerrillas that practically all the agents were compromised. One of them, Loyola Guzman, fearing more that she might betray her comrades during interrogation than she did for her own life, tried to commit suicide by throwing herself out of a third-floor window at the Ministry of the Interior. An awning broke her fall. But the Bolivian guerrilla mission was being steadily ripped apart on all sides.

With the inevitability of defeat hanging over them, the situation for the last remaining guerrillas slipped almost into the surreal. Around the 20th, having briefly seized a small settlement named Lusitano, they fled back into the jungle and found solace in a small orange grove. There they rested the night in a semi-delirious state before moving on. On 6 October, Che heard on his small portable radio that there were eighteen hundred men looking for them. The following day they were forced to detain an old lady whom they encountered for fear she might give them away. They took her back to her house, where she lived with one daughter who was almost bedridden and another who was a dwarf. The guerrillas paid them not to speak. That evening 'the seventeen of us set out under a slither of a moon', Che wrote. They left tracks behind them as they went, but they were in no condition to do anything about this. At two in the morning they stopped to rest 'because it was futile to continue . . . . Our refuge is supposedly between the Acero and Oro rivers.'

They did not make their refuge. On the morning of Sunday, 8 October, after marching all night, Che, half dead but dragging with him a small stash of books, as if he was still the twenty-three-year-old who had crossed the border from Peru, ordered the men to rest for the day in a ravine named Quebrada de Yuro. While they rested, the Ranger company that had recently graduated from the US Army Special Forces training camp in nearby Santa Cruz under the command of Gary Prado quietly took up positions on the heights surrounding the ravine. At midday Prado ordered an encirclement, and as Che's small group tried to break through they came under heavy automatic fire.

Che was shot in the leg as he fled. The only other comrade nearby, Willy, found him and helped him out of the line of fire, but the two of them walked straight into a group of four soldiers who were loading up a mortar. The soldiers ordered them to surrender. Che responded by firing back his carbine until a bullet from the return fire struck the barrel and rendered it useless. Not far off, the other guerrillas were being hunted down. There was nothing for it: the two of them had to surrender.

* * *

From Vado del Yeso, where he had been captured, Che was taken away to a village called La Higuera, gunfire still crackling around the ravine as his comrades fought on. There he was bound hand and foot, and trussed up against the wall of the village schoolhouse. Some time later he was interrogated by the deputy commander of the Vallegrande detachment of soldiers, Lieutenant Colonel Andrés Selich. The Bolivian officer accused Che of having 'invaded' his country. Che motioned with his head to the bodies of two Cuban *compañeros* who had been killed in the fight and were lying nearby. They had everything, but had come here to 'fight like dogs', he said.

'Are you Cuban or Argentine?' Selich pressed. 'I'm Cuban, Argentine, Peruvian, Ecuadorian, etc. . . . You understand,' Che replied, his wound still bleeding and his breathing noticeably audible but his irony not leaving him. Selich took notes of their conversation, which lasted about half an hour, then left him for the night. In the morning the village schoolteacher came, out of curiosity, to see Che. Her visit seemed to revive him a little. Che pointed to a grammatical error on the blackboard. And the place was filthy, he told her. She was too nervous to respond. When he called for her later, she did not come.

Later in the morning, Selich returned with Prado who tried to coax Che to 'speak badly about Fidel', but Che would not be drawn. All he would confess is that it had been their joint idea to come here. At 12.30 a message was radioed into the base from Bolivian high command in La Paz: 'Proceed with the elimination of Sr Guevara'; and at around 1 p.m. Mario Terán, the soldier who had been given the duty of killing him, stuttered into the fetid little room.

Terán found Che sitting against a wall. For some time, he didn't dare to shoot. All he could see was Che growing before him, he later recalled. He was 'big, very big, enormous'. But there was no escaping that the moment had come. His heart was racing. 'His eyes shone intensely. I was afraid he was going to jump on top of me and with a rapid movement, sever my arm off.' It was Che who brought him back to reality. 'Calm yourself man, and aim well,' he snapped. 'You're only going to kill a man.' But Terán seemed to think that wasn't true. And he already had his orders as to how to shoot. 'Avoid the face,' they had told him.

* * *

Later that afternoon, Che's body was strapped to the skids of a Bell helicopter and flown to the nearby town of Vallegrande. Already the townspeople and a few intrepid journalists were gathering after the army's morning announcement – made prior to Che's execution – that he had fallen in battle. As the helicopter landed, 'women in black dresses, men in wide-brimmed hats [and] little children surged towards the helicopter, and the soldiers on guard had difficulty in holding them back as the body was loaded into a car and rapidly taken to the hospital morgue.'

Seeing the diminutive-looking figure that he had become carried over to a wash-house, the journalists jostled for a view as he was set down amidst the throng of military personnel, photographers and onlookers. 'There was no longer any doubt,' one of them, Kumm, reflected. 'He was dead . . . . A soldier was holding a vessel with a white liquid above the body, and for a while I had the impression that they were administering a blood transfusion. The terrible stench of formalin made me realise my error. The body was being preserved to be displayed to the public and the world.' Initially they tried pumping it in through his mouth, but they found it easier to use one of the bullet holes instead. Then they washed him, cut and combed his hair and opened his eyelids so that the dead body looked more like the man he had once been.

It was a macabre but short-lived spectacle before the body was mysteriously secreted away – to where would not be known for more than thirty years. By the time Che's brother Roberto flew up to identify the body, only the hands remained, severed to provide proof that Che Guevara was indeed no more.

* * *

The news travelled fast. 'When reports of Che's death reached Fidel,' one of his bodyguards at the time recalled, 'all the Chiefs came round to Celia's house on Calle 11. Raúl, Ramiro. It was hard to see these men there, with their heads down, crying . . . . Celia came over to me and said: "Yes, it's confirmed."' But in fact in Havana, on the 9th, nothing was certain. And the following day things were, if anything, even less sure. There was talk of a scar on his left hand, Fidel said. But nobody could remember such a scar.

That evening Fidel, Raúl, Ramiro, Vilma, Celia and the others who had by then congregated at Fidel's house received the first photo from Bolivia. There was little similarity between the emaciated, goblin-like figure it depicted and the Che that everyone remembered. Fidel was one of those inclined to disbelieve it. But as the evidence mounted over the following days, and Fidel had anyone who might offer an expert opinion called in, the truth became ever more apparent.

On 15 October, after he had moved Aleida and the children into his own apartment to look after them, Fidel spoke on the television and radio. Over the previous two and a half years he had played much on the numerous claims that had circulated that Che had been killed. But this time, no one who saw Fidel's body language could be in any doubt. Che's death, Fidel confirmed, was 'bitterly true' and he recounted the 'painful' succession of cables by which the government had come to believe it as if they themselves were instruments of torture.

Some of the proof he now shared with the nation, holding up the photos. Here was his mule – 'just the way he used to ride them'; here his M-2 rifle – 'very accurate'; and of another he stopped to comment: 'Probably at that moment he had just made a joke with the person who was about to take the photo'. But the most convincing evidence beyond the photos, he confessed, was the unmistakeably awful handwriting of Che's captured diary. And indeed, as he read from some of the pages to have been made public by the Bolivian army as proof of his identity, Fidel had at times to stop when he reached the inevitable part that could not be read.

But Fidel was not just there to recount the death of his comrade-in-arms. He was there to make the case for the prosecution and to launch a new stage of the struggle, with his friend now playing the role of heroic martyr. It was only natural to turn any setback into the basis for a renewed push forward, and he had not been slow to recognise that his friend's image had begun its transformation into a symbol. And he accepted, as a point of necessity, the inevitable fact: that while in life it was Che who had tussled with countless others over that ideal of revolution that he saw embodied in Fidel, in death it would be he, Fidel, who would now have to fight for the revolutionary ideal embodied by Che. It would become one of the longest and most arduous of all his battles: a battle, at times, over the very soul of the revolution. 'Well, I have complied with this bitter task', Fidel said simply as he stood up to leave the studio at the end of his address.

With those words began what was perhaps Fidel's darkest hour, and quite possibly also Che's brightest. The national flag was ordered to be flown at half-mast for thirty days and on the night of the 18th, at a candlelit vigil in the Revolutionary Plaza attended by countless thousands, Fidel eulogised his friend once more. There was a breeze that wafted the flags beneath the giant sombre image of Che's face that had been pinned up around the Plaza. But all eyes in the crowd were on Fidel. 'They are mistaken when they think that his death is the end of his ideas,' he declared – still visibly stung – at the end of the vigil. His final marks were a variant, and a requiem, on the traditional revolutionary chant that by then followed any public speech on the island, and they were accompanied by a pained yet defiant expression. '*Hasta la Victoria Siempre! . . . Patria o Muerte! . . . Venceremos!*'

Fidel and Che's dream of a continent-wide revolution was over.

EPILOGUE

THE RELATIONSHIP BETWEEN Fidel and Che did not end that October of 1967. Not only was the fall-out from Che's death Fidel's greatest preoccupation for much of the following year, but Che's legacy would continue to haunt Fidel for the rest of his thirty-nine years in power. When asked a question about Che by a journalist many years later, Fidel stood up from his chair, 'inclined his head, leant forward with his knuckles pressed on to the lustrous wood of the table, and in a low voice, as if speaking to himself, he said to us: "I dream of Che a lot. I dream he is alive, in his uniform, I dream that we talk."'

In the months immediately following the death of his comrade, as he smarted at anyone he held even vaguely responsible, Fidel also watched observantly as around the world Che's image began to take on a life of its own. First in the wave of protests against Vietnam that autumn, then again in the uprisings of May 1968, Che's visage became a symbol of a whole era of protest. Fidel could do little to influence the students marching in Paris, or the veterans descending on the Pentagon in Washington, but in Cuba, at least, he sought to take control of how that symbol was being formed.

The Soviet leadership, who bore much of the brunt of Fidel's anger, greeted the news with a certain regret at the death of an undeniably committed and passionate revolutionary but also with a sense of relief that a dangerous heretic who had for some time been one of the greatest threats to their hopes of détente with the Americans had been removed from the scene. 'We raised a glass of vodka and a toast to "that difficult son of a bitch"', recalled a former US embassy representative in Havana, by then working in Moscow, of sitting down to hear the news with a high ranking Soviet official.

Aware of Fidel's anger, the Soviet leadership invited him to attend the fiftieth anniversary of the Bolshevik Revolution that October. Fidel not only refused to go, he sent a low-ranking Minister of Health in his stead. He also made no attempt to discourage the spate of rumours that sprang up that winter concerning the deterioration in relations between the two countries. While the Soviets celebrated their revolution in Moscow, Fidel had his now one official party newspaper, named after the invasion vessel, *Granma*, print a lecture on his and run a special feature entitled, somewhat pointedly, 'The Military Programme of Proletarian Revolution'.

The Soviets responded by refusing to deliver more fuel to Cuba. Fidel was forced to call for rationing, but even then he managed to frame at least one riposte: no fuel meant no traditional parade of Soviet-donated military hardware. Instead, Fidel said, we have the real revolutionaries, 'the units that represent the basic foundations of the revolution march[ing] past here. Our workers, represented by the *macheteros*.' He then proceeded to name 1968 the Year of the Heroic Guerrilla: 'Let this year be worthy of its name, worthy of Che's example in every respect,' he said.

Just a few days later the Soviets retaliated again, recalling Alexiev, who was so close to the Cuban leadership as ambassador, and replacing him with a diplomat who had greater experience in 'enemy' countries, Aleksander Soldatov. There would be no more 'sweetheart deals' for Cuba. Aníbal Escalante even made a brief reappearance on the scene, furnishing the Soviets with information on Fidel's government throughout the course of this Che-related spat.

Fidel had been lenient with Escalante in 1962, but when evidence of this new so-called 'micro-faction' surfaced he was in no mood to let him off again. '[T]his little island will always be a revolutionary wall of granite and against it all conspiracies all intrigues, and all aggressions will be smashed,' he had said the previous year. In a bruising and secret ten-hour indictment to the Central Committee – the sort of show trial Che loathed in which the entire government simply disappeared from view for three days of proceedings – Fidel had Escalante tried for treason and sentenced to fifteen years.

Typically, Fidel also used the occasion of Escalante's trial – his 'Secret Speech', as it would become known – to make some much broader points: first, that he stood firm to the vision of constant struggle that he had formulated with Che, and second, that nobody in his government should be thought of as a potential figurehead for a coup. Fidel had Raúl level most of these accusations. Described by some as an 'accusatory duet', it was also a clear first step on Raúl's path to playing a more prominent rearguard role for Fidel: a very similar position to that which Che had played so successfully until he left. But as Fidel said to a group of visiting intellectuals that same January, 'It will be difficult to find a human being who matches him.'

* * *

By the spring of 1968 Fidel seemed willing at last to move on. Henceforth, his line would always be somewhere between that offered by Che's example and that demanded by the Soviets, filtered always by his own principal objective to maintain power, to stay in control no matter what. Initially he committed the revolution once more to Che's ideas on 'moral incentives', but he would to and fro on this position throughout the remaining decades of his rule, always intuitively drawn by the ideas, always finding it hard to relinquish his own more pragmatic streak. At the same time Fidel gingerly sounded out the idea of some sort of rapprochement with the Soviets, and by the end of the following year, before the first anniversary of Che's death, he would even stand before a television audience justifying to the Cuban people, most of whom found it repulsive, why the Soviets had been right to send tanks in to crush the Prague Spring in Czechoslovakia.

By then it was clear that the death of Che had marked more than just the end of a friendship and a political partnership. A whole way of being revolutionary had also come to an end. 'It was like a cold-shower to those living in the euphoria of this exceptional period,' Regis Debray wrote some time after his eventual release. The CIA's new man in Havana concurred. He reported back that summer: 'Castro finds himself increasingly hemmed in. The loss of "Che" and the insurgency effort in Bolivia on the heels of the big LASO [Latin America Solidarity Organisation] splash has been a serious blow.' Others caught it too. Fidel wrote an introduction that summer to the publication of Che's Bolivian diary that a sympathiser in the Bolivian Interior Ministry had by then made available to him. No sooner was he finished than he met a journalist who noted that his face showed signs of stress. 'He was betrayed,' was all that Fidel said to him in a bitter tone of voice.

Fidel might well have felt that he too had been betrayed. Che's mission to Bolivia had been at once the culmination of his own ambitions and his greatest ever defeat. It had seen him launch a revolutionary movement across the continent of Latin America in open defiance not just of the Americans, but of the Soviets and of the Chinese too. This more than Bolívarian desire to bring a revolution to the entire Latin American continent, given shape and form and a means of being realised via his association with the restless figure of Che, was a revolutionary project that could not have existed outside their particular friendship. Theirs was indeed a revolutionary friendship. And with Che's death a moment had passed, Fidel knew it, and he would never approach the question of revolution in quite the same way again.

* * *

For more than four decades, Fidel has lacked the influence of Che Guevara in his life. But never has he escaped the image, much less the legacy, of his friend. Alberto Korda's famous photo of Che Guevara, his eyes set to the distance and the locks of his hair spilling out from beneath his beret, has been reproduced perhaps more than any other image in the world; it is a portrait that bristles with all the restless energy, the constant reinvention of the guerrilla fighter himself. And Fidel has used that image for all that it is worth often in ways that Che would not have approved of. He has pontificated before it, harangued and cajoled beneath it. He has alluded to it, tended to it and held it up as an image of the sacrifice required of his people. Che lives on, says one biographer 'in part because he had Fidel Castro as a press agent'.

But in fact, Che lives on because of how he became Che in relation to Fidel Castro and because it is ultimately in their relations with others that individuals must be judged. It was Aristotle who said that friendship could be based upon one of three things: utility, pleasure or goodness. But it was only the latter, Aristotle said, that was lasting. Fidel and Che were not the greatest of friends in any conventional sense of the term, but their friendship was based upon a distinctively modern version of this latter notion of goodness: goodness understood as the common good, what is perhaps better known as solidarity.

Fidel and Che's friendship, for all its ups and downs, was defined at heart by this common bond of solidarity. Such a bond does not encompass everything in a friendship, nor is it always necessarily present. But it is a measure of its worth. And rarely have its productive possibilities been seen more clearly than in the way that Fidel and Che shaped one another's vision of what a revolutionary was to be. Whatever one thinks of them as individuals, it is hard to deny that this bond existed between them and that consciously at times, instinctively at others, their conduct was shaped through it. Che modelled his vision of the 'New Man' in part upon Fidel, while Fidel modelled his archetype of the true revolutionary 'personal sacrifice and hard work' upon Che. They learned from one another, and they countered one another's forms of excess. And the fact that both men's stars seemed to dim when they parted suggests one thing: they may be two of the most iconic individuals of the twentieth century, but it is this common bond that underpins their individual acclaim. It seems right that it is so, for they achieved more together than they ever did apart.

ACKNOWLEDGEMENTS

THIS BOOK COULD not have been written without the interest and generosity of those who shared their stories, hunches, contacts and personal collections with me. I owe a special debt in this regard to a number of people in Cuba, particularly those who agreed to be interviewed. As ever, Edgar Montalvo, my unstinting *compañero*, was an enormous help and support. For assistance in contacting those who knew Fidel and Che and in accessing areas where I would otherwise not have been allowed I am grateful to Alfredo Guevara and his tireless assistant Camilo Pérez Casal. I was also put in touch with various people by Jesús Parra. Francisco Vitorero Acosta helped open up the world of Fidel's and Che's *escolta* to me, and Juan Borroto clarified much about Che's time at the Ministry of Industries. Juan Valdés Gravalosa and Jorge 'Papito' Serguera were each also generous with their time and consideration for my research. At the Council of State Historical Archives in Cuba I am grateful to Cuba's chief archivist Pedro Alvarez Tabio and Mario Mencía in particular, and to Efrén Gónzales and Heberto Norman Acosta. Igor Caballero, press attaché at the Cuban embassy in London, was enormously supportive of the whole project and understanding of my wilful pushing at doors that were not always quite ready to open.

The help and advice of Julia Sweig in Washington was crucial in helping to open doors later on in Cuba. Wayne Smith and

Sergei Khrushchev were both also kind enough to share their memories and to point up further leads, while the staff at Archives II in College Park were gracious and accommodating of my requests for large amounts of material in a short space of time. Kate Doyle and Mary Curry at the National Security Archive both gave helpful advice. In Moscow Anastasia Raevskaya provided generous and invaluable assistance, smoothing my requests to various archives and obtaining vital materials on my behalf. She also served as my interpreter and guide and translated with painstaking care each of the documents obtained for me. Along with Sergei and Dima, she helped make my time in Moscow particularly enjoyable. I am grateful also to Konstantin Boulich for having put us in touch. I must acknowledge Valery Kucherov, Director of RGANI, and Natalya Vladimirovnam at MID, both of whom ultimately processed my research requests and went to considerable effort to obtain the materials I needed.

Other people in different countries have provided further invaluable help. In Berlin, the tireless efforts of Deniz Değer in both obtaining and translating the documents I asked for was enormously helpful. Richard Nkulikiyinka also helped with some timely translations from there, as did Raphael Socha with his contacts. In Miami, I am grateful to Maria Estorino who generously gave of her contacts as well as her own expertise at the Cuban Heritage Center. The Argentine journalist Horacio López das Eiras was kind enough to share names and numbers with me, as well as pointing me in the right direction in Cuba and helping me to track down images for use in the book. For photocopying and sending me vast quantities of material I am extremely grateful to the staff at the John F. Kennedy Memorial Library in Boston and at Princeton's Firestone Library.

In the UK, my base for this research, I was given helpful early advice by Tony Kapcia at the Cuba Research Forum in Nottingham, by Steve Wilkinson at the Cuban Studies Institute and by Richard

Gott. For her on-call help translating archival indexes from the Russian and ferreting out names and numbers I am grateful to Sarah McArthur. The staff at the British Library helped me day in, day out, consistently meeting my demands for further material at the witching hour of all new orders for that day.

I must make special mention of my colleagues at the Department of Geography, Queen Mary, University of London for their constant support, understanding and advice. I am honoured to work alongside them. I am especially grateful to departmental cartographer Ed Oliver's work in producing the maps that appear at the beginning of the book. I am also indebted to a good number of other academics: James Dunkerley at the Institute for the Study of the Americas, Daniela Spenser at UNAM in Mexico, and Alan Ingram at University College London in particular. Kendra Peterson at CNN, Hector Ferreria and Esther Vanegas also provided useful assistance. The poem 'I had a brother'/ 'Che' on page ix is reproduced courtesy of the Herederos de Julio Cortázar, 2008.

This book really began in the conversations I had some time back with Nick Davies, then at Hodder, and my agent Georgina Capel. Since those early discussions, Georgina and her colleagues at Capel & Land have provided invaluable support at various stages of the process, for which I am truly grateful. Nick too has maintained an interest even though he moved on to take up a new position. After Nick's departure, Jocasta Hamilton and Rupert Lancaster took over the reins at Hodder with seamless despatch. Jocasta's eagle-eye helped identify the right format for a book that could all too easily have become utterly unwieldy, while Rupert and Laura Macaulay guided things through the closing stages when parallel lives gave way to twins for Jocasta. Esther Jagger has done a wonderful job copy-editing the text, clarifying it enormously in the process, Josine Meijer produced the picture sections.

As always my family have been a constant support and I am especially grateful to Katerini for making our life of paper piles, book towers and late dinners so much fun that it was possible to forget the encroaching mayhem. She, Duncan

Nelson, Elizabeth Day, Colin Holmes, Richard Gott, James Dunkerley and Tony Kapcia all found time to comment on earlier drafts, and their thoughtful and insightful comments were adopted in nearly every case.

A NOTE ON SOURCES

PREVIOUS BIOGRAPHIES OF Fidel Castro and Che Guevara have tended to rely primarily on the American archives. Some also encompass the Soviet perspective and some go as far as to incorporate European archival material, but relatively few include Cuban archival *and* interview material. Because of the nature of Cuba's transition from American to Soviet patronage, and of the diplomatic criss-crossing and sometimes plain simple plotting, it has always therefore been hard, for perfectly good reasons, to get a complete, balanced set of sources for the period covered by this book. In contrast, there is a glut of secondary material on Fidel, Che and the Cuban revolution. Some of it is very good and some is very bad, but all of it warrants reading in light of as much primary material as possible. I therefore tried very hard when researching this book to obtain as much first-hand material as I could, going back to the sources in a number of countries to ensure that my account of these two remarkable lives would be fresh and rigorously sourced. In view of this, a few words on my use of such material, how it relates to existing works and how it has shaped the book, seem warranted.

To narrate their young lives, I relied heavily on the recollections and reflections provided by the protagonists' families themselves. Che's family have been rather more forthcoming than Fidel's, but all these accounts need to be balanced against those provided by the men themselves (they each submitted to numerous interviews) and the archival record. Though at times it is necessary to excise the appearance of the men they would become from such memoirs (some of which are listed under Secondary Characters and Memoirs in the Select Bibliography), and to take into account the viewpoint of the authors in question, they none the less provide a good overview of two very different characters in the making. A number of recent publications based primarily upon interview material – such as *Ernestito Guevara, antes de ser el Che* by Horacio López Das Eiras and Rafael de la Cova's exhaustively researched account of the Moncada attack in *The Moncada Attack: Birth of the Cuban Revolution* – bring further testimonial material within reach of the biographer. The task in deciphering these years would seem henceforth to be one of interpretation and contextualisation; there is little especially new material to unearth. Nevertheless, some interesting material was made available to me by researchers at Havana's Council of State Office of Historical Affairs (OAH).

On the period in Mexico, the most extensive work has been carried out by OAH researcher Heberto Norman Acosta, son-in-law of one of the *Granma* fighters, in the two-volume *La Palabra Empeñada*. Also crucial for understanding the Mexico period is Garcini et al's recently released volume of photos, documents and commentary, *Huellas del Exilio: Fidel en México, 1955–56*. These books contain a wealth of archival and testimonial material: Acosta himself in *La Palabra Empeñada* has interviewed a vast number of figures involved, particularly in the 1980s and has produced an almost day-by-day account. My interview with Nikolai Leonov in Moscow was also helpful in understanding this period. Following Fidel's and Che's progress into the Sierra, I relied heavily on the records of the OAH archive photographed by Carlos Franqui before he left Cuba and now deposited at Princeton's Firestone Library. Julia Sweig's impressive monograph, *Inside the Cuban Revolution*, correlates some of these sources with those in the OAH itself, as well as providing absolutely essential reading for the period. Again, my own interviews with protagonists in Cuba complemented this material.

To recount the first years of the revolution I conducted further interviews in Cuba, Washington and Moscow. These accounts really come to life, however, in relation to the archival records held, primarily within record group RG-59, at the Archives II reading room in College Park, Maryland, along with documents held in the Foreign Ministry Archives (MID) and at the Russian Governmental Archive of Contemporary History (RGANI), both in Moscow. The former Soviet archives really pick up where the American ones tail off, at the end of 1961. At MID the documents for early 1961 are missing, but holdings then exist for October–December 1961, all of 1962 (except materials relating directly to the Missile Crisis, which have been transferred elsewhere) through until the end of 1965. At RGANI, there is likewise greatest coverage for the period 1962–5, though occasionally documents from outside this period can be sourced.

In order to contextualise these competing vistas on events in Cuba I found it useful to compare reports from the Americans and Soviets with other embassy observers on the island who remained throughout. In particular, the reports of the British embassy and the German Democratic Republic's embassy in Cuba often provided the means of getting close to events. A good deal of useful material in the form of reports, newspaper back issues, collections of the Cuban leadership's writings and so forth can be found at the José Martí National Library (BNJM) in Havana. The best material on this period is that held at the OAH in Havana, of course.

The chapters that comprise the denouement of the story were sourced from the archives referred to above. Additionally, I relied heavily on Che Guevara's two campaign diaries (of which numerous editions exist), cross-referenced with the diaries and memoirs of some of his comrades, notably the Cuban Harry Villegas (Pombo) and the Bolivian Inti Peredo. For insights into Fidel's personal life during this period I turned to a series of 'close-up' interviews with him by foreign journalists, such as appear in Lee Lockwood's *Castro's Cuba, Cuba's Fidel*. The broader picture of Fidel and Che striving to work together, while being steadily driven apart, emerges with reference to the CIA's own database of recently declassified materials, also held at Archives II in Maryland, and the wonderful collection of declassified materials at the National Security Archive in Washington (though much is available online). Online references in Foreign Relations of the United States (FRUS) and the Cold War International History Project (CWIHP) also help to put together the full picture of the two men's actions during these later years, as do the archives of the GDR Foreign Ministry in Berlin (PAAA). These latter documents are more comprehensive for the period 1965–8 than are the documents currently available in Moscow.

NOTES

Abbreviations

ARCHIVES II	Unites States State Department Records, College Park, Maryland
BL	British Library Microfilm Collection, London
BNJM	Biblioteca Nacional José Martí / José Martí National Library, Havana
CFCPFL	Carlos Franqui Collection, Firestone Library, Princeton
CHC	Cuban Heritage Center, Miami
CWIHP	Cold War International History Project, www.CWIHP.org (by permission of the Woodrow Wilson International Center for Scholars)
ECG	Ernesto Che Guevara
FBIS	Foreign Broadcasting Information Service, Castro Speech Database
FCR	Fidel Castro Ruz
FRUS	Foreign Relations of the United States
MID	Soviet Ministry of Foreign Affairs Archives, Moscow
NSA	National Security Archive, Washington DC
OAH	Oficina de Asuntos Históricos del Consejo de Estado / Cuban Council of State Office of Historical Affairs, Havana
OSA	Open Society Archives
PAAA	Foreign Ministry Archives (of the former GDR), Berlin
RGANI	Russian Governmental Archive of Contemporary History, Moscow
TSCJFK	Tad Szulc Collection, John F. Kennedy Memorial Library, Boston

Introduction

p.3 'unmatched', Szulc, *Fidel Castro: A critical portrait*, p.69

p.3 'in that small space . . . ', Castañeda, *Compañero: the life and death of Che Guevara* p.275

Prologue

p.5 Hershey bars and hams, Casuso, *Cuba and Castro*, p.125. Except where specified below, other details of the actual departure and crossing in the prologue come from Mencía, *Tiempos Precursores*, pp.316–17; Quirk, *Fidel Castro*, pp.119–23; Acosta, *La Palabra Empeñada*, Vol. II, pp. 439–64; Abreu, *Collado: Timonel del Granma*, pp.135–68

p.6 Silent embraces, the atmosphere, Franqui, *Camilo Cienfuegos*, p.76

p.6 Spies and pre-departure tensions, Faustino Pérez's account in Franqui, *Diary of the Cuban Revolution*, pp.121–4

p.6 Tracked by foreign intelligence, Outgoing Telegram, Gardner, Am-Embassy [Mexico City] to SecState [Washington], 2 November 1956, (Confidential), ARCHIVES II, 350.61 Box 6. I use Spanish acronyms, such as 'SIM' for Military Intelligence Service, throughout.

p.7 'you'll not get more than a dozen . . .' and 'she'll take ninety', cited in Quirk, *Fidel Castro*, p.119

p.8 'worth dying on some foreign beach . . . ', ECG, letter to his parents, cited in Guevara Lynch, *Aquí Va un Soldado de América*

p.8 'Is something going to happen?' and all other quotes in this paragraph, Gadea, *Ernesto: A memoir of Che Guevara*, p.158

p.9 Bounding up the gangplank, Acosta, *La Palabra Empeñada*, Vol. II, p.461

p.10 'We will bury you', Fursenko and Naftali, *Khrushchev's Cold War*, p.232; Khrushchev and Bulganin in India, 'Calcutta Greets Russians Wildly', *New York Times*, 30 November 1955

p.10 'The peoples of the East . . .', cited in Gene Overstreet, 'Soviet and Communist Policy in India', *The Journal of Politics*, Vol.20, No.1, February 1958, p.195; 'We did not know much . . .', Sergei Khrushchev (ed.), *Memoirs of Nikita Khrushchev*

p.11 Leaving the town, Faustino Pérez in Franqui, *Diario de la Revolucion Cubana*, pp.168–9

p.12 Revolutionary chants, Cuba Ruerzas Armadas Revolutionarias (ed.), *De Tuxpán a la Plata*, p.78

p.12 'This is lost!' and account of the storm, Faustino Pérez, in Franqui, *Diary of the Cuban Revolution*, p.122

p.13   Gangsters, *El Mundo*, 22 November 1959; see also Quirk, *Fidel Castro*, p.117

p.13   'alert, competent and fully capable . . .', in 'Statement by Batista Concerning Revolutionary Plotting', AmEmbassy [Havana] to State Department [Washington], 20 November 1956, ARCHIVES II, 350.61 Box 6, p.1

p.13   'rifles, machine guns, grenades . . .', Quirk, *Fidel Castro*, p.121 and Frank País and Félix Pena accounts in Franqui, *Diary of the Cuban Revolution*, pp.118–20; also Outgoing Telegram, confidential, J.L. Topping to State Department, 17 December 1956, ARCHIVES II, 350.61 Box 6, p.1

p.14   'I wish I could fly', Faustino Pérez account in Franqui, *Diary of the Cuban Revolution*, p.122

p.15   Landing of *Granma*, Faustino Pérez account in Franqui, *Diary of the Cuban Revolution*, p.123

p.15   'Some comrades . . .' and 'As soon as we reached . . .', Faustino Perez, 'De Tuxpán a las Coloradas', in René Ray, *Libertad y Revolución: Moncada, Granma, Sierra Maestra*, no page

p.15   'and after a while only half of us . . .', ECG, 'Interview with Jorge Massetti', cited in Bonachea and Valdes, *Che: Selected Works of Ernesto Guevara*, pp.364–5

p.15   'We were an army of shadows . . .', ECG, *Episodes of the Cuban Revolutionary War, 1956–1958*, pp.88–9

1. Faithful and the Pig

pp.20–1 Fidel's parents, Birán and surroundings, Betto, *Fidel and Religion*, pp.95–109; Ramonet, *Biografía a dos Voces*, pp.43–84

p.21   'tropical Mussolini' and background, Gott, *Cuba: A New History*, pp.129–30

p.21   'little Lord Fauntleroy', Coltman, *The Real Fidel Castro*, p.4

p.21   'savouring the sweet air . . .', cited in Quirk, *Fidel Castro*, p.562

p.22   shooting chickens, Quirk, *Fidel Castro*, p.10

p.23   'a dramatic looking girl . . .' and 'well read but unworldly . . .', Anderson, *Che Guevara: A revolutionary life*, p.4

p.23   'She was the first woman . . .', cited in Taibo II, *Guevara, also known as Che*, p.3

p.23   The birth certificate was faked, recording June, to cover Celia's having been pregnant before their marriage

p.24   'She had a very particular character' and 'It wasn't so much . . .', Guevara Lynch, *Mi Hijo el Che*, p.107

p.24   'difficult but happy', Guevara Lynch, *Mi Hijo el Che*, p.119

p.24   Cats and sandbags, Taibo II, *Guevara, also known as Che*, p.6

p.24 'two or three days later . . .', Enrique Martín, cited in Das Eiras, *Ernestito Guevara, antes de ser el Che*, p.87

p.25 'little creature' and the family's arrival in Alta Gracia, Das Eiras, ibid., pp.27–9

p.25 'impoverished aristocrats', ibid., pp.41–2

p.25 'often speak openly . . .', Clara Peña, cited in ibid., p.44

p.25 *You Can't Take It with You*, directed by Frank Capra, won two Oscars in 1938, ibid., p.159

p.26 Crumby pages, Fernando Córdova, cited in ibid., p.71

p.26 'Do like Guevara . . .', cited in ibid., pp.117–18. By then Ernesto was studying at Dean Funes school. Both periods are described in the greatest detail by Das Eiras

p.27 'Catalogue of Books Read . . .', Taibo II, *Guevara, also known as Che*, p.8

p.27 Illegible words, various places, but see Guevara Lynch, *Mi Hijo el Che*, p.260

p.27 'Your letters, very Guevara . . .', ECG, letter to his father, cited in Guevara Lynch, *Aquí Va un Soldado de América*, p.36

p.27 'I believe I have sufficient strength . . .' and Ernesto's handwriting, Guevara Lynch, *Mi Hijo el Che*, p.223

p.28 Santiago scene, Patrick Symmes, *The Boys from Dolores*, p.39

p.29 'Send me a ten dollar bill . . .', 'I didn't know . . .', 'Yeah, well. . . . He won the election . . .', Lundy Aguilar, cited in Symmes, *The Boys from Dolores*, p.66

p.29 'To be a Dolores boy . . .', Symmes, *The Boys from Dolores*, pp.70–1

p.29 'The mere acquisition of knowledge . . .', Father Luís Martín, cited in Allan Farrel, *The Jesuit Code of Liberal Education: Development and Scope of the Ratio Studiorum*, The Bruce Publishing Company, Milwarkee, 1938, p.402

p.30 '[T]hey got in your head . . .', Juan Rovira, TSCJFK, p.5

p.30 'Two boys who antagonised each other . . .', Symmes, *The Boys from Dolores*, p.66

p.30 'the little rooster . . .', Mario Cubenas, cited in Symmes, *The Boys from Dolores*, p.337

p.30 'When it came to sports . . .', Juan Rovira, TSCJFK, p.2

p.31 Rumours of bastardism, Symmes, *The Boys from Dolores*, p.336; though see also Szulc, *Fidel: A critical portrait*, pp.102–3

p.31 Jumping off the roof, José Ignacio Rasco, TSCJFK, p.3 and Symmes, *The Boys from Dolores*, p.148

p.31 'He had a photographic memory . . .', José Ignacio Rasco, TSCJFK, p.3

p.31   Intelligence and cramming, Juan Rovira, TSCJFK, p.2

p.32   'So, teacher, how do you think . . .', Tomás Granado, cited in Das Eiras, *Ernestito Guevara, antes de ser el Che*, p.108

p.33   'The two of us were very interested . . .', José Ignacio Rasco, TSCJFK, p.1

p.33   'tremendously shy', '[I]t wasn't easy . . .', Juan Rovira, TSCJFK, p.6

p.33   'a sort of verbal warfare', Coltman, *The Real Fidel Castro*, p.9

2. Zarpazo!

p.35   'I was sitting inside having lunch . . .', this and all reported speech from this encounter, Alfredo Guevara: interview with the author, Havana, 11 September 2007

p.36   Fidel's claim of radicalisation at university, FCR, 'En esta Universidad me hice revolucionario', Discurso en el Aula Magna de la Universidad de La Habana, 4 September 1995, OAH

p.36   'Down with Grau!', cited in Quirk, *Fidel Castro*, p.19

p.37   Fidel himself describes the plan to take the bell in a speech in April 1987, 'Castro addresses Fifth UJC Conference', http://www1.lanic. utexas.edu/la/cb/cuba/castro/1987/19870406

p.38   'a transcendental achievement . . .', Max Lesnick, TSCJFK, p.1

p.38   'one of the most colourful . . .', Max Lesnick, TSCJFK, p.2

p.40   'Ernesto had great affection for her . . . ' Celia Guevara de la Serna, cited in Cupull and González (eds), *Cálida Presencia: La amistad del 'Che' y Tita Infante a través de sus cartas*, p.13

p.40   Wednesday meetings and 'La Victoria', Tita Infante, cited in Cupull and González (eds), *Cálida Presencia*, p.109

p.40   'neither for, nor against . . .', Tita Infante, cited in Cupull and González, *Cálida Presencia*, p.109

p.40   'inflexible sectarians', Tita Infante, cited in Taibo II, *Guevara, also known as Che*, p.14

p.41   Crates of oranges, De la Cova, *The Moncada Attack: Birth of the Cuban Revolution*, p.10

p.41   'I bathe myself . . .', cited in Quirk, *Fidel Castro*, p.19

p.41   Dirty money, Pérez-Stable, *The Cuban Revolution: Origins, Course and Legacy*, p.50

p.41   'pseudo-revolutionary gangsterism', Raul Roa García, cited in De la Cova, *The Moncada Attack: Birth of the Cuban Revolution*, p.11

p.41   'no real ideological attachment', Max Lesnick, TSCJFK, p.2

p.42   'a revolutionary in the traditional . . .', Max Lesnick, TSCJFK, p.10

p.44   Lack of interest in Barral's case, Anderson, *Che Guevara: A revolutionary life*, p.54

p.44 Ernesto's literary tastes, Anderson, *Che Guevara: A revolutionary life*, pp.48–9

p.44 'I saw him . . .', Maria del Carmen Ferreyra, cited in Castañeda, *Compañero: The life and death of Che Guevara*, p.38

p.44 'For those green eyes . . .', ECG, cited in Castañeda, *Compañero: The life and death of Che Guevara*, p.38

p.45 'boring' old Buenos Aires, 'from these lands of beautiful . . .', and 'café coloured sirens', ECG to Aunt Beatriz, various letters, cited in Das Eiras, *Ernestito Guevara, antes de ser el Che*, p.218

p.45 'the intrigues of Creole Stalinism', Martin, *The Early Fidel: Roots of Castro's communism*, p.41, 'the climate of violence . . .', declaration of the FEU leadership, cited in De la Cova, *The Moncada Attack: Birth of the Cuban Revolution*, p.19

p.46 'Around these same days arrived in Bogotá . . .', Chief of Dept of Security, Colombia, cited in De la Cova, *The Moncada Attack: Birth of the Cuban Revolution*, p.22

p.47 'there appeared people . . .', FCR, in 'Castro Reveals Role in 9 April 1948 Colombian Uprising', FBIS 1982–04–09; see also Arturo Alape, *El Bogotazo: Memorias del Olvido*

p.47 'restless, impassioned', Alfredo Guevara, cited in De la Cova, *The Moncada Attack: Birth of the Cuban Revolution*, p.23

p.47 'quixotic, romantic, a dreamer . . .', FCR, cited in De la Cova, *The Moncada Attack: Birth of the Cuban Revolution*, p.23

p.48 'What April 9 lacked . . .', FCR, cited in Szulc, *Fidel: A critical portrait*, p.176

p.48 The Gangs' Pact, Szulc, *Fidel: A critical portrait*, p.189

p.48 'a demolishing denunciation . . .', 'absolutely stunning', staying at his apartment, Max Lesnick, TSCJFK, p.16

p.49 'Many times I saw him looking concerned . . .', Tita Infante, in Cupull and González, *Cálida Presencia*, p.109

p.50 'Salen Baby', ECG to Tita Infante, no date, cited in Cupull and González, *Cálida Presencia*, pp.22–3

p.51 'This country is that in which individual rights . . .', ECG, letter to his mother, 6 July 1952, cited in ECG, *The Motorcycle Diaries*, p.157

p.52 Ernesto's time in Miami, Granado, *Travelling with Che Guevara: The making of a revolutionary*, p.201

p.52 'He would spend fourteen hours studying . . .', cited in Korol, *El Che y los Argentinos*, p.72

p.52 'Wandering around our "America . . ."' and 'The person who wrote these notes . . . ' ECG, *The Motorcycle Diaries*, p.32

p.53 Fidel and Mirta's wedding, details from De la Cova, *The Moncada Attack: Birth of the Cuban Revolution*, pp.26–7

p.55 'too volatile, too unreliable', *Cuarteles,* 14 August 1952, p.28, BNJM

p.56 'impassioned, emotional, and sincere temperament', Virgilio Ferrer Gutiérrez, 'Nuestra Política es así', *Cuarteles,* 14 August 1952, p.44, BNJM

p.56 Fidel's investigative journalism, Mencía, *Tiempos Precursores* pp.114–21; the articles themselves were published in *Alerta* and republished in *Granma* on 9, 12 and 14 September 1995.

p.56 'voracious appetite . . .', 'palaces and pools' and 'corruption and moral misery', FCR, 'Prío rebaja la funcion de nuestras fuerzas armadas', *Alerta*, 28 January 1952, OAH

p.56 'I said that I would avenge . . . ', FCR, *Alerta*, 4 March 1952, OAH

p.57 The meeting with Batista, various sources, but see Coltman, *The Real Fidel Castro*, pp.56–7

p.58 '[T]he 10 March determined everything that came after', Raúl Chibás, TSCJFK, p.7

3. Bullets and Backpacks

p.59 'stepped out', FCR, cited in Szulc, *Fidel: A critical portrait*, p.206

p.59 First collaborators, Mencía, *Tiempos Precursores*, p.122

p.59 'When this young man began to talk . . .', Melba Hernández, cited in Szulc, *Fidel: A critical potrait*, p.216

p.60 Frenetic activity, Mencía, *Tiempos Precursores*, p.2

p.60 'We are going to take up arms . . .', FCR, cited in Szulc, *Fidel: A critical portrait*, p.231

p.60 The carnival, Marta Rojas, interview with the author, Havana, 9 November 2007, and Mencía, *El Grito de Moncada*, p.513

pp.61–4 The attack on Moncada, Mencía, *El Grito de Moncada*, pp.527–84, De la Cova, *The Moncada Attack: Birth of the Cuban Revolution*, pp.71–120 and Mencía, *Tiempos Precursores*, pp.140–51. Though I have consulted many sources on these events, the three references cited here were the most useful for reconstructing the assault on the barracks, including direct quotations, unless otherwise specified.

p.63 'hail of bullets', Severino Rosell interview, *Bohemia*, 7 October 1977, OAH

p.63 'Forward, boys', Szulc, *Fidel: A critical portrait*, p.268

p.64 Snow, wine and chickens, Ferrer, *De Ernesto al Che. El segundo y último viaje de Guevara por Latinoamérica*, p.68

p.65 'Alberto is now called Calica . . .' and 'a couple of odd-looking snobs . . .', ECG, *Back on the Road: a journey to Central America*, p.3

p.65 'semi-scientist, semi-bohemian . . .', Alberto Granado, foreword to ECG, *Back on the Road*, p.xi; see also *Entrevista a don Ernesto Guevara por Mario Mencia*, 16 July 1976, pp.8–9, OAH

p.65 'Minucha, I am losing him . . .' and 'When the train pulled out . . .', Matilde Lezica, cited in Cupull and González, *Ernestito, vivo y presente*, p.172

p.66 '[N]ight falls . . .', ECG, *Back on the Road*, p.4

p.67 'The best people of La Paz invite us to lunch . . .', ECG, cited in Anderson, *Che Guevara: A revolutionary life*, p.103

p.67 'The Indian continues to be . . .', ECG, *Back on the Road*, p.6

p.67 'The Shanghai of the Americas', ECG, *Back on the Road*, p.4

p.67 a 'tall, beefy man . . .', Anderson, *Che Guevara: A revolutionary life*, p.104

p.67 Rojo's story, Ricardo Rojo, *Mi Amigo el Che*, p.15

p.68 'the soldiers went looking for vengeance', Lieutenant Teodoro Rico, cited in De la Cova, *The Moncada Attack: Birth of the Cuban Revolution*, p.154

p.69 'Why didn't you kill me?' and 'I am not that kind of man', Szulc, *Fidel: A critical portrait*, p.276

pp.69–70 Journey to the courtroom, 'This is the most difficult case . . .', 'It is also the most important . . .' and 'Look at him, so tough . . .', De la Cova, *The Moncada Attack: Birth of the Cuban Revolution*, pp. 204–5

p.70 'the only solution to the present national problem', FCR, cited in De la Cova, *The Moncada Attack: Birth of the Cuban Revolution*, p.206

p.71 'Dr Fidel Castro is not sick', Melba Hernández, cited in De la Cova, *The Moncada Attack: Birth of the Cuban Revolution*, p.211

p.71 'The performance of the court . . .', FCR, cited in De la Cova, *The Moncada Attack: Birth of the Cuban Revolution*, p.211

p.72 'ton of bricks', ECG to Celia de la Serna Guevara, 22 August 1953, cited in *Back on the Road*, p.11

p.72 'As ever, the class spirit of the gringos . . .', ECG, *Back on the Road* p.29

p.73 'caught between the dodges and smirks . . .', ECG, *Back on the Road*, p.30

pp.73–4 At the Soda Palace Hotel, Severino Rosell interview, *Bohemia*, 10 October 1967, p.8, OAH

p.74 'In Guatemala I will improve myself . . .', ECG to Aunt Beatriz, cited in *Back on the Road*, p.29

pp.74–7 The court scene, bayonets fixed, Mencía, *Tiempos Precursores*, p.157;

folding chairs and the atmosphere, Marta Rojas, interview with the author, Havana, 9 November 2007

p.75 Creaking robe, Szulc, *Fidel: A critical portrait*, p.294

p.75 'Castro spoke at length . . .', Judge Adolfo Nieto Piñreio-Osorio, cited in De la Cova, *The Moncada Attack: Birth of the Cuban Revolution*, p.230

p.75 'even the soldiers . . .', 'Thank you' and 'Hopefully the country . . .', Marta Rojas, interview with the author, Havana, 9 November 2007

pp.75–7 'I must admit that I am somewhat disappointed . . .', Fidel's actual speech is reconstructed, in consultation with other sources, from http://www.marxists.org/history/cuba/archive/castro/1953/10/16.htm

4. The Monkey and the Bear

p.79 The 'electric' atmosphere, Rojo, *Mi Amigo el Che*, p.47

p.79 'McCarthyism Internationalised', Mario Mencía, *Bohemia*, 10 October 1975, OAH

p.80 'I am still following the donkey's path' and 'I haven't met a single interesting person . . .', ECG, letter to Aunt Beatriz, no date, cited in *Back on the Road*, p.38

p.80 Ernesto introduced to Hilda, Gadea, *Ernesto: A memoir of Che Guevara*, p.2

p.80 'Guevara made a negative impression on me . . .', Gadea, *Ernesto: A memoir of Che Guevara*, p.2

p.80 'a young aprista who, with my characteristic suaveness . . .', ECG, letter to his mother, April 1954, cited in Guevara Lynch, *Aquí Va un Soldado de América*, p.40

p.80 First impressions, 'those dark eyes' and 'I . . . knew that I was going to help him', Gadea, *Ernesto: A memoir of Che Guevara*, p.3

p.81 Mounting debts and moving on, see various letters in ECG, *Back on the Road*, pp.40–2

p.81 Early days of 'neither trouble nor glory', ECG, *Back on the Road*, p.40; and ECG, letter to Tita Infante, March 1954, cited in Cupull and González, *Cálida Presencia*, pp.53–4

p.81 'The Cuban exiles from the Moncada . . .' and Ñico's faith, Gadea, *Ernesto*, p.7

pp.81–2 'So, you're the Argentines . . .' and the party, from the account of Myrna Torres in Gadea, *Ernesto: A memoir of Che Guevara*, p.197

p.82 The missing eye, De la Cova, *The Moncada Attack: Birth of the Cuban Revolution*, p.233

p.82 'there seems to be good will on the part of the authorities', FCR, letter to his brother Ramón, no date, cited in Szulc, *Fidel: A critical portrait*, p.306

p.83 'tropical Siberia' and prison conditions, Szulc, *Fidel: A critical portrait* p.304

p.83 Place of a 'thousand screams', Pablo de la Torriente Brau cited in Mencía, *The Fertile Prison: Fidel Castro in Batista's Jails*, p.29

p.83 'At 5.00 a.m. sharp . . .', FCR, letter to unknown, 22 December 1953, cited in Mencía, *The Fertile Prison*, p.37

p.83 Prison schedule, Mencía, *The Fertile Prison*, pp.31–2

p.83 'Special assemblies shall begin at 7.45 . . .', Mencía, *The Fertile Prison*, p.33

p.84 'More than friends, we are brothers', Armando Mestre, letter to his uncle, no date, cited in Mencía, *The Fertile Prison*, p.36

p.84 'Those who learned how to handle weapons . . .', FCR, letter to unknown, 22 December 1953, cited in Mencía, *The Fertile Prison*, p.52

p.84 Law suits, Szulc, *Fidel: A critical portrait*, p.306

p.84 'It is hard for me to begin . . .', FCR, letter to René Guitart, 16 December 1954, cited in Conte Agüero and Bardach (eds), *The Prison Letters of Fidel Castro*, p.53

p.84 'I write with the blood of my dead brothers . . .', FCR, letter to Luis Conte Agüero, 12 December 1953, cited in Conte Agüero and Bardach (eds), *The Prison Letters of Fidel Castro*, pp.1, 6 and 12

p.85 'Are you completely healthy . . .' and the rest of this exchange, Gadea, *Ernesto: A memoir of Che Guevara*, p.24

p.86 'I felt very small when I heard the Cubans . . .', ECG, *Back on the Road*, p.45

pp.86–7 'buffoonish, provocative poses' and the rendition of the Freedom March, which would later become known as the 26 July March, Mencía, *The Fertile Prison*, pp.63–9, De la Cova, *The Moncada Attack: Birth of the Cuban Revolution*, p.235, and Szulc, *Fidel: A critical portrait*, p.309. This event took place on the morning of 12 February 1954. Pistolita's real name was Corporal Ramos

p.87 'short, chubby, and big bellied', Israel Tápanes, cited in Mencía, *The Fertile Prison*, p.67

p.88 'So you're the author of that piece of shit . . .', De la Cova, *The Moncada Attack: Birth of the Cuban Revolution*, p.235. Cebolla's real name was Salustiano Rodríguez

p.88 'They opened the door to my cell . . .', Agustín Díaz Cartaya, cited in Mencía, *The Fertile Prison*, p.68

p.88 'I forget all that exists in the world . . .', FCR, letter to his sister, 13

March 1954, cited in Conte Agüero and Bardach (eds), *The Prison Letters of Fidel Castro*, p.59

p.88 'I still have no light . . .', FCR, letter to unknown, 1 March 1954, cited in Mencía, *The Fertile Prison*, p.70

p.89 Communication within the prison, Szulc, *Fidel: A critical portrait*, p.312

p.89 Naty Revuelta, Mencía, *El Grito del Moncada*, p.267 and Szulc, *Fidel: A critical portrait*, p.231

p.89 'the hardest and purest of all the minerals', FCR, letter to Naty Revuelta, no date, cited in Quirk, *Fidel Castro*, p.62

p.89 'I'm going to chose carefully and calmly . . .', FCR, letter to Naty Revuelta, no date, cited in Quirk, *Fidel Castro*, p.62

p.90 'After knocking heads a good while with Kant . . .', FCR, letter to Naty Revuelta, 4 April 1954, cited in Mencía, *The Fertile Prison*, p.42

p.90 'I fixed up my cell Friday . . .', FCR, letter to Naty Revuelta, no date but likely 4 April 1954, cited in Mencía, *The Fertile Prison*, p.72

p.91 'How I would love to revolutionise this country . . .', FCR, letter to Naty Revuelta, no date but likely 4 April 1954, cited in Mencía, *The Fertile Prison*, p.134

p.91 'Maintain a soft touch and smile with everyone . . .', FCR, letter to Melba Hernández, 17 April 1954, cited in Conte Agüero and Bardach (eds), *The Prison Letters of Fidel Castro*, pp.15–16 and Acosta, *La Palabra Empeñada*, Vol. I, pp.32–4

p.91 'Already March of 1954 . . .', ECG, letter to Tita Infante, March 1954, cited in Cupull and González, *Cálida Presencia*, p.50

p.92 On reading and the 'agony of life', Gadea, *Ernesto: A memoir of Che Guevara*, p.36

p.92 Proposals of marriage, Gadea, *Ernesto: A memoir of Che Guevara*, p.41

p.93 'If she triumphs in her titanic struggle . . .', René Bedia, cited in Mencía, *The Fertile Prison*, pp.101–2

p.93 'initiate a criminal suit . . .', 'Mirta is too level-headed . . .' and 'It is the reputation of my wife . . . that is at stake', FCR, letter to Luis Conte Agüero, 17 July 1954, cited in Conte Agüero and Bardach (eds) *The Prison Letters of Fidel Castro*, p.xi

p.94 'Don't worry about me . . .', FCR, letter to his sister Lidia, 22 July 1954, cited in Conte Agüero and Bardach (eds), *The Prison Letters of Fidel Castro*, p.34

p.94 'Luis: Enclosed is the text . . .', FCR, letter to Luis Conte Agüero, no date, cited in ibid., pp.39–40

p.95 Which circle of hell to choose, Szulc, *Fidel: A critical portrait*, p.296

p.95 'Don't be impatient . . .', FCR, cited in ibid., p.317

p.95 Distributing 'History Will Absolve Me', Quirk, *Fidel Castro*, pp.71–3 and De la Cova, *The Moncada Attack: Birth of the Cuban Revolution*, p.236

p.96 The invasion and Castillo Armas in Honduras, Rodríguez, *Viajes y Aventuras del Joven Ernesto*, pp.301–4

p.97 'The planes came to bomb the city . . .', ECG, letter to his mother, 4 July 1954, cited in Herberto Norman Acosta, *El Libro del Che*, p.31, unpublished manuscript.

p.97 'Sons of bitches!', Rodríguez, *Viajes y Aventuras del Joven Ernesto*, p.303; see also Gadea, *Ernesto: A memoir of Che Guevara* p.48. Ernesto's opinion at this time was well summed up in a letter to his father: 'It seems to me that third positions don't achieve anything and the greatest knowledge of America increasingly convinces me of the fallacy of the Yankees', ECG, letter to his father, 6 May 1954, cited in Rodríguez, *Viajes y Aventuras del Joven Ernesto*, pp.295–6

p.97 'Ernesto was really pissed off . . .', Luis Felipe Béquer, cited in ibid., p.303

p.98 Citations from 'I Saw the Fall of Arbenz', Gadea, *Ernesto: A memoir of Che Guevara*, pp.53–6

p.98 'The embassies are full to the brim . . .' and 'The struggle begins now', ECG, letter to his mother, 4 July 1954, cited in Guevara Lynch, *Aquí Va un Soldado de América*, p.58

p.99 'I'm a little embarrassed to say but . . .', ECG, letter to his mother, cited in ibid., pp.58–9

p.99 'Here it has been very entertaining . . .', ECG, letter to Aunt Beatriz, cited in ibid., p.59

p.100 'I'm going to realise my artistic aspirations after all . . .', cited in Gadea, *Ernesto: A memoir of Che Guevara*, p.67

p.100 'The Guatemalan Dilemma' and 'The Working Class of the United States: Friend or Foe?' have both been recently published in María del Carmen Ariet (ed.), *America Latina: Despertar de un Continente*

p.101 'I have heard enough of Fidel . . .', Raúl Castro, cited in Szulc, *Fidel: A critical portrait*, p.35

p.101 'I . . . am prepared to re-enact the famous . . .', FCR, letter to his sister, 13 March 1955, cited in Conte Agüero and Bardach (eds), *The Prison Letters of Fidel Castro*, pp.59–61

p.101 'For there to be amnesty a priori . . .', FCR, letter to Luis Conte Agüero, no date, cited in ibid., pp.68–70

p.102 'I have a bohemian temperament . . .', 'Why should I wear linen *guayaberas* . . .' and 'You do not seem to be able to be satisfied . . .', FCR, letter to his sister Lidia, 2 May 1955, cited in ibid., pp.75–7

p.103 'I am not leaving Cuba . . .' and 'I have no ambitions . . .', FCR, cited in Garcini, Jiménez and Velis, *Huellas del Exilio: Fidel en México*, p.21

5. A Cold Mexican Night

p.108 Arrival in the fog and rain, Rodríguez, *Viajes y Aventuras del Joven Ernesto*, p.315

p.109 'The atmosphere one inhales here . . .', ECG, cited in Taibo II, *Guevara, also known as Che*, p.43

p.109 'The air of freedom is, in reality, a clandestine air . . .', ECG, cited in Guevara Lynch, *Aquí Va un Soldado de América*, p.149

p.109 'My aspirations haven't changed . . .', ECG, letter to Tita Infante, 29 September 1954, cited in Cupull and González (eds), *Cálida Presencia*, pp.58–9

p.109 'the city, or better said, the country of the *mordidas* . . .', ECG, letter to Aunt Beatriz, cited in Anderson, *Che Guevara: A revolutionary life*, p.161

p.110 'a typical clericaloid bourgeois education . . .', ECG, cited in ibid., p.162

p.110 Hilda's return, *Romeo and Juliet*, 'You and your dates . . .', Gadea, *Ernesto: A memoir of Che Guevara*, pp.84–7

p.111 'he wasn't much of a talker', Sánchez Pérez, cited in Acosta, *El Libro del Che*, p.52

p.111 '[H]e was very young, very thin . . .', interview with María Antonia González cited in ibid., p.54

p.112 Photos, poverty and reunions, Severino Rosell, testimony in *Bohemia*, 7 October 1977, pp.87–8

p.112 'Hilda came . . .', cited in Gadea, *Ernesto: A memoir of Che Guevara*, p.93

p.112 'I said no, that we should stay as little lovers . . .', ECG, cited in Anderson, *Che Guevara: A revolutionary life*, p.168

p.112 Raúl arrives, bullfighting, Taibo II, *Guevara, also known as Che*, p.55; cf. Efigenio Ameijeras in Franqui, *Libro de los Doce*, p.38

p.113 Leonov and the books, Nikolai Leonov, interview with the author, Moscow, 4 December 2007

p.113 'The sea beckons . . .', ECG, cited in Taibo II, *Guevara, also known as Che*, p.51

p.114 'I would like to be in that continent before . . .', ECG, letter to Tita Infante, 18 June 1955, cited in Cupull and González (eds), *Cálida Presencia*, pp.69–70

p.114 'I no longer believe in general elections . . .', FCR, *Bohemia*, 7 July 1955, threat of assassination, Juan Almeida, in Carlos Franqui (ed.), *Relatos de la Revolución Cubana*, p.19. Fidel's articles at this time included, 'Lo que iba a decir y me prohibieron', La Calle, 6 June 1955, p.1, 'Lo que iba a decir y me prohibieron por segunda vez', La Calle, 7 June, p.1, 'Mientes Chaviano', FCR, *Bohemia*, 29 May 1955. On 19 May the director of the radio channel Onda Hispano-Cubana was detained for simply transmitting a programme featuring Fidel and on 9 June, when a bomb went off in the Tasca de la Habana cinema, M26 members were detained. La Calle was closed down on 16 June

pp.114–5 'My body aches all over' and 'I feel more isolated than when they had me in solitary confinement', FCR in Claudia Furiati, *Fidel Castro: La historia me absolverá*, p.222

p.115 'I am leaving Cuba because all the doors of peaceful struggle have been closed to me . . .', FCR, cited in Quirk, *Fidel Castro*, p.86

pp.115–6 'Right now I am getting to grips with the revolutionary process . . .', FCR, letter to Médico, Mexico City, 14 July 1955; cited in Claudia Furiati, *Fidel Castro*, p.221

p.116 'Dear Doctora, I am going mad with impatience . . .', FCR, letter to Doctora, Mexico City, 24 July 1955; cited in Furiati, *Fidel Castro*, p.222

p.116 Seafood spaghetti and Ernesto watching Fidel, Furiati, *Fidel Castro*, p.224

pp.117–8 The meeting, and 'Cold Mexican nights', ECG, interview with Jorge Masetti, *Granma*, 16 October 1967. Biographers attribute surprisingly different dates for this event, some official Cuban sources positing September (though whether this refers to the friendship beginning then, or the meeting itself, is unclear). In 1971, in a speech in Chile, Castro himself suggested it was shortly after his arrival and Gadea also suggests it was early July. Jorge Castañeda, in his biography of Che suggests that numerous other biographers certainly have them together by the time of the 26 July celebrations. Most recently Julia Costenla, in *Che Guevara: La vida en juego*, p.73, puts it as early as 7 July, but this was when Fidel was just arriving in Veracruz. Given the circumstantial events of their meeting it seems most likely that they met after Fidel had been in Mexico for just three weeks, around 27–28 July. In affirmation that it was an association of convenience, of mutual interest in the idea of an adventure first, see Jorge 'Papito' Serguera, interview with the author, Havana, 10 November 2007

p.118 'it was Che Guevara's combative temperament . . .', FCR, cited in Lockwood, *Castro's Cuba; Cuba's Fidel. An American Journalist's Inside Look at Today's Cuba*, pp.162–3 p.119 'Ñico was right in Guatemala . . .' and all quotes in this paragraph, Gadea, *Ernesto: A memoir of Che Guevara*, p.102

p.119 'Dear sisters [*Queridas Hermanas*]', FCR letter to Melba Hernández and Haydée Santamaría, Mexico City, 2 August 1955, cited in Mencía, *Tiempos Precursores*, p.263

p.120 'Manifiesto No. 1 del Movimiento 26 de Julio al Pueblo de Cuba, 8 de agosto', 1955, and 'To those who accuse the revolution of upsetting the economy . . .', *Fondo: Fidel Castro Ruz*, No. 186, OAH, cited in ibid., pp.265–6

p.121 'every fortnight at the least', FCR, letter to Melba Hernández, Mexico City, Fondo: Fidel Castro Ruz, OAH, cited in ibid., p.269

p.121 'we shall sweep you and your clique of infamous murderers . . .', photostat of the 'Mensaje al Congreso de Militantes Ortodoxos' in Garcini, Jiménez and Velis, *Huellas del Exilio*, Appendix IV, no page

p.121 'Revolution! Revolution! Revolution!', Szulc, *Fidel: A critical portrait*, p.329

p.122 'This is for the baby', ECG, cited in Gadea, *Ernesto: A memoir of Che Guevara*, p.106

p.122 'I am going to have a child and I will marry Hilda . . .', ECG, letter to Tita Infante, cited in Anderson, *Che Guevara: A revolutionary life*, p.180; see also ECG, letter to his mother, cited in ECG, *Back on the Road*, p.94

p.122 A small, quiet wedding. This account comes from Acosta, *La Palabra Empeñada*, p.223; similar accounts, including 'short, flap-eared' treasurer, can be found in Anderson, *Che Guevara: A revolutionary life*, p.180, in Szulc, *Fidel: A critical portrait*, p.337 and in Taibo II, *Guevara, also known as Che*, p.56

p.122 'All [our] plans and prospects had changed, of course . . .', Gadea, *Ernesto: A memoir of Che Guevara*, p.110

p.123 'Hey Che, you're very quiet . . .' and rest of this exchange, Anderson, *Che Guevara: A revolutionary life*, p.180

p.123 'I'm your boy . . .', ECG, cited in Gadea, *Ernesto: A memoir of Che Guevara*, p.113

p.123 'not an automobile . . .', FCR, ibid., p.112

p.123 'We're mourning the developments . . .', ibid., p115

p.124 'The present American generation is obliged to take the offensive . . .', FCR, cited in Mencía, *Tiempos Precursores*, pp.277–8

p.125 ECG's encounter with Melba, Melba Hernández, cited in Acosta, *La Palabra Empeñada*, Vol. I, p.295

p.126 'We are digging trenches of ideas, but also trenches of rock . . .', FCR, speech at Palm Garden Hotel, 30 October 1955, cited in Furiati, *Fidel Castro*, p.233

p.126 'a radical and profound change in national life', FCR, cited in Szulc, *Fidel: A critical portrait*, p.341

p.127 'God and Caesar in one man', Szulc, *Fidel: A critical portrait*, p.244

p.127 'Don't touch that, Fidelito ...', FCR in ibid., p.343

p.128 'In the revolution, Martí said ...', FCR, Manifesto No. 2, *Fondo: Fidel Castro Ruz*, OAH, cited in Furiati, *Fidel Castro*, pp.234–5

p.128 Naty's trip to Miami, Acosta, *La Palabra Empeñada*, Vol.I, p.335

p.129 'I'm sorry, it's this disease that gets me out of sorts', ECG, cited in Taibo II, *Guevara, also known as Che*, p.60; on the trip, see also Gadea, *Ernesto: A memoir of Che Guevara*, pp.116–17

p.130 'most of what I've done is second rate and unoriginal', ECG, cited in Acosta, *Libro del Che*, pp.55–6

p.130 The poem appears in various places; this particular translation appears the closest and is from Anderson, *Che Guevara: A revolutionary life*, p.183

p.131 'He spoke with such certainty and naturalness ...', 'Yes, but first of all ...,' and 'It is true', in Gadea, *Ernesto: A memoir of Che Guevara*, pp.121–2

6. Fellow Travellers

p.132 'doctor Fidel Castro of hatching a subversive plan from abroad', in Furiati, *Fidel Castro* p.233

p.132 'each of us lives on less money ...', FCR, cited in Furiati, *Fidel Castro*

p.133 'humble, ordinary people ...', Casuso, *Cuba and Castro*, p.94

p.133 Che's preparations with anything that 'might be useful', Gadea, *Ernesto: A memoir of Che Guevara*, p.123

p.133 'neither a man nor a dollar', Bayo's memoirs cited in Szulc, *Fidel: A critical portrait*, p.325

p.133 'the gun and the lyre of the troubadour', introduction to Alberto Bayo, *Fidel te Espera en la Sierra*, Havana, 1959, p.4

p.134 'Come now, I thought ...', Bayo, cited in Szulc, *Fidel: A critical portrait*, p.326

p.135 'Fidel, we are not going to talk about politics ...', Melba Hernández, TSCJFK, p.172

p.135 Hildita's (Little Mao's) birth, Acosta, *La Palabra Empeñada*, Vol. I, p.432

p.135 'My communist soul expands plethorically ...', ECG, letter to his mother, 13 April 1956, cited in Guevara Lynch, *Aquí Va un Soldado de América*, p.130

p.135 'This girl is going to be educated in Cuba', FCR, cited in Szulc, *Fidel: A critical portrait*, p.353

p.135 'This is what was needed in the house' and 'For a moment it seemed to me . . .', ECG, letter to Tita Infante, 1 March 1956, cited in Guevara Lynch, *Aquí Va un Soldado de América*, p.129

p.136 Che's reasoning in taking part. A similar point is made by one of Che's biographers, Castañeda, in *Compañero*, pp.97–8: 'Everything suggests Guevara was fighting for an ideal of his own, and to be with Fidel, rather than for the Movement's actual programme or even the eventual transformation of Cuban society.'

p.136 'cactus, woods, and poisonous snakes', Casuso, *Cuba and Castro*, p.108

p.136 'an excellent shooter', Bayo's 'Evaluation in Firing Practice' on Che, photocopy of original document, Garcini, Jiménez and Velis, *Huellas del Exilio*, p.161

p.137 'We were terribly tired . . .' and 'Having had only a half orange each . . .', Melba Hernández, TSCJFK, p.223

p.137 Discipline and reviewing reports, Bayo, *Mi Aporte a la Revolución Cubana*, p.76

p.138 Che as a future leader. This claim is made in Acosta, *La Palabra Empeñada*, Vol. II, p.14, with reference to documents obtained by the Mexican authorities after the group's arrest and held today in the OAH archive, Havana

p.138 Days of 'talc' and 'toothpaste', Universo Sánchez, TSCJFK, p.24

p.138 Life as a 'concentration camp', from the diary of Tomás Electo Pedroso, one of the combatants, OAH: Fondo Expediente de la Procuradía General, cited in Acosta, *La Palabra Empeñada*, Vol. II, p.68

p.138 Fidel's aggressive support of Che, Acosta, *La Palabra Empeñada*, Vol. II, p.68

p.138 'confidence like that of an old friendship . . .', Faustino Pérez, cited in Acosta, *La Palabra Empeñada*, Vol. I, p.437

p.139 Accelerating plans, Pedro Miret, TSCJFK, pp.40–5

p.139 Observations of visitors to Fidel's lodgings, 'Report of Cuban Naval Attaché in Mexico, Nicolás Cartaya Gómez', cited in Acosta, *La Palabra Empeñada*, Vol. II, pp.14–15

p.139 Details of Fidel's arrest, Universo Sánchez, TSCJFK, p.31, FCR, in Borge, *Un Grano de Maíz*, and Furiati, *Fidel Castro*, p.245

p.140 The raid on María Antonia's, Acosta, *La Palabra Empeñada*, Vol. II, p.78

p.140 Casuso and Lilia arrive at Miguel Schultz detention centre, Casuso, *Cuba and Castro*, pp.91–2

p.140 'There were over fifty reporters . . .', Universo Sánchez, TSCJFK, p.41

p.141 'Lilia, who I had only been able to arouse . . .', Casuso, *Cuba and Castro*, pp.91–2

p.141 'by his look and bearing', and all other quotations in this paragraph, ibid., p.93

p.141 'if you should ever need it', ibid., p.93

p.141 'The simple elimination of a man . . .', FCR, Mexico, UPI, 3 July 1955

p.142 Two weeks in jail together, Acosta, *La Palabra Empeñada*, Vol. II, p191 and Castañeda, *Compañero*, p.93

p.142 'Up to now . . .' and 'Since you're so savage as to jail a woman . . .', Gadea, *Ernesto: A memoir of Che Guevara*, p.144

p.143 Che's responses to questioning, Acosta summarises Che's testimony in *La Palabra Empeñada*, Vol. II, p.105, based on the OAH: Fondo Expediente de la Procuradia files

p.143 'In these days of prison and in the previous ones . . .', ECG, letter to his mother, cited in Guevara Lynch, *Aquí Va un Soldado de América*, p.141

p.143 'days of sun . . .', Acosta, *La Palabra Empeñada*, Vol. II, p.248, cited from OAH, Fondo: Ernesto Guevara de la Serna, no.79

p.143 'without a shirt on . . . switching between Stalin and Baudelaire . . .', Carlos Franquí, in Das Eiras, *Ernestito Guevara, antes de ser el Che*, pp.315–16

p.144 Nikolai Leonov, interview with the author, Moscow, 4 December 2007

p.144 Fidel's decision to bring Che along, Borge, *Grano de Maíz*, p.257

p.145 'Having expressed his decision . . .', official note of the Secretaría de Gobernación de Mejico, cited in Acosta, *La Palabra Empeñada*, Vol. II, p.197

p.145 Fidel's visit to Casuso and 'but you must get rid of that friend', Casuso, *Cuba and Castro*, pp.101–5

p.146 'I would hardly consider my death more than a frustration . . .', and Hikmet's poem, ECG, letter to his parents, cited in Deutschmann (ed.), *Che en la Memoria de Fidel Castro*, p.20

p.147 Secret meetings with the communists, memorandum of conversation, USSR ambassador to Mexico A. G. Kulazhenkov with Cuban party leadership member Sánchez Cabrera and General Secretary of Mexican Communist Party Dionisio Encina, (strictly confidential), RGANI, Fond 5, Opis 28, Delo 440, pp.72–9

p.147 'no cheques' and 'the loan needs to be in proper cash', FCR, cited in Acosta, *La Palabra Empeñada*, Vol. II, p.181

p.148 'a bitter experience', FCR, speech in the Archivo Nacional del Partido, Carlos Marx Theatre, Havana, 8 February 1979, cited in Acosta, *La*

Palabra Empeñada, Vol. II, p.280; see also 'The Vengeful Visionary', *Time* magazine, 26 January 1959

p.148 Fidel–Prío conversation, Faustino Pérez, cited in Acosta, *La Palabra Empeñada*, Vol. II, p.281

p.148 'as part of her trousseau . . .', Casuso, *Cuba and Castro*, p.112

p.149 'Papa Castro is dead!', Furiati, *Fidel Castro*, p.255

p.149 'magnet for Cuba's top brass', Moruzzi, *Havana before Castro* p.98

p.150 'It is important to publish this . . .', FCR to Miguel Ángel Quevedo, OAH: Fondo, Fidel Castro Ruz, No.299, cited in Acosta, *La Palabra Empeñada*, Vol. II, p.365

p.150 'I just found out now . . .', ibid., p.266

p.151 'Yes, there is', Bauer Paíz testimony, *Bohemia*, No. 41, p.43

p.151 'To avoid pre-mortem patheticisms . . .', ECG, letter to his mother, cited in Anderson, *Che Guevara: A revolutionary life*, p.207

p.152 Gutiérrez Barrios delays his response, Fernando Gutiérrez Barrios, cited in Garcini, Jiménez and Velis, *Huellas del Exilio*, p.266

7. Mud and Ashes

p.153 The chapter title is derived from that of José Guerra Alemán's book *Barro y Cenizas: Dialogos con Fidel Castro y el Che Guevara*

p.153 Identifying the dead, outgoing telegram, J.L. Topping, Havana, to State Dept, 11 December 1956, 12 Noon, ARCHIVES II, 350.61 box VI

p.153 'whereabouts [of] Castro and other members landing group . . .', AmEmb, Havana, outgoing telegram, Gardner to State Dept, 17 December 1956, 4.30 p.m., ARCHIVES II, 350.61 box VI

p.153 Rumours and disbelief, confidential report from Oscar H. Guerra, American consul in Santiago to James Brown, consul general in Havana, ARCHIVES II, 350.61 box VI

p.153 The incident at Alegría del Pío, ECG, *Reminiscences of the Cuban Revolutionary War*, p.13

p.153 'almost impossible to land forces in sufficient numbers . . .', confidential report from Oscar H. Guerra, American consul in Santiago to James Brown, consul general in Havana, ARCHIVES II, 350.61 box VI

p.155 'terrorists', classified report, 'Revolutionary Outbreak in Santiago de Cuba; Related Events', J.L. Topping, Havana, to State Dept, 3 December 1956, ARCHIVES II, 350.61 box VI

p.156 Camilo makes an entrance, Franqui, *Camilo*, p.75

p.156 Travelling in groups and 'You pay for your life with such stupidity', testimony of Universo Sánchez, Franqui (ed.), *Relatos de la Revolución Cubana*, pp.38–44 p.156 Raúl Castro diary and the *asado* 'experiment', 28 January 1956, in *Granma*, Suplemento Especial, 17 January 1997, BNJM

p.156 'hunted look' and 'dirt, the lack of water . . .', ECG, *Reminiscences of the Cuban Revolutionary War*, p.32

p.157 'slip through [the army's] hands like soap', ECG, letter to Hilda, 28 January 1957, cited in Anderson, *Che Guevara: A revolutionary life*, p.229

p.158 'the possibility of [not] even the slightest skirmish', statement by Batista concerning revolutionary plottings, reaction by those accused and comments, AmEmb Havana to State Dept, classified, ARCHIVES II, 350.61 box VI

p.158 'tall man, thin, half bald, a simple dresser . . .', DePalma, *The Man Who Invented Fidel*, p.107

p.158 'making monkeys of the forces sent against them', situation in Cuba, AmEmb Havana to State Dept, 28 February 1957, ARCHIVES II, Havana Embassy General Records, 1956–58, box V

p.159 Llano leadership, Sweig, *Inside the Cuban Revolution*, pp.15–16

p.160 'general revolutionary strike as a capstone to the struggle', Frank País to Alberto Bayo, 15 May 1957, cited in Sweig, *Inside the Cuban Revolution*, p.13

p.160 'The situation was uncomfortable for the people and for [Eutimio] . . .', 'He lay there gasping a little while . . .', and 'We slept badly . . .'. These quotes are originally from Che's unedited diaries, made available to Jon Lee Anderson and cited extensively in his *Che Guevara: A Revolutionary Life*, here p.237. I refer to this source because the account differs from the sanitised version published as Che's 'authorised edition' by the Che Guevara Studies Centre in association with Ocean Press

p.161 'the timid stage of the revolution', ECG, in *El Cubano Libre*, No. 3, January 1958

pp.161–2 Comrade [Rigoberto] Silleros and Che's leading the men on his own for the first time, ECG, *Reminiscences of the Cuban Revolutionary War*, pp.88–96. See also the memo by Juan Almeida, 'Al Compañero Responsible' Sierra Maestra, Santiago de Cuba, 28 May 1957, CFCPFL, which confirms Che's account. Fourteen were injured in the El Uvero attack and eight died

p.162 'Listen, now you've arrived and from today . . .', Julio Martínez Paez in *Granma*, 25 November 1967, BNJM

p.163 País's centrality to the Movement. The very best account of this is in Sweig, *Inside the Cuban Revolution*, p.33

pp.163–4 'the abandonment of the [Ortodoxo] party . . .', US Dept of State

Joint Weeka Report no. 29, 17 July 1957, RG 59 737.00 (w)/7–1757, DSR, NA., cited in ibid., p.37

p.164 Che's 'promotion'. This account is based on my reading of the documents available in the Carlos Franqui Collection at Princeton's Firestone Library. The crucial letter is FCR to Frank País, 31 May 1957, CFCPFL

p.165 'I cannot convey to you the bitterness, the indignation . . .', Alejandro [Fidel], letter to Aly [Celia Sánchez], 31 July 1957, CFCPFL

p.165 'I believe you [should] take a strong stand . . .', ECG, letter to FCR, August 1957, CFCPFL

p.166 'All guns, all bullets, all resources to the Sierra!', and 'I would prefer a spy . . .', Alejandro, letter to Aly, 11 August 1957, CFCPFL

p.167 'thousands of leagues away from accepting . . .', Armando Hart to Carlos Franqui, reporting on Latour, cited in Sweig, *Inside the Cuban Revolution*, p.76

p.168 'a combat of positions, which must resist enemy attacks . . .', ECG, handwritten note to FCR, CFCPFL

pp.168–9 'News arrives with a cinematographic sequence . . .', ECG, letter to FCR, December 1957, cited in Anderson, *Che Guevara: A revolutionary life*, p.290

p.169 'I am very sorry not to have taken your advice . . .', ECG, letter to FCR, 9 December 1957, CFCPFL

pp.169–70 Che's analysis of events, Ramiro Valdés to FCR, 12 December 1957, 5.00 p.m., CFCPFL

p.170 'Fidel, if we see each other, or if I have the opportunity . . .', ECG, letter to FCR, 9 December 1957, CFCPFL

p.171 'I believe that your attitude of silence is not the most advisable right now' and other quotes in this paragraph, ECG, letter to FCR, 15 December 1957, CFCPFL

p.171 'for the record' and the Latour–Guevara exchange, René Ramos Latour, letter to FCR, 18 December 1957, CFCPFL

p.172 'Perhaps more in irony than in a coincidence of destiny . . .', FCR, letter in name of the 26 July Movement to the political leaders of the opposition based in Miami, 14 December 1957, CFCPFL

p.172 'One thing is clear . . .' and 'I await your news of new victories . . .', ECG, letter to FCR, 15 December 1957, CFCPFL

p.173 'an almost childlike face', Carlos María Gutiérrez, 'Conversación en la Sierra Maestra', *Brecha*, 9 October 1987

p.173 'It is the same everywhere . . .', ECG, 'No Bullet in the Chamber', *El Cubano Libre*, 3 January 1958

p.173 Fidel's political-historical strategy, Nicola Miller, 'The Absolution of

History', *Journal of Contemporary History*, Vol. 38, No. 1, pp.147–62, 2003

p.174 'I'll kill him . . .', cited in Meneses, *Fidel Castro*, p.60

p.174 'Che, if everything depends . . .', FCR, letter to ECG, 16 February 1958, CFCPFL

p.174 'Che, my soul brother . . .', Camilo to ECG, April 1958, CFCPFL; see also Anderson, *Che Guevara: A revolutionary life*, p.317

p.175 Meyer and Meneses visit, Quirk, *Fidel Castro*, p.161; cf. Meneses, *Fidel Castro*, various pp.

p.175 'Me and my colleagues were all Fidelistas', Robert Reynolds, lead desk officer for Cuba section, CIA HQ, cited in Sweig, *Inside the Cuban Revolution*, p.29

p.175 Bigart's report, 'Information Concerning Fidel Castro's 26th of July Movement', ARCHIVES II Cuba, Havana Embassy General Records, 1956–58, declassified, box V

p.176 'Can you imagine that . . .', FCR, cited in Meneses, *Fidel Castro*, p.66

p.176 'I tell Fidel that this meeting . . .', Celia Sanchez, cited in Sweig, *Inside the Cuban Revolution*, p.109

p.177 'In no way can one underestimate . . .', ECG, cited in Sweig, *Inside the Cuban Revolution*, p.120

p.177 'I don't think Fidel's last manifesto . . .', ECG, cited in Sweig, *Inside the Cuban Revolution*, p.120

p.177 'an atomic bomb', Sweig, *Inside the Cuban Revolution* pp.126–8

8. *Total War*

p.178 'tragic' and 'dark and bloody history', *New York Times* 'Cuba's Travail', (editorial), 11 April 1958, p.24

p.178 '[B]ands of armed youths entered the CMQ and Progresso radio stations . . .', *New York Times*, 'Havana Quieter: Regime and Union Say Strike Failed', 11 April 1958, p.1

p.179 Forty rebels and 'There is no general strike . . .', *New York Times*, 'Street Fighting Flares in Havana; 40 Reported Dead', 10 April 1958, p.1

p.179 Rebel safe houses and the fate of the 26 July attorney, Sweig, *Inside the Cuban Revolution*, p.153

p.180 'Let's talk for once . . .' and 'Who are the guilty ones?!' Raúl Castro, letter to FCR, 28 April 1958, CFCPFL

p.180 'I am the leader of this Movement and I have to assume the historic responsibility . . .', FCR, letter to Celia Sánchez, 16 April 1958, CFCPFL

p.181 'Che will go over there with me to take charge . . .', *Fidel y Che: trascen-*

dencia de una identificación, Lic. Ricardo Efrén González, Investigador Agregado, Oficina de Asuntos Históricos, May 2001, p.6, unpublished manuscript kindly shared with the author.

p.181 'bloodletting', Quirk, *Fidel Castro*, p.180, but the account of the meeting and its aftermath is from Sweig, *Inside the Cuban Revolution*, pp. 150–6

p.183 'If I'm not around try to respond to me via Che', FCR, letter to Celia Sánchez, 17 May 1958, 9.30, CFCPFL

p.183 'We've just solved the problem with the electric fuses . . .', FCR, letter to ECG, 17 May 1958, 9.35 p.m., CFCPFL

p.183 'Hopes that you will understand me? None . . .', FCR, letter to Celia Sánchez, 18 May 1958, 8.30 a.m., CFCPFL

p.183 'And you, why don't you make a short trip here?', FCR, letter to Celia Sánchez, no date, cited in Szulc, *Fidel: A critical portrait*, p.426

p.184 'It's been too many days since we spoke . . .', FCR, letter to ECG, 19 May 1958, 7.30 a.m., CFCPFL. One also gains a sense of Fidel's developing thought around this time, when he and Che shared much more time, from Homer Bigart's report which says that Castro told him the political platform was still 'nebulous' in February (it was evidently much clearer by May). See 'Information Concerning Fidel Castro's 26 July Movement', Foreign Service Despatch, 26 February 1958, ARCHIVES II, Cuba Havana Embassy General Records Cuba, 1956–58, declassified, box 5

p.184 Coffee harvest meeting and planes strafing, ECG, *Reminiscences of the Cuban Revolutionary War*, p.251

pp.184–5 'Either we must go there or they will come here . . .' and 'Exchanging tigers is no solution', outgoing telegram, confidential, Earl T. Smith, AmEmb Havana, to State Dept, 1 April 1958, p.4, ARCHIVES II, Cuba Havana Embassy General Records, 1956–58, declassified, box IV

p.185 'chaos and disorder', FCR, letter to Celia Sánchez, 2 June 1958, 5.45, CFCPFL

p.185 'Send me this, I will be there', 'I cannot read this . . .' and 'P.S., be careful . . .', FCR, letter to ECG, 1 June 1958, CFCPFL

p.186 'all a question of a bit of luck', FCR, letter to ECG, 12 June 1958, CFCPFL

p.186 'Although you left the code here I can't decipher the message . . .' and 'I am sending you the papers . . .', FCR, letter to ECG, cited in Ricardo Efrén González, *Fidel y Che: trascendencia de una identificación*, p.8

p.186 'As of yet I am not sending the men . . .' and 'If there is a detonator . . .', ECG, letter to FCR, 19 June 1958, CFCPFL p.187 The government offensive, confidential airgram, US Army attaché, American embassy Havana to Assistant Chief of Staff, Intelligence, Department of the Army, Washington, 11 August 1958, ARCHIVES II, Cuba Havana Embassy General Records, 1956–58, declassified, box 4

p.187 'Send to Che the complete message . . .', FCR, letter to Celia Sánchez, no date (but June 1958), CFCPFL

p.187 'Send help. Mortar shells are exploding near us', FCR, letter to ECG, no date, CFCPFL

p.187 American hostages, Vilma Espín, TSCJFK pp.52–54; 'anti-aircraft battery' in 'Documents Pertaining to Kidnapping of Americans by Rebel Forces in Oriente Province', confidential, Foreign Service despatch no. 19, 4 July 1958, but see also memorandum of conversation, 'Possible Release of More Kidnapped Americans', 6 July 1958, ARCHIVES II, Classified General Records, 350.61 box V

p.187 'Today we bombed the guardias!' and 'sound like a real goat', FCR, letter to ECG, 16 July 1958, 1.10 p.m., CFCPFL

p.188 'its spine broken', ECG, *Reminiscences of the Cuban Revolutionary War*, p.261; 'try and figure out . . .' and 'fanatical hardcore', confidential airgram, continuation of airgram AG no. 16–58, from US army attaché, American embassy, Havana to Assistant Chief of Staff, Intelligence, Department of the Army, Washington, 18 August 1958, ARCHIVES II, Classified General Records, 350.61 box V

p.188 Las Villas province was broken up into three smaller states after the revolution: Cienfuegos, Sancti Spíritus and Villa Clara.

p.189 The move westwards, 'streams that had become rivers' and 'from swampy rivers, or simply from swamps', ECG, *Reminiscences of the Cuban Revolutionary War*, p.263. Further details in this paragraph are from Jesús Parra, interview with the author, Havana, 11 September 2007

pp.189–90 'Dear Teté: I was so overcome to hear your voice after so much time . . .', Celia de la Serna Guevara, letter to ECG, cited in Anderson, *Che Guevara: A revolutionary life*, pp.327–8

p.190 'Fidel, I write you from the open plains', ECG, letter to FCR, 3 September 1958, CFCPFL

p.191 'The Fidelisms I've had to engage in . . .', ECG, letter to FCR, 8 September 1958, 1.50 a.m., CFCPFL

p.191 'time is not on my side and I must leave', ECG, letter to FCR, 13 September 1958, 9.50 p.m. CFCPFL

p.191 Fidel–PSP relations and opinions, Fabio Grobart, TSCJFK, p.24 and 'Conversation of Comrade Kulazhenkov with Cuban Party leadership member Sánchez Cabrera . . .', 21 December 1956, RGANI, Fond 5, opis 28, delo 440, reel 5185, pp.6–8

p.192 Book of Mao, Pardo Llada, *Fidel y el Che*, p.134

p.192 'Johnny come latelys', 'surrounding himself with communists', 'his most able Lieutenant' and 'especially in sabotage', confidential memorandum, 'Random Notes Gathered from Conversation with American Son-in-Law of Mr Manuel ARCA, Owner of "Central Estrada Palma", Oriente Province', ARCHIVES II, Santiago General Records, 1956–58

p.193 Fidel's suspicious silence on communism, Raúl Chibás, TSCJFK, p.26

p.193 'Che is extraordinary!', Pardo Llada, *Fidel y el Che*, p.131. Jorge 'Papito' Serguera, a close friend of both, speaks convincingly of the growing depth and intensity of the relationship between the two men, interview with the author, Havana, 10 November 2007

p.193 Air Cubana DC-3 hijacking, outgoing telegram, Earl E.T. Smith to SecState Washington, 6 November 1958; '[T]here are very definitely problems . . .', ARCHIVES II, Santiago General Records, 1956–58; and 'Request for Contact with Castro Movement', Park Wollam to State Dept, 16 December 1958, p.6, ARCHIVES II, Santiago General Records, 1956–58

p.193 Thefts of Mr Dodge's vehicles and other rebel incursions, 'Memorandum of Conversation between Mr Dodge and Mr Leonhardy', 5 November 1958, ARCHIVES II, Santiago General Records, 1956–58 and 'Confidential Memorandum of Conversation, Mr Riccardo Artigas [a close associate of Exile General García Tuñón] and Mr Wieland, Director, CIA', 15 November 1958, ARCHIVES II, Santiago General Records, 1956–58

p.194 'not up in the hills reading the bible', Sr Pérez-García in 'Memorandum of Conversation between Sr Luís Pérez-García [an exiled Cuban labour leader in Miami], Sr Antonio Santiago [an exiled Prío follower in Miami], and CMA representatives Leonhardy and Owen, 25 November 1958', confidential, ARCHIVES II, Santiago General Records, 1956–58

p.194 'rather be called sons of bitches than commies', in 'Debriefing of J. H. Schissler, Edward Cordes, Eugene P. Pilfeider, Roman Cecella, and Harold Kristjanson', 6 July 1958, ARCHIVES II, Cuba Havana Embassy, Classified General Records, 1956–1958, box V

p.194 'not a communist and well intentioned . . .', Felipe Pazos in 'Memorandum of Conversation, Dr Felipe Pazos [ex-President of the Cuban National Bank] and Mr Leonhardy [CMA]', 14 October 1958, ARCHIVES II, Santiago General Records, 1956–58

p.194 'This seems to me as authoritative a statement as we have . . .', handwritten note appended to 'Memorandum for the Files of October 3', ARCHIVES II, Santiago General Records, 1956–58

p.195 'Rebels, commanded by Camilo Cienfuegos in North and Che Guevara in South . . .', incoming telegram, no. 399, State Dept, 30 December 1958, 8.00 p.m., ARCHIVES II, Santiago General Records, 1956–58

p.195 'These people bore me . . .', FCR, cited in Quirk, *Fidel Castro*, p.185

pp.195–6 Che's progress, testimony of Oscar Fernández-Mell, *Granma*, 21 December 1967, p.2, BNJM

p.196 'In spite of everything . . .', ECG, cited in Anderson, *Che Guevara: A revolutionary life*, p.356

p.197 Oltuski encounter, Anderson, *Che Guevara: A revolutionary life*, p.347 and Oltuski, *Vida Clandestina*, p.194

p.197 Aleida and Che meeting, Anderson, *Che Guevara: A revolutionary life*, pp.356–61; Aleida March, in Enrique Oltuski (ed.), 'Un Che de este mundo', *Cuba Socialista*, No. 7, 1997, pp.87–9 and March, *Evocación: Mi vida al lado del Che*, pp.61–5

p.198 'a growing rift . . .', 'Castro is becoming increasingly annoyed' and 'Castro destroyed a communication . . .', in 'Confidential Memorandum of Conversation between Carlos Piad, Representative of the Cuban Exile Groups and Mr Wieland, Director, CIA', 19 December 1958, ARCHIVES II, Santiago General Records, 1956–58

p.199 Laying down arms and joining the rebels, confidential telegram, Santiago de Cuba to State Dept, No. 336, 15 December 1958, ARCHIVES II, Santiago General Records, 1956–58

p.199 'Sugar, of all things, is short in Manzanillo', in confidential memorandum, 'Random Notes Gathered from Conversation with American Son-in-Law of Mr Manuel ARCA, Owner of "Central Estrada Palma", Oriente Province', ARCHIVES II, Santiago General Records, 1956–58

p.199 'It's essential for you to realise . . .', FCR, letter to ECG, cited in Anderson, *Che Guevara: A revolutionary life*, p.363

p.200 The scramble to keep Fidel out of power, 'Memorandum of Conversation with Rivero Agüero', 26 November 1958, and 'Views of Dr Jorge García Montes on Cuban Situation', 12 November 1958; Agüero was then Batista's President Elect. Batista had also met with Ambassador Smith in July and assured him there would be honest elections, but the Americans were not really buying his account either. See outgoing telegram, AmEmb Havana to SecState Washington, 1 August 1958, ARCHIVES II, Havana Embassy General Records, box IV

p.200 Attack on the train, testimony of Ramón Pardo Guerra, *Granma*, 29 December 1967, p.2, BNJM

p.201 'gone in the night', *Time* magazine, 12 January 1959. As *Time* said of

Batista and his supporters, 'They knew that the jig, as well as the year, was up.'

p.201 'Night falls as we, the *barbudos* . . .', Franqui, *Family Portrait with Fidel*, p.3

p.201 'The rebels kept coming, with crucifixes hanging from chains . . .', Reinaldo Arenas, *Before Night Falls*, Penguin, London, 1994, p.45

p.202 'My mission, my commitment to Fidel ends here . . .', Núñez Jiménez, interview with Carlos Castañeda, cited in *Compañero*, p.142

9. A Hug and a Long Kiss of Years

p.205 This chapter title is taken from Celia de la Serra Guevara's last letter to her son during the war, Anderson, *Che Guevara*, p.328

p.205 The situation on 1 January, El Principe prison smashed open, outgoing telegram, AmEmb Havana to SecState Washington, 1 January 1959, ARCHIVES II, Cuba, Havana Embassy, General Records, 1956–58, declassified, box VIII

p.205 Che's decision to stay: Juan Borrotto, interview with the author, 10 September 2007

p.206 'The revolution begins now . . .', FCR, cited in Thomas, *Cuba: The pursuit of freedom*, p.710, and 'great avalanche', ECG, 'Discurso en el acto de entrega de premios a los cuarenta y cinco obreros más distinguidos en la producción en el Ministerio de Industrias', 30 April 1962, in Guevara, *Obras: 1957–67*, pp.136–153

p.206 'The man whose very name is a banner . . .', Quirk, *Fidel Castro*, p.215, citing *Bohemia*

p.207 'How am I doing?' and 'You are doing alright, Fidel', cited in Szulc, *Fidel: A critical portrait*, p.469

p.207 'I've been looking for you since . . .', Conchita Fernández, TSCJFK, p.67

p.208 'an inevitable step . . .', Casuso, *Cuba and Castro*, p.150

p.209 'the scorn of our formidable neighbour . . .', cited in Shnookal and Muñiz (eds) *José Marti Reader, Writings on the Americas*, p.119

p.210 PSP–M26 secret meetings, Alfredo Guevara, TSCJFK, p.72, Blas Roca, TSCJFK, pp.53–61 and Blas Roca, *Los Fundamentos del Socialismo en Cuba*, pp.180–1

p.210 'We are going to take the cake and turn it upside down', Alfredo Guevara, interview with the author, 11 September 2007

p.211 'he wouldn't have lasted three more months . . .', Juan Borroto, interview with the author, 10 September 2007

p.211 'Shit, now we're the government . . .' and 'Yes, things have really changed . . .', Blas Roca, TSCJFK, pp.53–4 p.212 'evil courtier' and 'practically monopolised his [Castro's] attention', in 'Memorandum of Conversation, confidential, Mr William A. Wieland, Director, CIA and Latin American Exile in the United States, Dept of State', 30 March 1959, ARCHIVES II, Cuba Havana Embassy General Records, 1959–61, declassified, box IV

p.213 'armed democracy', ECG, in Szulc, *Fidel: A critical portrait*, p.468; on the division of labour – 'Fidel saw to politics, Che to economics' Jorge 'Papito' Serguera, interview with the author, Havana, 10 November 2007

p.214 'If the Americans don't like what is happening . . .' and executions, FCR, cited in Szulc, *Fidel: A critical portrait* pp.482–3

p.214 'voluble, garroulous [sic] and impatient', in 'incoming telegram, Havana to Dept of State, confidential, 17 March 1959, ARCHIVES II, Cuba Havana Embassy General Records, 1959–61, declassified, box IX

p.215 Camilo's 'goodwill tour', 'every inch the frontiersman', *Washington Post*, 25 February 1959.

p.215 'more out of ignorance than malice aforethought . . .', W. G. Bowdler in 'Visit of Army Chief of Staff Camilo Cienfuegos to New York', ARCHIVES II, Cuba Havana Embassy General Records, 1956–58, declassified, box VIII

p.215 'Irritated by delays and counsels of caution . . .', P. Bonsal in incoming telegram, No. 686, from Havana to Dept of State, confidential, 17 March 1959, ARCHIVES II, Cuba Havana Embassy General Records, 1959–61, declassified, box IX

pp.215–6 'soul searching' and 'because of the political immaturity he has demonstrated', 'Entertainment of Fidel Castro', memorandum of Conversation, Mr Rubottom and Mr Russell Lutz, Grace Line, 24 March 1959, ARCHIVES II, Cuba Havana Embassy General Records, 1959–61, declassified, box IX

p.216 'because after all we have made enough sacrifices', FCR, cited in Casuso, *Cuba and Castro*, p.209

p.216 'Smiles, lots of smiles', Franqui, *Family Portrait with Fidel*, p.31

p.216 'We are not communists', 'laws and constitutions . . .', downtown Chinese restaurant, benzedrine and 'notable for an absolute lack of mutual understanding', Szulc, *Fidel: A critical portrait*, p.488

p.216 'almost wept', Casuso, *Cuba and Castro*, p.217

p.217 'looks upon Cuba as a sacrificial lamb . . .', W. G. Bowdler, 'Conversation with Sister-in-Law of Raúl Roa', 9 July 1960, ARCHIVES II, Cuba Havana Embassy General Records, 1959–61, declassified, box VIII

p.218 Working together at the Ministry, Francisco Vitorero, interview with the author, Havana, 7 November 2007 and Conchita Fernández, TSCJFK, pp.86–8

p.219 'Tell that SOB Castro I don't like it . . .', report of Congressman Adam Clayton Powell, 'Present Conditions in Cuba', ARCHIVES II, Cuba Havana Embassy General Records, 1959–61, declassified, box VIII, p.2

p.219 'significant changes [to be] made in top governmental positions', outgoing telegram, confidential, from AmEmb Havana to State Dept, 6 May 1959, ARCHIVES II, Cuba Havana Embassy General Records, 1959–61, declassified, box VIII

p.220 Che's impatience at the pace of change, Anderson, *Che Guevara: A revolutionary life*, p.422 and intelligence Information Brief, US Bureau of Intelligence and Research, 12 August 1959, ARCHIVES II, Cuba Havana Embassy, General Records, classified, 1959–61, box V

p.220 'a new phase', ibid.

p.220 'trusted lieutenant', ibid.

p.220 'I am the same old loner trying to find his way . . .' and other excerpts from this letter cited in Taibo II, *Guevara, also known as Che*, p.283

p.221 'hopes' for diplomatic relations and his public façade, incoming telegram, confidential, Rangoon to Secretary of State, US State Dept, 16 July 1959, ARCHIVES II, Cuba Havana Embassy, General Records, declassified, 1959–61, box V

p.222 'beatnik' appearance, 'incoming telegram, confidential, US State Dept from Belgrade', 20 August 1959, ARCHIVES II, Cuba Havana Embassy, General Records, declassified, 1959–61, box V

p.222 'I am pleased that you have liked the apples' and the Indian stopover, Llada, *Fidel y el Che*, p.141

p.222 Nasser on Che's grudge, 'Intelligence Information Brief, US Bureau of Intelligence and Research', 12 August 1959, ARCHIVES II, Cuba Havana Embassy, General Records, declassified, 1959-61, box V

p.222 'liquidating the privileges of a class but not . . .', in Mohamed Heikal, *Nasser: The Cairo Documents*. The Private Papers of Nasser, Mentor, London, 1973, p.304

p.222 Castro would say no, incoming telegram, confidential, US State Dept from Colombo, 10 August 1959 ARCHIVES II, Cuba Havana Embassy, General Records, declassified, 1959–61, box V

p.223 Che's contact with Soviet Embassy staff, 'Intelligence Information Brief, US Bureau of Intelligence and Research', 12 August, 1959, p.3 ARCHIVES II, Cuba Havana Embassy, General Records, Declassified, 1959-61, Box

V and 'Outgoing Telegram, Tokyo, secret', 23 July 1959, ARCHIVES II, Cuba Havana Embassy, General Records, Declassified, 1959-61, box V

p.223 'fullest coverage practicable', 'Outgoing Telegram, Confidential, US State Dept, 4 June 1959, ARCHIVES II, Cuba Havana Embassy, General Records, declassified, 1959-61, box V

p.223 'hopes' for diplomatic relations and 'not inconspicuous . . .', in 'Incoming Telegram, Confidential, Rangoon to Secretary of State, US State Department', 16 July 1959. ARCHIVES II, Cuba Havana Embassy, General Records, declassified, 1959-61, box V

pp.223–4 Chosing Cameras, Pardo Llada, *Fidel y el Che*, pp.158-9

p.224 Bonsal dinner party, in Philip Bonsal, *Cuba, Castro and the United States*, 1971

p.225 'We are now in a critical moment for the revolution . . .', Blas Roca, Hoy, 26 May 1959, p.7

p.225 'excommunication', Edward González, *The Cuban Revolution and the Soviet Union*, 1959-60, 1966, p.42

p.226 'Bonjour Tristesse', Casuso, *Cuba and Castro*, p.214

p.227 The Roa note is cited in González, *The Cuban Revolution*, p.52

p.227 'Because we have no safe planes . . .', ECG cited in Taibo II, *Guevara, also known as Che*, p.291

p.227 'All this is enough to satisfy . . .', ECG, cited in Taibo II, *Guevara, also known as Che*, p.296

p.228 'busy with Che Guevara . . .', Casuso, *Cuba and Castro*, p.185; Francisco Vitorero, in charge of many of the security details for the two men, tells of the hours he spent waiting as they deliberated behind closed doors, interview with the author, Havana, 7 November 2007

p.228 'It appears we have nothing more . . .' and Sukarno's visit, 'Memorandum: President Sukarno–Prime Minister Castro Interview', 23 May 1960, ARCHIVES II, Cuba Havana Embassy, General Records, declassified, 1959–61, box III

p.228 'They stayed until nine in the morning . . .', cited in Das Eiras, *Ernestito Guevara, antes de ser el Che*, p.22

p.229 Soviet trade fair, and Coke and Pepsi interest, Quirk, *Fidel Castro*, p.295

p.230 'warm organic', in 'Telegram of Head of the Revolutionary Government of the Republic of Cuba, Fidel Castro Ruz, to Head of the Cabinet of Ministers of the USSR, Nikita Khrushchev, 26 July 1960, Document 103, MID Publications, p.104; on trade agreements, 'Agreement of Trade and Payments between USSR and Republic of Cuba', ibid., Document 95, pp.87–9 p.230 'It's the honeymoon of the revolution . . .', Simone de Beauvoir, cited in Anderson, *Che Guevara: A revolutionary life*, p.468

p.231 'To conquer something . . .', ECG, cited in Taibo II, *Guevara, also known as Che*, p.300

p.231 Che's articles, 'El café, el petróleo, el algodón, el cobre y otras cuotas' (2 July 1960, *Verde Olivo*), 'El Payaso Macabro y Otras Alevosías' (10 April 1960, *Verde Olivo*), 'Los dos grandes peligros, los aviones piratas y otras violaciones' (22 May 1960, *Verde Olivo*). Many of these can be found in Matos (ed.) *Che Periodista*

p.232 'I just hope to Christ . . .', Ernest Hemingway, cited in Bonsal, *Cuba, Castro and the United States*, p.151

p.232 'down to the nails in their shoes', FCR, cited in ibid., p.151

p.232 Eisenhower adamant and his approach to Castro, Alan H. Luxenberg, 'Did Eisenhower push Castro into the arms of the Soviets', *Journal of Interamerican Studies and World Affairs*, Vol. 30, no. 1 (Spring, 1988), pp.37–71 and Geoffrey Warner, 'Review Article: Eisenhower and Castro: US–Cuba Relations, 1958–60', *International Affairs*, Vol. 75, no. 4 (1999), pp.803–17

10. Revolutionary Anatomy

p.234 Fidel's illness, rumours of being 'roaring drunk', J.L. Topping, Havana, to R.A. Stevenson, State Dept, 27 July 1960, ARCHIVES II, Havana Embassy General Records, declassified, box V

p.234 'absolute physical and mental rest' and 'for obvious political reasons, memorandum of conversation, W.G. Bowdler and Dr Enrique José Sandoval, 30 July 1960, ARCHIVES II, Havana Embassy General Records, declassified, box V

p.234 'malignant condition' and 'sedatives and drugs', outgoing telegram, Bonsal (Havana) to SecState (Washington), ARCHIVES II, Havana Embassy General Records, declassified, box V

p.234 'Possibility that Prime Minister Castro Underwent Psychiatric Treatment at Hands of Suspected Communist', Dr Roberto Sorhegui, memorandum for files, confidential, 29 July 1960, ARCHIVES II, Havana Embassy General Records, declassified, box V

p.234 Fidel's determination not to show weakness, 'Remarks made by Fidel Castro in Mid-September in Conversation with a close friend', memorandum to Ambassador Bonsal from attaché, 21 October 1960, ARCHIVES II, Havana Embassy General Records, declassified, box V

p.235 Working together for three days and nights, Conchita Fernández, TSCJFK, pp.88–9 p.235 Chibás flees the 'red indoctrination', cited at www.voy.com /87202/10/170.html

p.235 Fidel's contentedness at the changes and 'excellent sources close to Fidel Castro . . .', W.G. Bowdler to Ambassador Bonsal, 'Conversation with Sister-in-Law of Raul ROA', 9 July 1960, ARCHIVES II, Havana Embassy General Records, declassified, box V

p.236 The OAS meeting and Roa's condemnation, see Barry Sklar and Virginia M. Hagen, *Inter-American relations; collection of documents, legislation, descriptions of inter-American organizations, and other material pertaining to inter-American affairs*, Washington, US Govt Printing Office, 1972

p.236 Fidel's tearing of the treaty, Quirk, *Fidel Castro*, p.331

p.237 The Havana Declaration, FBIS [1962–09–02], available online at http://lanic.utexas.edu/la/cb/cuba/castro/1960/19600902.2

p.237 Fidel's gesturing to the PSP and a 'speech within a speech', Fursenko and Naftali, *One Hell of a Gamble: Khrushchev, Castro and Kennedy, 1958–1964*, p.59

p.238 Escalante's ambitions, González, *The Cuban Revolution and the Soviet Union*, pp.54–5

p.238 'More key world figures . . .' and 'red satellite chieftains', 'Mr K. and Castro', Universal-International News newsreel, 1960/09/19 (1960)

p.238 Fears of assassination, Szulc, *Fidel: A critical portrait*, p.524

p.238 'red hot', Franqui, *Family Portrait with Fidel*, p.83

p.238 'the place where the Cuban delegation arrived was where . . .', Carlos Rafael Rodríguez, TSCJFK, p.81

p.239 'I will be honoured to stay with the poor, humble people . . .', FCR, cited in Quirk, *Fidel Castro*, p.339

p.239 at the 'HOTEL THE—', ibid., p.337

p.239 'something of a bordello', Franqui, *Family Portrait with Fidel*, p.84

pp.239–40 'It will be the first time I attend such an assembly . . .', in 'Memorandum of Conversation, Soviet Ambassador Kudriatsev and Prime Minister of Cuba Fidel Castro Ruz', 15 September 1960, MID, Fond 104, opis 16 folder 116, No. 4

p.240 'Don't worry about it' and the exchange of cigars and vodka, Franqui, *Family Portrait with Fidel*, p.89 and Quirk, *Fidel*, p.340; see also Nikita Khrushchev, *Memoirs*, p.270

p.240 'Here you took our planes . . .', Quirk, *Fidel Castro*, p.343

p.241 'cordial, harmonious, [and based on] mutual cooperation', ECG, article in *Trabajo*, reproduced as 'Decisión Colectiva' in ECG, *Obras*, p.126

p.241 Granado's return, Granado, *Travelling with Che Guevara*, p.201

p.241 Fidel hopeful that Che might obtain the credits, 'Guevara Mission to Sino–Soviet Bloc', outgoing airgram, AmEmb Havana to State Dept, 21 October 1960, ARCHIVES II, Havana Embassy General Records, declassified, box V, p.2

p.241 Che flattered by the Soviets, incoming telegram, AmEmb Moscow to State Dept, 12 December 1960, ARCHIVES II, Havana Embassy General Records, declassified, box V

pp.241–2 Details of Che's visit and his 'satisfied, radiant look' in Red Square, Pardo Llada, *Fidel y el Che*, p.215. See also ECG, 'Informe de un viaje a los países socialistas', in *Obras*, p.113

p.242 Rumours of Che's argument with Raúl, incoming telegram, AmEmb Rio de Janeiro to State Dept, 28 October 1960, ARCHIVES II, Havana Embassy General Records, declassified, box V

p.242 The reception at the Kremlin and the champagne taking effect, Pardo Llada, *Fidel y el Che*, pp.216–21

p.243 'the thick world of Russian officialdom' and 'This is only for members of the Comintern' exchange, ibid., p.218

pp.243–4 Fidel's impromptu speech at the offices of *Hoy*, Fursenko and Naftali, *One Hell of a Gamble*, p.71

p.244 'We were uneasy because it put more pressure . . .', Sergei Khrushchev, interview with the author, by telephone, 20 June 2008

p.244 Che's asthma when meeting Mao, Pardo Llado, *Fidel y el Che*, p.162

pp.244–5 'Truly, China is one of those countries . . .', ECG televised conference, cited in ECG, 'Informe de un viaje a los países socialistas', *Obras*, p.111

p.245 'That did not exactly do him any favours', Sergei Khrushchev, interview with the author, by telephone, 20 June 2008

p.245 'humanitarian spirit' and the future lies with 'countries who fight for world peace . . .', ECG, 'Informe de un viaje a los países socialistas', *Obras*, pp.103 and 114

p.245 'The construction of socialism has to avoid this . . .', ECG, cited in Furiati, *Fidel Castro*, p.406

p.246 'droves of pink-faced, fair-haired burly young men', Barbara Smith, 'What's it Like in Cuba?' *Economist*, 13 April 1963, p.21

p.246 'Only the old communists and the Soviets know anything . . .', FCR, cited in Franqui, *Family Portrait with Fidel*, p.104

p.247 'lest absence US representatives give colour to charges . . .', Daniel Braddock, outgoing telegram, official use only, from AmEmb Havana to SecState Washington, 2 January 1961, ARCHIVES II, Havana Embassy General Records, declassified, box V

p.247 'but not with an official visit' and Fidel's aspirations for a visit to the USSR, 'Report on VLKSM (Komsomol) Delegation Visit to Cuban Republic', 1 February 1961, RGANI, Fond 89, opis 28, delo 5, p.9

p.247 Cuba's 'sincere and disinterested friends . . .', cited in Quirk, *Fidel Castro*, p.356

p.248 'Inside, one of the offices was a large pool of blood . . .', Martin, *The Early Fidel*, the door preserved, Betto, *Fidel and Religion*, p.187

p.248 'as angry as the sun was hot', Martin, *The Young Fidel*, p.10

p.249 'The imperialists cannot forgive us . . .', Blas Roca, TSCJFK, p.62

p.249 Che's experiences during the Bay of Pigs and the account of Aliushá and Sofía, Anderson, *Che Guevara: A revolutionary* life, p.508

p.249 Fidel writing his speech in the tank and other details, José Iñes, former Castro bodyguard, interview with the author, Havana, 8 November 2007; see also Szulc, *Fidel: A critical portrait*, pp.549–54

p.250 A new period in the revolution. Che wrote an article in September 1962 entitled 'El Cuadro, Columna Vertebral de la Revolución', in which he talks of such a periodisation in relation to the need to construct socialist work structures, ECG, *Obras*, pp.154–60

p.250 'Castro is not a communist but you can make him one', cited in Fursenko and Naftali, *One Hell of a Gamble*, p.134

p.251 Escalante's promotion of PSP candidates, Morray, *The Second Revolution in Cuba*, p.170 and Blas Roca, TSCJFK, pp.70–1

p.252 Fidel's more aggressive turn, FBIS 1961-07-28, 'Castro Speech on the Eighth Anniversary of 26 July'

p.252 'Castro was cynical re. basic goodness of man', telegram from AmEmb Havana to State Dept, 14 April 1959, cited in Falcoff (ed.), *The Cuban Revolution and the United States*, p.102

p.253 'Hey, you! What are you doing here . . .' and this exchange, José Iñes, former Castro bodyguard, interview with the author, Havana, 8 November 2007

p.253 Che as 'ascetic', Pardo Llada, *Fidel y el Che*, p.180

p.253 'Maybe you are not such son of a bitch . . .', ECG, cited in Oltuski, *Vida Clandestina*, pp.280–2. Much of my information about Che's activities at the Ministry comes from my interviews with Juan Valdés Gravalosa, Che's former aide, and with sugar expert and member of Che's circle Juan Borroto, both carried out in Havana in November 2007

p.254 the 'bashful' Emmita, Llovio-Menéndez, *Insider: My hidden life as a revolutionary in Cuba*, p.80

p.254 Hildita's visits to Che's office, Taibo II, *Guevara, also known as Che,* p.342; playing with Muralla, Juan Valdés Gravalosa, interview with the author, Havana, 8 November 2007

p.255 Che's speech at Punta del Este, ECG, 'Cuba no admite que se separe la economía de la política', in María del Carmen Ariet (ed.), *America Latina*, pp.272–306

p.256 'always imagining, always thinking, always developing plans', Carlos Rafael Rodríguez, TSCJFK, pp.21–2

p.257 'absenteeism and job slowdowns', State Dept research memorandum, 'Cuban Internal Political Situation', 20 November 1961, ARCHIVES II, Califano Papers, box III, folder 4

p.257 Fidel commits himself to Marxism–Leninism for life, Quirk, *Fidel Castro*, p.387 and Fursenko and Naftali, *One Hell of a Gamble*, p.72

p.257 'This absence of comment on Castro's open profession of faith is interesting . . .', British embassy, Moscow, to American Dept, Foreign Office, London, confidential, 3 January 1962, FO 371/162308, reel 23, BL.

p.257 'an act of political stupidity', confidential, inward saving telegram, from Mexico City to Foreign Office, London, departmental distribution, 8 January 1962, FO 371/162308, reel 23, BL

p.257 'treason', a view put forward by the Montevideo paper *Acción*, the chief organ of the Colorado opposition party. See British embassy Montevideo to American Dept, Foreign Office, London, restricted, 5 January 1962, FO 371/162308, reel 23, BL

p.257 'creeping coup d'état', Domingo Amachestegui, 'Cuban Intelligence and the October Crisis', in Blight and Welch, *Intelligence and the Cuban Missile Crisis*, p.92. On this, Fursenko and Naftali comment that 'Castro respected Escalante and did not oppose rumours that this old communist had actually eclipsed Raúl and Che as the second-most-powerful man in the revolution' (*One Hell of a Gamble*, p.163). Their wondrously sourced book is the authority on the political relationships of this period, drawing as it does on still inaccessible Soviet archives. They do not cite a particular document for this claim and I have not been able to obtain a copy of the reports from which they take this account, but it certainly rings true with the other circumstantial evidence of embassy reports and memoirs

p.258 'The up till now indispensable Fidel Castro . . .', British embassy Havana to [Prime Minister] Earl of Home, 11 January 1962, 'Cuba, Annual Review for 1961', FO 371/162308, reel 23, BL, p.9

p.258 'Is his hand still firmly on the tiller?' and 'stalking horse', George P. Kidd, Canadian ambassador, Havana, Cuba to Secretary of State for External Affairs, Ottawa, Canada, 16 December 1961, secret. FO 371/162308, reel 23, BL, p.1

11. *Hangman's Noose*

p.260 'are often prisoners of old dogmas . . .', memorandum of conversation, Soviet ambassador Kudriatsev and Fidel Castro Ruz, 10 February 1962, MID, Fond 104, opis 18, folder 121, no. 3, pp.71–8

p.260 'He practically cannot sleep . . .', memorandum of conversation, Soviet ambassador Kudriatsev and Aníbal Escalante, 21 February 1962, MID, Fond 104, opis 18, folder 121, no. 3, pp.116–18

p.261 'Those gentlemen who want to force their ideas on others . . .', FCR, cited in Hans Magnus Enzensberger, 'Portrait of a Party', *International Socialism*, No.44, July/August 1970, p.12

p.261 'extended vacation' and Escalante's fate, Quirk, *Fidel Castro*, pp.405–8

p.261 'We [will] have to work hard to overcome this dissatisfaction', memorandum of conversation, Soviet ambassador Kudriatsev and Blas Roca, 18 April 1962, MID, Fond 104, opis 18, folder 121, no. 3, p.30

p.262 'Sectarianism, dogmatism, clanism . . .' and 'the tactics of the game . . .', memorandum of conversation, Soviet adviser Belous and Prime Minister of Cuba Fidel Castro Ruz, 5 June 1962, MID, Fond 104, opis 18, folder 121, no. 3, p.101. Belous was later Soviet ambassador to Colombia (1971–7)

p.262 'Fidel Castro is a very impulsive person . . .', memorandum of conversation, Soviet ambassador Kudriatsev and Carlos Rafael Rodríguez, 4 May 1962, MID, Fond 104, opis 18, folder 121, no. 3, p.69

p.264 '*Compañeros*, all of you . . .', ECG, *Obras*, pp.152–3

p.264 'How does one actually carry out a work of social welfare . . .', ECG, *Obras*, pp.136–53

p.264 'should be satisfied with the absolute reward of doing his duty', ECG, cited in Llovío-Menéndez, *Insider*, p.81

p.264 'Individuals must disappear', ECG, ibid.

p.265 'He is a great leader . . .', ECG, *Obras*, pp.403–20

pp.265–6 Response to Khrushchev's proposal, comments of Emilio Aragonés in Brenner and Welch (eds), *Back to the Brink*, 1989

pp.265–6 Khrushchev's difficulties and the decision, Fursenko and Naftali, *Khrushchev's Cold War*, pp.430–4; cf. Fursenko and Naftali, *One Hell of a Gamble*, p.178

p.266 'things often hang on a thread, a detail . . .', FCR, transcript of the discussion at the Havana Conference in Blight, Allyn and Welch (eds), *Cuba on the Brink*, p.82

p.267 'greater success of our general affairs', cited in Fursenko and Naftali, *Khrushchev's Cold War*, pp.58–9

p.267 Raúl's nerves and signing the document, Anderson, *Che Guevara: A revolutionary life*, p.526

p.267 'While the people of Cuba would approve of your draft . . .', cited in Fursenko and Naftali, *One Hell of a Gamble*, pp.118–20

p.267 'We are not outlaws . . .', FCR, transcript in Blight, Allyn and Welch (eds), *Cuba on the Brink*, p.84

p.268 'If there is a problem . . .', ibid.

p.268 The Soviets and Americans step towards the brink, Fursenko and Naftali, *Khrushchev's Cold War*, p.455

p.269 'Even after five weeks in Oriente province . . .', British embassy Havana to [Prime Minister] Earl of Home, Her Majesty's consul in Santiago, Mr Collins, 23 August–27 September 1962, FO 371/162308, reel 23, BL

p.269 'secret, swift and extraordinary build-up . . .', Fursenko and Naftali, *Khrushchev's Cold War*, pp.468–72

p.269 'Well, things are clear, things are clear', FCR, transcript in Blight, Allyn and Welch (eds), *Cuba on the Brink*, pp.212–13

p.269 Fidel's cultivation of intelligence officers, Domingo Amechastegui in Blight and Welch, *Cuban Intelligence and the October Crisis*, pp.103–4

p.270 'Do you wish to say that we should be the first . . .', Fursenko and Naftali, *One Hell of a Gamble*, pp.272–3

p.271 'Dear Comrade Khrushchev, . . .' FCR to Khrushchev, 27 October 1962, cited in Blight, Allyn and Welch (eds) *Cuba on the Brink*, p.509

p.271 'knot of war', cited in ibid., p.5

p.271 Fidel's rage, Quirk, *Fidel Castro*, p.443

p.271 'box his ears', said to *Le Monde* editor Claude Julien in January 1963, cited in Quirk, *Fidel Castro*, p.448, cf. Fursenko and Naftali, *One Hell of a Gamble*, p.288

p.271 'allows for the question to be settled in your favour . . .', Khrushchev to FCR, 28 October 1962, cited in Blight, Allyn and Welch (eds), *Cuba on the Brink*, p.510

p.272 Not shooting down the plane, FCR to Khrushchev, 28 October 1962, cited in Blight, Allyn and Welch (eds), *Cuba on the Brink*, p.512. Fidel signed off this letter 'fraternally'. He would later confirm what he really meant to say: 'that is, questioning[ly] . . .'. See 'Fidel Castro's secret speech', cited in full in Blight and Brenner, *Sad and Luminous Days*, p.51

p.272 'Cuba will not lose anything by the removal . . .', FCR, cited in Fursenko and Naftali, *One Hell of a Gamble*, p.288

p.272 'It is not that some Cubans cannot understand . . .', FCR, cited in Fursenko and Naftali, *Khrushchev's Cold War*, p.494

p.272 'sallow, haggard and thin . . .', in British embassy Havana to [Prime Minister] Earl of Home, 1962, FO 371/168135, reel 23, BL

p.273 'We do not understand why we are being asked to do this . . .', FCR, cited in Blight, Allyn and Welch (eds), *Cuba on the Brink*, p.216

p.273 'clash of two superpowers . . .', Khrushchev to FCR, 30 October 1962, cited in ibid., pp.513–16

p.273 'Danger has been hanging over our country . . .' and all these quotes, FCR to Khrushchev, 31 October 1962, ibid., pp.517–19

p.274 'We mustn't underestimate the diplomatic means of struggle', cited in Blight and Brenner, *Sad and Luminous Days*, p.79

pp.274–5 'The USA wanted to destroy us physically . . .', 'But . . . we did everything . . .', 'You offended our feelings . . .' and 'It may cause difficulties . . .', 'Mikoyan Memorandum of Conversation', 8 November 1962, CWIHP

p.275 'Kennedy and Khrushchev are playing chess . . .', in memorandum of conversation, E. Pronsky with Havana University Professor Anastacio Cruz Mansilla, 6 November 1964, RGANI, Fond 5, opis 49, delo 759, pp.267–8

p.275 'shouting and unreasonable' and 'If the Cuban comrades do not wish to work with us . . .', cited in Fursenko and Naftali, *Khrushchev's Cold War*, p.503. 'When I return to Moscow . . .', cited in Blight and Brenner, *Sad and Luminous Days*, p.81

p.275 'I will never forgive Khrushchev, . . .' ECG, in memorandum of conversation, E. Pronsky with Havana University Professor Anastacio Cruz Mansilla, 6 November 1964, RGANI, Fond 5, opis 49, delo 759, pp.267–8

p.276 'Our only hope is to not give up . . . , Llovio-Menéndez, *Insider*, p.112

p.276 Fidel's 'pointed' absence and speculation on reasons, 'Central Intelligence Bulletin', 21 December 1962, daily brief, CIA database, ARCHIVES II.

p.276 'I do not . . . see these somewhat unorthodox excursions . . .', British embassy Havana to [Prime Minister] Earl of Home, 'The Cuban Crisis: Mr Mikoyan in Havana', 30 November 1962, FO 371/162409, BL

12. *Drowning Out of Courtesy*

p.277 'Our right to live is something which cannot be discussed . . .', text of letter dated 15 November 1962 from Prime Minister Fidel Castro of Cuba to Acting Secretary General U Thant, cited in Blight and Brenner, *Sad and Luminous Days*, pp.210–13

p.277 'we can now expect the decline . . .', ECG, in memorandum of conversation, A.I. Mikoyan with Oswaldo Dorticos, Ernesto Guevara and Carlos Rafael Rodríguez, CWIHP. The tenor of Che's response is partly explicable in terms of his 'inimitable' wilfulness – to the point of 'masochism': Jorge 'Papito' Serguera, interview with the author, 10 November 2007

p.278 'I am Minister of Industries, head of the western army . . .', ECG, cited in Oltuski, *Vida Clandestina*, p.289

p.279 'if a day comes when Guevara realises . . .' and 'scruples are sometimes harmful . . .', memorandum of conversation, A. Alexiev with Secretary of ORI National Leadership Minister of Industry Ernesto Guevara Serna, 25 February 1963, RGANI, Fond 5, opis 49, delo 652, pp.82–3

p.279 'Rumour in Havana had it that he had gone crazy . . .', Melba Hernández, cited in Taibo II, *Guevara, also known as Che*, p.363

p.279 '[T]he canebrake never ends', ECG, cited in Taibo II, *Guevara, also known as Che*, p.364

p.279 'Well, if you keep studying . . .', ECG, in Anderson, *Che Guevara: A revolutionary life*, p.567

p.280 'strange and moving drama of building socialism', in ECG, *Socialism and Man in Cuba*, p.7

p.280 Subversive plans against Cuba were outlined in such documents as 'General Pressures to Create a Contingency', 11 March 1963, ARCHIVES II, Califano Papers, box VI, folder 9. These were of a more consolidated, longer-term nature than the ad hoc, if imaginatively named, plans such as 'Operation Horn Swoggle', which would have tried to force down Cuban MiG aircraft by communication intrusion, and 'Operation Invisible Bomb', which planned to imitate American gunfire using the sonic boom of jet aircraft. Both were floated in memorandum to Brigadier General Edward G. Lansdale, USAF, Assistant to the Secretary of Defense, 2 February 1962, from William H. Craig, DOD Representative, Caribbean Survey Group, ARCHIVES II, Califano Papers, box 1

p.280 'form not substance' and 'arouses the reaction of Cuban leaders', memorandum of conversation, A. Alexiev with Organisational Secretary of ORI National Leadership, Emilio Aragonés, 23 January 1963, RGANI, Fond 5, opis 49, delo 652, pp.20–1

p.281 'With regard to the policy of peaceful coexistence . . .', FCR, cited in Fursenko and Naftali, *Khrushchev's Cold War*, p.429

p.281 'The present is for struggle . . .', in 'Fidel Castro Addresses PURS Meeting', FBIS, 1963-02-23

p.282 Castro's arrival, Blight, Allyn and Welch (eds), *Cuba on the Brink*, pp.223–6

p.282 'whistled, cheered, and stamped their feet', *Time magazine*, 'The Other Beard', 10 May 1963

pp.282–3 Fidel's speech in Volgograd, 'Meeting in Volgograd', FBIS, 1963-05-08 p.283 'I just wanted to touch him' and the gala evening, Ludmilla Stepanich, interview with the author, Moscow, 4 December 2007

p.283 'Leningrad was too beautiful to completely remember . . .', in 'Casto Returns to Moscow, Visits Kiev', FBIS, 1963-05-20

p.283 'fellow-feeling and love for us', in 'Speech in Irkutsk', FBIS, 1963-05-14

p.284 'Had the Americans agreed to withdraw their missiles . . .' and this exchange, FCR transcript from the Havana conference, cited in Blight, Allyn and Welch (eds), *Cuba on the Brink*, pp.223–5. A similar point was made by Sergei Khrushchev, interview with the author, 20 June 2008

p.284 'troublemaker', 'if there was a tradition of speeches . . .' and this exchange, memorandum of conversation, A. Alexiev with Minister of Industries Ernesto Che Guevara, 9 May 1963, MID, Fond 9, opis 5, delo 63

p.285 the 'primitive epoch of our management of the government', 'guerrilla tactics as a form . . .' and 'attempting to destroy "guerrillaism" . . .', in ECG, 'Against Bureaucracy', *Obras*, p.167

p.285 'invincible' and 'a communism which is based on the mandate of man', in 'Castro Farewell to Kiev', FBIS, 1963-05-22, 21 May 1963

p.285 'We are communists and our fate is bound . . .', in 'Castro 4 June Speech', FBIS, 1963–06–06

p.286 Sino–Soviet tensions, see Lüthi, *The Sino–Soviet Conflict: Cold War in the Communist World*.

p.287 'would be wrong to pin all their hopes . . .' and 'Revolution cannot be accelerated or made to measure . . .', Mikhail Suslov in 'Bureau of Intelligence and Research, Research Memorandum', 17 April 1964 secret, cited in Castañeda, *Compañero*, p.251

p.288 'We shall begin from this basis . . .', ECG, *Guerrilla Warfare: A method*

p.289 'The duty of revolutionaries . . .', ECG, ibid.

p.289 'ultrarevolutionary bordering on adventurism', Havana embassy Cuba to Moscow, 28 January 1964, cable no. 47784, RGANI, Fond 5, opis 49, delo 655

p.290 'If you want, I can use my good standing . . .', ibid. in Franqui, *Family Portrait with Fidel*, p.217

p.290 'Fidel would agree in principle with anything', ibid., p.32

p.290 Fidel's global vision, Furiati, *Fidel Castro*, pp.429–30

p.291 'Revolution can be made at any given moment . . .', 'Even in Argentina . . . ?' and 'Even in Córdoba . . .', Castañeda, *Compañero*, p.240

p.291 'There are institutions like that famous national bank . . .', in 'Castro Interview on Return from Soviet Trip', FBIS, 1963–06–06

p.292 'Fidel's recent speeches regarding . . .', memorandum of conversation,

O. Daroussenkov with Ernesto Guevara Serna, 27 August 1963, top secret, RGANI, Fond 5, opis 49, delo 654, pp.296–9

p.292 'our trade is maritime ...', memorandum of conversation, O. Daroussenkov with Ernesto Guevara Serna, MID, Fond 4, opis 9, delo 63

p.292 'Who is in the vanguard? ...', in 'Castro Defines the Theory of the Cuban Revolution: interview with Socialist Party weekly, *El Sol*, Montevideo', FBIS, 1963–05–10

p.293 'tactics in politics and tactics in revolution ...', Frank País to Alberto Bayo, 15 May 1957, cited in Sweig, *Inside the Cuban Revolution*, p.20

p.293 'slight, trim woman ...', Howard's attire and scotch and soda, Quirk, *Fidel Castro*, p.457

p.294 The Castro–Howard meeting, CIA briefing paper, secret, 'Interview of US Newswoman with Fidel Castro Indicating Possible Interest in Rapprochement with the United States', 1 May 1963, NSA; see also memorandum from Joseph Patchell to Joseph A. Califano, 'Castro Regime', ARCHIVES II, Califano Papers, box II, folder 16, pp.2–4

p.294 'Pushy Clairol blonde', *Time* magazine, 'No One Dodges Lisa', 25 October 1963

p.294 'Did you really tell him that ...', memorandum from Joseph A. Califano to various, 'Mrs Lisa Howard's Interview with Castro', 2 July 1963, ARCHIVES II, Califano Papers, box V, folder 4, pp.1–3

p.294 'Liza [sic] Howard definitely wants ...', CIA briefing paper, secret, 'Interview of US Newswoman with Fidel Castro Indicating Possible Interest in Rapprochement with the United States', 1 May 1963, NSA, p.3

p.295 The letter arrives while Kennedy in Dallas, Bamford, *Body of Secrets: Anatomy of the Ultra-Secret National Security Agency*, p.130

p.295 Johnson administration's change of policy toward Cuba, memorandum for the record, top secret, 'Meeting with the President on Cuba', 19 December 1963, ARCHIVES II, Califano Papers, box 6, folder 27

p.295 'I assured him we did not think ...' and 'A label is not an argument', memorandum of conversation, O. Daroussenkov with Minister of Industries Ernesto Guevara Serna, 20 December 1963, RGANI, Fond 5, opis 49, delo 760, pp.13–14

p.295 'Some members of National leadership are ...', memorandum of conversation, A. Anikin with Czech Socialist Republic Ambassador to Cuba Comrade Pavlicĕk, 4 January 1964, RGANI, Fond 5, opis 49, delo 762, p.28

p.295 'Chinese propaganda falls on fertile soil ...', memorandum of conversation, A. Anikin with chargé d'affaires of Poland to Cuba E. Siurus, 6 January 1964, RGANI, Fond 5, opis 49, delo 762, p.34

p.296 Fidel's visit to Khrushchev's dacha, Sergei Khrushchev, *Khrushchev on Khrushchev: an inside account of the man and his era*, also Sergei Khrushchev, telephone interview with the author, 20 June 2008

p.296 Soviet claws on Cuba, Skierka, *Fidel Castro*, p.165

p.297 'letting capitalism in through the back door', ECG, Ministry of Industries minutes, cited in Castañeda, *Compañero*, p.261

13. New Alignments

p.301 'There's an altiplano . . .', account from Menéndez in Anderson, *Che Guevara: A revolutionary life*, p.434

p.302 'Ever since he wrote . . .', Manuel Piñeiro, in Luis Suárez (ed.), *Che Guevara and the Latin American Revolution*, p.22

p.302 'It's not the century of Bolívars . . .', enclosure to Mr Brown's letter 1011/62 of 4 June 1963, 'Interview with Dr Castro', FO 371/162462, p.1

p.303 Che's turn to horse doctor remedies, Taibo II, *Guevara also known as Che*, p.374

p.303 'I kept looking at my watch . . .', ECG, Ministry of Industries minutes, cited in Castañeda, *Compañero*, p.264

p.303 'I greet you, Comrade Minister . . .', ECG to Regino Boti, undated (but October 1963), cited in Taibo II, *Guevara also known as Che*, p.377

pp.303–4 'Unfortunately, . . . apologies for the [current] system . . .', 'In this world it is you who knows me . . .' and 'in the difficult moments of the Cuban revolution . . .', ECG to José Medero Mestre, Havana, 26 February 1964, in *Obras*, pp.686–7. Emphasis ('*think*') is mine

p.304 'new era of international cooperation', in 'UNCTAD: Paving the road for trade and development into the 1990s – United Nations Conference on Trade and Development', *UN Chronicle*, December 1989

p.304 'the imperialistic policy of robbing weak countries', ECG cited at http://www.rcgfrfi.easynet.co.uk/ww/guevara/1964-dev.htm

pp.304–5 'Che Guevara, on the other hand . . .', memorandum from the Under Secretary of State (Ball) to President Johnson, Washington, 30 March 1964, FRUS, 1964–1968, Vol. XXXIII; see also 'Central Intelligence Agency Briefing Paper', SC No. 02971/64, FRUS, 1964–1968, Vol. XXXII

p.305 Lost in thought by the lakeside, Castañeda, *Compañero*, p.267

p.306 'This is a big mistake . . .' and 'Convince me . . .', memorandum of conversation, O. Daroussenkov with Minister of Industry Ernesto Guevara Serna, 29 April 1964, RGANI Fond 5, opis 49, delo 760, pp.65–6

p.306 'a den of meticulous bureaucrats', ECG, cited in Taibo II, *Guevara, also known as Che*, p.384

p.306 'Belous' mission, 'the thoughts expressed by Guevara . . .', 'Their speeches are not prepared beforehand . . .' and 'under the influence of emotions', memorandum of conversation, N. Belous with member of editorial staff of Cuba Socialista Fabio Grobart, secret, 13 May 1964, RGANI, Fond 5, opis 49, delo 757, p.72

p.307 'It is hard for the middle classes . . .', memorandum of conversation, O. Daroussenkov with Secretary of PURS national leadership Emilio Aragonés Navarro, secret, 4 June 1964, RGANI, Fond 5, opis 49, delo 758, p.153

p.308 Classes in political economy, 'accentuate the positive', 'listens carefully, generally agrees . . .', memorandum of conversation, E. Pronsky with Anastasio Cruz Mansilla, secret, 29 May 1964, RGANI, Fond 5, opis 49, delo 757, p.121

p.309 'neither she nor her mother . . .' and '[I]n general relations between them are poor', confidential memorandum, J. L. Topping, AmEmb Havana, 27 July 1960, ARCHIVES II, Cuba, Havana Embassy General Records, 1959–1961, declassified, box IV

p.309 Juana Castro defects and 'I knew you were going to ask me about this question . . .', in 'Juana Castro Ruz Acusa: La hermana de Fidel Castro, testigo de mayor excepción, denuncia los crimenes del Castro – Comunismo', *Cruzada Feminina Cubana*, Miami, 1964, p.29

p.310 Che's position weakens, 'The Fall of Che Guevara and the Changing Face of the Cuban Revolution', CIA report, 18 October 1965, ARCHIVES II, CIA database

p.310 'an atmosphere of the new man in the air' and Leon Felipe exchange, ECG to Leon Felipe, *Obras*, p.690; see also Victor Casaus (ed.), *Self Portrait: Che Guevara*, pp.223–5

p.311 'We sent the person closest to us', FCR, cited in Castañeda, *Compañero*, p.287

p.311 Moscow's strategic reappraisal post-Khrushchev, Fursenko and Naftali, *One Hell of a Gamble*, pp.353–5

p.312 'Here he confuses two terms . . .', ECG, notes on V. I. Lenin, photostat of a page from his Philosophical Notebooks, in Ariet (ed.), *America Latina*, pp.432–3

p.312 Conversations with Andropov and Korionov, Anderson, *Che Guevara: A revolutionary life*, pp.614–15

p.312 The 'highly secret extraordinary conference', memorandum of conversation, O. Daroussenkov with General Secretary of the Bolivian Communist Party, secret, 26 November 1964, RGANI, Fond 5, opis 49, delo 758, pp.310–11

p.312 Sponsorship of guerrillas the dominant issue, Furiati, *Fidel Castro*, p.440; Furiati takes this from her own conversations with Manuel Piñeiro

p.313 'We have learned from reliable sources . . .', in Johne (GDR ambassador) and Kulitza (the embassy's first secretary), 'Uber die Entwicklung der Republik Kuba im Jahre 1965 und einige Entwicklungstendenzen für das Jahr 1965', 21 January 1965, pp.9–10, 13–14, SED, DY30 IVA 2/20/270

p.313 'ask each speaker many questions . . .', memorandum of conversation, E. Pronsky with Secretary of Argentine Communist Party Victorio Codovilla, secret, 25 November 1964, RGANI, Fond 5, opis 49, delo 758, p.306

p.313 Che's meeting with Daroussenkov prior to leaving for New York, memorandum of conversation, O. Daroussenkov with Minister of Industry Ernesto Guevara Serna, secret, 8 December 1964, RGANI, Fond 5, opis 49, delo 758, p.308

p.314 'They internationalised the blockade . . .', FCR, cited in Ramonet, *My Life*, p293

14. *Straight Talking*

p.315 Bazooka attack and the knife-toting woman, *Time* magazine 18 December 1964; see also 'Bazooka Shells Fired at UN Buildings in New York; Misses by Wide Margin', *Chicago Tribune*, 12 December 1964, p.W1, and 'No clue is found to UN attackers', *New York Times*, 13 December 1964, p.1

p.315 'He lives a very dangerous life . . .', Radio Telefís Éireann report 'Che Guevara at Dublin Airport', 18 December 1964

p.315 Chess with the guards, Taibo II, *Guevara, also known as Che*, p.399

p.316 'This philosophy of despoilment . . .' and all quotes in these paragraphs from ECG, 'Colonialism is Doomed – Speech Delivered by Major Ernesto Che Guevara on September 11, 1964 at the United Nations Organisation', Republic of Cuba, Ministry of External Relations Information Department, BNJM, pp.6–20

p.316 'Dr Guevara, Washington has said . . .' and all quotes in these paragraphs, *Face the Nation* transcript, BNJM, p.30

p.317 Staying behind to talk with Szulc, in Szulc, *Fidel: A critical portrait*, p.599

p.317 'the imperialists were so surprised . . .', FCR 'Castro Speech on 6th Revolution Anniversary', FBIS, 1965-01-05

p.317 Lisa Howard's party, 'and would continue to do so', 'Meeting with Che Guevara, Cuban Minister of Industry', Exdis. drafted by Woods on 18 December, secret, FRUS, 1964–1968, Vol. XXXII p.318 Che's meeting with African ministers, memorandum of conversation, N. Belous with Director of Cuban Institute of Friendship with the People Masola, secret, 13 August 1964, RGANI, Fond 5, opis 49, delo 762, p.246. Among those present was A. M. Babu of Tanzania

pp.318–19 'Che: Sergio [del Valle] has just met me . . .', FCR to ECG, December 1964, cited in ECG, *The African Dream: The diaries of the revolutionary war in the Congo*, pp. xliv–xlv. Diocles Torralba was a minister in Castro's government in charge of sugar production. In 1989 he was imprisoned on corruption charges. Sergio del Valle was a leading figure in the Cuban army, a doctor and an intimate of Fidel

p.319 The Chinese show their displeasure, Abteilung Latein Amerika Akte A3363/4 PAAA Bestand MFAA, 0000301 Informationsbericht des ADR-Korrespondenten in Havana vom 03.03.1965: 'Die Meinung von Carlos Rafael Rodríguez', pp.301–2; cf. Carlos Rafael Rodríguez, TSCJFK, p.83

p.319 'President Nasser tended to dismiss them . . .' and all reported speech in this exchange, Heikal (ed.), *Nasser: The Cairo Documents*, pp.306–12

p.320 Jokes about Che's undiplomatic nature, Abteilung Latein Amerika Akte A3363/4 PAAA Bestand MFAA, 0000309: Brief der DDR Botschaft in Kuba an den Stellvertreter der Ministers für Auswaertige Angelegenheiten, Genossen Georg Stibli, Februar 22 1965, Vertrauliche Dienstsache No. 389/5, pp.308–9

p.320 'We talked, we debated' and [T]hey were not very happy', in Piero Gleijeses, *Conflicting Missions*: p.83

p.320 'haven for exiles . . .', CIA, special memorandum, 'Implications of Growing Communist Influence in URTZ', 29 September 1964, cited in Gleijeses, *Conflicting Missions*, p.84

p.321 Fidel sends message to the Soviets, Castro Speech on 6th Revolution Anniversary, FBIS, 1965-01-05

p.321 'We discussed his speech all night . . .', Ahmed Ben Bella, cited in Castañeda, *Compañero*, p.292; Jorge Serguera maintains that at least part of the influence behind Che's idea of a Third World bloc against both Americans and Soviets stemmed from Frantz Fanon's *The Wretched of the Earth*, a book he first read during the year of the Missile Crisis. Jorge 'Papito' Serguera, interview with the author, Havana, 10 November 2007

p.321 Che's speech as the 'last bullet', CIA intelligence brief 'The Afro–Asian Seminar', Directorate of Intelligence, Office of Research and Reports, March 1965, CIA database, ARCHIVES II; see also Lewis Diuguid, 'Guevara: A True Revolutionary', *Washington Post*, 11 October 1967

p.321 'How can it be mutually beneficial . . .', ECG speech to the Afro–Asian Conference in Algeria, in *The Che Reader*, pp.301–13

p.321 'many of the more extreme proposals', CIA intelligence brief 'The Afro–Asian Seminar', Directorate of Intelligence, Office of Research and Reports, March 1965, CIA database, ARCHIVES II

p.322 'discordant note' and 'would lead to a return to capitalism', in 'The Wave Breaks', *Hartford, Connecticut Times*, 29 March 1965

p.322 'Yes, edited by some unwitting fool . . .' and details on the Shannon stopover, Retamar, *Obras IV: Cuba Defendida*, pp.173–7

p.323 'Castro, Guevara and Camilo . . .', Jim Fitzpatrick, cited in Joe Ó Muircheartaigh, 'The Importance of Being Ernest', *Clare Champion*, 9 September 2005

p.324 'huge argument between el Fifo and el Che', Dariel Alarcón Ramírez ('Benigno'), cited in O'Donnell, *Che: La vida por un mundo mejor*, p.62; see also Ramírez, *Memorias de un Soldado Cubano*

p.324 'All right, the only alternative left . . .', Castañeda, *Compañero*, p.299. Castañeda's account is also derived from interviews with Benigno

p.324 Fidel not following the party line either, memorandum of conversation, V. Manko with Polish Press Agency Correspondent Miroslaw Ikonowicz, secret, 20 May 1965, RGANI, Fond 5, opis 49, delo 845, p.149

p.324 '[A]ll socialist countries have . . .', FCR, Live Speech by Prime Minister Fidel Castro at a 3 March 1965 Ceremony in the Central Park of Güines, FBIS, 1965-03-03

p.325 Secret training camps: these were known as 'Petis', standing for *Puntos de Entrenamiento de Tropas Especiales e Irregulares*

p.325 Fidel speaks of the Congo and Vietnam, Fidel Castro Speech at University, FBIS, 1965-03-14

p.325 'Which one?', Retamar returns the book, in Retamar, *Obras IV*, pp.176–7

p.326 'Adios Muchachos', this story from Juan Valdés Gravalosa, interview with the author, Havana, 8 November 2007

p.326 'hectic round of bittersweet farewells', ECG in *The African Dream*, p.9

p.326 Fidel's having been with Che, Francisco Vitorero, interview with the author, Havana, 7 November 2007

p.326 'You OK, Dreke?', this dialogue has been reconstructed from quoted material in Taibo II, *Guevara, also known as Che*, p.411

p.327 'With what right . . .', ECG, cited in Anderson, *Che Guevara: A revolutionary life*, p.532

pp.327–8 Che's letter to Fidel, *Carta del Che a Fidel*, Editorial Pablo de la Torriente, Havana, 2004, no page.

p.328 'Look after Che', FCR, in Taibo II, *Guevara, also known as Che*, pp.412–13

15. Red Letter Day

p.330 'under lock and key . . .', Richard Gott, foreword to ECG, *The African Dream*, p.ix

p.330 'The most difficult thing . . .', FCR, Letter to ECG, cited in ibid., p.xlviii

p.331 House arrest, out of the country etc., Abteilung Latein Amerika Akte A3363/3 PAAA Bestand MFAA, 0000216: Brief der DDR Botschaft in Kuba, Herr Johne, an den Stellvertreter des Ministers für Auswaertige Angelegenheiten, Genossen Georg Stibi, Vertrauliche Dienstsache No. 102, Juli 12 1965, pp.216–21

p.331 'It is likely that . . .', Piero Gleijeses, *Conflicting Missions*, p.91

p.331 Fidel's May Day speech, FCR, 'Castro Assails US Action in Dominican Republic', FBIS, 1965-05-03

pp.331–2 'Guevara's absence in the leadership . . .' and 'On the surface . . .', memorandum of conversation, A. Alexiev with Member of the National Leadership Carlos Rafael Rodríguez, RGANI, Fond 5, opis 49, delo 844, p.390

p.332 'support [of] liberation movements . . .', ibid.

p.332 'the relationship between us . . .', Abteilung Latein Amerika Akte A3363/3 PAAA Bestand MFAA, 0000216: Brief der DDR Botschaft in Kuba, Herr Johne, an den Stellvertreter des Ministers für Auswaertige Angelegenheiten, Genossen Georg Stibi, Vertrauliche Dienstsache No. 102, Juli 12 1965, pp.216–21

p.332 Rubbishing centralisation, FCR, 'Fidel Castro Speech on 26 July Anniversary', FBIS, 1965-07-27

p.333 'heatedly denounced' and the dog metaphor, CIA intelligence memorandum, 'The Fall of Che Guevara and the Changing Face of the Cuban Revolution' limited official use, ARCHIVES II, CIA Database, p.8

p.333 'In real life at present . . .', FCR, 'Castro Speaks at Award Ceremony for Canecutters', FBIS, 1965-07-26

p.333 'we had spent some months in searching . . .', memorandum from the Deputy Director for Coordination of the Bureau of Intelligence and Research (Williams) to the Assistant Secretary of State for Inter-American Affairs (Vaughn), 11 June 1965, FRUS, 1964–1968, Vol. XXXII, p.717

p.334 'I got him as a puppy . . .' and 'We could get to Florida . . .', FCR, in Lockwood, *Castro's Cuba, Cuba's Fidel*, p.60

p.334 'I want to do some hunting . . .', FCR, ibid., p.61

p.334 Sitting down to dinner and 'Oh, but they were the happiest times . . .', ibid., p.75

p.335 'At the present time I cannot answer . . .' and 'would be digging up the mystery', ibid., pp.342–3

p.336 'sudden escarpments, rushing rivers . . .' and 'the ideal terrain', Hoare, *Congo Mercenary*, p.239

p.336 'In reality, the lake is a kind of ravine . . .', ECG, *The African Dream*, p.12

p.336 Tutsis, Gott, foreword to ECG, *The African Dream*, p.xxx

p.337 'He kept talking . . .', ECG, *The African Dream*, p.15

p.337 'for me, personally . . . the saddest news . . .', ECG, *The African Dream*, p.24

p.339 'bright, sunswept day . . .', Lockwood, *Castro's Cuba, Cuba's Fidel*, p.8

p.339 'I'm just trying to remember how everything happened . . .', ibid. pp.10–11

p.339 'Comrade Guevara . . . who at times . . .', FCR, in 'Castro Speaks at Uvero Battle Commemoration', FBIS, 1965-06-02

p.339 Camilo and Che rushing through the canebrake, FCR, in 'Speech on Sugar Production', FBIS, 1965-06-09

p.340 'And now that I mention our comrade . . .', FCR, in 'Castro Speaks on Interior Ministry Work', FBIS, 1965-06-18

p.340 Changes of personnel, CIA intelligence memorandum, 'The Fall of Che Guevara', ARCHIVES II, CIA Database, p.8

p.340 'There is an absence . . .', FCR, in Deutschmann (ed.), *Che en la Memoria de Fidel Castro*, p.37

p.341 'dressed in black and verging on tears', *Time* magazine, 15 October 1965

p.341 'to have the only say . . .' and 'evidently taken great pains . . .', in Skierka, *Fidel Castro*, p.184

p.342 Machado Ventura's role as emissary, in Gleieses, *Conflicting Missions*, p.122

p.342 'Che was near me . . .', Martín Chivás, 'El Regreso de un Amigo', *Trabajadores*, 14 July 1997. Gleijeses in *Conflicting Missions* confirms this, citing the *Trabajadores* article and also quoting from his interview with Victor Dreke: 'I think Che knew that things in Zaire [then Congo] were going badly, and once Fidel read the farewell letter, he felt like it would be awkward to return to Cuba'

p.342 'a man from other climes', ECG, *The African Dream*, p.216

pp.342–3 'I received your letter . . .', ECG, letter to FCR, in ibid. pp.125–9

p.343 'We must to everything save for the absurd', FCR, letter to ECG, no date, cited in Furiati, *Fidel Castro*, p.448

p.344 'peasants fleeing, smoke rising', 'alone and perplexed' and 'desolate, sobering and inglorious . . .', ECG, in Archivo Personal, *The African Dream*, pp.216–17

p.345 'Well, we carry on . . .', dialogue from Anderson, *Che Guevara: A revolutionary life*, p.671. The real names of his interlocutors were: Harry Villegas (Pombo), Carlos Coello (Tuma) and José María Martínez Tamayo (Papi)

p.345 'roving incendiary', CIA intelligence memorandum, 'The Fall of Che Guevara', ARCHIVES II, CIA Database, p.5

p.345 'This is the history of a failure . . .', ECG, *The African Dream*, p.1

p.345 *'muy fuerte'*, Juan Borrotto, interview with the author, Havana, 5 November 2007

p.345 'There was an ongoing struggle with Fidel . . .', Castañeda, *Compañero*, p.327

p.346 Aleida's visit, see March, *Evocación*, pp.202–6

p.346 'The leaders of the revolution have . . .', ECG, *Socialism and Man*, pp.19–20

p.347 'all means available to support . . .', FCR, in CIA, Directorate of Intelligence, 'Current Intelligence Country Handbook, Cuba', secret, Directorate of Intelligence, July 1966, ARCHIVES II, CIA Database, p.5

p.347 'canny enough to keep his risks low' and 'We believe that . . .', ibid., p.5

p.348 'Where is Che? . . .', in Anderson, *Che Guevara: A revolutionary life*, p.683

p.348 'It is hard to believe in the sins . . .', memorandum of conversation, Y. Chestnoy with Bolivian Communist Party General Secretary, secret, 3 August 1964, RGANI, Fond 5, opis 49, delo 758, p.176

p.349 'new indications . . .', 'repeated his thesis . . .' and 'once again proclaimed . . .', CIA, 'Cuban Subversion in Latin America', secret, ARCHIVES II, CIA Database, p.10

p.349 'actually given meaningful support . . .', CIA Directorate of Intelligence, 'Current Intelligence Country Handbook, Cuba', ARCHIVES II, CIA Database, p.5

pp.349–50 'Events have overtaken my plans for a letter . . .', 'on any coolly objective analysis . . .', 'There is no question of principle . . .', 'I hope that these lines . . .', 'Did Marx, Engels, Lenin . . .' and 'We ourselves had to invest . . .', FCR, letter to ECG, ECG, *The African Dream*, pp.xlvi–xlix

p.350 'The idea, the plan, everything . . .', FCR, cited in Taibo II, *Guevara, also known as Che,* p.456

p.351 'I know you will be 38 ...', FCR, letter to ECG, ECG, *The African Dream*, p.xlix

p.351 'meticulously' hard work, in Suárez (ed.), *Che Guevara and the Latin American Revolution*, p.34

p.352 'I told them I wanted them to meet ...', FCR, in Ramonet, *My Life*, p.301

p.352 'Enjoy them, because when they're older ...', ECG, in 'Un Che de Este Mundo', *Cuba Socialista*, 1997, Vol. 7 p.88

p.352 'Mamá, I think that old man's in love ...', March, *Evocación*, p.235

p.352 'Fidel and Che talked together ...' and a 'simple farewell', Suárez (ed.), *Che Guevara and the Latin American Revolution*, pp.36 and 72

p.352 'Always cold, always less than you expected ...', ECG, *Back on the Road*, p.24

16. A Life and Death Foretold

p.354 Route to and arrival in Bolivia, Taibo II, *Guevara, also known as Che*, p.630

p.355 'My only one, ...', ECG, letter to Aleida March, cited in March, *Evocación*, p.237

p.355 'Che was seated ...', Inti Peredo, 'My Campaign with Che', p.322. Originally written while he was in hiding after the Bolivian campaign and shortly before his murder, Peredo's memoir can be found in the full English version in ECG, *The Bolivian Diary*, Hereafter Peredo, *My Campaign*

p.356 Che's argument with Monje, Peredo, *My Campaign*, p.340

p.357 'hostile region, characterised by ...', Harris, *Death of a Revolutionary*, p.101

p.358 'We have all been disturbed ...' and 'message of solidarity ...' FCR, 'Castro Speaks at Havana University Graduation', FBIS, 1966-12-20

p.358 'And our special warm message ...', FCR, 'Castro Marks 8th Anniversary of Revolution', FBIS, 1967-01-03

p.359 'He talked about us in a way ...', ECG, *The Bolivian Diary*, p.64

p.360 'Latin America's Vietnams ...', Richard Gott, *Guardian*, unmarked news cutting, British Library, date unknown

p.361 The guerrillas attack, Harris, *Death of a Revolutionary*, p.112

p.361 'talked like parrots', ECG, *The Bolivian Diary*, p.111

p.361 'Everything gives the impression ...', ECG, *The Bolivian Diary*, p.118

p.362 Aleidita at the May Day event, Taibo II, *Guevara, also known as Che*, p.516

p.362 'Almeida passed the mantle ...', ECG, *The Bolivian Diary*, p.146. All short Guevara quotes from here on are from this source p.362 'This revolution will never be . . .', in Kevin Devlin, 'Castro's Place in the Communist World', 1967, OSA, box 14, folder 1, report 84

p.363 '[T]he Cuban leadership', in 'Brief der DDR-Botschaft in Havanna an das MfAA', cited in Skierka, *Fidel Castro*, p.187

p.363 'playing the role of judge . . .', in 'Antwort der Kommunistischen Partei Venezuelas', cited in Skierka, *Fidel Castro*, p.187

p.363 'What right?' CIA, intelligence information cable, background of Soviet Premier Aleksei Kosygin's Visit to Havana, October 1967, http://www.companeroche.com/index.php?id=106

p.364 Che's 'Message to the People of the World', handwritten note appearing in *Granma*, 2 December 1967, p.12, BNJM

p.365 'surprise visit . . .', Mexican embassy in Havana, confidential report no. 559, 'Visita a Cuba del Premier Ministro Soviético Alexei Kosygin, 26–30 June, 1967', from Kate Doyle, *Double Dealing: Mexico's Foreign Policy Toward Cuba*, Electronic Briefing Book, National Security Archive, Washington, DC, 2003

p.365 'direct evidence of Cuba's encouragement . . .', memorandum of conversation, The President and USSR Chairman Kosygin, 25 June 1967, FRUS, 1964–1968, Vol. XIV, document 235

p.365 'a little upset with Castro', recording of telephone conversation between President Johnson and [former President] Dwight D. Eisenhower, 25 June 1967, 9.44 p.m., FRUS, 1964–1968, Vol. XXXI, documents 44–71

p.365 'serious, thoughtful, clever leader . . .', memorandum of conversation, O. Daroussenkov with PURS national leadership secretary, Minister of Industry Ernesto Guevara Serna, secret, 16 October 1964, RGANI, Fond 5, opis 49, delo 758, pp.265–6

p.365 Castro–Kosygin meeting, on context see 'The Russians Were Coming: The Soviet Military Threat in the 1967 Six-Day War', Isabella Ginor, *Middle East Review of International Affairs*, Vol. 4, no. 4, December 2000, p.52; 'in Cuba to reprimand Castro', 'Visit to Cuba of Soviet First Minister Alexei Kosygin', Mexican embassy in Havana, confidential report no. 559, *Double Dealing: Mexico's Foreign Policy Toward Cuba*, Electronic Briefing Book, National Security Archive, Washington DC; 'virtual ultimatum', Blight and Brenner, *Sad and Luminous Days*, p.126; cf. *Time* magazine, 'Stopover in Havana', 7 July 1967

p.365 'Kosygin and Fidel talked . . .', 'Kosygin then asked Fidel . . .' and 'especially bitter', Oleg Daroussenkov, the only translator present at the meeting, interview with Blight and Brenner, cited in *Sad and Luminous Days*, p.125

p.366 'supporting the local party . . .', Oleg Daroussenkov, cited in Castañeda, *Compañero*, p.384

p.366 Fidel lectures Kosygin on Latin American history, CIA, intelligence information cable, Background of Soviet Premier Aleksey Kosygin's Visit to Havana, October 1967, http://www.companeroche.com/index.php?id=106

p.366 'excellent progress', Karol, *Guerrillas in Power* pp.343–4

p.367 Last chance to get to Argentina, Harris, *Death of a Revolutionary*, pp.135–6

p.368 'The history of Cuba . . .' and banners at the OLAS conference, Geyer, *Guerrilla Prince*, p.316

p.368 'fluttered in luminous letters . . .', Karol, *Guerrillas in Power*, p.364

p.369 'those who want to make the revolution . . .' and the OLAS, FCR, in Karol, *Guerrillas in Power*, pp.379–87

p.370 'Yes, the more I think of it . . .', 'Very well . . .', 'I wonder what sort of world . . .' and 'We are not building socialism . . .', cited in Karol, *Guerrillas in Power*, p.385

p.371 Tania's body, Harris, *Death of a Revolutionary*, p.149

p.371 The bounty on Che, ECG, *The Bolivian Diary*, p.233

p.371 'the seventeen of us set out . . .' and 'because it was futile . . .', ECG, *The Bolivian Diary*, pp.253–4

p.372 Che's capture, Gary Prado debrief, ARCHIVES II, CIA Database, p.153

p.373 'Are you Cuban or Argentine?' and 'speak badly about Fidel, ibid.

p.373 'proceed with the elimination' and Prado's role, ibid.

p.373 The execution, O'Donnell, *Che*, pp.13–14

p.374 'women in black dresses,' Bjorn Kumm, 'Guevara is dead, long live Guevara', *Transition*, No.75/76, p.34

p.374 'There was no longer any doubt' and 'He was dead . . .', ibid., pp.34–5

p.374 Formaldehyde and bullet holes, Richard Gott, interview with the author, London, 17 July 2007

p.374 'When reports of Che's death . . .', 'all the Chiefs . . .' and 'Yes, it's confirmed', José Iñes, former Castro bodyguard, interview with the author, Havana, 8 November 2007

p.375 'bitterly true' and all quotes from Fidel's appearance on television, 'Comparición por Fidel Castro Ruz, 15 October 1967', pp.7–10, BNJM

p.376 'They are mistaken when they think that his death . . .', FCR, 'Discurso Pronunciado en la Velada Solemne . . .', *Granma*, 2 December 1967, p.5, BNJM

Epilogue

p.377 'I dream of Che a lot . . .', FCR, in Jorge Timossi, 'Los Sueños de Fidel', cited in Costenla, *Che Guevara: La vida en Juego*, p.11

p.378 'We raised a glass of vodka . . .', Wayne S. Smith, interview with the author, Washington, 13 March 2007

p.378 'The Military Programme of Proletarian Revolution', *Granma*, 1 November 1967, p.2

p.378 'the units that represent the basic foundations . . .', FCR, in 'Fidel Castro's 2 January Speech on Anniversary', FBIS, 1968-01-03

p.378 'Let this year be worthy . . .', ibid. See also Abteilung LateinAmerika/ Sektor Cuba, Akte C1226/77, PAAA Bestand MFAA, 000105, pp.105– 38: Gaspraech Castros in der 'El Mundo', vom 13 Jan. 1968, 'Der USA-Imperialismus – der Hauptfeind der Menschheit'

p.378 'sweetheart deals', Blight and Brenner, *Sad and Luminous Days*, p.133

pp.378–9 '[T]his little island . . .', FCR, cited in ibid., p.131

p.379 Fidel affirms militant revolutionary path, in Kevin Devlin, 'Castro Strikes at Communist "Microfaction" in a Challenge to Moscow', 1968-2-6, OSA, 93-3-103.

p.379 'accusatory duet', Blight and Brenner, *Sad and Luminous Days*, p.135

p.379 'It will be difficult . . .', Abteilung LateinAmerika/Sektor Kuba, Akte C1226/77, PAAA Bestand MFAA, 000105, pp.105–38: Gespraech Castros in der 'El Mundo', vom 13 Jan. 1968, 'Der USA-Imperialismus – der Hauptfeind der Menschheit'

p.380 'It was like a cold shower . . .', cited in Blight and Brenner, *Sad and Luminous Days*, p.131

p.380 'Castro finds himself . . .', in 'Memorandum from William G. Bowdler of the National Security Council Staff to the President's Special Assistant (Rostow)', 18 December 1967, FRUS, Vol. XXXII, 1964–1968, p.747. See also SNIE, 'Cuba: Castro's Problems and Prospects Over the Next Year or Two', 27 June 1968, ibid., p 752

p.380 'He was betrayed', Saul Landau, 'Filming Fidel': A Cuban Diary, 1968', *Counterpunch*, 16/17 December 2006

p.381 'in part because he had Fidel . . .', Fontova, *Exposing the Real Che Guevara*, p.xxviii

p.381 'personal sacrifice and hard work', Quirk, *Fidel Castro*, p.405

SELECT BIBLIOGRAPHY

Biographical Works

Anderson, Jon Lee, *Che Guevara: A revolutionary life*, Bantam Books, London, 1997

Betto, Frei, *Fidel and Religion*, Simon & Schuster, New York, 1987

Castañeda, Jorge, *Compañero: The life and death of Che Guevara*, Bloomsbury, London, 1998

Coltman, Leycester, *The Real Fidel Castro*, Yale University Press, New Haven and London, 2003

Costenla, Julia, *Che Guevara: La vida en juego*, Edhasa, Buenos Aires, 2007

Franqui, Carlos, *Family Portrait with Fidel*, Cape, London, 1983

Furiati, Claudia, *Fidel Castro: La historia me absolverá*, Plaza y Janés, Barcelona, 2003

Gadea, Hilda (trans. Carmen Molina and Walter I. Bradbury), *Ernesto: A memoir of Che Guevara*, W. H. Allen, London, 1973

Geyer, Georgie Anne, *Guerrilla Prince: the untold story of Fidel Castro*, Little, Brown, New York, 1991

Korol, Claudia, *El Che y los Argentinos*, Dialéctica, Buenos Aires, 1988

O'Donnell, Pacho, *Che: La vida por un mundo mejor*, Editorial Sudamericana, Buenos Aires, 2003

Quirk, Robert, *Fidel Castro*, W. W. Norton, New York, 1993

Ramonet, Ignacio *Biografía a dos Voces*, Random House Mondadori, Barcelona, 2006

Ramonet, Ignacio, *My Life*, Penguin, London, 2008

Skierka, Volker (trans. Patrick Camiller), *Fidel Castro*, Polity Press, Cambridge, 2006

Szulc, Tad, *Fidel: A critical portrait*, First Road Press, New York, 2000

Taibo II, Paco Ignacio, (trans. Michael Robers), *Guevara, also known as Che*, St Martin's Press, New York, 1997

Youths

Alape, Arturo, *El Bogotazo: Memorias del Olvido*, Casa de las Americas, La Habana, 1983

Bonachea, Rolando and Nelson Valdes (eds), *Revolutionary Struggle, Volume I of the Selected Works of Fidel Castro, 1947–58*, MIT Press, Cambridge, Massachusetts, 1972

Conte Agüero, Luis and Anne Louise Bardach (eds), *The Prison Letters of Fidel Castro*, Nation Books, New York, 2007

Cupull, Adys and Froilán González, *Ernestito, vivo y presente,* Editora Política, Havana, 1989

Cupull, Adys and Froilán González (eds), *Cálida Presencia: La amistad del 'Che' y Tita Infante a través de sus cartas*, Editorial Oriente, Santiago, Cuba, 1997

Das Eiras, Horacio, *Ernestito Guevara, antes de ser el Che*, Ediciones del Boulevard, Córdoba, Argentina, 2006

De la Cova, Antonio Rafael, *The Moncada Attack: Birth of the Cuban Revolution*, University of South Carolina Press, Columbia, SC, 2007

Granado, Alberto (trans. Lucia Awarez de Toledo), *Travelling with Che Guevara: The making of a revolutionary*, Random House, London, 2003

Guevara, Ernesto (trans. Patrick Camiller), *Back on the Road: A journey to Central America*, Harvill Press, London, 2001

Guevara, Ernesto, *The Motorcycle Diaries*, Fourth Estate, London, 2004

Guevara Lynch, Ernesto, *Mi Hijo el Che*, Editorial Planeta, Barcelona, 1981

Guevara Lynch, Ernesto, *Aquí Va un Soldado de América*, Sudamerican-Planeta, Buenos Aires, 1987

Martin, Lionel, *The Early Fidel: Roots of Castro's Communism*, Lyle Stuart, Inc., Secaucus, 1978

Mencía, Mario, *El Grito del Moncada*, Editora Política, Havana, 1986

Mencía, Mario, *Tiempos Precursores*, Editorial de Ciencias Sociales, Havana, 1986

Mencía, Mario, *The Fertile Prison: Fidel Castro in Batista's Jails*, Ocean Press, Melbourne, 1993

Ray, René, *Libertad y Revolución: Moncada, Granma, Sierra Maestra*, Havana, 1959

Rodríguez, William Gálvez, *Viajes y Aventuras del Joven Ernesto*, Editorial de Ciencias Sociales, Havana, 2002

Rojo, Ricardo, *Mi Amigo el Che*, Editorial Jorge Alvarez, Buenos Aires, 1968

Mexico and the War

Abreu, Norberto Collado, *Collado: Timonel del Granma*, Casa Editorial Verde Olivo, Havana, 2006

Acosta, Heberto Norman, *La Palabra Empeñada*, Vols I and II, Oficina de Publicaciones del Consejo de Estado, Havana, 2006

Alemán, José Guerra, *Barro y Cenizas: Dialogos con Fidel Castro y el Che Guevara*, Fomento Editorial, Madrid, 1971

Bonachea, Ramón and Marta San Martín, *The Cuban Insurrection, 1952–1959*, Transition, New Brunswick, NJ, 1974

Casuso, Teresa, *Cuba and Castro*, Random House, New York, 1961

Cuba. Fuerzas Armadas Revolucionarias (ed.), *De Tuxpán a la Plata*, Editorial Orbe, La Habana, 1979

DePalma, Anthony, *The Man Who Invented Fidel: Cuba, Castro and Herbert L. Matthews of the New York Times*, Public Affairs, New York, 2006

Escobar, Froilán and Félix Guerra, *Che: Sierra Adentro*, Ediciones Unión, Havana 1982

Franqui, Carlos, *El Libro de los Doce*, Instituto del Libro, Havana, 1967

Franqui, Carlos (ed.), *Relatos de la Revolución Cubana*, Editorial Sandino, Montevideo, 1970

Franqui, Carlos, *Diario de la Revolucion Cubana*, R.Torres, Madrid, 1976

Garcini, Otto Hernández, Antono Núñez Jiménez and Liliana Núñez Velis, *Huellas del Exilio: Fidel en Mexico, 1955–1956*, Casa Editora Abril, Havana, 2004

Guevara, Ernesto, *Episodes of the Cuban Revolutionary War, 1956-1958*, Pathfinder, 1996

Guevara, Ernesto, *Reminiscences of the Cuban Revolutionary War*, Ocean Press, Melbourne, 2006

Guevara, Ernesto and Raúl Castro, *La Conquista de la Esperanza: Diarios inéditos de la guerrilla Cubana*, Diciembre 1956–Febrero 1957, Editorial Joaquín Mortiz, Mexico City 1995

Hart Davalos, Armando, *Aldabonazo*, Editorial Letras Cubanas, Havana, 1997

Mencía, Mario, *Tiempos Precursores*, Editorial de Ciencias Sociales, Havana, 1986

Meneses, Enrique (trans. J. Halero Ferguson); *Fidel Castro*, Taplinger, New York, 1966 and Faber, London, 1968

Sweig, Julia, *Inside the Cuban Revolution: Fidel Castro and the urban underground*, Harvard University Press, London, 2002

Together in Power

Arcos Bergnes, Ángel, *Evocando al Che*, Editorial Ciencias Sociales, Havana, 2007

Ariet, María del Carmen (ed.), *America Latina: Despertar de un continente*, Ocean Press, Melbourne, 2003

Bender, Lynn Darrell, *The Politics of Hostility*, Inter American University Press, Hato Rey, Puerto Rico, 1975

Blight, James and David Welch, *Intelligence and the Cuban Missile Crisis*, Frank Cass, London, 1998

Blight, James and Philip Brenner, *Sad and Luminous Days: Cuba's struggle with the Superpowers after the Crisis*, Rowman and Littlefield, Boston, 2002

Bonachea, Rolando and Nelson Valdes, *Che: Selected Works of Ernesto Guevara*, MIT Press, Massachussets, 1969

Bonsal, Phillip, *Cuba, Castro and the United States*, University of Pittsburgh Press, Pittsburgh, 1971

Borge, Tomás, *Un Grano de Maíz*, Fondo de Cultura Económica, Mexico City, 1992

Borrego, Orlando, *Che: El camino del fuego*, Imagen Contemporanea, Havana, 2001

Brenner, Philip, and David Welch (eds.) *Back to the Brink, Proceedings of the Moscow Conference on the Cuban Missile Crisis, January 27–28, 1989*, University Press of America, Boston, Massachusetts, 1989

Castro, Fidel, *The Second Declaration of Havana*, Pathfinder Press, New York, 1994

Falcoff, Mark (ed.), *The Cuban Revolution and the United States: A history in documents, 1958–1960*, US – Cuba Press, Washington DC, 2001

González, Edward, *The Cuban Revolution and the Soviet Union, 1959–1960*, University of California Press, Los Angeles, 1966

Guevara, Ernesto, *Guerrilla Warfare: A method*, Foreign Languages Press, 1964, Peking

Guevara, Ernesto, *Obras: 1957–1967, Tomo II* Casa de las Americas, Havana, 1970

Guevara, Ernesto, *La Guerra de Guerrillas*, Fondo de Cultura Popular, Lima, 1973

Guevara, Ernesto, *Socialism and Man in Cuba*, Pathfinder Press, Canada, 2006

Karol, K.S., *Guerrillas in Power*, Cape, London, 1971

Lüthi, Lorenz, *The Sino–Soviet Conflict: Cold War in the Communist World*, Princeton University Press, Princeton, 2008

Matos, José Martínez (ed.) *Che Periodista*, Editorial Pablo de la Torriente, Havana, 1968

Morray, J.P., *The Second Revolution in Cuba*, MR Press, New York, 1962

Núñez Jiménez, Antonio, *En Marcha Con Fidel, 1962*, Editora Ciencias Sociales, Havana, 2005

Sáenz, Tirso, *El Che Ministro: Testimonio de un colaborador*, Editorial de Ciencias Sociales, Havana, 2005

Following Their Own Paths

Bamford, James, *Body of Secrets: Anatomy of the Ultra-Secret National Security Agency*, Anchor Books, New York, 2002

Casaus, Víctor (ed.), *Self Portrait: Che Guevara*, Ocean Press, Melbourne, 2004

Cupull, Adys and Froilán González, *De Ñacahuasú a la Higuera*, Editora Política, Havana, 1989

Deutschmann, David (ed.), *Che en la Memoria de Fidel Castro*, Ocean Press, Melbourne, 1998

Fernández, Alina, *Alina: Memorias de la hija rebelde de Fidel Castro*, Plaza y Janes Editores, Barcelona, 1997

Fontova, Humberto, *Exposing the Real Che Guevara*, Sentinel, New York, 2007

Gleijeses, Piero, *Conflicting Missions: Havana, Washington and Africa, 1959–1976*, University of North Carolina Press, Chapel Hill, 2002

Guevara, Ernesto (trans. Patrick Camiller), *The African Dream: The diaries of the revolutionary war in the Congo*, Harvill Press, London, 2000

Guevara, Ernesto, *The Bolivian Diary*, Ocean Press, Melbourne, 2006

Harris, Richard, *Death of a Revolutionary: Che Guevara's last mission*, W. W. Norton, New York, 2000

Kumm, Bjorn. 'Guevara is Dead, Long Live Guevara', *Transition*, No. 75/76, Anniversary Issue: Selections from *Transition*, 1961–1976 (1997), pp.30–38

Lockwood, Lee, *Castro's Cuba; Cuba's Fidel*, Westview Press, New York, 1990

Mina, Gianni (trans. Mary Todd), *An Encounter with Fidel*, Ocean Press, Melbourne, 1991

Saldaña, Roberto, *Fertile Ground: Che Guevara and Bolivia*, Pathfinder Press, New York, 1997

Taibo II, Paco Ignacio, Froilán Escobar and Félix Guerra, *El Año en Que Estuvimos en Ninguna Parte*, Editorial Joaquín Mortiz, Grupo Planeta, Mexico City, 1994

Secondary Characters and Memoirs

Álvarez Tabío, Pedro, *Celia: Ensayo para una biografía*, Oficina de Publicaciones del Consejo de Estado, Havana, 2004

Bustos, Ciro, *El Che Quiere Verte; La historia jamás contada del Che*, Javier Vergara Editor, Buenos Aires, 2007

Costenla, Julia, *Celia: La madre del Che*, Editorial Sudamericana, Buenos Aires, 2004

Debray, Régis (trans. John Howe), *Praised Be Our Lords: The autobiography*, Verso, London, 2007

Ferrer, Carlos, *De Ernesto al Che. El segundo y último viaje de Guevara por Latinoamérica*, Editorial Marea, Buenos Aires, 2005

Franqui, Carlos, *Diary of the Cuban Revolution*, Viking Press, New York, 1980

Guevara, Alfredo, *Revolución es Lucidez*, Ediciones ICAIC, Havana, 1998

Franqui, Carlos, *Camilo Cienfuegos*, Editorial Seix Barral, S.A., 2001

Heikal, Mohamed, *Nasser: The Cairo Documents. The Private Papers of Nasser*, Mentor, London, 1973

Khrushchev, Sergei, *Khrushchev on Khrushchev: an inside account of the man and his era*, Little, Brown and Company, London, 1990

Khrushchev, Sergei (ed.), *Memoirs of Nikita Khrushchev* (trans. George Shriver), Penn State University Press, University Park, 2004

Llovio-Menéndez, José Luis, *Insider: My hidden life as a revolutionary in Cuba*, Bantam Books, New York, 1988

March, Aleida, *Evocación: Mi vida al lado del Che*, Editorial Planeta Colombiana, Bogotá, 2008

Oltuski, Enrique, *Vida Clandestina*, John Wiley and Sons, San Francisco, 2002

Oltuski, Enrique, *Pescando Recuerdos*, Casa Editorial, Havana, 2004

Pardo Llada, José, *Fidel y el Che*, Tribuna de Plaza y Janés, Barcelona, 1988

Ramírez, Dariel Alarcón, (with Elisabeth Burgos), *Memorias de un Soldado Cubano: Vida y muerte de la revolución*, Tusquets Editores, Barcelona, 2003

Retamar, Roberto Fernández, *Obras, IV: Cuba Defendida*, Editorial Letras Cubanas, Havana, 2004

Rojas, Marta (ed.), *Testimonies about Che*, Editorial Pablo de la Torriente, Havana, 2006

Villegas, Harry, *Pombo: A man of Che's guerrilla*, Pathfinder Press, New York, 1997

On Cuba

Domínguez, Jorge, *Cuba: Order and Revolution*, Belknap Press, London, 1978

Dumont, René, *Cuba: Socialism and Development*, Grove Press, New York, 1970

Gott, Richard, *Cuba: A new history*, Yale University Press, New Haven, 2005

Kapcia, Antoni, *Cuba: Island of Dreams*, Berg, Oxford, 2000

Pérez Jr, Louis, *Cuba under the Platt Amendment, 1902–1934*, University of Pittsburgh Press, Pittsburgh, 1986

Pérez-Stable, Marifeli, *The Cuban Revolution: Origins, Course and Legacy*, Oxford University Press, Oxford, 1994

Thomas, Hugh, *Cuba: The pursuit of freedom*, Picador, London, 2001

States, Revolutions and the Cold War

Andrew, Christopher and Oleg Gordievsky, *KGB: The Inside Story of its Foreign Operations from Lenin to Gorbachev*, Hodder & Stoughton, London, 1990

Andrew, Christopher and Vasili Mitrokhin, *The KGB and the World: The Mitrokhin archive*, Allen Lane, London, 2005

Blight, James, Bruce Allyn and David Welch (eds), *Cuba on the Brink: Castro, the Missile Crisis and the Soviet Collapse*, Rowman & Littlefield, New York, 2002

Debray, Régis, *Revolution in the Revolution: Armed struggle and political struggle in Latin America*, Greenwood, Westport, CT, 1980

Dunkerley, James, *Dreaming of Freedom in the Americas: Four minds and a name*, Inaugural Lecture, Institute for the Study of the Americas, London, 2004

Fursenko, Alexander and Timothy Naftali, *One Hell of a Gamble: Khrushchev, Castro, and Kennedy 1958–1964*, W. W. Norton, New York, 1997

Fursenko, Alexander and Timothy Naftali, *Khrushchev's Cold War*, W. W. Norton, New York, 2006

Gott, Richard, *Rural Guerrillas in Latin America*, revised ed., Penguin, Harmondsworth, 1973

Huberman, Leo and Paul Sweezy (eds), *Régis Debray and the Latin American Revolution: A collection of essays*, Monthly Review Press, New York, 1968

Hylton, Forrest and Sinclair Thomson, *Revolutionary Horizons: Past and Present in Bolivian Politics*, Verso, London, 2007

Joseph, Gilbert and Daniela Spenser, *In From the Cold: Latin America's new encounter with the cold war*, Duke University Press, Durham, NC, 2008

Roca, Blas, *Los Fundamentos del Socialismo en Cuba*, Ediciones Populares, Havana, 1961

Shnookal, Deborah and Mirta Muñiz (eds.) *José Martí Reader, Writings on the Americas*, Ocean Press, Melbourne, 2001

Skocpol, Theda, *States and Social Revolutions: A comparative analysis of France, Russia and China*, Cambridge University Press, Cambridge, 1979

Suárez, Luis (ed.), *Che Guevara and the Latin America Revolution*, Ocean Press, Melbourne, 2006

Miscellaneous: Times, Places and Happenings

Childs, Matt D., 'An Historical Critique of the Emergence and Evolution of Ernesto Che Guevara's Foco Theory', *Journal of Latin American Studies*, Vol. 27, No.3 (October 1995), pp.593–624

Estrada, Alfredo José, *Havana: Autobiography of a city*, Palgrave Macmillan, Basingstoke, 2007

Hoare, Mike, *Congo Mercenary*, Robert Hale, London, 1967

Moruzzi, Peter, *Havana before Castro: When Cuba Was a Tropical Playground*, Gibbs Smith, London, 2008

Symmes, Patrick, *The Boys from Dolores*, Pantheon Books, New York, 2007

Various, *Cartas del Che*, Editorial Sandino, Montevideo, 1969

451

PICTURE ACKNOWLEDGEMENTS

akg-images: 13 below. Camera Press: 1 below, 7 above, 10 above. Corbis: 1 above, 4 below, 6 below, 11 below, 12 above, 16. Courtesy of the Cuban Heritage Collection, University of Miami Libraries, Coral Gables, Florida: 2 above, 3 above, 5, 6 above, 7 below, 11 above, 14, 15. Getty Images: 9. *New York Times*/eyevine: 8. Magnum Photos: 2 below (Rene Burri), 4 above (Rene Burri), 12 left (Rene Burri), 12 right (Elliott Erwitt), 13 above (Marc Riboud). Prensa Latina: 10 below.

Every reasonable effort has been made to acknowledge the ownership of the copyrighted material included in this volume. Any errors that may have occurred are inadvertent, and will be corrected in subsequent editions provided notification is sent to the author.

INDEX